Digital Echoes

Sarah Whatley • Rosamaria K. Cisneros
Amalia Sabiescu
Editors

Digital Echoes

Spaces for Intangible and Performance-based
Cultural Heritage

Editors
Sarah Whatley
Centre for Dance Research
Coventry University
Coventry, UK

Rosamaria K. Cisneros
Centre for Dance Research
Coventry University
Coventry, UK

Amalia Sabiescu
Institute for Media and Creative
Industries
Loughborough University London
London, UK

ISBN 978-3-319-73816-1   ISBN 978-3-319-73817-8   (eBook)
https://doi.org/10.1007/978-3-319-73817-8

Library of Congress Control Number: 2018938998

Cover illustration: Antonio Arcos / Alamy Stock Photo

Printed on acid-free paper

This Palgrave Macmillan imprint is published by the registered company Springer International Publishing AG part of Springer Nature.
The registered company address is: Gewerbestrasse 11, 6330 Cham, Switzerland

FOREWORD

What is essential in any artistic revolution, in which I would suggest digital arts practice and its linkage to live performance can be situated, is its capacity to communicate, as Heidegger suggests, 'what is' and 'what matters'. Significant art practice shows 'what is' present and what is appearing in its historical moment and reveals 'what matters' and what counts within that world. In our postdigital condition, what appears is the intangible and its potentiality, virtuality and immanence. What matters is how our shared cultural heritage, our history, is constructed within that intangibility. The phenomena of the intangible, be it a human voice, which rises to be heard and then fades into silence, a body in performance splendidly isolated in time and space, or the domain of virtual communications that circulate in seeming timelessness, remain the ground upon which our current cultures are articulated and represented. This important volume, *Digital Echoes*, works to understand that process and those phenomena conveyed through arts practice and research, specifically in the areas of dance, performance and somatic practices.

What is of concern to the editors and contributors of this book are the phenomena of the gathering of the posthuman subject within, and in collaboration with, the grounds of technological communications and representations. These events of 'performing subjects in the spaces of technology' are responding to the new cultural construction that is both organic and technological, corporeal and intangible, with an increasing awareness of the seepage between these states of being. What the editors of this collection are keenly aware of, and what is lucidly acknowledged by the various authors in this fine book is the fact that at the heart of the construction of any shared cultural heritage lie its technologies of representation. Our cultural heritage, intangible or otherwise, which is essentially, our history, and the manners in which that history is 'recovered, transmitted, created, curated, and presented' within a postdigital culture are inseparable and exist in a continuum. Digital technologies are not only the transmitters of our shared intangible cultural heritage, they are the cultural heritage itself. From the landscapes of social media to the portraits of technologically-enhanced dance, performance and somatic practices, this timely book addresses these phenomena in methods that are engaging, provocative, and stimulating.

Although the authors of the individual chapters represent a variety of Universities and Research Centres, much of the work contained in this volume has found its inspiration through the Centre for Dance Research (C-DaRE) at Coventry University, which has established itself as leader in the field of Dance and Performance Research. The Centre's engagement with performance philosophy, digital culture and multiple points of contact across the spectrum of issues related to dance and somatic practices are wide-ranging and enlightening. A significant contribution to that leadership have been the series of symposia named 'Digital Echoes', which have served as a vital resource to the members of the wider dance, performance and somatic practices research community. This volume places in hand a portion of the output of the Centre's and the symposia's crucial contributions to practice-based arts research and thought.

Digital Echoes: Spaces for Intangible and Performance-based Cultural Heritage is an essential and informed engagement with the critical issues of postdigital culture as witnessed through the practice, research and thought of the body in performance. These lived bodies, being present in the events of performance, are the fundamental components of the situation of our lives. These bodies echo throughout the digital spaces and are the fundamental elements and the basis of the intangible cultural heritage that makes our world. The intangible is grounded on the corporeal. This book is an invitation to consider, within a reflection of the notion of an intangible cultural heritage constructed via digital technologies and performance practices, what is and what matters within this postdigital condition.

Trinity College Dublin   Matthew Causey
The University of Dublin
Dublin, Ireland

Contents

NOTES ON CONTRIBUTORS

Suparna Banerjee is an independent scholar, artist and dance writer from India. She obtained her PhD in Dance Studies from the University of Roehampton, UK. Her research interests include South Asian dance, digital performance, the politics of identity, dance ethnography, site-specific dance and critical pedagogy. She has taught many undergraduate and postgraduate courses in the USA and contributed to developing dance curricula for the undergraduate liberal education programme in India. She is trained in Bharatanatyam dance and her choreographies have been showcased in many countries. Her writings on dance have appeared in peer-reviewed journals.

Adam Benjamin Plymouth University, UK was joint founder of *CandoCo Dance Company* and a pioneer of integrated dance, author of *Making an Entrance: Theory and practice for disabled and non-disabled dancers* (Routledge 2002). He went on to create the award-winning *Tshwaragano Dance Company*, the first South African dance company integrated on both racial and disability lines and more recently helped establish the first professional integrated company in Japan: *Company-Kyo*. Adam is an award-winning choreographer and a National Teaching Fellow at Plymouth Conservatoire, where he advised on the design of the new fully accessible theatre *The House*. www.adambenjamin.co.uk.

Hetty Blades is a Research Fellow in the Centre for Dance Research (C-DaRE) at Coventry University. Her research considers philosophical questions posed by the circulation and transmission of dance works and practices. She has worked on projects funded by AHRC and the European

Commission and was Researcher in Residence at the Digital Catapult in 2016. Hetty is widely published, including in *International Journal of Screendance* (2017), *Performance Philosophy* (2017, 2016), *Choreographic Practices* (2016) and *Performance Research* (2015), and is Editorial Assistant for *Journal of Dance and Somatic Practices.*

Hing Chao International Guoshu Association, has been involved with heritage conservation since 2001 and is known for his wide-ranging work with nomadic cultures and Chinese martial studies. A pioneer in the use of new media for Chinese martial arts, he co-founded 'Hong Kong Martial Arts Living Archive', the first-ever Kung Fu digital archive, which has to date spawned two major exhibitions: *300 Years of Hakka Kung Fu: Its Digital Legacy and Future* (2016), and *Lingnan Hung Kuen Across the Century: Kung Fu Narratives in Cinema and Community* (2017). Hing has also written a number of articles and books on China's indigenous sports and nomadic cultures.

Rosamaria K. Cisneros is an artist, dancer, choreographer, and curator who works at Coventry University's Centre for Dance Research. Rosamaria is involved in various EU-funded projects which aim to make education accessible to vulnerable groups and ethnic minorities, and part of cultural heritage projects that bring dance and digital technologies together.

Jerri Daboo is Associate Professor of Performance in the Department of Drama at the University of Exeter. She has been researching and writing about performance and the cultural history of British South Asian communities for fifteen years. She is currently working on two new related monographs: *Staging British South Asian Culture: Bollywood and Bhangra in British Theatre* (Routledge), and *Beyond the Broadway: Performance, Culture and Social Change in Southall* (Peter Lang).

Scott deLahunta As a Senior Research Fellow at Coventry University and Deakin University's Deakin Motion.Lab, Scott deLahunta (PhD) continues his work as a writer, researcher and organizer on a range of international projects bringing performing arts with a focus on choreography into conjunction with other disciplines and practices. deLahunta is currently the Project Leader for Motion Bank, a new four-year project (2010–14) of The Forsythe Company providing a broad context for research into choreographic practice.

Matt Delbridge University of Melbourne/City University Hong Kong, actively researches many areas including: actor training, motion capture, performance capture, animation, theatre history, cultural heritage, scenography, technology studies and stage production. He has published articles in *SCENE, ISPA, Animation Practice, Process and Production, Body Space Technology* and *Nordic Theatre Studies*. He is the author of *Motion Capture in Performance: An Introduction* (Palgrave Macmillan, 2015), and *Theatre & Technology* (2018). He regularly consults and delivers masterclasses in Motion Capture and Digital Performance environments in Scandinavia, Europe and Asia, and is an Adjunct Professor in the School of Creative Media, City University Hong Kong.

Mathew Emmett Plymouth University UK, is an experimental architect, artist, composer and academic. He works across constructs of hybrid space, site-responsive installation, data-generated sound and emerging technologies. Among other collaborations and international commissions Emmett works with the avant-garde artist Eberhard Kranemann, choreographer Adam Benjamin, Perception Lab and Charles Jencks with performances in Japan, Germany and the Place, London. In June 2016 Emmett performed *Sender Receiver* using a digitally augmented bullroarer to communicate with *This Is Where We Are*, a data-driven digital sculpture created by i–DAT at the opening of the new Switch House at Tate Modern. http://www.mathewemmett.com.

Kerry Francksen is an independent artist, researcher and educator. Her work spans the intersections of live and digital performance practices and her specialist interest areas include dance and media and interdisciplinary and collaborative creativity. She has a PhD in Performance and Digital Art, and her work has been performed and screened nationally and internationally. She regularly collaborates with artists from other disciplines, including long-standing partnerships with composer Dr Simon Atkinson, filmmaker Laura McGregor and composer/media artist and creator of the award-winning software *Isadora* Mark Coniglio. She is also Co-director of DAPPER, a cross sector network, supported by De Montfort University.

Laura Griffiths is Senior Lecturer in Dance in the School of Film, Music and Performing Arts at Leeds Beckett University. She has a PhD in Dance and Archival practices, facilitated through an AHRC funded Collaborative Doctoral Award in partnership with the University of Leeds and Phoenix Dance Theatre. Broadly, her research interests include the relationship between dance and the archive, the role of the body and the digital in archival processes and performance. Professional industry experience has encompassed project management within the arts, dance teaching in community settings, lecturing and research project assistance. Laura sits on the board of Dance HE (www.dancehe.org.uk).

Kate Hennessy is a Professor at Simon Fraser University's School of Interactive Arts and Technology. She is a cultural anthropologist and director of the Making Culture Lab, where she explores the role of digital technology in the documentation and safeguarding of cultural heritage, and the mediation of culture, history, objects and subjects in new forms. Her video and multimedia works investigate documentary methodologies to address Indigenous and settler histories of place and space. She is an assistant editor of *Visual Anthropology Review* and co-founder of the Ethnographic Terminalia curatorial collective, which explores the borderzones between ethnography and artistic practice.

Sarah Kenderdine researches at the forefront of interactive and immersive experiences for galleries, libraries, archives and museums. In widely exhibited installation works, she has amalgamated cultural heritage with new media art practice, especially in the realms of interactive cinema, augmented reality and embodied narrative. In 2017, Kenderdine was appointed Professor of Digital Museology at the École polytechnique fédérale de Lausanne (EPFL), Switzerland where her new laboratory for Experimental Museology (eM+, http://emplus.epfl.ch) explores the convergence of aesthetic practice, visual analytics and cultural big data. Sarah is also director and lead curator for EPFL's new art/science initiative ArtLab (https://artlab.epfl.ch).

Teodora Konach Currently a PhD candidate at the Jagiellonian University in Cracow, Poland, Teodora Konach received a MA in European Studies (Warsaw University) and a MA in Cultural Management (Jagiellonian University). Initially from a music background, her interests range from legal issues to arts sociology, management, policy and into international comparisons. Her research interests lie in the fields of arts education, intangible cultural heritage and the local and global dynamics of safeguarding of cultural heritage. She works at the Chancellery of the Polish President as an expert on cultural policy and was awarded the Polish Ministry of Culture scholarship 'Mloda Polska'.

Alvin Eng Hui Lim is Assistant Professor in the Department of English Language and Literature at the National University of Singapore. His research explores notions of media, spirit possession and spirituality in religious practices. He is currently working on two projects: a monograph on digital media and religion titled *Digital Spirits in Religion and Media: Possession and Performance* and a long-term research on island practices, performers and spirits. He is also Deputy Director of the Asian Shakespeare Intercultural Archive (a-s-i-a-web.org).

John McCormick is recognized as one of the pioneers of new media dance, motion capture and telematic performance. He was awarded an Australia Council Fellowship in 2007–8 for real-time motion capture and networked performance. John has collaborated on works worldwide, including at peak festivals ZERO1SJ, SIGGRAPH, Melbourne Festival and The Venice Biennale.

Lydia Nicholson University of Tasmania is a PhD candidate in History at the University of Tasmania. She has a Bachelor of Creative Arts (Drama) with Honours (First Class) from Flinders University, a Masters of Museum Studies from the University of Sydney, and an industry background in theatre, museum theatre and heritage interpretation.

Adrian Palka is a Senior Lecturer in the School of Media and Performing Arts at Coventry University. Adrian's research interests are in the fields of inter-disciplinary performance/installation as well as the cultural politics of Central and Eastern Europe. His work spans performance practice-as-research, pedagogical innovation and reflective writing. Since 1996 he has collaborated with Berlin artists Robert Rutman and Wolfram Spyra, incorporating Rutman's musical sculptures, the Steel Cello and Bow Chime in sound performances and installations, with a current emphasis on memory and postmemory (www.palkadiaries.com). He is currently working on the trilogy 'Iron Curtain' a multi-media reminiscence event to commemorate the fall of the Berlin Wall, in the Museum fuer Jugend[widerstands], Berlin. (ironcurtain.coventry.ac.uk).

Liana Psarologaki is a Senior Lecturer and the subject area leader for Art, Architecture and Design at the Department of Arts and Humanities, University of Suffolk, and is based in the UK. She holds a PhD from the University of Brighton (2015) sponsored by UCA, a Masters in Architecture from the National Technical University of Athens (2007), and practiced architecture before receiving an MA in Fine Art from UCA

Canterbury (2010). Her research contributes to the criticism on the aesthetics of contemporary art practice, and art and design pedagogy. Dr Psarologaki is a RIBA, ARB and TCG chartered architect, a Fellow of the Royal Society of Arts and continues to publish and exhibit internationally.

Amalia Sabiescu is a communications researcher affiliated with the Institute for Media and Creative Industries at Loughborough University London. She conducts interdisciplinary research at the interface between information and communication technology (ICT), culture and development studies. Her main research interests are in investigating the integration, use, and impact of ICT in cultural and creative practice, community contexts, and intersections with issues of citizen voice, agency, and social inclusion.

Jeffrey Shaw (Professor, 1944 Melbourne) has been a leading figure in new media art since its emergence from the performance, expanded cinema and installation paradigms of the 1960s to its present day technology-informed and virtualized forms. In a prolific career of widely exhibited and critically acclaimed work he has pioneered the creative use of digital media technologies in the fields of virtual and augmented reality, immersive visualization environments, navigable cinematic systems and interactive narrative. Shaw was co-founder of the Eventstructure Research Group in Amsterdam and founding director of the ZKM Institute for Visual Media Karlsruhe. In 2003 Shaw was awarded the prestigious Australian Research Council Federation Fellowship and returned to Australia to co-found and direct the UNSW iCinema Centre for Interactive Cinema Research in Sydney from 2003 to 2009. At iCinema he led a theoretical, aesthetic and technological research program in immersive interactive post-narrative systems, which produced pioneering artistic and research works such as Place-Hampi and T_Visionarium, the latter shown at the Biennale of Seville in 2008. In September 2009 Shaw joined City University in Hong Kong as Chair Professor of Media Art and Dean of the School of Creative Media (SCM). Professor Shaw has a position at UNSW as co-director of the iCinema Centre for the purposes of academic and research co-operation with CityU. He established a SCM research facility at the Hong Kong Science Park in 2010.

Rebecca Stancliffe is a Postdoctoral Researcher in Learning and Participation at Trinity Laban Conservatoire of Music and Dance where she also teaches release-based contemporary technique and dance history and culture on the undergraduate and postgraduate programmes. Rebecca is currently completing her PhD at the Centre for Dance Research (C-DaRE) at Coventry University. Her thesis examines video annotation as an analytic practice for dance, its roots in analogue forms such as movement notation and choreographic sketchbooks, and how it informs the way movement is seen, analysed, interpreted and understood.

Caitlin Vincent is a PhD researcher at Deakin University in Melbourne, Australia. Her work examines the use of digital and 3D stereoscopic scenography in opera productions in the twenty-first century.

Jordan Beth Vincent is a Melbourne-based dance historian and critic, and a Research Fellow in the areas of live performance and new technology at Deakin University's Deakin Motion.Lab. Since 2008, Jordan has reviewed dance, circus and physical theatre for *The Age* newspaper and other dance publications.

Kim Vincs is a Professor at Swinburne University of Technology. Kim is a choreographer and interactive dance artist who develops new ways of investigating and creating dance using digital technology. Her research brings together scientific, technological and artistic methodologies to develop new ways of creating dance performance.

Charlotte Waelde The focus of Charlotte Waelde's work lies at the interface between intellectual property law (particularly copyright) and changing technologies, the changes in the law wrought by those technologies, and the impact that those changes have on the way that the law is both perceived and used by the affected communities. Her work reaches out into other domains including intangible cultural heritage, human rights, competition law, international private law and the regulation and promotion of new technologies more generally as they intersect with her core interests.

Ben Walmsley lectures and researches in audience engagement, arts management, arts marketing and cultural policy in the School of Performance and Cultural Industries at the University of Leeds. Prior to his academic career, he was a Producer at the National Theatre of Scotland. Ben is Director of the National Summer School for Arts Fundraising and Leadership and recently evaluated the national Arts Fundraising and Philanthropy Programme. Ben is the Co-editor of *Arts and the Market* and has published widely in a number of leading journals. He is currently running an AHRC network for audience research and completing a monograph on audience engagement, which will be published by Palgrave Macmillan in 2018.

Rachel M. Ward is completing her PhD at Simon Fraser University's School of Interactive Arts and Technology with a focus on digital anthropology, experimental ethnography and virtual reality (VR). She earned her Master's degree in Social Anthropology from the London School of Economics and, as a Rotary Ambassadorial Scholar, a postgraduate degree in Visual Anthropology at the Australian National University. She has also completed material culture training at the American Museum of Natural History and Smithsonian Institution. She has produced several film projects, including socio-cultural documentary shorts about Appalachian music, punk ('DIY') cultures and Air Jordan collectors.

Sarah Whatley is Director of the Centre for Dance Research (C-DaRE) at Coventry University, UK. Her research interests extend to dance and new technologies, intangible cultural heritage, somatic dance practice and pedagogy, dance documentation, and inclusive dance practice; she has published widely on these themes.

Heather Young Reed is a dancer, teacher and historian. She holds a BFA and PhD from York University in Toronto, and an MA in Choreography from the University of Leeds. Heather spent a year working at the Juilliard School in New York before returning to York to pursue a PhD in Dance Studies. Her doctoral research focused on the restaging of contemporary dance, and investigated the ways in which various modes of documentation intersect in the practices of recording, transmitting and preserving choreographic works. She is currently a lecturer on both undergraduate and graduate dance courses at the University of Lincoln, UK.

CHAPTER 1

Introduction

Sarah Whatley, Rosamaria K. Cisneros,
and Amalia Sabiescu

This volume emerges out of a series of established annual symposia hosted by C-DaRE (Centre for Dance Research) at Coventry University, 'Digital Echoes', which over six years has attracted a wide cross-section of the cultural heritage, artist and scholar community worldwide. The series began with a clear focus on the interrelationship between dance and digital technologies, in particular how digital technologies support different documentation strategies including digital archives. Throughout six editions, the focus has expanded to include a broad cross-section of the creative and cultural industries. This expansion also contributed to placing dance and performance practice in dialogue with forms of intangible heritage such as storytelling and music. Whilst the focus of Digital Echoes contributions was firmly established on the digital, these dialogues opened up questions regarding boundaries and relationships between different forms of arts and culture, which predate the digital. One critical aspect emerging from the Digital Echoes symposia is that there is a need to consolidate the body of knowledge that both relates and critically examines differences between

S. Whatley (✉) • R. K. Cisneros
Centre for Dance Research, Coventry University, Coventry, UK

A. Sabiescu
Institute for Media and Creative Industries,
Loughborough University London, London, UK

© The Author(s) 2018
S. Whatley et al. (eds.), *Digital Echoes*,
https://doi.org/10.1007/978-3-319-73817-8_1

present-bound, traditionally-rooted and future-oriented artistic and cultural practices as a step towards a firmer understanding of the role and the impacts associated with the intervention of digital environments on creative practice and audience engagement with arts and culture.

Intended as a contribution in this direction, this edited volume provides a compendium of innovative cases and practices, as well as critical, historical and theoretical approaches examining the integration of digital environments in the creation, documentation, circulation and reception of arts and culture, with a focus on intangible and performance-based cultural heritage. A thorough engagement with the relationship between performing arts and cultural heritage, which is only sparsely treated in the literature through an interdisciplinary lens, contributes to consolidating a much-needed set of conceptual frameworks for drawing connections between historical, contemporary and future artistic and cultural practices. The volume is not limited to a strictly academic perspective but takes a horizontal approach which brings in the voice of artists and practitioners, as well as creative professionals that blend practice and research. This enables us to offer an overview of innovative creative practice as it is currently being cultivated, accompanied by reflexive, theoretical and critical perspectives necessary to expand the corpus of knowledge around initiatives, achievements and developments many of which are still emerging, singular in their approach and achievements. Whilst emergent, the authors are careful to acknowledge where these activities are rooted in or take influence from texts that have established a lively discourse for describing and analysing digital performance. Several cite key references, including Steve Dixon's 2007 text *Digital Performance: A History of New Media in Theatre, Dance, Performance Art, and Installation*, and Philip Auslander's much cited theory of 'liveness' (1999). Other texts that provide a contextualizing framework for this collection include Sita Popat's *Invisible Connections: Dance, Choreography and Internet Communities* (2006), her co-authored text with Jonathan Pitches, *Performance Perspectives: A Critical Introduction* (2011), and the more recent jointly edited volume by Popat and Salazar Sutil, *Digital Movement: Essays in Motion Technology and Performance* (2015). Another volume that has emerged since Digital Echoes in 2015 and shares some concepts with this collection is Maaike Bleeker's edited collection that has a primary focus on dance: *Transmission in Motion: The Technologizing of Dance* (2016). Matthew Causey, our keynote speaker at the Digital Echoes 2015 edition, became an important influence for many when preparing their chapters. Two of his texts are particular reference points: *Theatre and Performance in Digital Culture: From Simulation to Embeddedness* (2007), and his jointly edited volume with Emma Meehan and Neill O'Dwyer, *The Performing Subject in the Space of Technology: Through the Virtual Towards the Real* (2015).

The connection between intangible and performance-based cultural heritage, which is central to this book, has combined with reflective practice relatively recently, considering as well that notions of intangible cultural heritage (ICH) have made their entry into established cultural heritage vocabularies less than half a century ago. The first systematic definition of ICH was formed in 2003, in the UNESCO Convention for the Safeguarding of Intangible Cultural Heritage. The definition, purposefully broad, insists on the dynamic and co-creative nature of ICH as the sum of cultural and spiritual forms that are developed, cultivated, and transmitted intergenerationally in the midst of a community or society, providing the members with a sense of identity, belonging, and historical continuity. A list of ICH domains is provided, which spans forms from oral traditions and performing arts to craftsmanship, music, traditional knowledge and ritual practices. The UNESCO Convention marks the recognition of ICH as a fundamental aspect of humanity's collective heritage. This also marks a point in time when understandings of heritage started to shift, from an almost exclusive focus on tangible and material aspects of it, to a more inclusive conception that integrates intangible and immaterial aspects.

The chapters in this book engage with varied forms of ICH, from music and storytelling to dance, theatre and martial arts. Despite their labelling as ICH, all these forms also have distinctive characteristics, which compel us to think differently about how we may engage with, preserve and transmit them. For instance, dance fills a unique place in ICH as an ephemeral art, frequently described as an act of disappearance (Phelan 2003), which draws its meaning and communicative power from the relation with an audience in the moment when it is being performed. This ephemeral quality also poses unique issues regarding the preservation and transmission of dance, as the knowledge embedded in its creation and performance is strongly embodied, and difficult to capture within notation and representation systems.

The focus of this book is on the intervention of digital technologies in all aspects related to the recovery, creation, transmission, curation and preservation of ICH. We take digital technology to encompass the tools, devices, and infrastructures that enable the representation of information in the binary system made of 0 and 1 digits. Beyond this functional perspective, we acknowledge as well the role of digital technology as a mediating mechanism that can profoundly intervene in and affect all processes involved in the continuum of cultural heritage creation and transmission. It is not in the scope of this book to provide a systematic overview of these spaces of intervention, but rather to use illustrative cases to point to tendencies and trends that are bound to have profound implications for the future of creative, artistic and cultural management, transmission and preservation practices. Thus, the chapters selected for this book each engages with one or more of these intervention areas, blending a perspective anchored in practice, with a critical, reflexive or theoretical overlay. We can illustrate the profound impacts of digital technology by looking at some instances of its intervention in relation to the multiple processes involved in how dance enters the public domain and sustains itself, whether through analogue methods, digital code or a combination of both. In creative practice, digital technology can provide new ways of thinking about the dance making process, adopting for instance computational or algorithmic patterns in the choreography, or using digital tools to create new choreographic pieces. The same can be true for the documentation, preservation, audience engagement and transmission of dance.

Cases of digital technology interventions are provided throughout this book for arts and culture forms from different geographies and cultural settings, from Europe, as well as the Americas, Australia and Asia. This enables us to take a broad perspective to reflect on the implications that digital interventions have on ICH engagements, its curation and transmission and how these are contextualized in developments we have witnessed in cultural institutions and heritage management, such as:

- Blurring boundaries between contemporary arts and heritage, but also between different forms of art and culture, creating new bridges and ways of relating between the material, the immaterial, and the digital.
- Shifts from conceptions of heritage focused on the past to conceptions of heritage that attribute it a quality of liveness, through audience engagement in the present moment, often through digitally mediated environments.
- Transitions from centralized to decentralized forms of curation and management in Galleries, Libraries, Archives and Museums (GLAMs).

These developments eventually impact on creative practice and on creative professionals and artists, to name just some of these influences:

- The increasing contemporary relevance of cultural heritage for the creative industries, in which it acts as a source of inspiration and creativity for new generations of creative professionals.
- Changing notions of author, creator, and creativity associated with digitally mediated choreographies and performance forms.
- Greater synergies among diverse art forms (such as visual and performing arts), leading to new opportunities for inspiration and creative practice and novel art forms and sources for content.
- Intellectual Property (IP) issues raised by the increased possibilities for digital reproduction and circulation of arts and culture forms and collaborative forms of creation, but also novel opportunities such as new business models for creative businesses and professionals.

1.1   BOOK STRUCTURE

The volume features sixteen chapters that together treat four broad themes, focused respectively on critical and reflexive engagements, digital interventions in time and space, documentation and preservation, and authorship and legal aspects.

Part I: Critical and Reflexive Engagements opens up the volume with an interdisciplinary exploration of the interplay between performance-based cultural heritage and the digital, bringing in perspectives from psychology, aesthetics, body-based performance and audience studies. In Chap. 2, Laura Griffiths and Ben Walmsley discuss the intervention of digital environments in creative processes for enabling dialogues between creative practitioners and audiences. Suparna Banerjee in Chap. 3 explores Freudian theories of the uncanny in relation to two contemporary choreographies and how they link to broader questions around performance politics and culture. The section closes with Kerry Francksen's Chap. 4, which shifts the focus to an embodied perspective as represented by the performing artist. She makes a case for embodied ways of knowing and creating in relation to digital technologies, and illustrates it in the examination of two choreographic pieces. This close, attentive reading of the interplay between body and technology in movement practice enables her to reflect critically on the impact technology has on the dancer.

Part II: Space, Time and Memory: Digital Interventions examines the process and implications associated with digital interventions over a range of intangible heritage forms, from folklore and contemporary dance to war memoirs and performance art. Whilst different forms of artistic practice and cultural heritage can be identified in the contributing chapters, in practice the cases examined therein all converge in pointing how boundaries between contemporary arts and heritage, and between material and immaterial cultural forms are increasingly blurred. Adrian Palka's Chap. 5 traces a digital journey to recover and reclaim family and cultural memory. Palka shows how a war diary can inspire on-location elusive arts interventions, but also have more enduring echoes in digital representations and the evocation of historic events. In Chap. 6 by Liana Psarologaki, museums—sites of material culture—are invested with qualities of ephemeral and new temporalities through digital and performance arts interventions. Ward and Hennessy's Chap. 7 looks into how intangible and tangible heritage boundaries blur in interactive installations that use a token of material culture to access intangible heritage recordings and documentation. And Benjamin and Emmett's Chap. 8 provides a fine analysis of how relations between space and movement, acoustics and sociality acquire new dimensions and qualities in an experimental dance piece that explores the spatial qualities of sound.

Part III: Preserving the Intangible: New Tools and Documentation Strategies examines digital tools, environments and strategies for documentation and preservation of cultural heritage beyond their most obvious, functional role, foregrounding notions of present-bound engagement, memory activation, and manifestation of identity and belonging. Jerri Daboo (Chap. 9), shows how engagement with cultural heritage through digital mediation interrelates with issues of identity and belonging in diaspora communities. Alvin Eng Hui Lim (Chap. 10), argues that digital archiving of performance-based cultural heritage can go beyond mere reproduction, and be invested with all the 'hallmarks of theatrical performance', creating its own event whilst engaging with audiences over the digital medium. Rebecca Stancliffe (Chap. 11), examines how different annotative approaches can be employed to capture and communicate movement intentions and illuminate fine nuances of choreographic knowledge and improvisational techniques. Heather Young Reed's Chap. 12 on video documentation suggests that the value of video records for body-based performance lies not in mere archival storage, but in their use as living archives, to activate memories and bring to life a corporeal experience as lived and inscribed in the kinaesthetic memory of the performer. Chapter 13 by Chao, Delbridge, Kenderine, Nicholson and Shaw looks into the use of 3D video and motion capture to record and annotate Kung Fu practice so that elements of speed, force and motion are rendered.

Part IV: Authorship, Ownership and Legal Aspects discusses open questions and challenges brought by digital mediation of artistic and cultural practice, including changing notions of 'creator' and 'author', and the tensions between intellectual property rights and the increased opportunities for artistic inspiration and creative interpretation opened up by digital and networked environments. Teodora Konach (Chap. 14) examines the existing intellectual property rights laws from the perspective of intangible cultural heritage and proposes improvements based on museum practice. In Chap. 15 by Jordan Vincent and colleagues, the notion of 'spin-off' is discussed at length in the context of publishing and broadcast media and in dance. In Chap. 16 Hetty Blades delves into the subtle question of 'authorship' in dance, providing examples and case studies featuring Flemish choreographer Anne Teresa De Keersmaeker. We come back to legal aspects in the final Chap. 17 by Charlotte Waelde, which considers the problems discussed in the previous two chapters within the context of copyright law.

References

Auslander, Philip. 1999. *Liveness: Performance in a Mediatized Culture*. Oxon: Routledge.

Bleeker, Maaike, ed. 2016. *Transmission in Motion: The Technologizing of Dance*. London: Routledge.

Causey, Matthew. 2007. *Theatre and Performance in Digital Culture: From Simulation to Embeddedness*. Oxon: Routledge.

Causey, Matthew, Emma Meehan, and O'Dwyer Néill, eds. 2015. *The Performing Subject in the Space of Technology: Through the Virtual, Towards the Real*. Palgrave Studies in Performance and Technology. Basingstoke: Palgrave Macmillan.

Dixon, Steve. 2007. *Digital Performance: A History of New Media in Theater, Dance, Performance, and Installation*. Cambridge, MA: MIT Press.

Phelan, Peggy. 2003. *Unmarked: The Politics of Performance*. Oxon: Routledge.

Pitches, Jonathan, and Sita Popat. 2011. *Performance Perspectives: A Critical Introduction*. Basingstoke: Palgrave Macmillan.

Popat, Sita. 2006. *Invisible Connections: Dance, Choreography and Internet Communities*. Oxon: Routledge.

Popat, Sita, and Nicolas Salazar Sutil, eds. 2015. *Digital Movement: Essays in Motion Technology and Performance*. Basingstoke: Palgrave Macmillan.

PART I

Critical and Reflexive Engagements

Considering the Relationship Between Digitally Mediated Audience Engagement and the Dance-Making Process

Laura Griffiths and Ben Walmsley

2.1 Introduction

This chapter offers some original empirical insights into emerging modes of audience engagement with dance, which highlight the role of digital environments for the reception and circulation of culture across multiple arts practices and audiences. The discussion focuses on the intervention of the digital into the creative practices and processes of making contemporary dance. In so doing, it considers the impact that a digital platform designed to share work-in-progress can have upon an artist's process and reviews the potential of digital platforms for engaging audiences in cultural practices such as dance-making.

This chapter will explore the integration of audience feedback via a digitally mediated platform during the creative process of three new pieces of dance. It will critically review how attempts to forge empathetic

L. Griffiths (✉)
School of Film, Music and Performing Arts, Leeds Beckett University, Leeds, UK

B. Walmsley
School of Performance and Cultural Industries, University of Leeds, Leeds, UK

© The Author(s) 2018   11
S. Whatley et al. (eds.), *Digital Echoes*,
https://doi.org/10.1007/978-3-319-73817-8_2

relationships between artists and audiences through digitally mediated interactions intersect with and intervene in the dance-making process. The chapter is based on the findings of a National Endowment for Science, Technology and the Arts (Nesta) funded project, which enabled the authors to collaborate with the Leeds-based dance agency Yorkshire Dance and with a digital partner, Breakfast Creatives. The project was funded under Nesta's Digital R&D Fund for the Arts, which supported the development, testing and analysis of a responsive online platform that we called *Respond*. The platform was designed to mediate interaction between audiences and artists, taking the former on a structured journey of collaborative critical enquiry to deepen their insights into the development of new dance works. The platform adapted the acclaimed Critical Response Process (CRP), a feedback technique for soliciting feedback designed to support the needs of the artist/maker of work and develop effective modes of critical enquiry (Lerman and Borstel 2003).

By critically reviewing the process and findings of the study, which was conducted in 2014 by the two authors, the chapter will consider the wider implications for audience engagement of digitizing what is essentially an artist-led and -focussed process of critical enquiry. The discussion draws upon key insights developed through scrutiny of qualitative research data gathered through the established audience research methods of focus group discussion, depth-interviews and netnography. The chapter invites new perspectives on the appropriation of technology for developing relationships between dance artists and audiences whilst also highlighting the potential of such a platform for informing and shaping a shared understanding of cultural value and heritage between artists and audiences. The chapter contributes to this book through exploring tensions and possibilities for cultural engagement through harnessing technology in a meaningful and collaborative way.

2.2   Background and Context

The research context for the project emerged through the increased attention and value that is placed upon developing audiences' contextual insights or "readiness to receive" (Brown and Novak 2007) and through evolving definitions and processes of co-production and co-creation (Grönroos 2011; Walmsley 2013). Indeed, when presenting emerging findings from this research project, it is towards the shifting and ambiguous notions of co-production and co-creation that audiences' questions have primarily been addressed. However, the main focus of this chapter is to explore the implications of digital engagement with audiences during artistic development for *artists*.

The project was also initiated as a response to the relatively low Target Group Index (TGI) for contemporary dance in Yorkshire. In response to this demographic challenge, one of Yorkshire Dance's key objectives remains to build and develop a region-wide infrastructure for dance whilst also fostering creativity and innovation. Similar projects such as BAC's (London's Battersea Arts Centre) *Scratchr* model have explored co-creation through digital collaboration between artists, audiences and producers with a view to better equipping artists, producers and audiences for co-creative roles (Meyer and Hjorth 2013). This aim was explored via an online space (www.scratchr.net) designed for the sharing of creative ideas, essentially an online collaboration space, which also set out to enable relationships between artists, the venue and their audiences. The *Scratchr* project findings suggested that audiences were more motivated to use other social media platforms to engage in dialogue rather than scratchr.net. This motivated us to design a responsive platform that would attract and engage participants in a sustained critical dialogue.

The *Respond* project stemmed from the activities of Yorkshire Dance in supporting a broad range of practitioners from across the region and developed organically from their frequent face-to-face application of the CRP technique to support artistic development. Responding directly to the stated aims of the Nesta R&D Fund, our project shifted the focus of the technique from the artist to the audience, with a view to creating a more bespoke audience engagement platform. This gave rise to a number of healthy tensions regarding to what extent *Respond* constituted an artist or audience focussed tool.

2.3   Liz Lerman's Critical Response Process and Its Place in the Creation of Dance Works

The *Respond* platform (see www.respondto.org) translated CRP to the digital realm and thus shifted the facilitation of the technique that ordinarily takes place in a live context towards a more automated and autonomous process managed via an online platform. *Respond* enabled direct communication back and forth between the artist and online participants via a highly structured process (see below). Like its live counterpart,

Respond provided the audience with privileged access to an artist's creative process. But the online process was mediated through automated responses and input from a facilitator in order to mirror how CRP functions in a "real-life" environment, where it is facilitated by a trained and/or experienced intermediary.

CRP was developed by Liz Lerman in the USA during the late 1980s with the aim of supporting the development of artistic practices, initially in dance-making. CRP traditionally functions as a feedback system based on the principle that the best possible outcome from a response session is for the maker to want to go back to work. The process has proved valuable for multiple creative endeavours and collaborative relationships within and beyond the arts. Since its inception, CRP has been embraced by a diverse range of stakeholders, including dance-makers, art-makers, educators, conservatoires, theatre companies, museums, orchestras, scientists and science centres. The core aims of CRP are as follows:

- to inform and develop a more reflexive approach to artistic practice;
- to deepen dialogue between makers and audiences;
- to facilitate enhanced learning between teachers and students.

CRP involves a four-step process that aims to minimize and contain personal opinions, personal aesthetics and biases (Lerman and Borstel 2003). The four key steps that promote constructive dialogue between artist and audience are delineated as follows:

1. *Statements of meaning*: This step involves the respondent commenting upon what was exciting, evocative, challenging, memorable, compelling or stimulating about the work.
2. *Artist's questions*: The artists ask the audience questions about their work. Lerman and Borstel (2003) suggests that if artists ask questions first about the intent of their work, the respondents will be better able to frame the discussions around the needs of the artists.
3. *Neutral questions*: The audience asks neutral questions about the artist's work. Questions are considered to be neutral when they do not have an opinion couched in them.
4. *Sharing opinions*: The audience state their opinions, subject to permission from the artist. The usual form is "I have an opinion about *x*; would you like to hear it?" The artist then has the option to decline opinions for any reason (Lerman and Borstel 2003).

Ordinarily, the CRP process takes place following a live sharing of work-in-progress where spectators are configured in a circle and the four step process is implemented by a facilitator (and note-taker) who polices each step to ensure that each step is followed and assures the coherency of the overall process. The circular arrangement is recommended for the Critical Response Process "because it runs contrary to certain conventions of learning and leadership in the dance field—for example, that dancers enter a room and face front to receive direction from the teacher or choreographer" (Borstel 2003, 8).

CRP provides clarity on what artists are dealing with in their creative endeavours and subsequently enables the work to be successful through an increased sense of clarity around the artistic intention behind the work. CRP helps to build work as it assists in overcoming habits and preconceived ideas and prompts artists to reflect closely on their creative process.

For the purpose of *Respond*, CRP was facilitated via an online platform. The artists each made a short film documenting their works-in-progress and shared this online for a week. Yakira's documentation was shared with a "closed group" of thirty participants who had identified themselves as either frequent attenders of contemporary dance (seeing more than four performances per year), infrequent attenders (seeing between one and four performances per year) or non-attenders (never seeing contemporary dance). Alternatively, Synge's film was made public via the online *Respond* platform for a potential global "open audience" to engage with. *Respond* brokered direct communication between the artists and each individual participant through a process of exchange that followed the CRP format. The project team assisted in the facilitation of these interactions, and qualitative data was gathered through the documented exchanges between artist and audience member. This process was repeated at a later stage in the development of the work and depth interviews were undertaken with a selection of participants and with the artists who shared their work via the platform (Fig. 2.1).[1]

In translating Lerman's process to the digital world, our project encountered a number of challenges, not least that of maintaining momentum amongst a diverse group of participants from non-attenders to established dance artists. CRP traditionally reverses the hierarchies inherent in feedback for dance artists, as it is primarily audience focused. Developed with a research focus on how cultural value (and ultimately, therefore, cultural heritage) might emerge as a result of co-creative relationships,

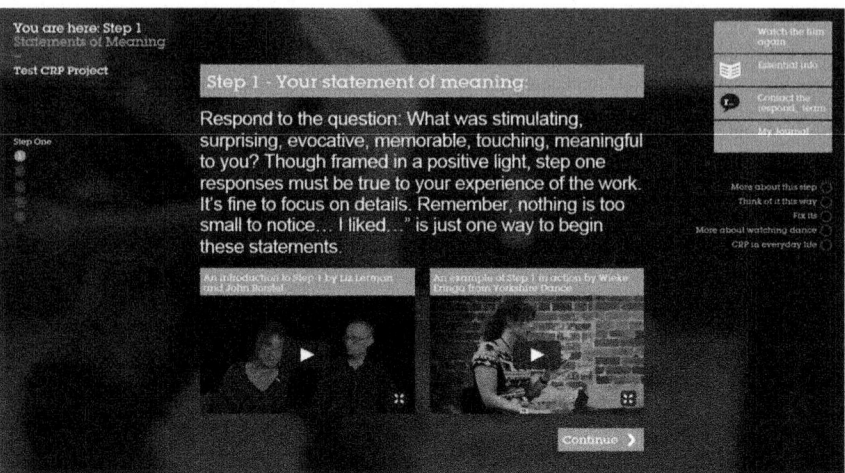

Fig. 2.1   The *Respond* platform (screen-shot of Step 1)

Respond sought to expand the dimensions of CRP into an audience engagement tool. However, some of these challenges ultimately transpired to be benefits, which surmounted some of the pernicious restrictions and barriers inherent to face-to-face communication in live time. For example, the lack of a spatial context and the shift from spoken to written feedback opened up new possibilities to foster a more democratic culture of constructive critical exchange. As Whatley and Varney (2010) have argued: "Web technologies have a tendency of flattening" what they refer to as the "temporal qualities" or the "raw" nature of materials (p. 60). These authors relate this process to dance and in particular to the process of *making* in their contention that:

> the rehearsal process is by its nature a collaborative process, subject to all kinds of influences that are necessarily of the moment. But what is discarded and what is kept is an unseen, un-explained cognitive process; a unique intuition that resides within both the choreographer and the dancer/s, which might be termed "choreo-cognition". (Whatley and Varney 2010, 60)

Whatley and Varney recognize that aspects of "choreo-cognition", if exposed and disseminated, can prove valuable in providing data for the researcher. Whilst Whatley and Varney are concerned with strategies for documentation and digital preservation on otherwise intangible dance heritage, the *Respond* project adds a new dimension to the potential value inherent to sharing the creative process. As such, the project substantiates the work of Miranda Boorsma (2006), who highlights the vital role that audiences play in processes of artistic reception and argues that the arts consumer is not a passive recipient of art, but an important co-producer of value.

2.4   Creating Empathetic Audience Relationships

In the context of this book, this chapter emphasizes how new modes of audience engagement with digitally mediated dance-making processes can assist in creating more empathetic audience relationships. The use of the online environment to facilitate audience reception has particular implications for dance, which is traditionally experienced as a live performance practice. The visual experience of watching dance pulls the observer into feeling, through empathetic engagement with the bodily action and the motivation inherent in the movements (Foster 2011, 156–7). This observation derives from the writings of dance critic John Martin (1939) and has continued to inform more recent investigations into the role of kinaesthetic empathy in dance spectatorship.

The work of Dee Reynolds and Matthew Reason (2010, 2012) offers useful insights into the multiple modes through which audiences engage with and reflect upon dance performance, including kinaesthetic, empathetic and musical engagement, social experience and intellectual reflection (2010, 55). These authors suggest that "kinaesthetic responses are a key source of pleasure and motivation for many dance spectators" (ibid., 42). Furthermore, Susan Foster emphasizes the centrality of the moving body to empathetic engagement as a result of the body's "affinity with cultural values" (2011, 218). These ideas provide a context for understanding the empathetic perspectives through which dance is primarily received and *Respond* both adds to and problematizes these multiple layers of empathy.

The specific function of *Respond* as a feedback mechanism that utilized the online environment alters traditional modes of spectating whereby bodily exchanges are not facilitated through a shared space but an online interface. Existing research into web-based choreography reveals that it is possible for audiences to engage in dance-based learning through Internet communications (Popat 2006). In addition, practices of "web-based choreography" suggest that the Internet can prove a valuable tool and resource for audience experience and engagement with dance (as is evident in the work of Mark Coniglio, for example). Similarly to Popat's research into the possibility of supporting the creative process via Internet dialogues, this research focused upon the time of making, which is ordinarily privately endured by the artistic team. Recent innovations into documentary practices in dance reveal the value associated with the multiple aspects of process. Increased interest in embodied knowledges or aspects of "choreo-cognition" are becoming increasingly apparent within web-based platforms. Scott deLahunta and Bertha Bermudez have explored the increase in artists' involvement in developing unique approaches to the documentation and transmission of their work, which largely depend on the digital interface (2010). Projects such as *Inside Movement Knowledge*, *Motion Bank* (The Forsythe Company), Siobhan Davies' *Replay* and *Double Skin/Double Mind*, to name but a few, encompass:

> a wealth of dance-related material while also allowing for new modes of interacting with this material, new modes of navigating through it, understanding it, selecting and recombining it, pulling information from it, and putting it to new (creative) uses. (Bleeker 2010, 4)

Such projects offer insights into the otherwise hidden components of the dance-making process and reveal that these new ventures are enabling traditionally less tangible forms of choreographic heritage to become more commonplace. Whilst such projects incorporate the use of rehearsal footage, digitally annotated notations, scores and materials that are intrinsic to the choreographic process, *Respond* adds a layer of audience dialogue into the milieu of choreographic process.

The complexity of kinaesthetic empathy as described by Reason and Reynolds is further problematized when translated to a digital environment, especially as the three dance works that have been part of the *Respond* project were not specifically "web-based" choreographies. As Susan Leigh Foster explains, "the dancing body in its kinaesthetic specificity formulates an appeal to viewers to be apprehended and felt, encouraging them to participate collectively in discovering the communal basis of their experience" (2011, 218). This sense of communality has been considered essential to audience engagement via the digital, according to Popat, in that the construction of "group-ness" in an online context is what facilitates dance-based learning and can support the creative process (2006, 117–18).

The implications for creating empathetic audience relationships via the means of a digital platform illuminate the possibility for communal experience and highlight the inevitability of co-creating value. In particular, the tensions between co-presence and asynchronous online exchange reveal how such modes of engagement afford different types of empathetic relationships. Whatley explains that "the presence of a 'live dancer' involves the viewer sensing the dancer's effort, breath and weight in a more immediate, co-present way" (2012, 266). In contrast, when a dancer's body is mediated through a screen, the viewer is required to "perform" in a different way in order to engage with the work, such as activating a mouse or using a keyboard. Whatley explains that the relationship between the work and the viewer through the use of technology suggests that modes of virtual engagement implicate the watcher in the viewing "as co-creator, thereby active in realising the work" (ibid., 267). Moreover, for artists, as deLahunta and Shaw explain, increased approaches for "looking inwards" at their process helps the choreographer in the form of a "self-demystification" of their own practice, enabling them to deepen their own understanding (2006, 53). The digital manifestation of CRP facilitates this depth of understanding, as it forces artists to excavate their process and through the addition of a shared dialogue contributes to the artists' and audiences' ability to decipher and engage with the work (Interview with Lucy Suggate, 14 September 2015).

The platform provided an opportunity to explain that there don't have to be "secrets" withheld regarding the dance-making process and provided audiences with a sustained introduction into the work. It was also implied that the process had enabled the artists to understand and engage with expectations and misunderstandings with regards to the work as it "confirmed suspicions" that the work might be "baffling" and this could be pursued in dialogue via the platform. Among the expectations was the idea that the platform might assist in unlocking or providing "new avenues of awareness to explore in future work" (Interview with Hagit Yakira, 6 December 2015). It was anticipated that the platform would enable time for "the formulation of ideas and for connections between concepts to emerge in a way that is not possible in the live context of CRP" (Interview with Lucy Suggate, 14 September 2015).

2.5   Engaging Audiences Digitally

There is arguably a current trend to overstate audience's desire to co-create artistic work. There are a limited number of studies into co-creation in the arts, but a recent study of co-creating theatre by one of the authors (Walmsley 2013) found that the desire to create work alongside artists was restricted to a relatively small and niche segment of the audience. For the purpose of this chapter, it is important to distinguish between co-creation and co-production. Grönroos (2011) maintains that "co-creation" should be applied to processes of audience reception and sense-making and defines "co-production" in terms of consumers participating in the production phases of an artistic product or event. So, co-creation is perhaps best understood as a creative philosophy that provides audiences with a cognitive and emotional stake in artistic work rather than a productive role.

To date, very little research has been dedicated to the digital engagement of audiences. One of the most significant contributions to this emerging area of research is provided by Lynne Conner (2013) who illustrates the myriad benefits of digital engagement, including its ability to empower and embolden audiences by safeguarding their anonymity. Conner also notes that online engagement can incorporate important periods of silence, which "slow the pace and allow for a redistribution of power among the speakers", thus democratizing discussion and enhancing the meaning-making (p. 79). Significantly for this particular study, Conner's research also illustrates that effective audience engagement focuses on process rather than outcome, which serves to vindicate further the adoption of Lerman's CRP into the audience reception process.

Our empirical work with *Respond* participants provided some rich qualitative accounts of the impact of the digital platform on audiences. Several participants noted that *Respond* helped to peak their anticipation, which served to confirm the findings of Brown and Novak's (2007) study that determined a causal link between anticipation and positive impact in the performing arts. As one of our participants put it: "I had been worried that the process would hinder my enjoyment of the performances, but actually it made me very excited to already be a little aware of what was to come."

Other participants shed light on how digital engagement can facilitate reflexivity and develop a positive etiquette of critical response. For example, one infrequent attender fed back her feelings that the *Respond* process:

wasn't asking me to be knowledgeable; it wasn't asking me to give facts or figures or esoteric arguments or similes or whatever. It was actually asking me to *respond* to something; and I think to do that you actually had to be very mindful and very humble. And I thought that was a really good thing. It was something I wasn't expecting...

What is perhaps of particular interest in the context of this book is how this facilitation of mindful response can exert a positive influence on artistic practice and address notions of cultural heritage and value.

2.6   THE ARTIST'S PERSPECTIVE

The use of *Respond* as a digital feedback platform was a new venture for all the artists involved and their anticipation of what this could afford illustrated the value that each placed upon establishing constructive dialogues with audiences. Much of the appeal of the platform resides in the opportunity to understand how audiences perceive artists' work. But it is important to note that the platform marks a departure from more traditional uses of digital technologies for marketing activities, which mainly occurs via social media platforms. Instead, *Respond* became a vehicle for shared constructive and creative dialogue. Among the expectations was the idea that the platform might assist in unlocking or providing "new avenues of awareness to explore in future work" (Interview with Hagit Yakira, 6 December 2014). It was anticipated that the platform would enable time for "the formulation of ideas and for connections between concepts to emerge in a way that is not possible in the live context of CRP" (Interview with Lucy Suggate, 14 September 2015). Alongside these potential benefits of the platform, a number of complexities inherent to sharing the work during the making process emerged in relation to the digital content and function of the feedback dialogue. In particular, the tensions between what benefitted the artist and the audience/responder highlight the impact that the digital environment can have upon the creative process and the facilitation of deeper, more "mindful" audience engagement.

The CRP technique connects both the makers and the responders of an artwork through a process of response. The three artists referred to in this chapter (Lucy Suggate, Robbie Synge, Hagit Yakira) identify CRP as being central to the process of uncovering "secrets" about the work, or more specifically, allowing the concepts inherent to the process to emerge in and through the shared online dialogues. As Lucy Suggate explained, CRP is "a productive tool to make the work better" as:

> it helps me realize *how* I want to engage with audiences [...] to build work and overcome preconceived ideas, it prompts me to look more into *process*. [...] CRP gives me clarity on the work that I'm presenting. There's something about that clarity that allows the work to be successful [...] there's an artistic clarity. (Interview with Lucy Suggate, September 14, 2015)

This perspective was also echoed by Robbie Synge, who explained that the process helped him to make the kind of work that he wanted to make. In addition, Yakira noted that the ordinarily private process of creating work is an intellectual journey and that she hoped by "making the ideas public as soon as they are conceived [...] they can be both clarified and deepened" (Interview with Hagit Yakira, 6 December 2014). The sense of immediacy implicit in Yakira's comment here is significant in relation to the shift in facilitation of CRP from the live to digital context. One key complexity was the timing and participation: as opposed to when feedback is shared live, the sense of immediacy does not translate to the digital platform. Participants reported that they missed the "dopamine hit" they get from other digital platforms (such as social media); and because the CRP was facilitated asynchronously, the artists missed the moments of real-time dialogue that they would get through a live facilitation of CRP (Fig. 2.2).

When using *Respond* the artists were required to prepare two video clips for use in two separate phases of the platform testing. The way in which this intervened in the process offers insights into how the online relationship with audiences is developed and into artists' different approaches to sharing their works-in-progress. Susan Melrose has argued that "all performance-making processes are relational" in the sense that they are constructed around the presence of an imagined spectator, materially positioned (2007). This relationality, as Melrose argues, dislocates the performance because it is "neither here nor there, but in more than two places, and differently, at once".

This perspective resonates with the mode through which the artists were required to present their work via the platform, meaning that a work within a work as such was offered as an insight into the development. Each artist approached the task of showing work-in-progress via video quite differently. For Yakira, it was important that she consciously placed herself within the footage so that the audience would "see the relationship, [...]

Fig. 2.2 Robbie Synge, *Douglas* © Yorkshire Dance/Sara Teresa

see the dialogue, [...] see the way I think, then [...] see how it comes along with the dance. I think it creates more personal relationships with the work, to me, with the whole thing" (2014). In contrast, Synge's clips offered a narrative and were framed as "artistic offerings" (Interview with Robbie Synge, 6 December 2014) often not filmed in a traditional dance space (i.e. in a village hall and in outdoor rural locations).

The dramaturgy behind the videos themselves therefore became an important consideration for the artists, who geared it towards assisting the audience's understanding of their own creative narratives. In particular, Suggate suggested that the process of selecting material for a film of a targeted length (approximately five minutes) directly impacts upon the scope of the feedback and how much she is able to probe her audience in relation to the overall work. These factors contribute to an emphasized distinction between the experience of spectating and experiences of performance-making and performing, both in and in the lead-up to the event (Melrose 2007). For Suggate, the audience are not watching *the* piece of work but function as observers in a research process. Therefore, the terms within which the work is received is not only subject to the binary of live/digital but performance-making/performing; and through discussion with the artists it became evident that this distinction begins to overlap as a result of the shift from an "imagined spectator" to the presence of a spectator via the online environment.

Based on the findings of this project, it is thus arguable that the application of CRP to the digital context exerted a more sustained impact upon the creative process than the application of a live CRP. This is because of the artists' ability to return to the online feedback, to re-read and reflect back upon their own and others' comments. Suggate (Interview with Lucy Suggate, 14 September 2015) suggested that this offered a more reflexive process, providing her with an "external eye" in the process. It was also suggested that a live CRP process can sometimes feel confrontational and formal whereas in this digital manifestation the tone was more informal and the depth of feedback was greater. The function of the platform also offered a sense of support and legacy for the works-in-progress. Synge reported that the more time the responders invested, the more rewarding this was for him, supporting Conner's (2013) contention that the slower-paced mode of digital engagement can enhance the process of meaning-making.

All of the artists appreciated the access to feedback in written form, claiming that this more tangible form of documentation functioned as a type of choreographic notebook, which also contributed to a more sustained period of reflection upon the process and development of their work. The artists appeared to benefit from the process of writing questions for the digital environment instead of formulating these in the live context. The translation of the process into a digitally mediated feedback loop forced the artists to articulate their questions and responses with more care and consideration, making them more "honed and reflexive" (Suggate 2015). Suggate also welcomed the fact that *Respond* enabled her to capture her work digitally and to create a living archive of her process. Similarly, Synge commented that the platform has provided him with "a timeline of a process" that is invaluable for future development of the work.

For Suggate, the ultimate aim of CRP is to determine a shared interpretation of a piece of dance: she describes this as "a process of *alignment*", which enables her to "filter the feedback". This perception chimes closely with and Bourriard's definition of "relational art" as "intersubjective encounters [...] in which meaning is elaborated *collectively*" (cited in Bishop 2004, 54, original italics).

2.7 Development of Dance-Making Practice

All three artists reported that the use of the platform for gaining feedback on their work offered the necessary space for reflection and the ability to prepare considered responses. This is something that has been perceived as a key strength of the online platform as opposed to live CRP, where dialogue is more dynamic and succinct. The digital facilitation allowed for a different mode of expression that was considered more expansive and reflective. Synge (2014) also claimed that the mode of participation and engagement was "more generative".

The way in which the audience commentary became present within the dance-making environment is significant as it marks a shift away from the spectator as an "imagined presence" (Melrose 2007) towards a more co-present engagement. This was particularly the case for dance artist Hagit Yakira who selected some of the audience feedback to share with the dancers, musicians and costume designers also involved in the work. The process of reading comments to the artistic team during the rehearsal process inevitably increases the visibility of the audience at the time of making. Yakira explained that the commentary was selected based upon how closely it related to what she was trying to achieve in the work and therefore constructed a positive dialogue between the studio activity and the online commentaries.

Managing the role and expectations of audiences also emerged as a central concern amongst the artists. As Suggate (2015) pointed out, "the audience are not watching *the* piece of work [...] they are observers in a research process". This insight develops Suggate's notion of the artist-as-researcher and challenges the concepts of co-creation and relational art described above. In the case of Robbie Synge's work, *Douglas,* some of the responders began expressing concerns towards the final stages of the process about whether or not the work would be ready in time for the performance date. Such behaviour further illustrates how the platform enabled more empathetic relationships to emerge through heightened sense of investment in the creative process. Yakira also commented that she was aware of her responsibility to the audience in her selection of "something safe" for them to see and also in her acknowledgement that: "They wanted to help and they wanted to take part [...] there's a willing that comes from a good place."

Yakira's suggestions reveal that she was less influenced by what audiences actually said but more so about considering how to "invite audiences in". The strength of the process for Yakira was rooted in the way in which it encouraged her to reconsider the language she used to describe her work and how to ask questions of her audiences. These findings further support the distinction between the co-creation and co-production of value that marks a shift in the reception of value as something that can be understood as a shared process of alignment between artist and audience, afforded via processes of digital engagement such as that offered in *Respond*.

2.8   IMPLICATIONS

The various ways within which the audience feedback intersected with the artists' process is indicative of how this mode of engagement has the potential to inform the development of a dance work and provide audiences with a significant and meaningful stake in choreo-cognition. However, the three artists claimed that they were unclear as to how engaging with audiences in this way had impacted upon their creative decision-making. This suggests perhaps that responsive platforms of this nature might function more effectively as tools of co-creation (of value) rather than co-production (of product). Nonetheless, the process has clearly enabled an awareness of the work "beyond geography" and an understanding of how to communicate with audiences by constructing appropriate processes, etiquettes and discourses around their work and by co-creating value through enhanced and more empathic audience relationships.

Another key implication stemming from this work is the challenge of securing funding for digital engagement, which not only emerged as a highly labour intensive process but also demanded significant marketing and facilitation resources. The study also highlighted the need to address artists' skills gaps and lack of confidence in digitally capturing their creative process through ongoing professional development. This is a sector-wide issue that impinges on cultural policy and on aspects of cultural heritage.

2.9   CONCLUSION

There are indications from this case study that digital engagement can encourage both artists and audiences to take responsibility in their various roles of creating and receiving culture and in making sense and deriving meaning from their artistic experiences and endeavours. Digital platforms such as *Respond* have an advantage over traditional face-to-face exchanges in that they can capture and document the creative process as it happens. This implies a democratization of cultural memory and heritage, as the focus shifts from output (or product) to process, and the documentary voice broadens from that of the artist to a collaborative dialogue between the artist and their audience (sometimes facilitated by a cultural intermediary). This in turn serves to give audiences a stake not only in what cultural heritage *is*, but, perhaps just as importantly, in who *decides*. On a broader level, this more democratic artistic exchange can serve to shape and determine cultural value by establishing an empathetic relationship where sense is made of a work through the artist–audience relationship.

The findings of this project could have significant implications for artists and arts organizations. The platform demonstrated potential for audience development and enrichment alongside the clear potential to shift artist–audience relations well beyond standard transactional processes into a more artistic, human, dialogic realm that exemplifies Miranda Boorsma's (2006) conception of co-creation, whereby audiences give "meaning to the artefact by means of their imaginative powers" (p. 85).

There is consensus from the artists engaged in the process that there is no clear correlation between the creative choices made and the audience feedback, and therefore the role of co-production is not particularly apparent from the activities within this project. The main value for the artists and audiences was inherent in the way in which the platform encouraged a more "considered", "deep", honest", "structured", "succinct" and "mindful" critical responses than a verbal, face-to-face exchange.

NOTE

1. Artist Interviews:
   Robbie Synge, Saturday 6 December 2014. Yorkshire Dance, Leeds.
   Hagit Yakira, Saturday 6 December 2014. Yorkshire Dance, Leeds.
   Lucy Suggate, Monday 14 September 2015. Yorkshire Dance, Leeds.

REFERENCES

Bermudez, Bertha, and deLahunta, Scott. 2010. [NOTATION] *rtrsrch* 2 (2). Accessed 7 November. http://insidemovementknowledge.net/reference/reading/.

Bishop, Claire. 2004. Antagonism and Relational Aesthetics. *October* 110: 51–79.

Bleeker, Maaike. 2010.What If This Were an Archive? [NOTATION] *rtrsrch 2* (2). Accessed 7 November 2015. http://insidemovementknowledge.net/reference/reading/.

Boorsma, Miranda. 2006. A Strategic Logic for Arts Marketing: Integrating Customer Value and Artistic Objectives. *The International Journal of Cultural Policy 12* (1): 73–92.

Borstel, John. 2003. Liz Lerman Dance Exchange: An Aesthetic of Inquiry, an Ethos of Dialogue. *Animating Democracy.* Accessed 30 October 2015. http://animatingdemocracy.org/sites/default/files/documents/labs/dance_exchange_case_study.pdf.

Brown, Alan S., and Jennifer L. Novak. 2007. *Assessing the Intrinsic Impacts of a Live Performance.* San Francisco, CA: WolfBrown.

Conner, L. 2013. *Audience Engagement and the Role of Arts Talk in the Digital Era.* New York: Palgrave Macmillan.

Department for Culture Media and Sport. 2007. *Culture on Demand: Ways to Engage a Broader Audience.* London: Department for Culture, Media and Sport.

Foster, Susan Leigh. 2011. *Choreographing Empathy: Kinesthesia in Performance.* Oxon: Routledge.

Grönroos, Christian. 2011. Value Co-creation in Service Logic: A Critical Analysis. *Marketing Theory 11* (3): 279–301.

deLahunta, Scott, and Norah Zuniga Shaw. 2006. Constructing Memory: Creation of the Choreographic Resource. *Performance Research* 11 (4): 53–62.

Lerman, Liz, and John Borstel. 2003. *Liz Lerman's Critical Response Process: A Method for Getting Useful Feedback on Anything You Make, from Dance to Dessert.* Takoma Park, MD: Liz Lerman Dance Exchange.

Martin, John. 1939. *Introduction to the Dance.* New York: Dance Horizons.

Melrose, Susan. 2007. Not Yet, and Already No Longer: Loitering with Intent Between the Expert Practitioner at Work, and the Archive. Accessed 16 October 2015. http://www.sfmelrose.org.uk.

Meyer, Eric T., and Isis Hjorth. 2013. *Digitally Scratching New Theatre. London's Battersea Arts Centre Engaging Via the Web.* London: Nesta.

Popat, Sita. 2006. *Invisible Connections: Dance, Choreography and Internet Communities.* London: Routledge.

Reason, Matthew, and Dee Reynolds. 2010. Kinesthesia, Empathy, and Related Pleasures: An Inquiry into Audience Experiences of Watching Dance. *Dance Research Journal 42* (2): 49–75.

Reynolds, Dee, and Matthew Reason, eds. 2012. *Kinesthetic Empathy in Creative and Cultural Practices.* Bristol: Intellect Ltd.

Scratchr. n.d.. http://www.scratchr.net. Accessed 15 October 2015.

Walmsley, Ben. 2013. Co-creating Theatre: Authentic Engagement or Inter-legitimation? *Cultural Trends* 22 (2): 108–118.

Whatley, Sarah. 2012. The Poetics of Motion Capture and Visualization Techniques: The Differences Between Watching Real and Virtual Dancing Bodies. In *Kinesthetic Empathy in Creative and Cultural Practices*, ed. D. Reynolds and M. Reason. Bristol: Intellect Ltd.

Whatley, Sarah, and Ross Varney. 2010. Siobhan Davies Dance Online: The Digital Archive and Documenting the Dance Making Process. In *Capturing the Essence of Performance*, ed. N. Leclercq, L. Rossion, and A. Jones. Brussels: Peter Lang.

CHAPTER 3

Performing the Uncanny: Psychoanalysis, Aesthetics and the Digital Double

Suparna Banerjee

3.1 INTRODUCTION

Bharatanatyam, an Indian "Classical" dance, was revived, renamed and reconstructed in the 1930s from Sadir, a dance form which was originally practised by temple dancers (*devadasi-s*)[1] of South India in the late nineteenth and early twentieth centuries (Meduri 1996; Srinivasan 1985; Soneji 2010).[2] Broadly speaking, the aesthetics of Bharatanatyam pivot on two techniques: *nritta*, the abstract form of dancing, abounds in metrical sequences and rhythmic steps and *abhinaya* is the interpretative dance in which the textual meanings are articulated through codified gestures and facial expressions. Its repertoire, popularly known as *margam*, largely draws on temple rituals and mythological tales about Hindu gods and goddesses, but has been adapted to suit different contexts and audiences over the past century. Widely practised in diasporas across nations, today Bharatanatyam dance has attained the status of a global dance form (Meduri 2004; O'Shea 2007). Every year several international and national festivals include traditional Bharatanatyam dance performances to keep on this rich cultural heritage. Although coded as classical, this dance form has undergone and continues to undergo transformations alongside historical,

S. Banerjee (✉)
Independent Scholar, Pune, India

© The Author(s) 2018
S. Whatley et al. (eds.), *Digital Echoes*,
https://doi.org/10.1007/978-3-319-73817-8_3

contextual and technological shifts as well as the unique perspectives of different choreographers, both locally and globally.

In Britain, since the 1990s, choreographer Shobana Jeyasingh has contributed significantly to contemporanising Bharatanatyam dance by introducing various movements that are laced with histories and cultures, digital techniques and films, and consequently, her works have been the subject of academic attention (Briginshaw 2001; O'Shea 2008). Over the past decade, post-Jeyasingh artists including Nina Rajarani, Mayuri Boonham, Ash Mukherjee, Divya Kasturi, Shane Shambhu, Kamala Devam, Seeta Patel and Shamita Ray, who are trained in Bharatanatyam dance along with many others, have also continued to push the edge of this tradition, drawing on multi-disciplines, hybrid dance techniques and media arts (Banerjee 2014).

In the new millennium, the celebration of the digital body in contemporary works could be surprising to many, due to the deep-rooted training of the "live" body[3] in Bharatanatyam or any Classical dance for that matter. Given the importance of the "*angasuddhi*"[4] and the "sanskritised body" (Coorlawala 2004)[5] in the core of Bharatanatyam, choreographies that combine this cultural heritage dance form with cutting-edge technology undeniably call into question the ontology of such practice. While theorising on technology and the body, scholars have contended that technological interactivity could, presumably, make us implicate a presence despite an actual absence. Sociologist Jean Baudrillard argues that "simulation threatens the difference between the 'true' and the 'false', the 'real' and the 'imaginary'" (1994 [1981], 3). Postmodern subjectivities have thus become indefinable due to this technological reproduction, which pose a challenge to the notion of the authentic body as well as one's identity.

In my attempt, while conducting fieldwork as a part of my doctoral study in London and other cities in Britain, I was attracted to watch contemporary/Bharatanatyam practice[6] by post-Jeyasingh practitioners that have been barely explored in the literature. My broad aim was to investigate how the boundary of Bharatanatyam dance tradition is negotiated through the inclusion of new themes, techniques, tools and genres in the contextualised setting (Banerjee 2014). Looking specifically at digital performances,[7] I observed how the use of the engineered body, technically known as the "digital double" (Dixon 2007),[8] is precisely one of the ways Bharatanatyam dance is re-articulated. My attention was captured by the way the digital body has blurred the following binaries: home/unhomely, familiarity/unfamiliarity, real/unreal, me/not-me and life/death. Furthermore, a mystical interplay between corporeality and the simulated image invoked phantasmagoria. The uncanny doubles emerged, confronted the live subjects on the stage and unexpectedly disappeared to return even more intensely for dramatic effect. This dualism of presence and absence created cognitive dissonance, inducing a vulnerable sensation of mystery. In my mind, the question was not whether the digital body would gradually supplant the "live" body, but the ways place(s), time and geometry in addition to gravity collided in the "digital space" to create new aesthetics. All these factors would affect the gaze of the audience and thus warrant a new methodological framework for analysing such works. This chapter therefore opens up a space for examining the way the "uncanny" can be utilised as a choreographic as well as a research device and goes on to discuss how new dance aesthetics are reconfigured through digitisation of the body, thereby bringing in a critical lens to this study.

The concept of the "uncanny" was first theorised by psychiatrist Ernst Jentsch, who defined it as a "sensation of psychical uncertainty" (1996 [1906], 6), and later, it was developed by psychoanalyst Sigmund Freud in his seminal essay *Das Unheimliche* [*The Uncanny*] (1955 [1919]). Freud noted that *das Unheimliche* (adj. *Unheimlich*), the original German expression for "the uncanny", is derived from the word "*Heimlich*", which means "native", "familiar" and "belonging to the house".[9] Phenomenologically, the uncanny is something which "is undoubtedly related to what is frightening" (Freud 1955 [1919], 219). In his discussion, Freud also mentioned it as an aesthetic category which in its broad sense is the study of "the qualities of feeling" as opposed to the narrow sense, the study of the "theory of beauty" (1955 [1919], 219). Whilst situating the concept of the "uncanny" into the core of psychoanalysis, Freud centred his discussion primarily on the following qualities, such as the uncanny nature of animism, the double, omnipotence of thought, the discrepancy between the real and the unreal, the return of the repressed and the relationship with the dead. Therefore, when speaking of the uncanny, there is a sense of fear in the psyche, the haunting thoughts, the visceral experience of the presence of a dark spirit that perturbs.

Academic research on the uncanny has remained diverse, ranging from the fields of literature (Botting 1991; Johnson 2010; Labriola 2002) to film studies (Linville 2004; Spadoni 2007) and from architecture (Vidler 1992) to visual arts (Kligerman 2007). At the beginning of the twenty-first century, literary theorist Nicholas Royle's *The Uncanny* (2003) and artist Mike Kelley's *The Uncanny* (2004), published on the occasion of his exhibition in the Tate Gallery Liverpool, brought together significant attention to the discourse on the uncanny, including its links with a theoretical, critical and creative practice. Theatre scholars have also endeavoured to define methodologies and theoretical approaches for a greater understanding of the intersection of the digital performance and the uncanny. For instance, media studies scholar Matthew Causey (1999) posits the digital double within the concept of the uncanny, informed by a psychoanalytic Lacanian position that proposes the double as the split self.[10] Drawing on the Freudian notion of the uncanny, media theorist Steve Dixon categorises the digital double as an "alter-ego" which is a "darker embodiment" (2007, 250), haunting the real self.

Returning to my field experience, I am reminiscent of how the danceworks simultaneously reveal the lure and dismay of the impact of technological splitting of artistic selves through the use of digital tools. Later, when interviewing the artists, I was curious to know why they adopted the digital tools and what their doubles represented (Banerjee 2014). While video-recording their interviews, I was enraptured by their account of why their doubles recur as haunting memories and how they mirror artists' imagined selves. For instance, I noted how Divya Kasturi's double in *NowHere* dramatised the impossibility of stabilising identity due to her constant travelling across borders and also her search—"where do I belong?" On another occasion, when researching through the internet, I came across another hauntingly beautiful piece *Last One Standing* (2009) by Seeta Patel and Kamala Devam in which the artists employed their doubles for portraying the existential struggle of people living in urban cities through black humour whilst reinforcing the unresolved question— "who shall be the last one standing in the game of life?". After I expended my energies further into exploring these insights in-depth, I realised that the digital doubles were used also to demonstrate their varied psychological conditions, including in-betweenness, frustrations, fear and a deep pain of loss.

Despite a widespread interest in the "uncanny" and the double in films and theatre, scarcely any scholarly attention has been paid to approaching contemporary/Bharatanatyam practice adopting the psychoanalytic optic. I therefore suggest that engaging with the uncanny as a method needs no apologetic stance. The research questions that are investigated here include: what are the various elements that contribute to the uncanny spectacle, and how can the uncanny be appropriated as an aesthetic tool? Finally, aligning with the theme of the anthology, I am interested in analysing how far these techno-human additions in these new works reconfigure the practice of contemporary/Bharatanatyam dance.

For the purpose of this chapter, I focus on the two aforesaid choreographies: *Last One Standing* (full length: 15 minutes) and *NowHere* (full length: 50 minutes). I have selected them primarily because both are overpoweringly enigmatic and stage temporal suspensions at domestic sites. Both construct an unpredictable universe in which boundaries collapse, in-betweenness constitutes everyday life; where nothing is under control, and the uncertainty abounds. Methodologically, the dance analysis does not rely much on movement descriptions, rather my superseding intention is to examine how the uncanny can be appropriated both as a research and a choreographic tool. During discussions, I draw on my background as a Bharatanatyam dancer, a teacher and also as a researcher whose interest lies in investigating how the borderline between theory and practice is negotiated through the interface of flesh and the engineered body. Although I do not elaborate on any subjective experiences, I occasionally draw insights from them in support of my arguments.

Building on the Freudian uncanny and my readings of the choreographies and interviews, I demonstrate that the digital doubles not only uncover the concealed uncertainty due to transnational migration but also act as a psychoanalytic lens to express all kinds of dualities, dialectics and identity crises of the artists. Contrastingly, I also reveal that the doubles do not always symbolise their repressed thoughts or traumatic complexities, but illustrate the transcendent, elevated sides too. Towards the end of this chapter, a critical discussion centring on the aesthetic alterations eventually leads us to comprehend how the scope of Bharatanatyam dance as a cultural heritage has been expanded through the technological doubling. We arrive at an understanding where the uncanny as a methodology is not only connected with the politics of the body and identity, history, aesthetics and technoculture, but also to our life itself.

3.2   ANALYTICAL LENS: THE UNCANNY

In his discussion, Freud clearly marked the uncanny as a kind of anxiety, and noted the paradoxical fact that people derive aesthetic pleasure from being anxious.[11] He was the first to draw attention to the lexical ambivalence of its etymology: *Heimlich*, as stated earlier, is something that makes us feel "at home" because it is familiar, and its negation *Unheimliche* would obviously produce a feeling of alienation and otherness. However,

Freud resisted drawing a simple conclusion: "what is 'uncanny' is frightening precisely because it is *not* known and familiar" (1955 [1919], 220, italics in original). It was then that he came across philosopher Friedrich Wilhelm Schelling's definition of the term "*unheimliche*" as something which has "*remained...secret and hidden but has come to light*" (quoted in Freud 1955 [1919], 224, italics in original). Schelling's definition provided Freud with an initial inspiration to build an aesthetic theory surrounding the uncanny and its effects. The uncanny is something that was familiar once, but is now estranged by the process of repression. So, at its core, it is paradoxical; it conceals and reveals a subject at the same time.[12] As we shall see shortly, the technique of defamiliarisation is adopted to engage the audience in the process of re-seeing the familiar. We enter into a fictional land, away from a familiar world, which is disquieting, yet comforting because the uncanny world becomes familiar as soon as we begin to identify ourselves with the subjects' stories.

As stated by Freud, the proper site of the uncanny is the domestic space ("*das Heim*" or the home). While discussing the significance of the uncanny in buildings, architecture academic Anthony Vidler argues that the uncanny is inextricably bound up with urbanism: "the uncanny, as Walter Benjamin noted, was also born out of the rise of the great cities, their disturbingly heterogeneous crowds and newly scaled spaces" (1992, 4). Figuratively, the houses of the characters, more precisely the living rooms, have been important sites for staging the uncanny as their geographical displacements transform the native domain as alien. I return to this to demonstrate how in-betweenness and confusion of "home", national boundaries and haunting memories, which has also been the origination of ghosts and Gothic novels, have rendered the uncanny in *NowHere*.

Throughout his discussion, Freud posited the double as a dark figure that conveys a sense of duplication, double meanings, dreadful occurrences and recurring reminiscences. Some of the darker elements which appear in literature and films include demonic entities, aliens, ghosts, dolls, intruders in the home and more. Drawing on psychoanalyst Otto Rank, Freud commented that a sense of the uncanny foregrounds in the idea of a "double" (the Doppelgänger),[13] which is an "uncanny harbinger of death" (Freud 1955 [1919], 235). Having its lineage in folklore and occult culture, the double has been a seductive device in literature (Rogers 1970; Slethaug 1993), and also in horror films (Schneider 2004). As referred earlier, the Dixonian definition of the double as "alter-ego" represents the darker and "the schizophrenic self" (2007, 268). Causey however observes that the phenomenon of the uncanny recurs through the subject's experience of seeing "the self as other in the space of technology" (2006, 17). In a similar vein, philosopher Avital Ronell comments: "The more dreadfully disquieting thing is not the other or an alien; it is, rather, yourself in oldest familiarity with the other, for example, it could be the Double in which you recognize yourself outside of yourself" (1989, 69). How the subject/object split acts as an instrument by which these artists articulate different levels of experience is demonstrated later.

Citing instances from literary works and patient case studies, Freud further contended that the sight of mutilated body parts provokes an uncanny sense of terror. In analysing E.T.A. Hoffman's story, *The Sandman*, Freud catalogued several images including "[d]ismembered limbs, a severed head, a hand cut off at the wrist,...feet which dance by themselves—all of these have something peculiarly uncanny about them, especially when, as in the last instance, they prove able to move themselves in addition" (1955 [1919], 244). I demonstrate shortly the way both the danceworks under examination overflow with severed limbs, which symbolise the haunting memories of the characters, leaving them plagued by uncertainties in the midst of dismal urban conditions, which steer them towards a bleak prognosis, either in the form of death or spiritual insecurity.

Furthermore, Freud associated dismemberment with the castration complex: "A study of dreams, phantasies and myths has taught us that anxiety about one's eyes, the fear of going blind, is often enough a substitute for the dread of being castrated" (Freud 1955 [1919], 231). Apart from mentioning the Oedipal myth, the nature of these "dreams, phantasies and myths" has however not been discussed in detail. As argued by Freud, castration anxiety is a repressed fear that returns in strangely familiar appearances to unnerve us. In practice, castration anxiety functions more on a metaphoric level. As we shall eventually unfold, onscreen mutilated body images or onstage dismembered inanimate bodies have a tangled connection to fear, cultural menace, haunting memory and the artist's struggle for identity, especially in *NowHere*.

Another provocative theme in Freud's essay is the implication of death. We experience the uncanny in death because it confronts us without prior intimation. The concept of death, while familiar, is enigmatic precisely because the aftermath is ambiguous. According to Freud, the uncanny is associated with the concept of death and the return of the dead. Both Freud and his disciple Otto Rank viewed the "double" as an expression of one's desire for immortality. Rank's "immortal double", a "magic self" (Rank 1958 [1941], 102), is a catalyst to create art and to control the mysteries of life and death. So, the double can function both as "an energetic denial of the power of death" and the "harbinger of death" (Freud 1955 [1919], 235). I shall return to this later to discuss how the culminating scenes in both pieces examined appear to be spectral; they are about the perception of the living and the experience of the dead, and the mystery of being there and not-there.

3.3   THE CHOREOGRAPHIES

3.3.1   Last One Standing

The metaphor of "playing a game" has been associated with theatre for some time;[14] borrowing from this tradition, *Last One Standing* dramatises two game players' encounters as opponents, their attempts to safeguard vulnerabilities and their tactics for survival in an urban city. A duet created by Kamala Devam and Seeta Patel, it features film sequences by Maria Åkesson, and Jason Sweeney has composed most of the musical score. The movement canvas juxtaposes isolated *adavu*,[15] codified hand gestures and the art of mime from the Bharatanatyam tradition with movements, including throwaways, swings, sharp curves, angled hip movements and long leg stretches from Western contemporary dance. Using limited narratives and a few onscreen texts, it builds up a core of the slumbering uncanny underneath an idyllic surface of "humour". Throughout, the performers are careful not to shatter the illusion that the spectators are merely watching a game; rather, all are claustrophobically retained in the game. It ends with a precarious blend of fear and perplexity, divided between time and space, life and death, fiction and reality.

In its exposition, we see the invasive nature of the interior, where two players build tension around a table on which wooden blocks are piled up (Fig. 3.1). By concealing other objects in the living room and keeping the walls in the dark, it submerges location and history, creating a greater sense of homelessness within domesticity. An unknown, disembodied male voice announces the rules: "The game is played with 54 wooden blocks. The blocks are stacked in a tower formation [...] The game ends when the tower falls in any significant way. The loser is the person who makes the tower fall." As the piece progresses, we comprehend that this game symbolises the unrestrained competitiveness of the surrounding

Fig. 3.1 Two game players in combat. *Last One Standing* (2009) by Seeta Patel and Kamala Devam. Performers: Seeta Patel and Kamala Devam. Photograph: Simon Richardson

society at large. The house becomes a spatially disordered site where the boundary between interior and exterior is blurred.

Gradually, the choreographic plot sharpens the ambiguities of the game. The players operate as if they exist in an ethical vacuum where they learn about life through a coded programme. As opponents, they try to manipulate its result unlawfully, but offer undisputed support the moment they experience torment at the hands of an unseen power. All the boundary-blurring visuals of indeterminacy or veiled deception make it strangely attractive. Dread and humour, although on opposite sides of the emotional axis, are brought out together with subtlety. Seeing Patel's sudden collapse is extremely distressing because of its obscurity, but the way she lifts herself from the ground, then pats her skirt to ward off the dirt to resume the game is comical.

By the end, both are restless to finish the game. A sense of dread is experienced when a set of creepy hands wants to dissemble the tower. Devam and Patel shy away from providing concrete explanations on whose hands these are or why they are trying to manipulate and destabilise. We feel frustrated when the players undergo complete annihilation onstage as we expect them to be the ones who can rise up, disregarding all frailties and trivialities of life. Their cause of death or destruction remains undisclosed, but what is hinted is "a fundamentally unlivable modern condition" (Vidler 1992, x) which "cannot be pinned down or controlled" (Royle 2003, 15–16). Royle claims that: "Uncanniness entails a sense of uncertainty and suspense, however momentary and unstable. As such, it is often to be associated with an experience of the threshold, liminality, margins, borders, frontiers" (2003, vii). The oscillation between life and death is what renders it as liminal.

Throughout, the piece fails to give us any clue about who the players are; instead, there is apprehension that we are, or could be, them and there is no escape from playing this game in life. It is at this point that the uncanny precipitates, and when the horror beneath the surface (death or destruction) is finally exposed, we realise that it has always existed and is prowling in every sphere of urban living. The music fades away, but what remains is the wisdom of the anonymous male voice: "There are no real winners. It is just a game!"

3.3.2   NowHere *(2011)*

Divya Kasturi's *NowHere* evokes how shifting national boundaries, cultural pluralities, spiritual faithfulness and fragmented selves have resulted in a re-evaluation of what it means to feel "at home" and "nowhere" in a postmodern world. Performed by Kathak dancer Urja Thakore and Kasturi herself, this piece centres on a confining psycho-geographical space, wrapped by a hesitant feeling of in-betweenness and the repressed politics of identity. Music composition is by John Marc-Gowens, and lights and sets are orchestrated by Anthony Hateley and Helen Murphy respectively.

In this piece, Kasturi largely borrows from two Indian Classical dance techniques (Bharatanatyam and Kathak)—intricate footwork, hand gestures, repetitive spins and theatrical elements. However, she gradually moves out of the traditional canon, symmetry and gravitational rule to weave a complex texture of time and space: a crystalline geometry contrasted with the fluidity of Western release technique.

Broadly divided into two scenes, *NowHere* adopts the element of Freudian theory as its core theme: the "home", the boundary of which is blurred through doublings and troubled perceptions. In homes, furnishings, such as a sofa and curtains, remind us of an excess of intimacy and affection. Likewise, rich tapestry and home decor in the opening scene apparently make Kasturi feel at home. The living room of Kasturi's dance master at upstage brings the remnants of her past—an archive where she accumulates time and brings objects with which she feels an affinity. Four mysterious, headless figures, draped in Kasturi's intricately woven dance costumes, are cognitively threatening (Fig. 3.2) because they incite in the spectators the mental activities behind these physical structures. By subtly hinting at the in-between identities and fear associated with mutilating limbs, these beheaded figures estrange Kasturi from her familiar face, creating an unnerving visual of something neither dead nor alive.

Fig. 3.2 Headless inanimate figures in *NowHere* (2011) by Divya Kasturi. Performer: Divya Kasturi. Photograph: Simon Richardson

In this scene, Kasturi recounts anecdotes from her dance classes, maiden performances and travels in English, occasionally interspersed with her mother language (Tamil). The setting represents the remainder of her home, but does not resemble it fully, in a way similar to Freud's assertion of the familiar becoming strangely unfamiliar. A net curtain, which was intended to draw a line between her "past and present life" (Kasturi, Skype interview, 4 April 2014), represents the threshold between the old and new home. Theorists have also considered the issues of "liminality" in connection with the uncanny (Royle 2003, 2). Liminality is "neither here nor there, betwixt and between" (Turner 1974, 232), much akin to Kasturi's new home, which is neither "here" (Britain) nor "there" (Chennai, India). The choreographic matrix comprises a series of different dance sequences: back and forth, up and down, fast and slow along with the sweeping hand gesture that reflects the ebb and flow of the tides, all underscore shifting boundaries. The margin oscillates, bearing a potential to set Kasturi on an odyssey—a quest for her new home as well as her new artistic self to emerge.

The second scene takes us back to Kasturi's homeland, this time not through the homely decor but the digital space. Silence builds tremendous trepidation as we wait for the inevitable sound. Projected on the backdrop, Chennai's Parthasarathy temple, which stands isolated from the world, seems haunting. Kasturi silently enters the stage; her sudden, forceful stomps against her echoing voice effectively rouse strangeness. Random sounds from the busy streets of Chennai and London intrude into the space of stillness, diverting attention. The film sequence of the cityscape is faded out by a hazy pair of animated doubles, while we see Kasturi performing a series of energy releasing movements onstage. She wriggles with her ripped identities, but is hemmed in a non-existent space "nowhere". Her animated double symbolises haunting memories of her mistaken identity, from which she cannot recover (Fig. 3.3). In fact, here the double theatricalises the darker presence of those who raised a boundary against the idea of her performing Kathak (a North Indian Classical dance form) as a "Tamil" (South Indian) woman.

Towards the end, the stage space appears huge with Kasturi's enormous double. She dreams of her utopian home with this hyperbolic image, where the two worlds meet: the world of "here" and the world of "there"; and the utopian bridge connecting both, yet existing nowhere. The penultimate scene condenses mystery with Kasturi's sudden disappearance,

Fig. 3.3 Double as alter-ego in *NowHere* (2011) by Divya Kasturi. Performer: Divya Kasturi. Photograph: Simon Richardson

while her reverberating chants create an inexorable unease. Bathed in blue light, the temple stands still. Whether she has found her new "home" or returned to her old one remains obscure. The fading blue light drowns our cognition; the phantom trace of darkness gradually disperses, bringing us back to reality.

3.4   THE UNCANNY STAGE/DOUBLE/PSYCHE

The Freudian uncanny is closely associated with the domestic space of the home, as discussed above. None of these characters are at home in their worlds; at the core is a fundamental insecurity: the rise of a newly established class of nomad artists, feeling homeless in a new land in the midst of unknown masses. They are always at the margins, whether between (dis)located homes (in Britain/India/the USA) and languages (Tamil/English) or between professions (choreographers/travellers/game players) and dance practice (Eastern/Western). In *Last One Standing*'s apparent ordinary and benign locus, its slightly tawdry domestic setting, the characters are monitored at every moment, positioned by a gaze which they cannot tame. Being American, Devam sees British culture as the "Other".[16] Her unhomely feeling is connoted through communication in her daily life in London: "British culture has lots of subtexts which they don't want to mention. The presence of subtexts is always there in communication that happens in our daily life" (Skype interview, 11 March 2013). By bringing up the subtext, the storyline (un)masks the trauma of a colonial past, the scars of which go unseen.

The realm of the uncanny is equally a perfect setting for Kasturi's piece. The boundary of (un/)homely is a hybrid experience, the feeling being never able to find the exact place. In her words: "Sometimes, when I am 'there' [India] I think of 'here' [Britain] and vice versa. So there is [...] a co-existence that is both pleasurable and chaotic at once [...]" (email communication, 7 April 2014). Strangely enough, choreographically, what Kasturi presents is a cultural uncanny, that is, she clings to her cultural past and simultaneously, possesses a strong desire for assimilating new traditions. It is this in-betweenness, generated by the simultaneity of two opposite feelings, that defines the "uncanny".

In his essay, Freud argued that "an uncanny effect is often and easily produced when the distinction between imagination and reality is effaced" (1955 [1919], 244]. Patel asserts that the double has been her "twin" (email communication, 1 March 2013). So, on one hand, she affirms the "Lacanian mirror stage" (Lacan 1977 [1949]) in the process of discovering the self in her double. On the other hand, the title (*Last One Standing*) results in a deep split: where Patel becomes an object of the speaking subject (a player in a game). The frame between Patel's world and the fictional world gets porous, giving rise to a feeling of strangeness, attuned to what Causey (2006) and Ronell (1989) believe. Despite the "darker" presence of the doubles, Devam and Patel enigmatically present the imagined, future selves of the players/artists who want to conquer the existential game of life in a light-hearted manner. They display comic vanity in overlooking the game of life where "there are no real winners" (recorded male voice, *Last One Standing*). I argue that the doubles here, along with the "darker embodiment", have also underlined a hyperbolic expression of future desire which can conquer life through a hopeful self yet to come. Such portrayal unquestionably pushes the interpretations of the Freudian uncanny double and the Dixonian double as "alter-ego".

In several close-ups in *Last One Standing*, the bodies appear fragmented: face, hands, legs and fingers; which brings us back to Freud's idea of uncanniness incited by the visual of detached body parts. It becomes difficult to believe that the truncated hands are fictional; rather they invoke us to sense a malevolent plotting by some unseen power. We feel asphyxiated at the thought of getting entrapped in the hands of destiny, from which none can escape. Elsewhere in this piece, a forceful leg thrust to displace the arranged wooden blocks arrests the trauma of a postmodern world, where disorientation reigns (Fig. 3.4). Such images arouse a sense of anxiety because we at once become aware of our struggle in real life, which, according to Freud, is a prerequisite for the construction of the uncanny.

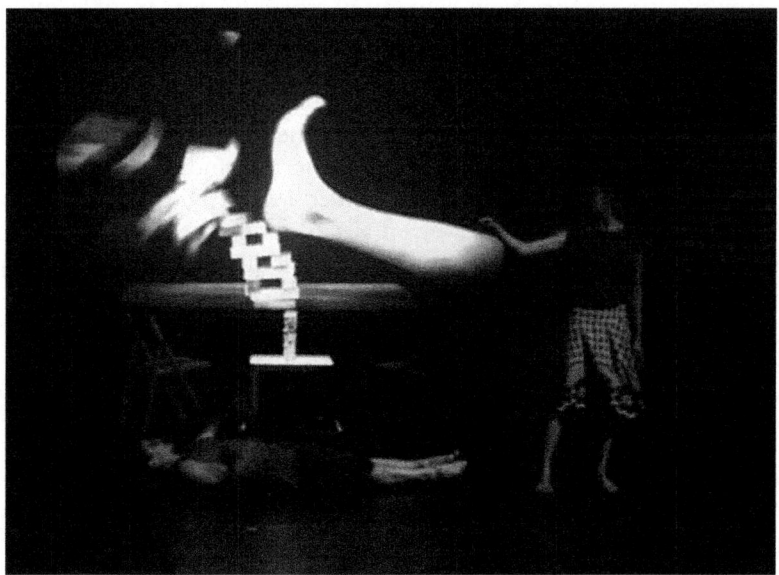

Fig. 3.4 A dismembered leg thrust in *Last One Standing* (2009) by Seeta Patel and Kamala Devam (video still). Videography: Maria Åkesson

Dismembered limbs also deconstruct the Freudian notion of castration in *NowHere* in which the opening scene is obsessed with the four headless figures, signifying Kasturi's disjointed memories. Having no eyes is a perfect allegory of how vision is cognitively removed to defamiliarise Kasturi from her past, and also challenge the audience's gaze. The element of uncertainty emanates not only from the blurring boundary of organic and inorganic, but also of past and present. Also, Kasturi's severed hands "that danced by themselves" serve as a metonymy for her struggle for freedom of expression as an artist. She also deepens the meaning of torn limbs by unveiling her inability to fit in either in her "there-I" or "here-I". This disjuncture ("there-I" and "here-I") reverberated my status then as a doctoral researcher in Britain. I was the first woman in the entire history of my family, to reside abroad alone, leaving my husband back "home" (India). Torn between two nations and underpinned by class-constrained gender roles associated with international travels, the negotiation between my fragmented selves (professional/personal, artist/researcher) often made me disconcerted. Echoing Royle's argument that the uncanny represents "what is happening within ourselves, to ourselves, to the world" (2003, 2), we become aware that the uncanny functions more than evoking horror; rather, it invokes individual subjectivity and how we make sense of our existence. Transcending the bounds of theory and practice, the uncanny is not merely a reflection of the human psyche, but our life stories.

An important trait of the uncanny is the erasure of the boundary between animate and inanimate objects, the real and the unreal (Freud 1955 [1919]; Jentsch 1996 [1906]; Vidler 1992). Drawing on Jentsch, Freud suggested that the uncanny entails "doubts whether an apparently animate being is really alive; or conversely, whether a lifeless object might be, in fact, animate" (Jentsch cited in Freud 1955 [1919], 226). In *NowHere* the four headless figures are endowed with human subjectivity, offering the spectators an illusory feature of identity in the inanimate. At times, Kasturi's animated doubles have rendered her somewhat beyond recognition. In the light of Freudian psychoanalysis, the effect is to leave the audience uncertain of the extent to which the animated skirt costume delivering spins (seen in Kathak dance) in slow motion is a real dancer. As told by Kasturi: "[...] I chose to use my visuals to refer to this 'other' person dancing inside my mind while physically there was the 'real me'" (email communication, 16 April 2013). The juxtaposition of the familiar with the unfamiliar is unnerving, because it transports us swiftly into Kasturi's unconscious.

Feeling uncomfortable and estranged even in one's body is the crux of the uncanny as Royle argues: the uncanny "may be construed as a foreign body within oneself, even the experience of oneself as a foreign body..." (2003, 2). When Thakore's head peeps behind Kasturi's costume, it offers the audience an illusion of Kasturi's suppressed self as a Kathak dancer (Fig. 3.5). Her body assimilates two conflicting principles of dance aesthetics, underpinned by the politics of provincial identity (North versus South Indian). What haunts Kasturi is not a ghost, but a limitation that was imposed on her as an artist by the people—a cultural inheritance to which I can very well relate. Often, my identity as a Bharatanatyam dance artist is challenged for a similar reason. As my ancestral roots lie in the State of West Bengal (Eastern India), many have questioned about my interest in Bharatanatyam and not Odissi, another Indian Classical dance that also has its origin in Eastern India. The artist/audience/researcher borderline collapses; we begin to see the double as a collective experience that occurs somewhere on the margins of art and life.

Fig. 3.5 The uncanny head peeps out in *NowHere* (2011) by Divya Kasturi. Performers: Divya Kasturi and Urja Thakore. Photograph: Simon Richardson

As mentioned above, for Freud, the double duplicates life of the subject. Through doubling, life is "a preservation against extinction" (Freud 1955 [1919], 235), and simultaneously, the double is also the forerunner of the subject's death. Coming to the danceworks, what is most striking is the way the choreographers provocatively bring in the element of death in *Last One Standing*. The doubles do not assure immortality, but bring forth death. Strangely enough, the ambiguous death of the characters brings an end to the world of the game. Through this climax, a sense of helplessness is built up, the torment of which is inescapable. In fact, the viewers are alerted that they can never shirk from enduring such postmodern conditions. I argue that the culminating visual clearly erases the line between life and death, allowing consciousness and unconsciousness to overlap, but never to reconcile.

A symbolic life/death dichotomy in *NowHere* throws it open for critical scrutiny. The menacing absence of Kasturi's real and digital selves in the last scene seems particularly acute. Paradoxically, Kasturi's disembodied voice positions herself inside and outside the text. We wait anxiously and wordlessly, but Kasturi never reappears; for Kasturi, "nowhere" is a psycho-geographic destination from which return is impossible. The deadly terror of being in "nowhere" roots from Kasturi's dislocation, invoking a certain degree of "home-sickness" (Freud 1955 [1919], 245), yet concealing an intensified psychic conflation of womb (nostalgia for motherland) and tomb (destruction of her old self). What does virtual space (of the temple) represent then—spiritual void, inner psyche or the space afterlife? The blue-lit temple functions as the unconscious realm in which the "repressed" memories are amassed before they "return". Finally, virtual space submerges into darkness, which buries Kasturi's haunting thoughts, never to be heard again. I argue that this scene rouses uncanniness as the line between life and (spiritual) death, presence and absence, familiarity and strangeness, and homely and alien is entirely blurred, which is also in agreement with what Freud mentioned.

3.5   Human-Computer Interface: Shifting Aesthetics

In this section I briefly discuss how various transformations are brought into practice by the addition of new technologies. In both danceworks, the classical treatment of the body is displaced, giving rise to techno-human subjectivity. Traditional body posture, which is conceived as geometrical shapes, gets deconstructed along with the superimposition of real architecture with urban digital spaces. The artists' bodies in bits and pixels have succeeded in portraying the complex abstractions of the inner psyche. The digital doubles function to fray identities, while the juxtaposition of live action and animated double creates the effect of coexistence rather than a synthesis, as we have seen in *NowHere*. With these slits, Devam, Patel and Kasturi have given the audience deeper knowledge about the redefinition of the body being affected by technology—especially techniques of replicating the self as "twin" and the "Other"/"other". The transformation of flesh into data offers the choreographers a new relationship, allowing an osmotic flow from one side of the membrane (flesh) to the other (screen). The interface between human being and technology functions as a double-edged sword: it causes a split between the mind and the body; simultaneously, it integrates the mind and the body for us to make sense of ourselves and our environment. Dance criticism, I argue, is thus founded on the dialogic relation between the organic/digital, the whole/fragmented body.

Technically, hybridity has resulted from either conglomeration or juxtaposition of Bharatanatyam with Western dance styles as well as with other Indian dance forms. Although these pieces borrow gesticulations and facial expressions from ancient Indian theatrical practice, they are not as stylised as what is found in traditional genres (say a padam or a varnam).[17] *Mukhaja abhinaya* (facial expression), one of the significant components in Bharatanatyam dance to lead the audience towards the evocation of *rasa*,[18] is minimally utilised. Poetic texts, dominant in *rati bhava* (feeling of erotic love) or *bhakti bhava* (religious sentiments), are supplanted by postmodern themes of travels, shifting homes, liminality and existential crisis. The titles of these danceworks have accordingly changed from the traditional to the topical (Banerjee 2009, 2017).[19]

The traditional Bharatanatyam repertoire has an innate connectivity with temple architecture (Balasaraswati 1978); however, by situating contemporary practice against urban cities, the artists have irrefutably altered the sacred imperative of Bharatanatyam dance. Usually, in a traditional performance, a solo dancer's body predominantly occupies the centrestage. With the juxtaposition of real and digital bodies, the stage becomes "polycentric" (Lopez y Royo 2010, 118) which, in turn, makes the audience's gaze multicentred. Set in contrast to a cyclical progression of a rhythmic structure called *tala*, these choreographies have devised multiple temporalities to reveal fragmented lives of "here" and "there" of the artists (Banerjee 2014).

By defying the linearity of time, these works are successful in embroidering a new "spatio-temporal aesthetic" (Banerjee 2015). For some, new technologies might be dystopian, leading to the disjuncture of classical aesthetics, however they create room for artistic subjectivities, which many of us in today's world of digital communication can relate to and appreciate.

3.6   Conclusion

Appropriating the psychoanalytical lens of the uncanny to read two contemporary/Bharatanatyam choreographies, the chapter has woven theory, practice and research together and the way they inform each other. More specifically, it has investigated the curious intertwining of the uncanny with the digital double and discussed how the pieces under scrutiny have successfully implemented the device of the uncanny through the art of doubling, defamiliarising, animating the live body, actions of dismembering limbs and effacing the line between life and death. We have seen how the uncanny as a liminal border permits conscious and unconscious to simultaneously exist, but never to be completely blended. Drawing on practice, we have also noted how these techno-human subjectivities expand the notions of the "authentic" and the "sanskritised body", giving rise to a new sense of aesthetics and performance legitimacy. This chapter has further revealed how the connection between the artists' inner psyche and the viewers' senses has broadened the psycho-visual aesthetics of contemporary/Bharatanatyam practice. By breaking down the boundaries between the self and the other as well as the spectator and the performer, the choreographies have connected the organic to the digital, the fictional to the personal and the experiential to the social. It is this aesthetic appropriation, rather than merely presenting the content of horror or the frightening visuals, which makes the danceworks extremely appealing.

Acknowledgements A fragment of this chapter appeared in my doctoral thesis, and I am thankful to my doctoral supervisors—Andrée Grau, Ann R. David and Avanthi Meduri—for their generous advice. Later, it was substantially developed and presented at the Digital Echoes Symposium at Coventry University in 2015. I wish to extend my gratitude to Sarah Whatley and Matthew Causey for their comments on my presentation. Thanks are also due to the reviewers who provided constructive feedback, Jingqiu Guan, Jessica Fiala and Pritika Agarwal for lending their critical eyes on my writing and the artists (Divya Kasturi, Kamala Devam and Seeta Patel) for their enthusiastic support.

Notes

1. Married to gods, *devadasi*-s lived in temples and performed services to the deities. To know more about the history of *devadasi*-s, see D. Soneji, *Unfinished Gestures: Devadasis, Memory, and Modernity in South India*; S. C. Kersenboom, *Nityasumangali Devadasi Tradition in South India*; A. Meduri, *Nation, Women, Representation: The Sutured History of the Devadasi and Her Dance*.

2. As the revivalist movement of the Indian arts in the 1930s was configured by the nationalist imagination of a "pure" and "sacred" tradition, the reformers had excluded *devadasi*-s from it because of their fallen status in society. Therefore, the "classicisation" of Bharatanatyam, although elevated the form on the national platform, had uprooted the original dance practice (Srinivasan 1985). In postcolonial India, the reformers further tried to elevate its national image by seeking a lineage with the most valued retrieved Sanskrit text on Indian dramaturgy *Natyasastra* (Srinivasan 1985), thereby "sanskritising" the Bharatanatyam dance tradition (Coorlawala 2004).

3. Performance scholars have debated the presence of a digitally reproduced body in a "live" performance. For a critical discussion, see P. Auslander, *Liveness, Performance in a Mediatized Culture*, and P. Phelan, *Unmarked: The Politics of Performance*.

4. In dance classrooms, the term *angasuddhi* ("purity of limbs") is used for indicating the coordination of various body parts for delivering a perfect rendition of movements within a given unit of time. It has also gained currency as an object of criticism in Bharatanatyam recitals due to being used as a measure of overall performance skill.

5. Bharatanatyam dance has a deeply ingrained theory that "physicality is contradictory to refinement" (Coorlawala 2004, 56), as noted in the Kalakshetra style founded by Rukmini Devi. As a socio-cultural construct, the "sanskritised body" aims to uphold cultural values and moral standards along with the demonstration of authentic technique, appropriate costumes and repertoire (Coorlawala 2004).

6. The slash used between "contemporary" and "Bharatnatyam" is to indicate the juncture of two concepts. By situating these new works within this node, I intend to articulate that the border between "contemporary" and "classical" is ever-changing and thus liminal.

7. A digital performance is a new genre that incorporates computer technologies into production and in which the movements of the performers are confronted with the stage and projected spaces, blurring the boundaries of the flesh and engineered bodies. To know more about digital culture and performance, see C. Beardon, and G. Carver, *New Visions in Performance:*

The Impact of Digital Technologies, S. Broadhurst, and J. Machon, *Performance and Technology: Practices of Virtual Embodiment and Interactivity*, S. Dixon, *Digital Performance: A History of New Media in Theater, Dance, Performance Art, and Installation.*

8. In this chapter, the "digital body", the "digital double", "doubles", "techno-human bodies" and the "engineered body" are used interchangeably.

9. Sigmund Freud, "*The Uncanny*," in *The Standard Edition of the Complete Psychological Works of Sigmund Freud, Volume XVII (1917–1919): An Infantile Neurosis and Other Works*. Ed. and trans. James Strachey (London: The Hogarth Press and The Institute of Psycho-Analysis, 1955 [1919]), 220, 222.

10. Matthew Causey, *Screen Test of the Double: The Uncanny Performer in the Space of Technology* (1999), 394.

11. Freud, *The Uncanny*, 219.

12. Ibid., 220–6.

13. As a twin, a shadow or a mirror image of the central character, *doppelgän-ger* in gothic narratives is used to delineate an undiscovered self or the darker side of the character.

14. For example, see Samuel Beckett's *Endgame* [*Fin de Partie*] (1958 [1957]) that portrays the existential crisis of people through the ambiguity of a game of chess, making the distinction between the rationality of the game of chess and the irrationality of the theatre of absurdity imprecise.

15. In Bharatanatyam dance, an *adavu* is the integrated movement of hands and feet, performed to metrical syllables.

16. The upper case for the word "Other" is only used when it denotes the postcolonial discourse.

17. Both *padam* and *varnam* in the Bharatanatyam repertoire are rich in mimetic technique. The former is a lyrical composition, dominates either in the erotic or spiritual mood, and is sung to a particular melodic mode called *raga*. It is devoid of metrical recitations and rhythmic movements, while the latter is intricately weaved, featuring both thematic and abstract dance movements.

18. Originally a Sanskrit word, *rasa* means juice or something that is to be tasted. In *Natyasastra*, *rasa* is used as a gustatory metaphor—an object of taste that is produced in a theatrical production (Barlingay 1981). Over the years, this term has seeped into the domain of Indian Classical dance as an object of criticism, especially for appreciating a thematic piece.

19. See also K. Katrak, *Contemporary Indian dance: new creative choreography in India and the diaspora* and S. Kothari, *New Directions of Indian Dance* for further discussions.

REFERENCES

Auslander, Philip. 1999. *Liveness, Performance in a Mediatized Culture*. London and New York: Routledge.

Balasaraswati. 1978. On Bharata Natyam. *Dance Chronicle* 2 (2): 106–116.

Banerjee, Suparna. 2009. Quest for Authenticity in Indian Classical Dance: Innovations and Hybridization of Bharatanatyam on [the] Global Stage. *The Global Studies Journal* 2 (3): 75–86.

———. 2014. *Emerging Contemporary Bharatanatyam Choreoscape in Britain: The City, Hybridity and Technoculture*. PhD diss., University of Roehampton.

———. 2015. Performing/Writing Heterotopia: Dislocated Places and Fragmented Temporality. In *Writing Dancing/Dancing Writing, Proceedings SDHS-CORD Joint 2014 Conference*, SDHS Web Publication, pp. 15–25.

———. 2017. *Classical Dance Takes a Global Spin in the New Age*. Accessed 29 April 2017. http://www.wionews.com/south-asia/classical-dance-takes-a-global-spin-in-the-new-age-14989.

Barlingay, Surendra Sheodas. 1981. What Did Bharata Mean by Rasa? *Indian Philosohical Quarterly* VIII (4): 433–456.

Baudrillard, Jean. 1994 [1981]. *Simulacra and Simulation*. Translated from French by Sheila F. Glaser. Ann Arbor, MI: University of Michigan Press.

Beardon, Colin, and Gavin Carver, eds. 2004. *New Visions in Performance: The Impact of Digital Technologies*. Abingdon: Swets and Zeitlinger.

Beckett, Samuel. 1958 [1957]. *Endgame: A Play in One Act, Followed by Act Without Words, a Mime for One Player (Vol. 96)*. Translated from French by Samuel Beckett. London and New York: Faber & Faber.

Botting, Fred. 1991. *Making Monstrous. Frankenstein, Criticism, Theory*. Manchester: Manchester University Press.

Briginshaw, Valerie A. 2001. 'Hybridity and Nomadic Subjectivity' in Shobana Jeyasingh's 'Duets with Automobiles'. In *Dance, Space and Subjectivity*, 97–109. New York: Palgrave.

Broadhurst, Susan, and Josephine Machon, eds. 2006. *Performance and Technology: Practices of Virtual Embodiment and Interactivity*. New York: Palgrave Macmillan.

Causey, Matthew. 1999. Screen Test of the Double: The Uncanny Performer in the Space of Technology. *Theatre Journal* 51 (4): 383–394.

———. 2006. *Theatre and Performance in Digital Culture: From Simulation to Embeddedness*. London and New York: Routledge.

Coorlawala, Uttara A. 2004. The Sanskritized Body. *Dance Research Journal* 36 (2): 50–63.

Dixon, Steve. 2007. *Digital Performance: A History of New Media in Theater, Dance, Performance Art, and Installation*. Cambridge, MA: MIT Press.

S. BANERJEE

Freud, Sigmund. 1955 [1919]. The Uncanny. In *The Standard Edition of the Complete Psychological Works of Sigmund Freud, Volume XVII (1917–1919): An Infantile Neurosis and Other Works.* Edited and translated from German by James Strachey, 217–256. London: The Hogarth Press and The Institute of Psycho-Analysis.

Jentsch, Ernst. 1996 [1906]. *On the Psychology of the Uncanny.* Translated from German by Sellars Roy. *Angelaki: A New Journal in Philosophy, Literature, and the Social Sciences* 2: 7–21.

Johnson, Laurie R. 2010. *Aesthetic Anxiety: Uncanny Symptoms in German Literature and Culture.* Amsterdam: Rodopi.

Katrak, Ketu H. 2011. *Contemporary Indian Dance: New Creative Choreography in India and the Diaspora.* Basingstoke: Palgrave Macmillan.

Kelley, Mike. 2004. *The Uncanny.* Cologne: Walther König.

Kersenboom, Saskia C. 1987. *Nityasumangali Devadasi Tradition in South India.* Delhi: Motilal Banarsidass Publishers.

Kligerman, Eric. 2007. *Sites of the Uncanny: Paul Celan, Specularity and the Visual Arts.* Berlin: Walter de Gruyter.

Kothari, Sunil. 2003. *New Directions in Indian Dance.* New Delhi: Marg Publication.

Labriola, Patrick. 2002. Edgar Allan Poe and E.T.A. Hoffmann: The Double in William Wilson and The Devil's Elixirs. *The International Fiction Review* 29: 69–77.

Lacan, Jacques. 1977 [1949]. *Ecrits: A Selection.* Translated from French by Alan Sheridan. London: Tavistock Publications.

Linville, Susan E. 2004. *History Films, Women, and Freud's Uncanny.* Austin: University of Texas Press.

Lopez y Royo, Alessandra. 2010. Indian Classical Dance: A Sacred Art? *The Journal of Hindu Studies* 3 (1): 114–123.

Meduri, Avanthi. 1996. *Nation, Woman, Representation: The Sutured History of the Devadasi and Her Dance.* PhD thesis, New York University.

———. 2004. Bharatanatyam as a Global Dance: Some Issues in Research, Teaching, and Practice. *Dance Research Journal* 36 (2): 11–29.

O'Shea, Janet. 2007. *At Home in the World: Bharata Natyam on the Global Stage.* Middletown, CT: Wesleyan University Press.

———. 2008. Unbalancing the Authentic/Partnering Classicism: Shobana Jeyasingh's Choreography and the Bharata Natyam 'Tradition'. In *Decentring Dancing Texts: The Challenge of Interpreting Dances*, ed. Janet Landsdale, 38–54. Basingsoke: Palgrave Macmillan.

Phelan, Peggy. 1993. *Unmarked: The Politics of Performance.* New York: Routledge.

Rank, Otto. 1958 [1941]. *Beyond Psychology.* New York: Dover Publications.

Rogers, Robert. 1970. *A Psychoanalytic Study of the Double in Literature*. Detroit: Wayne State University Press.

Ronell, Avital. 1989. *The Telephone Book: Technology, Schizophrenia, Electric Speech*. Lincoln: University of Nebraska Press.

Royle, Nicholas. 2003. *The Uncanny*. Manchester: Manchester University Press.

Schneider, Steven Jay, ed. 2004. *Horror Film and Psychoanalysis: Freud's Worst Nightmare*. Cambridge: Cambridge University Press.

Slethaug, Gordon. 1993. The History of the Double: Traditional and Postmodern Versions. In *The Play of the Double in Postmodern American Fiction*, 7–32. Carbondale: Southern Illinois University Press.

Soneji, Davesh, ed. 2010. *Bharatanatyam: A Reader*. New Delhi: Oxford University Press.

Spadoni, Robert. 2007. *Uncanny Bodies: The Coming of Sound Film and the Origins of the Horror Genre*. Berkeley and Los Angelos: University of California Press.

Srinivasan, Amrit. 1985. Reform and Revival: The Devadasi and Her Dance. *Economic and Political Weekly* 20 (44): 1869–1876.

Turner, Victor. 1974. *Dramas, Fields, and Metaphors: Symbolic Action in Human Society*. Ithaca: Cornell University Press.

Vidler, Anthony. 1992. *The Architectural Uncanny: Essays in the Modern Unhomely*. Cambridge, MA: MIT Press.

CHAPTER 4

The Implications of Technology in Dance: A Dancer's Perspective of Moving in Media-Rich Environments

Kerry Francksen

4.1   INTRODUCTION

This chapter considers how technology can affect some of the landmark activities of dance making and explores the implications of moving in media-rich environments, specifically from the perspective of the dancer. With the ubiquitous use of technologies in performance practices more generally, which has been variously termed digital performance, mediated performance or performance and new technology (Bailey 2007), the ways in which we now create, capture and experience movement is changing. In digital dance performance most specifically, there are a number of practical concerns that can affect the ways in which dancers generate and then perform their movements. This is because a dancer's role is not just a matter of generating appropriate movement material for a particular choreographic intention or purpose. Rather, in digital performance environments her movements are also subject to further analysis and modification through

K. Francksen (✉)
Independent Artist, Researcher, and Educator, Leicester, UK

S. Whatley et al. (eds.), *Digital Echoes*,
https://doi.org/10.1007/978-3-319-73817-8_4

technological means, i.e. her movements become necessary for generating additional visual and/or aural information. This has direct implications for the types of movements that are created, not least because a dancer moving in media-rich environments is required to identify with and then generate movement as part of a technologically driven situation.

There is now a considerable collection of work that includes the integration of technology into time-based theatre arts (see Dixon's seminal text *Digital Performance* 2007, for example), along with an expanding repertoire of dance and theatre companies, both in the UK and abroad, who use new media technologies in their performance work (AΦE, Aakash Odedra, Chunky Move, DV8, Klaus Obermaier, Motion House Dance Theatre, Phoenix Dance Theatre, Random Dance, Troika Ranch et al.). The term digital performance is largely understood to describe works where technology constitutes a key element within the performance. As Steve Dixon describes, "We define the term 'digital performance' broadly to include all performance works where computer technologies play a key role rather than a subsidiary one in content, techniques, aesthetics, or delivery forms" (2007, 3). Digital dance performance therefore falls into this category. Much research and experimentation has taken place in these areas, and it is clear that the incorporation of technology is proving rich grounds for the creation of new performance models.

Nevertheless, a number of underlying tensions exist for anyone wishing to combine live performance and technology. The main thrust of the conversations surrounding new media technologies and performance tend towards the apparent tension between the seemingly separated worlds of the live and the mediated. This is predicated on the view that technology, because of its pervasive cultural qualities, tends to overpower and dominate when placed within a live performance setting. Put simply, on the one hand there are advocates for the beneficial impact technology is having on our potential to adapt, develop, access and share performance, in contrast to those who argue that technology's presence can alienate us from some of the fundamental characteristics of live performance, namely live bodies performing in space and time. Principally, a central concern for any director, choreographer, actor, dancer etc., working in this area is how best to utilize technology in the context of a developing and ubiquitous digital culture where technology is seen as a dominant medium.

Many scholars, including Philip Auslander, who discusses the cultural dominance of the digital in his seminal text *Liveness: Performance in a Mediatized Culture* (2008), have explored such concerns. He states:

> The notion that, working together, stage and screen can convey a fuller sense of what it is to be human than either can alone is premised on the assumption of their working together as complementary equals, an assumption that still underlies much performance work that incorporates both live and screened bodies. (2008, 40)

Auslander's critique is based on the cultural phenomenon of a live event being understood in the context of its subsequent mediation. The analysis he draws is that the cultural dominance of the digital far outweighs the historical claim that live performance is somehow more authentic. Auslander's contention is that we have become estranged from what live actually means, i.e. we are increasingly drawn, if not even more enamoured, by the representation of such events as they become manifest in digital form. As a result, he posits that we should look to accept a screen-based presence as essentially live in nature. This is, according to Auslander, because we live in a world already saturated by technology. The cultural dominance of the digital, as signified here by Auslander, has therefore become highly significant for artists wishing to explore live and digital materials together in performance.

Since his original text a variety of scholars have extended the somewhat binary discussions between the apparent conflict between what is live, in contrast to what is digital or deemed virtual[1] (for example see Broadhurst 2007; Benford and Giannachi 2011; Manning 2009). Through such discussions it is clear that our digital heritage is not only opening up new platforms and possibilities for accessing and experiencing art, but it is urging art makers to ask deeper questions concerning the fundamental characteristics of performance. As Susan Broadhurst describes, some "digital practices indicate an increased potentiality for new artistic creativity rather than emptiness...they indicate a redefinition of 'meaning'" (2007, 15). In accordance with Broadhurst, and in commonality with those artists listed above who explore technology as a fundamental component within their performance making, my own explorations have sought to consider a "redefinition of 'meaning'", which comes from the dancer's ability to perceive a "new artistic creativity" (ibid.) as she moves within a technologically-rich environment.

By presenting some reflections on the embodied experiences of the dancer, my aim in this chapter is to highlight the potential for technology to transform movement making. To do this, I focus on digital dance performance that makes use of video-based technologies as an essential component within the live dance event. This has been besides using video as a tool for preservation and documentation, or indeed as part of the scenography or peripheral characteristics of the dance (which are, of course, as equally important). This discussion comes largely from my own desire as a dancer and choreographer to explore the complex nature of combining choreographic practice with digital processing. Through my own practice, I have discovered that engaging with technology as an implicit agent in the creation and formation of movement, a dancer can be encouraged to re-engage, at a fundamental level, with how she generates and essentially perceives movement. By doing this my intentions have been to test and extend further some of the ongoing questions and theories surrounding the intriguing, yet potentially problematic, relationships that exist in the combination of new media technologies and live performance. My discussion takes account of some of these difficulties and posits that a dancer's awareness of such concerns is vital for understanding movement in the context of our increasingly technologized age.

4.2   Embracing Technology into the Creative Fold

The pervasive nature of technology therefore requires us to acknowledge concerns, which are both real and virtual in nature. Matthew Causey usefully describes this as the "maturing of a digital culture" where such an "awareness that contemporary subjectivity is one that dwells within both the virtual and the real" (2015, 1) has become part of the fundamental building blocks for how we understand and appreciate performance. This is particularly relevant given the ways in which we now experience and access cultural activities more generally within contemporary Western societies. Accordingly, a dancer moving within a digital environment must not only concern herself with the job of creating and managing movements for a particular aesthetic or creative concern (as she might in a more traditional choreographic situation for example), but she must also contemplate how best to generate movement content with the added consideration of working alongside technological processing and within a cultural context where technology is an essential component for how we perceive and interact in our everyday lives.

As Johannes Birringer usefully states:

Addressing "interaction" as a spatial and architectural concept for performance, therefore, means shifting the emphasis away from the creation of steps, phrases, "combinations" or points on the body that initiate movement, away from the dancer's internal bodily awareness...into her environment, to a not-given space but a constructed, shifting relational architecture that influences her and that she shapes or that in turn shapes her. (2003, 90)

The idea that a dancer is moving within a "shifting relational architecture" (ibid.), suggests that her position in the work is indeed changing. Not least because this new hybrid real and virtual space, in Causey's terms, is both recognized and then acted upon by her in the context of her movement's digital mediation. In effect, this changing situation necessitates that she adapts and similarly changes because, as Birringer mentions, the environment which she shapes "in turn shapes her" (ibid.). Likewise, it is also suggestive of a necessity to recognize how a dancer's fundamental understanding of making movements is becoming transformed. For the purposes of this discussion, I would like to make a case for returning to "the dancer's internal bodily awareness" (ibid.) as a way to try and understand how technologically rich environments can transform dance practice.

This also implies that our technological era asks of us more fundamental questions in terms of how we identify and understand artistic processes. As Liesbeth Groot Nibbelink and Sigrid Merx state in their chapter, "Presence and Perception: Analysing Intermediality in Performance":

The clash between digitally influenced perceptions and embodied presence manifests itself particularly as a disturbance of the senses and results in a blurring of realities. Theatre makers often deploy digital media in live performance in order to disturb clear-cut perceptual distinctions between fictional and real, physical and virtual, live and pre-recorded and so on. (2010, 218)

Because of such disturbances it would seem that a shift in our very understanding of the characteristic qualities of what constitutes a dance and by association what types of movement a dancer generates is necessary, especially since technology is now integral to the ways in which we experience and perceive the world. Discussing such influences is therefore important given the current digital landscape in which choreographers and dancers are now having to function. This is supported by Mariella Combi who states:

> There is a gap between the speed at which digital technology is developing and the slow pace at which cultural models and their inherent values are changing. For example, time and space are perceived in different ways on the net and in real life, although the perception of the web is slowly influencing the perception in real life. (2016, 5)

By thinking more generally about the ramifications of using technology in performance and in terms of understanding the cultural adaptations, or potential gaps that are being brought about by our technological age, I propose that technology can offer a dancer exciting opportunities to transform the ways in which she creates movement. Presenting the experiences of the dancer as key to such an understanding offers further evidence for the ways in which our digital culture can help us to advance the inherent values of performance making. This is particularly relevant in the context of dance's heritage, which is intrinsically based on live bodies moving in real space and time. This chapter therefore makes a case for technology's potential to not only develop the ways in which we share and view art more generally, but for how technology's affordances are influencing the fundamental characteristics of artistic process and movement practice.

4.3   MOVING IN MEDIATED ENVIRONMENTS: RE-ENGAGING IN PROCESSES FOR MOVING

By thinking about how technology can be used to open up exciting possibilities for alternative cultural models, in my own work I have been concerned with how a dancer might actually approach this within the studio setting. One such approach has to do with opening up perception and experience. As scholar Stamatia Portanova describes, "the main problematic idea associated with digital technology remains how to analyse and reproduce the external shape, as well as the internal nature, of a gesture" (2013, 12). What is interesting to note here is the difficulty of representing the internal nature of a gesture, or otherwise said the difficulty of how best to signify any underlying intention, which the dancer might be trying to communicate. This is in addition to replicating or presenting the external form of a dancer's body (the shape of her torso as represented through figure animation software for example). As Portanova proposes in her book *Moving without a Body: Digital Philosophy and Choreographic Thought* (2013), technology's historical role for capturing the fleeting nature of dance on account of its ephemeral character, can be thought of differently when it is considered as a mechanism for opening up perception and experience. This is besides technology's facility to archive and preserve a dance, which has since passed and seemingly disappeared.[2]

By utilizing technology in this way, a dancer's sense of agency comes from her perception of digital materials, significantly as they become part of the actualization of her movements. So, rather than making sure that her movements syncopate in time with a video or a musical score for example, which can be as equally compelling,[3] the ways in which she experiences and perceives the evolving dance is thus centred on how all of the materials present afford her different choices and opportunities to move. Crucial here is the fact that she is not adhering to a set mode of choreography, but rather she is responding in the moment to what it feels like to move within a technologized environment. In this type of scenario she is attending to the development of both live and digital materials concurrently. Furthermore, by utilizing technology creatively in order to disrupt or to help re-engage the dancer with her processes for moving, my own works have sought to open up how, what and why she creates what she does because of her experiences of responding to technological information. As well as being useful for capturing, preserving and disseminating dance, video-based technologies (when used to inspire movement) can motivate a dancer to think and move differently.

To that end, my own interests have been focused on exploring image processing technologies and the projected image as an integral part of the dancer's creative process. Steve Dixon supports this when he says:

> In live multimedia theatre, projection screens or video monitors frame additional spaces, this time in two dimensions…Yet despite the flatness of the screen frame, projected media can in one important sense offer far more spatial possibilities than three-dimensional theatre space. (2007, 335)

As Dixon describes, technology offers additional possibilities for thinking about alternative spatial and/or temporal dimensions. By managing the creative process across both live and digital platforms, such alternative spatial and temporal possibilities then became imaginable within the studio setting. Thus, by thinking about how to make and then re-imagine movement in both a live and digital context as part of the dancer's creative

process, my own work explores alternative methods for activating movement. This resulted in a positive willingness to perceive altering qualitative, and more importantly, spatial and temporal dimensions. As Nathaniel
Stern writes, "we must forget technology and rather study the quality of
our movements with them, and the techniques we rehearse in and around
them" (2013, 21). However, rather than forgetting technology, my own
work reveals how such encounters can offer rich grounds for enhancing,
extending and enlivening the act of moving.

The exploration of image processing therefore not only offered additional stimuli for the dancers' to respond to, it positively opened up the
possibility for thinking about dancing within alternative spatial and temporal dimensions. A key question that arose from this was, can the flow of
data move as usefully backwards and forwards to the dancer as her movements arise in both live and digital space and time? Through such questioning it was important to try and understand how moving in digitally
rich environments might inspire the dancers to make transformed choices
about their dancing.

4.4   Transformed Choices: Digital Environments

Following on from this, my own explorations have centred on how a
dancer might deal with the almost insurmountable task of having to compose and create movement across these two very different dimensions. To
do this, my explorations have been focused on encouraging the dancers to
conceive of their position in the work as central to how the evolving technological landscape is both constructed and then managed. This position
necessitated that they engage in the process beyond a requirement to
merely create movements to "fit" or work within a defined technological
structure. More exactly, the purpose for making movement came from the
dancers developing embodied appreciation of how their movements were
both transformed and then enlivened through technological manipulation. This could be described as Stern has suggested, as "more than an
isolated sense, that data has materiality, that bodies are always present with
the machine" (ibid.).

I therefore propose that a dancer's sense of her own agency, as she
responds to her own digital self (as will be examined shortly in a discussion
of a piece titled *Modulation_one*, 2014), suggests that a more synergistic
relationship between bodies and technologies can be realized when a
dancer concentrates her perceptual, embodied and kinaesthetic sensibili-

ties as part of an active and emerging encounter. This is in addition to capturing or preserving the dance, or by asking her to respond or work in opposition to the digital. By integrating technology into the dancer's perceptual process, and by virtue into her and an audience's awareness of any emerging relationship between the movement and the image, the use of video-based technologies can become part and parcel of, what Yehuda E. Kalay has described as, the "believability" (2008, 7) of a work.

Before I discuss *Modulation_one* in more detail, I wish to place this in relation to my own experiences of being directed in interactive media-rich performance environments. In the past, some of my encounters with technology have left me with the feeling that the dancer is somewhat removed from certain elements of the creative process. Namely, she is useful mostly in terms of her abilities to formulate movements for a particular effect. In other words, the dancers tend to be excluded from the technological side of the process because they are needed to activate changes (wearing a motion capture suit, or actuating movements that can be tracked for example), which are then processed and fed back into the computer. In one sense, it has been a practical dilemma to overcome. For that reason, the potential to move not only becomes restricted by the technology, but any opportunity to explore a different movement outcome is stymied by the necessity for activating certain technological requirements. Therefore, any exploration for the dancer in terms of exploring alternative qualities, rhythms, or patterns that might be developed in the movement itself is overpowered by the need to input data into the system. This necessitates her action only in so far as she is needed to activate the technology and not because she wishes to follow an emerging artistic or creative impulse. As scholar Scott DeLahunta advocates, the best way to overcome this is to work collaboratively with dancers so that:

> The choreographic and computational processes are both informed by having arrived at this shared understanding of the constitution of movement... [which] can exist in both its own terms (physical) as well as in the symbolic abstractions necessary in order to use these techniques of gesture modeling, simulating, learning, following etc. with the computer. (2006)

Yet, as we found out, using technology in this way within the studio is trickier to manage. This was because the dancers were faced with having to initiate movements in a live context whilst simultaneously having to address any digital representation or mapping of her movements in digital space. This is challenging because each respective area is defined by its own sets of principles. For one, the laws and physical properties of real space are at odds with the principles of digital/virtual space, which is not bound by the same laws. As we grappled with managing our live movements in tandem with any subsequent digital manifestation, we realized that we needed to think differently about making our movements. This was because we were having to respond to both our physical and technological desires.

Consequently, we began to manage the process not as two separate activities, i.e. making a movement which is then fed back into the computer for further processing, but as a process which slipped backwards and forwards between making, performing, observing, programming, etc. What we found was that by responding to how it felt to make a particular movement, whilst simultaneously perceiving and experiencing the movement's qualities differently as it re-appeared technologically, both our practical choices (actually creating the movement) and technological decisions (how that movement was then re-interpreted and changed through the software) became intertwined. Importantly, the dancers in *Modulation_ one*, were not only responsible for creating the movement content, they were also responsible for offering further suggestions for how to manipulate and develop the technological environment. As a result, the dancers' responses were crucial to both the practical and technological concerns for the work, which in turn became part and parcel of the overall process for generating the movement and the image. Throughout this work, the role of the dancer included that of a technologist, choreographer and performer. Intentionally, programming and designing within the technological environment became informative of how and why the dancers made particular creative decisions, which in turn transformed the technological parameters of the work also. This was also heightened because the dancers were acutely aware of, and in my own case responsible for, the overall programming of the image. Again, in order to challenge normative models of performer–technologist relationships (where technologists are brought in to work with and alongside dancers), it was important that the dancers were fully engaged in how the creative decision-making processes both differed and interconnected across these roles. Having to make decisions that were both technological and embodied therefore became instructive of the overall movement trajectory and thus enriched the dancer's experience of moving. This is usefully illustrated in the following case study.

4.5 CASE STUDY: *MODULATION_ONE:* A BRIEF DESCRIPTION

Modulation_one presented two dancers (myself and dance artist Jodie Davis) moving and improvising within a visual and sonic landscape (see Fig. 4.1). The performance area, which was defined by the positioning of

Fig. 4.1 *Modulation_one*, Atkinson and Francksen (2014). Photograph: Laura McGregor

two transparent screens (see Fig. 4.2), established a physical space in which the dancers could move. Over a period of around 25–30 minutes, images of the dancer's movements then appeared variously on to each one of the transparent screens. These images, which had been captured in the first instance by filmmaker Laura McGregor, had been subject to a further process of manipulation by me and Jodie using Mark Coniglio's Isadora software[4] during the rehearsal process. By way of a brief description for the construction of the image, we used specific tools within the software to manipulate and explore alternative qualities such as, changing the image's luminosity or pixilation slowly over time, as well as using cross fades, and by layering one image on top of another (see Fig. 4.3) to inspire a variety of movement sequences. These sequences were determined by each dancer's desire to explore and change her evolving relationship to the image. Each sequence of movement and image was interchangeable and could play out at differing times and/or via different combinations throughout the performance. The dancers' decisions to alter how and when the image might appear and/or disappear on to each one of the screens, or how and when they might physically interact with each other, or move spatially for example, was therefore determined by her technological and embodied impulses. By using Coniglio's software as a key element within the

Fig. 4.2 *Modulation_one*, Atkinson and Francksen (2014). Photograph: Kerry Francksen

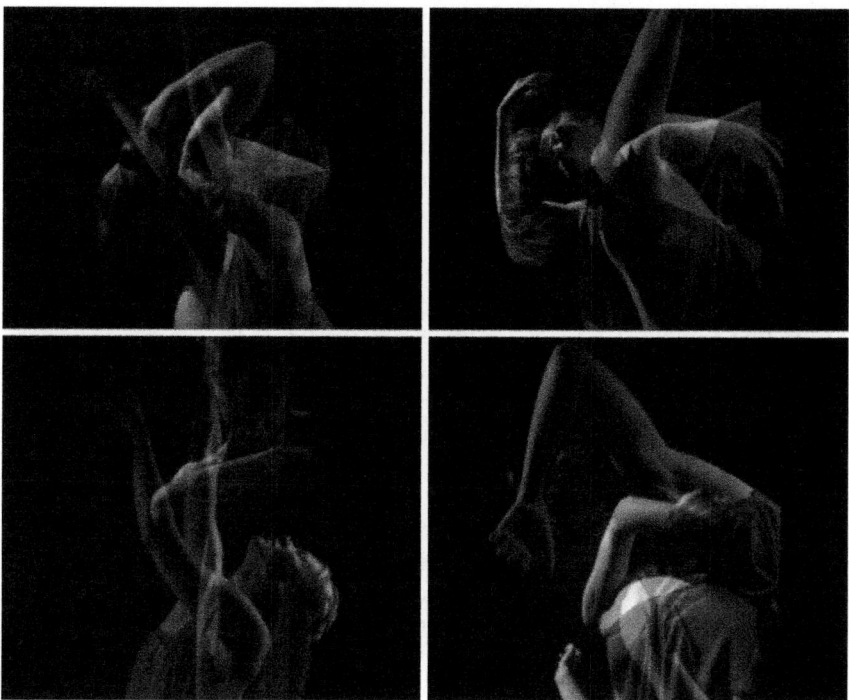

Fig. 4.3 Sequence of stills from the projected image, *Modulation_one* (2014). Photograph: Kerry Francksen (2014)

devising process we were able to continually affect the characteristic qualities of the environment, which then became instructive for the overall imperatives of the work.

During the performance, the dancers were also simultaneously immersed in an electroacoustic sound landscape, which they could also respond to as and when they felt appropriate. The acousmatic[5] landscape, composed by Simon Atkinson poetically brought together sounds that were not representative, i.e. recognized as the sounds of instruments or "known" sounds, such as the breath of the dancer. In fact, the sonic landscape was designed in such a way as to elicit an experience of the spatialization of sound, where undulating tones and rhythmic changes in pitch quite literally repositioned themselves across and though the space. This had a direct relationship to the ways in which the dancers expressed their movements and correlated to the evolution of the image. Crucially, the role of the dancer was not to dance with the images or to the sound, rather she was invited to observe and respond to an ever shifting and evolving landscape. The resulting performance emerged through the coalescence of varying combinations of images, sounds, tones, gestures, qualities and so on. In point of fact, the performance environment was constructed in such a way as to make it almost impossible for the dancer to dance with or to the images and sounds, and yet she was utterly central to how all of the elements ultimately came together.

The image, which had been sensitively captured by McGregor prior to any further manipulation in Isadora, was also filmed in such a way as to emphasize and elicit varying details of each dancer's movements (for Jodie the articulation of her back and for me the curvature of my neck and clavicle). This was done using close-up shots, and by slowing the image to almost half speed. The dancers were therefore presented with a series of continuously changing images, which presented her with a trace of one particular movement's features for example, but which had importantly undergone a further process of qualitative manipulation. Through such a process, the dancers were continuously observing and responding to a series of changing qualities within the movement, the images and the sound. This presented them with a transforming view of their body, or bodies—a close-up image of an arm, or the implication of a shape that represented parts of a torso or neck for example—which provided them with a suggestion of what the movement might be, but which was importantly part of an ongoing process. The images and sounds were thus representative of a particular movement's trajectory (i.e. changes in quality or pace) but importantly they did not present a direct copy of what the dancer was doing. In a sense they were dancing within a continuously changing landscape that appeared to be at once both tangible and intangible.

4.6   Dancing Amidst the Tangible and Intangible

This created an observable landscape where the dancer could attend to any number of connections, which might appear between her live movements, the evolving image and the emerging sound, depending on where, when, how and why she felt compelled to move. Crucially, she was given the option to make creative choices about what movement response might be appropriate depending on what she was most drawn to in that moment. For example, she might change her positioning depending on the evolution of one of the looping images, or she might feel compelled to respond with a particular gesture because she was drawn to a shift in the sound's quality. By creating an environment that was not necessarily fixed in choreographic terms (where a particular movement sequence might be designed to coalesce with a particular crescendo, or to combine with a particular image for example), made it possible for the dancers to let go of their usual desires and responsibilities for constructing movement material to adhere to a particular choreographic intention. Her decisions were thus key to any emerging coalescence of materials as she attended to them variously and concurrently across live and digital spaces (in both a real sense—i.e. attending to the act of making movements in real space and time—and in a digital/virtual sense—i.e. attending to her perception of how a movement fuses with a digital gesture or as a sonorous echo—for example).

Consequently, the clarity, shape and density of some of the images or sounds seemed to become markedly stronger or changed, depending on how and when the dancer decided to connect or disconnect her live movement with a particular live and/or mediated/aural gesture. This was possible in both spatial terms, such as paying attention to the scale or size of the image, or by changing her placement in relation to the screen or to her fellow dancer for example. Similarly, she could attend to the spatialization of the sounds, or respond to a temporal change in the speed of the image, or adapt to the tempo of her fellow dancer's movement trajectory. This process resulted in a variety of changing relationships and connections between the movement, images and sound because of where she was directing her attention. Different features therefore became more prevalent at different times. Crucially this made her sensitive and able to respond perceptively to any new or emerging connections. It was, then, only through the creative decisions and choices she made in the moment of performance, that such connections became explicit both to her, to her fellow dancer, and importantly, to her audience. This placed the dancer's sense perceptions at the very heart of the work's resulting outcomes.

What this created was a sense that she was interconnecting with materials that were both live and digital in nature. Opening up the movement process to encompass both live and digital materials, therefore encouraged the dancers to respond iteratively through a process of moving, responding, refining, moving, responding, programming and so on and so forth. Relating to the visual and aural landscape in this way not only changed her relationship to the images and sounds, which in turn encouraged her to keep attending and responding sensitively to the evolving performance, it categorically placed her at the centre-fold of the works meaning and emergence. That is not to say that the movement, image and sound could not be experienced in their own right. To the contrary, each constituent element was indeed rich and exciting in its own terms. Yet, what was palpable in this work was how clearly the dancers were able to make decisions in order to effect a particular change in quality or rhythm, most significantly as the work was unfolding in front of them. If we return briefly to Auslander's claim made at the beginning of this chapter, the dancer was by no means subservient to the dominance of the digital, and they were by no means controlled or useful only in service of generating a technological outcome. In point of fact, the dancers in *Modulation_one* were fully present and able to manage their own position and role within the work significantly from a position of influence and attention.

In terms of a methodology it was clear that responding and remaining attentive to such an emerging situation, is what empowered the dancer to activate movements between the two seemingly strained worlds of the live and the digital. One of the most significant elements for this was how the image and sound were considered both in terms of their formation (i.e. their characteristic qualities) and in terms of how they were integrated into the dancers' sense perceptions. In such a scenario, the screened image began to offer alternative rhythms and possibilities, which the dancer could either respond to or not. This is counter to Kalay's claim that, "The screen acts as a barrier, engendering a sense of detachment that encourages disbelief" (2008, 6).[6] Moreover, in contrast to this and to some of the concerns raised earlier in this chapter regarding the potential of technology to alienate us from the qualities of a live performance, the divide between the physical properties of the body and what could otherwise be seen as the detached qualities of an image on the screen, was suspended. This was because the dancers' attention to their movements arose out of a strong perceptual experience of their movement as a physical, digital and sonorous entity. As such, this work began to challenge the apparent tension between the live and the digital because they were concerned with noticing and experiencing the changing qualities of a dance, which they were influencing in both live and digital space. Moreover, their sense of moving across both domains became part of the reason for how, and more importantly why, they felt compelled to move.

This approach, which uses the dancer's thought processes as a central focus, echoes with Portanova's premise of perception. This also points towards appreciating the imaginative and creative qualities of bodies and technologies when they are conceived of together. Susan Broadhurst supports this by saying:

> It is my belief that technology's most important contribution to art is the enhancement and reconfiguration of an aesthetic creative potential which consists of interacting with and reacting to a physical body, not an abandonment of that body. (2011, 149)

Consequently, rather than abandoning the body and giving it the status of activator or actuator, creating opportunities for the dancer to craft her movements in this way, irrespective of whether they are live or digital, was significant for addressing the tensions between the two seemingly disconnected worlds. Correspondingly, working in this way informed and encouraged particular reactions and performative behaviours that were not only practical and technological, but also fully embodied. Importantly, the decisions the dancers made in terms of responding to the visual and aural materials was born from the desire to experience the dance, as Elizabeth Grosz would describe, as being in the flesh.[7] The creative process therefore involved striking a balance between responding to certain visual and aural imperatives, whilst simultaneously tackling the creative and performative challenges of being immersed within a technological environment. Moreover, it was based upon the dancer's ability to be creative and to engage with her movements as they became manifest as both live and digital in nature.

4.7   CONVERGING IN LIVE AND DIGITAL DOMAINS

From the outset, the intention for *Modulation_one* was to inspire the dancers to interpret and engage with the technology in such a way as to cultivate alternative meaning, and to stimulate new ways of moving in relation to the digital. Consequently, the function of the technology was not merely used for operating visual and/or sonic materials, neither was it used to preserve or fix the dance, rather it was used to inspire a situation for invention and play. The emphasis on such a process, which by its very nature encouraged the generation of ideas without a particular end goal, was also very important. As a result, the creative methods adopted were focused on creating varying parameters (through the technology), as a means to stimulate a set of responses, which could, in turn, encourage a continual and continuing connection between all of the related elements in the moment of performance.

What became important for the dancers was how to create movements that could influence different aspects of the emerging relationship between bodies, images and sounds. The impact of having to move in response to an echo, or to a trace of an image or sound, is what began to dictate not only practical decisions, such as prescribing an alternative direction and/ or enabling a new choice of quality or rhythm, but the dancers also began to ask more conceptual questions. In a reflection from an early investigation I described not really knowing "where my body was" (Francksen 2011). The feeling of moving was somehow extended, or continued, as the dancers became intrigued with being part of a visual and sonic landscape. Likewise, the dancers were not watching their screened presence, they were moving with the sense that their fleshy bodies were enveloped in a strange duet, which happened to cross between the live and the digital. In this way, the digital was not only informative of how and why the dancers made certain movement choices, but it also became entangled into her experience of moving. So rather than merely developing new movements in order to continue the technological process, the interrelationships between the doing (responding to the environment) and the strange experience of dancing amidst all of the textural materials present, began to affect how and why the dancers moved.

What became significant was the experience of moving as both a live and digital body. In further support of this, fellow dance artist Jodie Davis described in relation to one exploration, "It's real…the digital me is real… I want to keep it real…I am constantly surprising myself and wanting to be surprised."[8] Jodie's description of the experience of moving with her digital echo as something that was real and surprising is counter to what Kalay has described as a representation encouraging disbelief (2008, 6). To the contrary, such a situation continually inspired the dancer to re-engage at a fundamental level with the hows and whys of making movement in a truly embodied way. As a result, she became intent on experiencing something that was not only "surprising", but also extremely tangible and affecting.[9] This was besides constructing movement into an appropriate form in order to correspond to a particular choreographic idea.

This is akin to Dee Reynolds concept of the "dance's body" and *not* the dancer's body—as suggested by Susanne Langer, and developed further by Reynolds. As Langer states:

> The dance is an appearance, if you like, an apparition. It springs from what the dancers do, yet it is something else…But these powers, these forces that

seem to operate in the dance, are not physical forces of the dancer's muscles, which actually cause movements taking place. The forces we seem to perceive most directly and convincingly are created for our perception: and they exist only for it...Anything that exists only for perception, and plays no ordinary, passive part in nature as common objects do, is a virtual entity. (1951, 341–2)

This usefully extends the earlier discussion of the problematic relationships between what is seen to be live and digital. As Langer describes here, the idea of "something else" (ibid.) springing from the dance is what began to happen in *Modulation_one*. The dancers described this as switching backwards and forwards between states of "me", "her", "it", and "us". This also helped to problematize the notion that her fleshy body was somehow autonomous and separate from the digital.

In summary, the significance of establishing an environment that could empower the dancer to make fresh decisions about her movement choices, as part of an emerging mediated landscape, was an important finding for the practice. This occurred by using video-based technologies not as a tool to preserve or memorize the dance, but as an essential stimulus for provoking the dancer to make further creative and expressive decisions.

4.8   Concluding Thoughts

In conclusion, using technology, and in particular using video-based technologies, to inspire a new sense of a movement's trajectory and to express the internal nature of a gesture through both live and digital means, is what stimulated the dancers to think differently about how and why they moved. As Kalay mentions, "Rather than how can the new technology assist the practice and how to avoid its pitfalls, the question to be asked is how can the affordances provided by the new technology change the practice itself?" (2008, 9). In *Modulation_one* the ability of the dancer to embrace other forms of media into her consciousness did indeed begin to change the practice itself. This resulted in essential changes to the characteristics of her movement content, which meant that she was able to renegotiate how and when to move in relation to the digital. As a consequence, she became the centre-fold for any re-interpretation of the dance. Moreover, it was through the dancer's developing skills and abilities in perceiving the changing and altering states, that the dance became more about a developing "subjectivity...that dwells within both the virtual and the real" (Causey 2015, 1).

By enabling the dancer to conceive of such digital representations besides merely preserving and memorizing what has passed, I argue that it is possible to think of technology as part of the "vibrant life" (Kalay 2008, 1) of the dance itself. Using technology in this way provides us with a richer understanding of how a dancer might be able to engage in a fresh perceptual experience, which is fundamentally transformed through technology. In my own work the digital was not useful as a re-presentation or digital accompaniment to the dancers' movements, rather it became integral to how the dancer perceived and re-engaged with the works meaning. Furthermore, the image was not there to replace or record what happened, it was instructive of the tangibility of the event; in so much as it was tied up with the perceptual and somatic experiences of the dance's emergence. Kalay supports this when he says: "Digital media could be utilised for much more than re-creation and re-presentation of physical entities. It has the capacity to become a tool to capture both the tangible and the intangible essence" (2008, XV).

As such, it was the complexities of having to make movement amidst the live and the digital that inspired the dancer to re-engage, at a fundamental level, with the changing characteristics of her movement—or as it could also be understood as a shift in attention towards something extremely affecting.[10] In this type of situation the act of dancing itself became "intensified" (Mackendrick 2004). This is because traditional strategies and processes for making movement were problematized and hitherto were altered through the use of technologies in a truly transformative way. For those choreographers and dancers wishing to move beyond the more traditional combinations of live performance and digital projection, using video-based technologies as part of the creative process can indeed inspire a dancer to think and move differently.

NOTES

1. One of the defining features of digital performance is the possibility to combine live theatre practices (i.e. the management of performers, actors, dancers) with digital processing tools (film, video, projection, etc.), which also includes the use of virtual and/or augmented reality. Virtual in this context refers to a technologized form of representation, via a camera or through an online portal for example, and in relation to animated virtual figures such as avatars. For an alternative view of the virtual, please see Brian Massumi's definition in terms of perception and experience. He

states, "For the present is lost with the missing half second, passing too quickly to be perceived...This requires a reworking of how we think about the body, something that happens too quickly to have happened, actually is virtual" (2002, 30).

2. See Peggy Phelan's discussion in her book *Unmarked: The Politics of Performance* (1993) where she discusses the actualization of movement, which is at once both vital for "its coming into being" (1993), but transient in its always becoming absent.

3. For an exemplar of movement and technology working as part of a well-timed and structured choreography with digital images and sound see Motion House's performance *Scattered* (2009).

4. "Isadora is a real-time software tool to support the creation of interactive live performance work for installation or stage and is programmed primarily to manipulate digital video" (DeLahunta 2005, 31).

5. See http://ears.pierrecouprie.fr for Pierre Couprie's definition of acousmatic sound.

6. Kalay discusses "We have been conditioned from childhood to disbelieve what we see on the screen—otherwise, it would be hard to watch gory films and play vicious computer games" (2008, 6).

7. Flesh here corresponds to what Elizabeth Grosz's discusses as "The concept of the flesh is developed as an 'ultimate notion'" (Merleau-Ponty 1968, 140), not the union or compound of two substances, but 'thinkable by itself'" (1994, 139)".

8. Jodie Davis. 2014. Interview with K. Francksen on 13.03.14. De Montfort University, Leicester (documentation in possession of author).

9. Affecting is referred to here in accordance with Susan Melrose, who writes, "It is 'affecting and being affected' which seems to challenge certain in(ter)ventions specific to the digital economy" (2011, 8).

10. I use the term "affecting" here not merely to denote an emotional response; rather this discussion also aims to align itself with those discourses where the "so-called affective turn" (Reynolds 2012, 126) implies affect as inherently embodied.

References

Auslander, Philip. 2008. *Liveness: Performance in a Mediatized Culture.* Oxon: Routledge.

Bailey, Helen. 2007. Ersatz Dancing: Negotiating the Live and Mediated in Digital Performance Practice. *International Journal of Performance Arts and Digital Media* 3 (2–3): 151–165. http://www.tandfonline.com/doi/abs/10.1386/padm.3.2-3.151_1.

Benford, Steve, and Gabriella Giannachi. 2011. *Performing Mixed Reality*. London: The MIT Press.

Birringer, Johannes. 2003. Dance and Interactivity. *Dance Research Journal* 35 (2): 89–111.

Broadhurst, Susan. 2007. *Digital Practices: Aesthetic and Neuroesthetic Approaches to Performance and Technology*. Basingstoke: Palgrave Macmillan.

———. 2011. Intelligence, Interaction, Reaction, and Performance. In *Performance and Technology: Practices of Virtual Embodiment and Interactivity*, ed. Susan Broadhurst and Josephine Machon, 141–152. Basingstoke: Palgrave Macmillan.

Causey, Matthew. 2015. General Introduction. In the After-event of the Virtual. In *The Performing Subject in the Space of Technology: Through the Virtual, Towards the Real*, ed. Matthew Causey, Emma Meehan, and Neill O'Dwyer, 1–8. New York: Palgrave Macmillan.

Combi, Mariella. 2016. Cultures and Technology: An Analysis of Some of the Changes in Progress—Digital, Global and Local Culture. In *Cultural Heritage in a Changing World*, ed. Karol Jan Borowiecki, Neil Forbes, and Antonella Fresa. Switzerland: Springer International Publishing.

DeLahunta, Scott. 2005. Isadora 'Almost Out of Beta': Tracing the Development of a New Software Tool for Performing Artists. *International Journal of Performance Arts and Digital Media* 1 (1): 31–46. http://www.tandfonline.com/doi/abs/10.1386/padm.1.1.31/1.

———. 2006. *Co-descriptions and Colaborative Composition*. Opening presentation at Choreographic Computations (a NIME06/IRCAM workshop), Paris, 4 June.

Dixon, Steve. 2007. *Digital Performance: A History of New Media in Theatre, Dance, Performance Art, and Installation*. London: MIT Press.

Francksen, Kerry. 2011. *Rehearsal Documentation*. Leicester: De Montfort University (Documentation in Possession of Author).

———. 2014. *Modulation_one*. Kerry Francksen and Simon Atkinson, Leicester: De Montfort University.

Grosz, Elizabeth. 1994. *Volatile Bodies: Towards a Corporeal Feminism*. Bloomington: Indiana University Press.

Kalay, Yehuda E. 2008. Introduction. Preserving Cultural Heritage Through Digital Media. In *New Heritage, New Media and Cultural Heritage*, ed. Yehunda E. Kalay, Thomas Kvan, and Janice Affleck, 1–11. London: Routledge.

Langer, Susanne. 1951. The Dynamic Image: Some Philosophical Reflections on Dance. In *The Dance Has Many Faces*, ed. Walter Sorell. New York: World Publishing.

Mackendrick, Karmen. 2004. Embodying Transgression. In *Of the Presence of the Body: Essays on Dance and Performance Theory*, ed. Andre Lepecki, 140–156. Middletown: Wesleyan University Press.

Manning, Erin. 2009. *Relationscapes: Movement, Art, Philosophy*. Cambridge: MIT Press.

Massumi, Brian. 2002. *Parables of the Virtual: Movement, Affect, Sensation*. Durham: Duke University Press.

Melrose, Susan. 2011. Bodies Without Bodies. In *Performance and Technology. Practices of Virtual Embodiment and Interactivity*, ed. Susan Broadhurst and Josephine Machon, 1–17. Basingstoke: Palgrave Macmillan.

Merleau-Ponty. 1968. *The Visible and the Invisible*. Evanston: North Western University Press.

Nibbelink, Liesbeth Groot, and Sigrid Merx. 2010. Presence and Perception: Analysing Intermediality in Performance. In *Mapping Intermediality in Performance*, ed. Sarah Bay-Cheng, Chiel Kattenbelt, Andy Lavender, and Robin Nelson. Amsterdam: Amsterdam University Press.

Phelan, Peggy. 1993. *Unmarked: The Politics of Performance*. London: Routledge.

Portanova, Stamatia. 2013. *Moving Without a Body: Digital Philosophy and Choreographic Thoughts*. London: MIT Press.

Reynolds, Dee. 2012. Kinesthetic Empathy and the Dance's Body: From Emotion to Affect. In *Kinesthetic Empathy in Creative and Cultural Practices*, ed. Dee Reynolds and Matthew Reason, 123–136. Bristol: Intellect.

Stern, Nathaniel. 2013. *Interactive Art and Embodiment: The Implicit Body as Performance*. Canterbury: Gylphi Lim.

PART II

Space, Time and Memory: Digital Interventions

Bark and Butterflies: Redeeming the Past— Digital Interventions into Post-Memory

Adrian Palka

5.1 Introduction

When my old Polish father died in Leeds in 2008 I didn't know what to do with his memory. Neither his personal instructions nor cultural traditions gave me a clue. As post-war agnostic-atheists confronted with death, my family and I had no established bereavement rituals or forms of remembrance. As a result, his funeral was held in an anonymous council crematorium and his ashes remained in an urn at the undertakers for seven years. All remembrance became DIY, personal and private.

The morning after he died, I woke up and was taken over by a fit of automatic writing. I grabbed a pen and the nearest paper I could find, which was a sheaf of medium-sized yellow Post-it notes. On them I compulsively wrote down a set of instructions and messages which seemed to come from my father. Some of them were guidance about my life, others were instructions on what to do *when* I returned, on his behalf, to Siberia, where he had been exiled as a teenager in the Second World War. The instructions read, 'travel light', 'mix with and befriend the locals', 'you may get cold but make sure you never stay wet'.

A. Palka (✉)
School of Media and Performing Arts, Coventry University, Coventry, UK

© The Author(s) 2018
S. Whatley et al. (eds.), *Digital Echoes*,
https://doi.org/10.1007/978-3-319-73817-8_5

His death confirmed what we already knew, that surviving his exile from Poland to Siberia and adapting to his subsequent displacement to England, were the defining stories of his life. I was personally dissatisfied by the oblivion implied by entirely private forms of remembrance and was convinced that the story of his life held wider public significance. Dealing with his memory inevitably involved engaging with these stories. My decision was to use the inherited diary as a means to explore his story artistically, building on previous work, with the aim to somehow tell it publicly within my roles as an artist and academic, in the *Palka Diaries* project.[1]

This chapter is a part of a series of reflective commentaries on this project. Here the theme is our artistic practice as research en route during our expedition, focusing on the process and context through which we produced digitally facilitated memorial forms, as a work of contemporary art.

5.2   BACKGROUND: THE *PALKA DIARIES* PROJECT

My father Jan Palka was a Polish displaced citizen, who settled in England at the end of the Second World War, following exile to Siberia and military service in the Middle East and Italy. Along with up to 1.7 million Polish people, my father and grandfather, Zygmunt Palka, were forcibly deported from Lwow (now Lviv in Ukraine) in Eastern Poland to Siberia, on orders from Stalin, as part of a genocidal campaign to Sovietize Polish society.[2] My grandfather died while under arrest by the NKVD[3] and my father was released when the Soviets allied with the West in 1941. He made his way, like 200,000 other deportees to Polish divisions[4] to join the British Army in the Middle East.

My father's double exile—first to Siberia, and then to England—was at the core of his identity and the central narrative of his life, the majority of which was lived in the UK, in Leeds. On his death, my sister and I inherited a diary which tells the story of his forced deportation with his father, Zygmunt, to Stalin's Gulag in Siberia in 1940. Reading the diary in detail impelled me to return to Siberia following in the diary's footsteps, as artistic research for a project about his life following the disturbed psychological promptings of the automatic writing. This was also based on a strong conviction, supported by experts and peers, that the diary and the story it contained were of historical significance and public interest (see Fig. 5.1).

With funding from the Heritage Lottery Fund (HLF) 'All Our Stories' scheme and Coventry University, I embarked on the *Palka Diaries* project

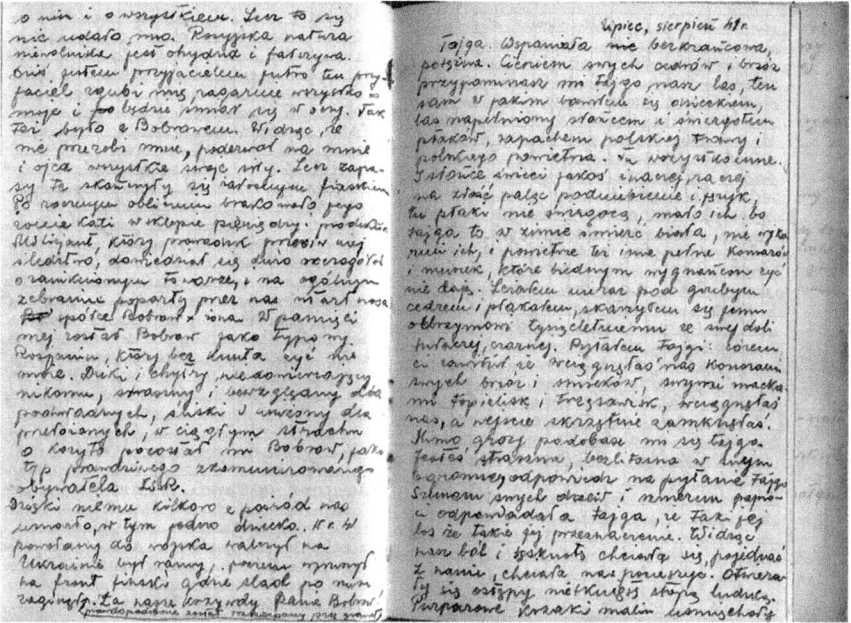

Fig. 5.1 The diary. Photograph: Adrian Palka and Wolfram Spyra

which set out to document the diary and explore its content. In 2013, sound artist and musician Wolfram Spyra, and musician/translator Roksana Vykaluk and I retraced the steps of the journey recounted in the diary. We travelled 5000 kilometres by train and then 100 kilometres by car, deep into the Siberian forest (taiga) to the area where my father and grandfather had been imprisoned. The aim of the trip was to collect impressions and gather photos, videos and audio recordings for future performance and educational projects around this story and its meanings. We also planned to make spontaneous multimedia performance interventions on the way using the equipment we took with us, both as artistic research and as independent performance gestures. While the object of the trip was not to specifically explore digitality, the inherent qualities of our digital tools transformed them into a medium of expression, defining the process and product of our work as well as the future contexts in which it would be shown.

On return to the UK, we (re)presented our journey and our artistic responses to it via a number of media and platforms: the multimedia installation *Bark and Butterflies* and accompanying exhibition, web documentation www.palkadiaries.com, HLF Historypin documentation, *Exile to Leeds*, a short film for an exhibition at Leeds City Museum, as well as schools talks and university lectures. In this chapter, I explain the rationale behind the project and assess how and why digital equipment facilitated our artistic work and its public expression.

5.3   RETURN TO THE GULAG

Siberia, for many, is synonymous with Hell, 'a God forsaken, frozen Hell' (Taylor 2012, 4), a landscape haunted by death.[5] So why would anyone want to go back to a place where their relatives were murdered, starved, worked to death and left to die?[6] Why return to places whose purpose was to erase your ancestors from history, and by default deny your own future existence? Why and how should this culturally specific and highly personal experience of return be put into the public domains of cultural heritage, the arts and education in the UK?

Stalin's deportations of Polish people from Eastern Poland to the Gulag in 1940–1 has a significant place in Polish cultural heritage. Alongside other Second World War atrocities such as the Katyn[7] massacre, it was experienced as a national trauma and its legacy is still felt by survivors and their descendants. As noted, the deportees numbered up to 1.7 million people, a tiny percentage of whom returned to post-war Poland. Of the approximately 200,000 who managed to leave Russia and join the British forces, some 80,000, including my father, settled in the UK after the war. Sixty thousand migrated to Australia, and several thousand to Canada, the US, South Africa and South America.

To the Polish, Siberia is not simply a geographical place, it is a symbolic landscape entwined within dominant national myths: primarily, the national historic struggle with Russian imperialism and the related romantic cult of Polish Messianism.[8] Many survivors refer to their imprisonment in Siberia, when they were in fact in other parts of Russia. Though officially suppressed during the communist period 1945–89, the story of the deportations is part of popular knowledge, national history and remembrance in contemporary Poland, even though the majority of survivors lived in the diasporas.

The complexity of positioning the memory of this historical episode lies in the fact that the deportations were based on a collective national identity, but the living memory of a Polish national trauma was held outside Poland in the diaspora, complicating the context in which the story could be transmitted and represented.

Official suppression under Soviet rule and local disinterest in the UK meant that knowledge of the deportations was not part of the public postwar cultural narrative in either the East or the West. Writing in 2013 about their resettlement in 1940s and 1950s Britain, Zosia and Jurek Biegus state, 'our English friends had absolutely no idea' (Biegus and Biegus 2013, iii). There were few representations of the Polish deportations in the UK media. The best-known English language account is the book *The Long Walk* (1956), narrated by Gulag survivor Slawomir Rawicz and ghost-written by *Daily Mail* journalist, Ronald Downing.[9] Otherwise, the tale has existed primarily in the private sphere of émigré families and in the memories of the individual survivors.[10]

In my own family, the Siberian episode is an elemental narrative. It is a story of extreme hardship and loss which defined my father's life and, by default, that of my mother, sister and me. It reverberates through our narrative of family, and in many ways, is ingrained within our identities. Our mealtimes were laced with tales of starvation, our walks in the country were endurance tests fuelled only with dry bread and water; shopping trips to Tescos exercises in Asiatic bartering. Eighteen months in a Siberian labour camp was my father's cure-all for society's ailments. When suffering from, and surviving, throat cancer in his late seventies, he commented, 'Hitler didn't get me, Stalin didn't get me, so this won't get me either.' The anecdotes are legion.[11]

My father's story of his exile, during his lifetime, was entirely oral. There were no photos, no history books. The most intangible form of heritage, it was a set of mental images, words and attitudes. The story arrived in my father's voice, in English with a Polish accent, in vivid images, pithy anecdotes, dark jokes. Sometimes delivered as short, immediate references, at other times, three-hour-long monologues, particularly on hikes through the Yorkshire Dales. It entered my consciousness in fragments and was latently present throughout my life, like a disturbing subsonic note, which could erupt at any time. Similarly, writer Ewa Hoffman describes her parents' wartime memories appearing as 'emanations', emotional eruptions which took on the character of 'fairy tale, nightmare or myth' (Hoffman 2004, 6–9). In their affective character and frame of reference, these stories exceed the historical record of the facts on which they are based and it is widely argued, most prominently by Marianne Hirsch, as will be discussed next, that they belong to the intersubjective realm of memory transmission, rather than the objective factual base of family history.

5.4   The Diary

The diary my family inherited from my father supplied us with a written narrative of this personal epic. In it the story of exile was recounted, both by him and his father, giving facts, observations, details, emotions. It also supplied a tangible object for us to keep and share with others. In this way, the story took its first step out of family discourse and the realm of imagination, into the material and social world.

The diary had sat for sixty years in a sideboard in Leeds and would only occasionally be brought out. It was written in a spidery hand in Polish and my sister and I were neither able nor encouraged to read it. It was surrounded by an aura of brooding sanctity as the last physical link with our murdered grandfather. When my father died, the diary fulfilled a similar role for us, linking generations both as an object and as a story; a precious family heirloom and the narrative base of the *Palka Diaries* project.

The project was predicated on a return to the Gulag, following in the diary's footsteps. The motivations and intentions behind this return were several and overlapping. The primary aim of the trip was to engage with the family story told in the diary and in so doing to find the means to tell it further within my capacities as artist and lecturer. This urge to bring the story into the public domain was driven by private grief and the associated urge to make sense of my father's life, as well as a conviction of the wider historical value of its contents. Additionally, I wanted to change the character and status of the story, to shift the received images and words in my imagination through an artistic re-working, and in so doing to give it a public presence in the UK.

5.5   Inter/Generational Trauma

Jay Winter and Emmanuel Sivan, in their study *War and Remembrance*, point out that the inheritor generations, that is, 'younger people, uninitiated into the actual experience, can carry emotion laden stories very effectively. For some, carrying a survivor's narrative can approximate survivorship itself' (Winter and Sivan 1999). This observation points to the complex intergenerational and intersubjective overlays of memory and identity associated with wartime stories, which are at work in this project, and also suggests the important role they have in shaping appropriate forms for second-generation retellings.

These relationships have been elaborated and theorized by Marianne Hirsch in relation to the Holocaust which she argues is a 'limit case' of the intergenerational transmission of Second World War trauma. Hirsch posits that the second-generation processing of Second World War traumas constitutes a form of belated memory or *post-memory*, which transcends family history and is particularly prevalent in post-war diasporas:

> Post-memory describes the relationship that the 'generation after' bears to the personal, collective and cultural trauma of those who came before—to experiences they 'remember' only by means of the stories, images and behaviours among which they grew up. But these memories were transmitted to them so deeply and affectively as to seem to constitute memories in their own right. Post-memory's connection to the past is thus actually mediated not by recall but by imaginative investment, projection and creation. (Hirsch 2012, 5)

She argues that it is the very living connection to the survivors and the affective link of family that defines second-generation projects as a form a memory work; less the recall of historical fact than personal creative explorations of conditioned affective and psychological forms.

These studies provide a useful model through which to consider our Siberian expedition. Hirsch discusses the work of a number of second-generation artists who have addressed their inheritance of their parents' sufferings and the artistic strategies they deploy. An example of this work in the UK is the hybrid post-memoir, *Living with the Holocaust* (1996) by the *Guardian* columnist Anne Karpf. Karpf describes the psychological and psychosomatic problems she suffered as a result of her experience of her parents' Holocaust stories and memories as an 'awful, involuntary mimetic obsession'. Another example is the prize-winning book, *Maus, Vol. 1* (1986) by cartoonist Art Spiegelman, which subtly interlaces postwar suburban American life with war memory in an idiom appropriate to him as the second-generation interpreter, and poignantly subtitled, 'My Father Bleeds History'.

This complex overlay of intergenerational, intersubjective experience entangled our project too, shaping its processes and results. Our Siberian trip was *my* journey into *their* journey. On one level, the purpose was social and cultural; an attempt to record and present the landscapes and sites of this history, to illuminate and illustrate it for others, and at the same time to bring this experience to life for them. I also wanted to find a creative response to my father's story, which would enable me to move beyond its received form. In this sense, the journey and the artworks we produced both in Russia and when we returned to the UK were an attempt to convey the nature of the experience for the deportees and the trauma it created in their lives, as well as the subsequent intergenerational impact on their descendants. In so doing, we aimed to document and communicate this submerged cultural history so that it becomes a recognized part of the official and popular knowledge of the Second World War and its aftermath.

5.6   THE JOURNEY

In June 2013, we set off to retrace the journey narrated in the diary. We left as closely as possible to the original date on which they left which was 1 July. Their journey took eighteen days in one train, ours took six days by several trains on the same route, starting from Lwow in Eastern Poland (now Lviv in the Ukraine), to Bijsk in the Altiskij Kraj region of Siberia. Wolfram, Roksana and I had collaborated previously on multimedia performance/installations evoking memories, themes, moods and atmospheres from Eastern Europe including *Kick the Bucket: the Dustbin of History* (2006),[12] *Dislocation* (2007),[13] and *S5: In the Driver's Cab of History* (2008) (see Fig. 5.2).[14]

The team left with no concrete artistic plans, simply the intention to gather impressions for future works and to somehow use the archival materials en route as ephemeral performance gestures. To do this, we transformed each of our train compartments into a studio-laboratory, using digital equipment including computers, cameras, speakers, projectors, as well as mobile phones and LED torches. We took with us digitized images of the original handwritten diary text, transcriptions in English, recordings of readings of the text by Polish actors in Polish as well as digitized photos of my father, Jan and grandfather, Zygmunt.

Our practice was made possible by the portability of the digital equipment and the ease with which we could instantaneously switch from recording to

Fig. 5.2 The map. Photograph: Adrian Palka and Wolfram Spyra

playback mode, and process sound and image in real time while travelling. The artistic experiments took the form of structured improvisations with projections of archival images and playbacks of recordings as well as live feeds and real-time recordings of the journey. These occurred in the corridors, on the windows, out of the windows, on the undercarriage of the train, on passing station platforms, rolling stock, buildings and trees. An overall structure was provided by the unfolding of the journey and the diary narrative, with artistic improvisations created by our responses to chance situations and combinations of environments en route.

My interest, as principal investigator and family member, was to connect with the story and, through the act of travelling the same path as my family members, to work out how to communicate the story in a way that enabled people to understand its physical and emotional impact and consequences for individuals, as well as its political and cultural significance. For me, seeing the landscapes described in my father's stories and narrated in the diary was a critical first step. My intuition was that the journey itself would transform the images and post-memories I had absorbed from my father's story. Staying open to all possibilities enabled high levels of spontaneity in the production of artistic response.

5.7   Interventions

5.7.1   *Performed Readings and Projections*

Our first interventions were live readings from the diary, in English, by me, either at the places mentioned in it or as close to them as possible; these were documented on video. We had no explicit rationale for the performance, except that it explicitly connected our journey with that of my father and grandfather. With portable pico projectors, we projected images of the diary script on to the walls, windows and furniture of the train carriage and onto my face and clothes as I read (see Fig. 5.3).

The effect was dual. The light of the projector illuminated and emphasized the features of the carriage, while simultaneously covering them with images of the text. This juxtaposition was striking and was one we would develop. However, projecting onto me, while reading in English, reinforced the paradox of our journey. It immersed me in the narrative, bodily, through the physicality of reading, illuminated in the image of the words.

Fig. 5.3   Readings 1. Photograph: Adrian Palka and Wolfram Spyra

Yet the content of the readings and context of the journey highlighted disjunction rather than connection. Our luxury, their privation; our freedom, their incarceration; their Polishness, my Englishness. The sound of my voice reading in English and the images projected on me, on reflection, seemed inauthentic.

The Russia outside the window was also disjunctive. The diary described poverty, squalid shacks and shoeless peasants. While we saw the timeless expanse of forests, steppes and great rivers of Russian legend, we also passed through the flourishing modern towns and plush new stations of modern Russia, which separated our experience from theirs. While passing through Kiev we experimented with projecting my reflection, illuminated by torchlight onto the train window while reading from the diary. A ghostly reflection of my face and the sound of live reading was seen over the passing cityscape of cars, tower blocks, petrol stations and shops. The ghostly layering of the images was striking and useful, but in this situation, ghostly images of me, were, again not appropriate.

We also experimented with projecting images of the passing landscape and maps of it onto my torso wearing a white shirt while reciting from the diary. Again, in retrospect the image was visually striking; however, by chance there was reference in the text to people on the stations attempting to buy shirts. The reference to 'shirt' made the contrast between the abjection of the original and the indulgence of our efforts seem tasteless. At this stage, it felt wrong to place me and my experience of our journey at the centre of the experiments. The original experience of my father and grandfather asserted its power in our present and drove us to experiment in other directions.

This response reflects a problem at the heart of post-memory work, which lies in the gap between the experience of the original victims and survivors and the responses of the second generation. The urge is to connect to an experience whose effects have been passed down to you, but which is not your own. Hirsch suggests that the urge to return to traumatic sites in the second generation is both 'connective' and 'incommensurable', as a 'fractured encounter between generations, between cultures, and between mutually imbricated histories occurring in a layered present' (Hirsch 2012, 206). Sitting in comfort surrounded by food and drink, mobile phones and expensive equipment, the gulf between the two journeys was insuperable, the conditions incomparable. Nevertheless, our creative aim was to find a way to connect to and make public the trauma of the original deportees using our artistic and digital resources.

5.7.2   Projections and Photos

As the journey progressed we turned away from positioning me in relation to the diary narrative and concentrated on positioning the original text and images of Jan and Zygmunt within our journey. Our strongest urge was to return their presence symbolically to the landscape which had been intended to erase them. Literally, we wanted to shed light into the darkness at the heart of this story. To do this, we projected images of Jan and Zygmunt through the window of the train into the night, onto passing trains, bridges, buildings, telegraph poles. Projected onto the carriage window, the images had a comforting immediacy, as if they were travelling with us in the compartment. The window acted simultaneously as a screen, a frame and a site. It was physically necessary to make the images appear, but with none of the neutrality associated with screen; instead, it was layered with the symbolic resonances of this specific journey. For all the ephemerality of the light projections, this felt to us like the symbolic heart of the matter, them and their journey revisited, both in actuality and virtually.

5.7.3   Speakers

In the daylight, we set up speakers and played back readings of passages of the diary text in Polish, with a projected image of Zygmunt on its surface which we filmed. The sound of the text in the original, juxtaposed with the simple ambient sounds of the journey, the rattle of the train and the chatter of children in the corridors, combined with the archaic flickering sepia image was like an eerie return, a phantasmagoric voice from beyond the grave, the speaker like a headstone, the image reminiscent of ceramic memorial photos of the deceased which can be seen in cemeteries throughout Poland.

5.7.4   Projection

At night, we opened the window and hanging outside with the projector, projected their images onto the passing landscape. This produced other effects. At every step, any interaction resonated with symbolic meaning to us, as every step of our journey could be related back to the original journey, either literally or metaphorically. The darkness of the night became the darkness of the story, the grubbiness of the window, the banality within the evil. The frame of meaning-making we had built for ourselves

Fig. 5.4 Window projections. Photograph: Adrian Palka and Wolfram Spyra

constantly produced sparks of connection to the journey made by Jan and Zygmunt. The creative challenge was to find ways of expressing these significances beyond the personal (see Fig. 5.4).

Projecting out of the window produced a more violent and dramatic effect than the daytime versions. The deafening metallic clatter of the train, the cold gale, and the dark and sudden appearances of bridges, tunnels and telegraph poles created an undertone of danger and potential violence, all captured on video.

The projections of their images dispersed into the expanses of darkness outside and then suddenly came into vivid focus on passing trains, buildings and tunnels, giving them a violent assertiveness. The images articulated challenge, the two isolated figures, the tender weave of light and shadow, projected into night-time vastness, defying the darkness.

5.7.5   Klub

The final stage of the journey was several hours by road into the depths of the forest (taiga). We followed the text of the diary and stopped at the sites mentioned in it. The site of their camp no longer existed—it had been abandoned and reverted to forest—so we followed the road in its general direction until we reached a dilapidated village called Novoiushino. Here we made contact with the local administration. They welcomed us and, as unexpected guests, they offered us the village social club (*klub*) to spend the night in.

The club was a dilapidated building with forlorn traces of former use. There was a huge room with a crooked table tennis table, the ceiling decorated with deflated balloons from a former party. There was a main room with a stage, an antiquated PA and stage lights. The walls were decorated with wallpaper of photographic images of the birch forest. This was deep Russia. As a remnant of its former role as a school, there was a small wardrobe of theatrical costumes, some of which we put on. Roksana and our local driver Marina were transformed by this change of costume into figures from Russian folklore. In this space, where we were offered our own private theatrical environment, despite exhaustion, we staged an intervention which extended the techniques we had developed on the train.

We positioned one of the speakers from the PA in the middle of the stage, projected Zygmunt's image onto it and played back readings in Polish as we had done in the train carriage. The women in their folkloric costumes simply sat and listened. It was as if Zygmunt had returned and Russia itself was listening to his story.

Novoiushino was the last settlement before the wilderness of the taiga began. Our final goal was to enter the forest and see the landscape which my father had described to me so many times. Villagers drove us into the forest, warning us about its dangers, and we made our final intervention. We projected my father's image onto my hand held against a birch tree, while playing recordings of a poem he had written in the diary. The poem expressed the pain of his situation and his awe at the power and beauty of the taiga; it was addressed to the taiga (see Fig. 5.5).

My father had always told me that, while alone in the forest, he had eaten the bark of birch trees to survive. As with my grandfather in the *klub*, we returned Jan's voice from beyond the grave to the Siberian vastness and audio-visually merged his memory with the secret of his survival, his antidote to death: birch bark. We collected shards of it as found objects from our expedition to be included in later work.

The bark shards relate to the epiphanous moment of our trip, which is when we were confronted by swarms of butterflies in the taiga. Again, this connected to my father's stories of starvation and of having to eat butter-

Fig. 5.5 Taiga projection. Photograph: Adrian Palka and Wolfram Spyra

flies to survive, which he had told at home in Leeds and which symbolized his survival. I had never understood quite what he meant, but the swarms of large butterflies gave a concrete reality to his story. I simply placed the DVD camera on the ground next to where swarms of butterflies were feeding and filmed them. This image was the prize find of the entire trip.

5.8 Reflections

The concept of 'journey' was the entire foundation of this project. It was a literal journey, a creative journey, and a symbolic journey into family and historical narrative. More problematically it was a journey into a journey. The mythic power of the original story, at least personally, lies in how the experiences it relates constitute a battle with death, which defined and explained my father's life. The struggle between death and life is the referent of every incident and observation on both journeys and the landscape of Siberia, the landscape haunted by death, its symbol.

For me, the journey was not a literal re-creation or re-enactment—I did not suffer the same hardships as my father, and was never in danger of dying—but it was a way of grounding his stories in the reality of place. This embodied and emplaced experience, now inscribed with his powerful story of human struggle, was simultaneously a personal and a political/ cultural journey of discovery, understanding and release. The affective potential of the artworks we produced—both *in situ* and when we returned—lies in the tensions, correspondences and disjunctions between our journey and theirs.

Accordingly, our creative resources for the interventions were explicitly limited to materials related to the diary: images of my father and grandfather, images of the diary text, sound recordings of the text, and of course, the actuality of journey.

In her elaboration of the theory of post-memory, Hirsch gives considerable attention to the role of the photograph in the artistic interventions of the second generation. The photograph, in her view, represents a paradoxical connection with the past but also an irreversible finality. It also offers an object on which personal projections of desire and identity can play out:

> More than oral or written narratives, photographic images that survive massive devastation and outlive their subjects and owners, function as ghostly revenants from an irretrievably lost past world. They enable us, in the present, not only to see and touch that past, but also to reanimate it by undoing the finality of the photographic 'take'. (Hirsch 2012, 36)

She goes on to say that, given the emotional charge of post-memory work, the 'fragmentariness and the two-dimensional flatness of the photo make it especially open to narrative elaboration embroidery and to symbolisation' (Hirsch 2012, 37). For us, the recent developments in digital/LED portable projection technologies allowed us to extend the physical reach of family photographs by projecting scanned images onto sites en route and thereby extend their symbolic potential too.

Critical writing on the art of projection emphasizes its capacity to interrogate space and to suggest 'filmic counterworlds', to the extent argued by Knapstein that 'ultimately all film images are phantasmagoria' (Jaeger et al. 2006, 11).

This accorded with our experience. As every point on the journey manifested the story within the diary and associated personal narratives, our projection of the photographs into ambient space generated images saturated with meaning. In our private experience, the images of Jan and Zygmunt, their sepia patina of the past projected onto the passing landscape, reanimating them and accompanying us on our journey: as 'ghostly revenants', as Hirsch suggests. Projecting photos framelessly onto the symbolic landscapes within which we were immersed penetrated the suggestive 'subtle beyond' and 'blind space' outside the photographic image described by Barthes (1981) in *Camera Lucida*, and rendered our themes of life and death in terms of the light of the LED bulb and the darkness of the Siberian night.

The digital equipment allowed us to manipulate, reconfigure and blur art forms and media in the audiovisual overlays of photos and diary text in real time. Using hand-held equipment, we were deploying filmic techniques in and on a real-time, three-dimensional environment. The visual layering, the fade, the dissolve, the filmic metaphor of the train window, the combining and montage of immediate environment with image and sound, created an eerie continuity and contiguity of past and present, of mediated archival image, concrete reality, remembered and imagined pasts. The digital co-mingling of image, sound and site generated a synaesthetic, phantasmagorical present, placing my father's original oral account and the written text into a digitally re-mediated imaginative register.

Our interventions externalized the stories; projected them out of the complex, interwoven interior space of family discourse, into the world, and then re-immersed us in them. In the world of the train carriage, we created a memory/memorial space for ourselves, a kind of digital phantasmagoria, a dream-mare in which the faces and voices of the dead accompanied us[15] as 'ethereal emanations' from our equipment. For several days, the confined interior of the carriage resembled an externalized disturbed state of mind, as the spatial, temporal and symbolic coordinates of the story imploded under the density of their digitized presence.

The digital reconfiguring of the scanned text and photos as projected image offered us both immersive and invasive possibilities, with corresponding identificatory or objectifying effect. Jan and Zygmunt were both returned to Russia. No longer made invisible by official suppression, they were assertively 'writ large' on the spaces and places through which we travelled. The text of the diary, its archaic hand-written Polish script projected into our environment, immersed us in the symbolic past world of its story. The words swaying and crawling on the carriage walls, floors, beds, fittings, dominating, reclaiming the carriage, as if they were letting no one and no thing forget. The images illuminated and silently interrogated official history, almost taunting the train carriage with the words of those who had been destined to annihilation. The projections of word-processed transcriptions and English translations helped us to understand the text better, draw parallels between our journey and theirs, between our idioms and theirs. Our attempts to understand the reality of my father's and grandfather's journey was grounded by a more literal understanding of the facts as written in the diary and the places we were passing.

As Peter Weibel observes, projection facilitates 'the invasion of space by the visual image' (Weibel 2002, 43), and this implicit aggression was present in the taunting silence of Jan and Zygmunt's words as image, and by the projection of their portraits into the passing landscape. At night, the portrait photos projected out of the train window dissolved into the surrounding blackness as a 'pure gleam which falls into the void' (Blunck 2002, 57) and then when it struck a passing ridge, lamp-post, train, suddenly bounced back—whole, complete, staring, a challenging, spectral emanation from the void. At every juncture, our work was saying, we are back, in life, in memory and despite your hell, we prevailed. Similarly, the sound recordings of readings of the text lifted the words from the page into ambient space, invoking the presence of the writers, the layering of voice and the familiar, timeless clatter of the moving train, producing a sound track connecting our worlds with theirs.

In this way, the pervasiveness of our digital images and sounds, the faces and voices of the dead merging with ambient space, had engendered an intense immersive space in the train carriage. The audiovisual recombinations destabilized and imploded spatial, temporal and symbolic coordinates in an overlay of the digital and empirical reality, for the performative enactment of the complexities of this post-memory.

By the time we left the train and headed into the taiga and the *klub*, the contours of our artistic method were becoming firmer: experiments with my presence receded and attempts to *evoke* their journey had been evolved into attempts to *invoke* it. Our focus became their images and their words, telling their stories, now, witnessed by us as well as by a mythic Siberia, personified by the forest to which my father's poem was addressed and by the women in folkloric costumes in the *klub*.

Finally, our experience *in situ*, looped back into the family stories of childhood, by reference to the bark which we collected and the butterflies we filmed and brought back to the UK.

5.9   BARK AND BUTTERFLIES: SIBERIA IN A SUITCASE

On our return, our task was to work out a way to retell the story through the methods which had evolved on our journey. Back home, we edited the materials we had collected and produced a website (www.palkadiaries.

com) about the entire project, which included detailed documentation of our journey and a section which explained the creative process. The problems of retelling these stories lies in the post-memory paradox of the existence of the epic in the domestic; that is, of the memory of unspeakable hardship immersed in quotidian routines and the slippage between the

Fig. 5.6 Bark and butterflies shed. Photograph: Adrian Palka and Wolfram Spyra

events of an imagined, but also real, past and the attempt to live a reality distant in time and place (see Fig. 5.6).

For me, simply seeing the Russian landscapes was the first step in a process of concretization, taking the story out of imagination and remembered family conversations. Travelling to Siberia transformed the 'God forsaken, frozen Hell' of imagination and stereotype. What we saw was verdantly beautiful, bearing an uncanny resemblance to our own beloved Yorkshire Dales. Not only was this a process of demystification, but of familiarization, looping correspondences and bridging worlds of memory. The climax of our expedition was seeing the butterflies, which we collected as a found image. This acted to bridge my memories of the family breakfast table of childhood with my father's exile, and our experience of the reality of Siberia. Though our experiences were incommensurable, these images forged the connections I sought, and the bark and the butterflies which saved his life became the symbolic material which would sustain his memory.

We had worked with a syncretic bricolage method, imaginatively shaping and reassembling divergent and multiple materials, and this continued on our return and in the final work. *Bark and Butterflies* is a combination of sound and image, of digitized photos merged with found materials and found footage and set to the sounds of voice, countryside and train, which illuminated my father's stories of survival, of eating birch bark and migrating butterflies. This combination of digital and actual materials acted as a three-dimensional metaphor of my father's exile.

The installation took the form of a tall wooden shed clad in bark. In the shed, there was a tatty leather suitcase containing a pile of shards of birch bark which we had brought back from Siberia. On the bark chips, images of the butterflies in the taiga fluttered over the rough contours of the wood. A superimposed photo of my father's young face peered out of the suitcase. His poem to the taiga in Polish emanated from a speaker beneath the bark and a whispered translation in my voice in English was played simultaneously through a speaker on the wall. The positioning of the speakers produced an effect like headphones in which the voices sounded inside the listener's head, rather than exteriorized in ambient space. The found materials gave authenticity to the sense of place within the installation, and the bilingual rendition of the taiga poem, recited in Polish and English, represented the cultural displacement central to the exhibit, with the bodily intimacy of a whisper.

The leather suitcase (the train carriage too) is a stock image of Second World War refugeehood.[16] Despite the highly personal nature of the project, it also tells a common story and Hirsch notes that in the attempt to find appropriate forms for post-memory work, second-generation artists often fall back on 'familiar and often unexamined cultural images' or 'pre-established expressive forms' (Hirsch 2012, 39). The value of this strategy is that it underlines the fact that this experience is not only individual, but was experienced by millions.

Jay Winter observes that mass death provokes 'timeless questions' in the bereaved and the survivors (Winter 1995, 224). The urge to remember prompts universal questions about death and life, pondered in pain, and expressed in memorial activities. Questions which in the immediate aftermath of my father's death I had not really been able to respond to, but through the Siberia trip had begun to address.

As the journey progressed, our work had shifted from *evocation* to *invocation*, and the original gestures of challenge and experiments with identification moved towards rituals of remembrance. The spectral qualities of video projection combined with the sound of Polish voices recounting in their words, generated the illusion of their presence. The carriage became like a spiritualist phantasmagoria of summoned spirits.[17] It was at once a fantasy space fulfilling my personal desire for the dead to live, and also an increasingly devotional space. We transposed this devotional atmosphere and affective space into the installation which, despite other possible readings, had the character of a memorial shrine.

While our intention had been to extend our enclosed family discourse into new forms through artistic experiments, both the journey structure and the memorial process, I would argue, elicited what Turner refers to as the 'root' paradigmatic form of the *pilgrimage* (Turner and Turner 1978). We had loosely used the term in our preparations, but the character of our experience en route lent it more accuracy, authenticity and rigour.

We undertook a long journey, which was framed as a research trip but acquired the form of a pilgrimage, rendering the audiovisual interventions into devotional acts of remembrance and connecting our lives to the lives of the dead. Culturally disconnected from a tradition of memorial images, words and forms beyond family discourse to refer to, we unwittingly created our own DIY version of an ancient, archetypal, paradigmatic form and applied it to our private mythology around my father's and grandfather's exile, in a form of 'self-sacralisation' (Luckmann 1996).

In retrospect, the digital interventions we made were analogous to pilgrimage activities, engaging with 'shrines, images, liturgies, ritual circumambulation of holy objects' (Turner and Turner 1978, 8). In this journey, after Turner, the pilgrim (artist) 'becomes the redemptive tradition' and the redemptive form, aesthetic. Emerging from the journey, back home, the installation *Bark and Butterflies* becomes a permanent artistic shrine of self-styled 'sacred' images, relics and prayers, testifying to the miracle of survival and circulating in a permanent, redemptive, electronic infinity of remembrance, for anyone to visit.

Notes

1. See www.palkadiaries.com, the project documentation website. My grandfather Zygmunt kept a wartime diary, a section of which offers a detailed account of the forced journey he and his son (my father Jan) endured from eastern Poland to Siberia. Jan kept and maintained the diary throughout his further travels during the war, hence the overall project title being *The Palka Diaries*.
2. Following the Molotov–Ribbentrop Pact (1939), Poland was dismembered and occupied by the Germans in the West and the Russians in the East.
3. NKVD is the Narodnyi Komissariat Vnutrennikh Del (People's Commissariat for Internal Affairs), a ministry of the Soviet government responsible for security and law enforcement which was formed on 7 November 1917, later becoming the Ministry of Internal Affairs (MVD) on 19 March 1946.
4. The so-called Anders Army.
5. This theme is present in sources as various as Dostoevsky's *House of the Dead* (1861–2, reprinted 1979), and Colin Thubron's travelogue, *In Siberia* (1999).
6. The account of Zygmunt's final arrest appears on page J67 of the diary transcription on www.palkadiaries.com.
7. Mass assassination of Polish officers and intelligentsia.
8. The Romantic doctrine of the martyrdom of Poland.
9. The book has sold 500,000 copies since then, has been translated into twenty-five languages and has ever been out of print. In 2010, it was adapted into the film, *The Way Back* by Peter Weir.
10. Herling-Grudziński's *A World Apart* was published in English in 1951 with a preface by Bertrand Russell, but was not a best-seller.
11. There are too many to tell. My favourites are his habit of berating hapless young politicos attempting to sell the *Socialist Worker* in the shopping centres of Leeds, with stories of his 'long holiday in Russia, courtesy of Stalin'. Also, one Christmas, he and I ignored the festivities and went for a long hard walk in the Yorkshire Dales in the driving rain. On the way back, we called in on some of his friends from work. The entire family was dozing in

front of the TV after Christmas lunch. We entered dripping wet into their stupor. A Dalmatian dog suddenly leapt up in front of the TV, disturbing the slumbering grandmas, prompting my father to remark, 'Ah, a Dalmatian, I ate one of those when I was in Siberia.'

12. A form of sonic coconut shy in which the public threw stones at several oil drums triggering sampled sounds on the theme of the collapse of the communist system.

13. A site-specific sound performance which used the fragmented acoustic of Coventry Cathedral as a metaphor for the psychic dislocations of war and refugeehood.

14. A sonorized multi-screen film examining post-1989 Berlin.

15. More dream than nightmare, as we weren't filled with fear, but there was fear in the text.

16. One of the most immediate examples being the sculpture dedicated to the Kindertransport at Liverpool Street station, and also at Friedrichstrasse station in Berlin.

17. Winter (1995) notes the rise of these practices in post-First World War Britain.

REFERENCES

Barthes, Roland. 1981. *Camera Lucida*. New York: Hill and Wang.

Biegus, Zosia, and Jurek Biegus. 2013. *Polish Resettlement Camps in England and Wales 1946–1969*. Rochford: PB Software.

Blunck, Annika. 2002. Towards Meaningful Spaces. In *New Screen Media: Cinema/Art/Narrative*, ed. Martin Reiser and Andrea Zapp, 54–63. London: British Film Institute Publishing.

Dostoevsky, F. (1861–2) 1979. *House of the Dead*. London: Dutton Adult.

Herling-Grudziński, Gustaw. 1951. *A World Apart*. London: Heinemann.

Hirsch, Marianne. 2012. *The Generation of Post Memory: Writing and Visual Culture After the Holocaust*. New York: Columbia University Press.

Hoffman, Eva. 2004. *After Such Knowledge: Memory, History and the Legacy of the Holocaust*. New York: Public Affairs.

Jaeger, Joachim, Gabriele Knapstein, and Anette Husch. 2006. *Beyond Cinema: The Art of Projection: Films, Videos and Installations from 1965 to 2005*. Ostfildern: Hatje Cantz.

Karpf, Anne. 1996. *The War After: Living with the Holocaust*. London: Heinemann.

Luckmann, Thomas. 1996. The Privatization of Religion and Morality. In *Detraditionalization: Critical Reflections on Authority and Identity*, ed. Paul Heelas, Scott Lash, and Paul Morris, 72–86. Oxford: Blackwell.

Rawicz, Slavomir. [Ronald Downing]. 1956. *The Long Walk: A Gamble for Life*. New York: Harper and Brothers.

Spiegelman, Art. 1986. *Maus, Vol. 1. A Survivor's Tale: My Father Bleeds History*. New York: Pantheon.

Taylor, Elizabeth. 2012. *Next Stop Siberia*. Guildford: Grosvenor House.

Thubron, Colin. 1999. *In Siberia*. London: Chatto & Windus.

Turner, Victor, and Edith Turner. 1978. *Image and Pilgrimage in Christian Culture*. New York: Columbia University Press.

Weibel, Peter. 2002. Narrated Theory: Multiple Projection and Multiple Narration. In *New Screen Media: Cinema/Art/Narrative*, ed. Martin Reiser and Andrea Zapp, 42–53. London: British Film Institute Publishing.

Winter, Jay. 1995. *Sites of Memory, Sites of Mourning: The Great War in European Cultural History*. Cambridge: Cambridge University Press.

Winter, Jay, and Emmanuel Sivan. 1999. *War and Remembrance in the Twentieth Century*. Cambridge: Cambridge University Press.

CHAPTER 6

Chorotopical Art: Mediating the Atmospheres of Cultural Sites to Create a New Spatial Logic

Liana Psarologaki

6.1 INTRODUCTION

Art and architecture have been considered by many as distinct practices that respond to different logics and inherit rationales of diverse scope and intention. They have been however interconnected particularly in the context of artistic place and space making. Rosalind Krauss's essay "Sculpture in the Expanded Field" (Krauss 1979) made a critical contribution the establishment and expansion of theories and practices that consider the sculptural place of architectural ontology and characteristics with the introduction and acknowledgement of the term installation art, which implies the decentrification of the oeuvre d'art highlighting the importance of the spatial architectonics that contextualize it. Claire Bishop, in the prolific *Installation Art: A Critical History* associates the term installation art with the viewers' entering a space in order to appreciate the artistic qualities and presence of the work (Bishop 2005, 6), rendering therefore the viewers' empirical reading as constitutional to the work (2005, 10).[1]

L. Psarologaki (✉)
School of Arts, Design and Humanities, University of Suffolk, Ipswich, UK

© The Author(s) 2018
S. Whatley et al. (eds.), *Digital Echoes*,
https://doi.org/10.1007/978-3-319-73817-8_6

107

On the other hand, philosopher Peter Osborne in his book *Anywhere or Not at All: The Philosophy of Contemporary Art* (Osborne 2013) agrees that installation art is a term now limited to its curatorial reference. The chapter contributes to the theories around a prominent era when architecture is "a term without which contemporary art would be hard-pressed to continue to exist" (Osborne 2013, 141). The chapter highlights that art and architecture as spatial practices become defined as in tangent, driven by the formation of spaces that share ontological aspects of both.[2] The chapter will define these as "chorotopical art" (Psarologaki 2016a, b), an expression critically synthesizing the Greek terms choros (space) and topos (locus) (Psarologaki 2016a). Chorotopical art aims to create spatial experiences in a state of becoming localized events embedded in the architectural reality of culturally defined sites, rather than to produce aesthetic phenomena within institutionalized gallery settings (Psarologaki 2016b, 119).

Various terms are already in use in attempts to identify this genre of spaces: "Kunst am Baum" (=Art on Building/Architecture) (Fernie 2006), "Warped Space" (Vidler 2000), "Raumkunst" (Architecture/Space Art), "Creatress of Space" or "Spatial Creation" (Raumgestalterin or Raumgestaltung respectively) (Vischer et al. 1994), "Sculptural Architecture or Architectural Art" (Fernie 2006). Experimental terms might also include "meta-chorical art", "space-generic art" or "site-generic art", "artiecture" or "imarchitecture"—following the pattern of Gordon Matta-Clark's Anarchitecture (Ursprung 2011) and SITE's De-Architecture (1980). It is interesting that in the book *Two Minds: Artists and Architects in Collaboration* (Fernie 2006) the chapter on pertinent art practices is entitled "Things" in contrast to "Buildings" and "Groundscapes", which are titles of previous chapters in the same book.

In the same context, Peter Osborne argues that the meaning of site is neither institutional nor archaeological, but instead constructive (Osbourne 2014). The material expression of chorotopical art practice does not demand a gallery but embraces a cultural site; a place of history and heritage that will form part of the ontological construct of an artwork that has a sociocultural agenda. Site, in this case, becomes a critical term to frame the vocabulary of this larval practice. The reliance on the site then, in the context of this investigation becomes more circumstantial and situational. Contemporary chorotopical art repositions site-specificity, and site actively contributes to the experience as material and immaterial locus. It imposes a set of cultural and social parameters and the synergy of those in the context of space creation. It moreover presents an index of non-substance related attributes that a specific place holds when becoming a site for artistic intervention maintaining its historical, stylistic, at times monumental, character. As Miwon Kwon says, "site for art begins to diverge from the literal space of art and the physical condition of a specific location" (Kwon 2004, 19).

Sites of chorotopical art are culturally defined loci that inherit complex topologies and change over time. They are palpable, active organs that produce relational dynamics. A cultural site acts and reacts within time, it allows and blocks out changing constantly and depends on intensive and extensive qualities of space. This is closely related to Gilles Deleuze's theory of the "fold" (Deleuze 1993) and Leibniz's notion of the "membrane" (Vidler 2000, 219–34). In the theory of the "fold" or "le pli", a folding is a condition of multiplicity and singularities, of simultaneous interiority and exteriority. "It open(s) up to thereby enable something other to happen", as Marcus Doel notes (Doel 2000, 132). Extending Doel's theory with reference to ontology, one may argue that site opens up, enabling something to become. The site facilitates the play between the somatic and mental, the inherited and new, the actual and virtual.

Virtuality becomes more intense because "we can never know its reality directly or completely, but we can be sure that it has reality outside our perceptions of it" (Massumi 1992, 53). If we follow Massumi and his argument that the "virtual and the actual are co-resonating systems" (Massumi 1992, 65) and reflect the intensive qualities of spatial events, each intensity can be seen as actual or virtual. Actual intensities can be differentiated to virtual intensities by the existence of form and substance yet the actual is

> the only destination that the virtual has. Its only end is an endless becoming-actual of immanence through extension to our dimension and it's made of spatiotemporal composition. (Massumi 1992, 66)

In the context of chorotopical art, virtual and actual do not form a binary system; they dynamically co-exist. Intensities are neither actual nor virtual per se, but on the contrary create actual–virtual realities. A typology of intensity becomes thus subject to the territorialization, topology and the level of intimacy felt in space, making the distinction between virtual and actual obsolete and obscure.

The role of the architectural site as place of cultural heritage is very important in the making and critical examination of a spatial practice that is inscribed in the historical context of places and at the same time materialized in contemporary media and methods. The inherited aesthetic qualities in chorotopical art maintain the anthropological and geopolitical element visible. This contributes to the presence of the actuality (actual reality) that is recognizable, and often familiar. For instance, a spatial intervention in the interior of a gothic cathedral—however imposing—will be perceived as inserted in a particular historical or religious calibre, which may challenge the presence, but ontologically enhances the gravitas and value of the artwork carrying connotations and visual reference as traces of the past, preserved exactly to do so as a place of heritage.

On the other hand, new media and the systematic use of technology in the making of spatial practices, particularly related to architecture, expand the possibilities in the creation of virtual realities. The latter may respond to the topology of the site as host, embracing (or opposing) its cultural or historical configuration. The preservation and perception of the site as place of heritage is critical. It sustains and promotes the role of the site, as the fundamental component in the empirical making and reading of the space. Avoiding the institutional character of the gallery, it does not detract the notion of the place for art being a destination for a visitor.

The analysis of two case studies that follows aims to critically involve the topological significance of cultural heritage in the ontology of the chorotopical. It will offer the framing of the ontology of chorotopical art in practice, with a particular focus on defining the role of architectural site that is originally a place of cultural heritage in the formation of actual–virtual reality.

6.2   The Canterbury Cathedral Water Tower

The first case study is *Hydor* (2013): an ephemeral intervention conceived and developed for the water tower of Canterbury Cathedral. The culturally heavy surroundings of the cathedral cloisters filter the spiritual atmosphere of the interior towards the freshness of the gardens and vice versa. The geometry and order of the passage that the visitors walk to reach the cloisters, first allow a part perception and then reveal the whole of the installation. The intervention consists of two different parts. The first is physical: a mist-maker situated in the middle of the site towards the cloisters. The second shows footage of the mist-maker, projected on the floor of the hallway that leads to the water tower. The projection shows the top view of the mist-maker out of scale; an alienated image that is difficult to compre-

Fig. 6.1 Liana Psarologaki (2013) *Hydor*, Canterbury Cathedral installation view

hend. On the other hand, the actual object provides sensory immediacy and becomes blended into the archaeological journey of the visitors and pilgrims (Fig. 6.1).

The development of *Hydor* started with the audio-visual documentation of the physical object in the studio and the digital manipulation of the output using specialized software. The LED water atomizer (mist-making device using ultrasound) was recorded whilst in operation under different light conditions and from a variety of standpoints. The documentation provided a heightened perception of the object and space by distorting the scale and the view as well as amplifying the sound it is producing.

The virtual as defined by Massumi (2002) was explored in practice during the development and installation on-site. The projection becomes a spatial virtuality as the postproduction of a physical object (Fig. 6.2). The complexity of this virtual–actual folding is addressed by Massumi in a commentary on Deleuze's ontology, where he notes that "[a]s the actual contracts a set of virtual states into itself at a threshold state, the virtual dilates" (Massumi 1992, 65). The process of recording may have taken place off-site whilst the projection is set up on-site. Still the in-situ presence of the actual object implies a temporal connectivity between object and projection, actual and virtual, place and intervention. The production

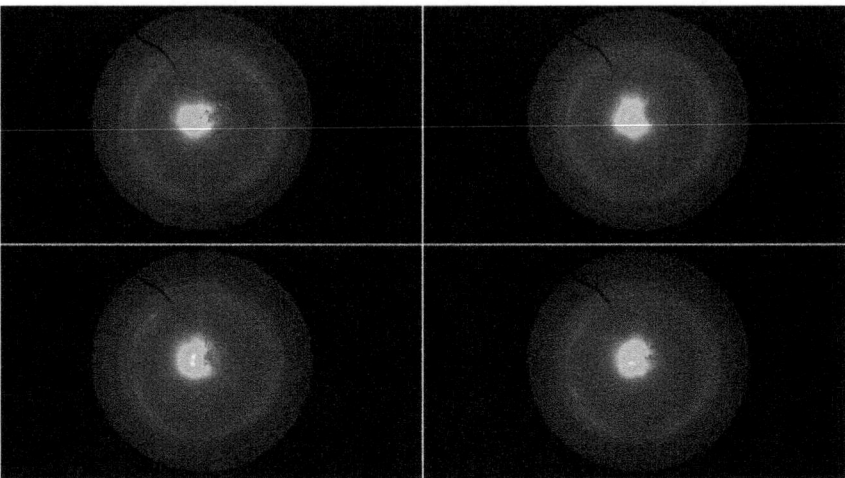

Fig. 6.2   Liana Psarologaki (2013) *Hydor*, time lapse extracted from notational video

forces of each part of this virtual–actual folding reflect on the intensity of the topology produced. The scale and ambiguity of projection as well as the sound that reflected on the Cathedral wall surfaces created an intensity that would override the immediacy of the actual presence of the object.

Whilst the studio testing of *Hydor* defined its formal articulation (colour, scale, object view), in-situ testing revealed it afforded different intensities depending on the positioning of the projection on the architectural elements of the cloisters hallway: vaulted ceiling, walls and floor. The architectural character of the site defined the intervention, which subsequently recalibrated the architectural space. The presence of water in the AV projection was implied, impressed and virtual yet more intense than the actual presence of water in the physical object. The superimposition of the projection on the architectural space interrupted the journey of the visitors who were intrigued and bemused (Fig. 6.3).

The actual mist-maker was placed at the centre of the water tower as an affirmation of its absolute circular order. The water emitted a cloud of mist illuminated by blue light and although visually and physically engaging, it was less spatially intense than the projection, which stood out as an ephemeral event. The actual object only merged physically with the site as a small-scale imposition with its presence implying that the projection pre-

Fig. 6.3 Liana Psarologaki (2013) *Hydor*, Canterbury Cathedral, installation views with audience engagement

sented a recorded live streaming. The intensity of the mist-maker effect was surprisingly fragile and depended on situational factors such as the natural climate and light conditions. On a windy day the mist barely formed small swirls in the air just above the water surface; otherwise soaring as a low level thick cloud around the pillars around the water tower. During a bright sunny day, the intervention remained subtle waiting to be discovered by the curious visitor. Late in the evening, the light of the mist-maker became more distinct, reflecting on the stone surfaces. Standing out in the darkness of the surroundings, it lit up the space like a blue firefly, trembling as the water surface waved producing a drizzle (Fig. 6.4).

The superimposition of site and intervention towards the mediation of a specific experience in space was only successful because of the poetics and agenda of the surrounding space. It accumulated the population of viewers who were already inserted in the context of exploring the space and facilitated a historical and spiritual context that felt imperative and natural. This resonated the visitors' affect on the unexpected encounter with the intervention, which appeared strangely yet harmoniously positioned in the architecturally heavy surroundings. The fact that the site being a place of cultural heritage afforded very little modification challenged the poetics of the intervention at the same time framing the boundaries of chorotopical art in practice.

Fig. 6.4 Liana Psarologaki (2013) *Hydor*, Canterbury Cathedral, installation view from the water tower

6.3   THE CRYPT OF ST PANCRAS PARISH CHURCH LONDON

The second case study[3] is on the development and realization of site-specific project *Cryptopology* (2014), a project developed in the Crypt of St Pancras Church, London that manifests the environmental moment of chorotopical art (Psarologaki 2016a). *Cryptopology* created a self-contained space embedded in the imposing architecture of the site. Staging an experience was abandoned in the favour of framing a socially and culturally embedded event. The architectural envelope became a critical component of the work from an archaeological and contextual aspect as the site afforded very little expansion and alteration. While its entrance partially maintains the transitional feel of the urban fabric in central London, the interior of the Crypt exists in a state of stillness and self-encapsulation. The monumentality of an institutionalized art gallery or museum space like Tate Modern's Turbine Hall is very far from the atmosphere sustained by the Crypt as an architectural envelope; a place preserving its flavour of former lives; a "trace" in time (Eisenman 2007). The qualities inherited by the site not only become part of the intervention but also indicate its limits and nature. There is no longer a necessity for the physical space of the site to play an institutional role for the artwork and its role is no longer that of a host. *Chorotopical art* changes the ontology of both artwork and site by creating new spatial approaches and methodologies. The material as such expression becomes secondary to the spatial effect facilitated by both object(s) and site.

The spectacle of technologically mediated art forms creates a crisis in the theorization and understanding of art. Subtly embedded in the lived and socially framed construct of the everyday, the reality of chorotopical art is an actual–virtual reality experienced in a more-than-aesthetic way. It intensifies the gathering the world around oneself and the projection of oneself into space that has been a place (Psarologaki 2016a). The postmodern world promotes the fragmentation of the senses, which are gradually becoming mediated by technological devices once used only to "record sensuous experiences...beyond the immediate reach of the bodily senses" (Rodaway 1994, 175). The sensuous geography of chorotopical art is however spatially and architecturally synthesized to impose receptive atmospheres. There is no medium specificity, as the fabric of site becomes the raw material for the lived event to occur within.

Inserting independent sound sources to create a 3D sound effect composed a complex soundscape. A set of four fans was installed in vertical formation at the entrance of an open wall chamber facing towards the central passage. The fragile structure was suspended from a beam and held in place by thin fishing wire. The mechanism remained invisible, only making its presence felt by creating white noise and a slightly bemusing airflow. The noise of the fans located in between the two sound sources interrupted the looping water dripping soundtracks and marked a threshold to the interior soundscape. The stream of air created an invisible yet immediate threshold that interrupted the movements of the visitors. Artificial fog made airflow patterns visible and temporarily distributed the fog in the interior. Air drastically contributed to the visual part of the intervention. The bright white beams of light directed from floor to ceiling were given flesh by the mist and created temporal gates at once dissolving into darkness and reappearing in the mist.

The mediated airflow also sustained different temperature conditions. An enclosure of warmth—in a self-contained chamber in the Crypt—lit by the glow of a heater was every now and then cut through by a light breeze of air that brought swirling clouds of mist in. The contrast between temperature conditions was clearly defined. The way the sensory stimuli were received and translated into affect depended very much on the internal timing of the experience (rhythms, duration and movement). The more time one spent inside, the deeper the engulfment became, the more explicitly articulated the boundaries and environmental variations became.

Cryptopology relied on the architectural and cultural context of the site, the synthetic parameters of the intervention (rhythms esoteric to the work) but also the audience, particularly the interaction of bodies and space. Air again played the role of a situational mediator. The fragile topologies created were subject to the ever-changing and non-patterned airflows determined by the visitors' movement, speed and direction, as well as the correlations of movements, and subsequently the number of receptive visitors being in situ at the same time. The climate of the exterior occasionally penetrated the Crypt walls, through small ventilation oculi and the heavy entrance gate that remained half open. The fresh breeze from outside merged the airflow of the fans installation and moved the mist in unpredictable directions. Occasionally the entrance was covered by thin mist revealing the atmosphere of the interior to the passers-by.

Cryptopology started with an exploratory site visit that mapped the existing conditions of the site as architectural order and perceptual geography as well as a number of pragmatic factors such as architectural services and technical feasibility. The culture of the site as a place of heritage and historical gravitas was specifically studied against its former function, considering the building as what Eisenman calls a "writing" (2007), vis-à-vis an architectural ruin that is not bound to its original programme anymore but has instead become virtuality by changing function, use and contextual connectivity over time. The interconnectivity of the rooms sometimes becomes marginal, with spaces almost turning their backs on each other. The proportions of the corridors entail the potential of framing thin streams of airborne spatial qualities such as scent or sound. The canonical symmetry on plan is felt as an implication for the absolute order between the earthly and the divine and the rhythmical is both a preconception and immanence. The rhythms observed become the link between the noetic and the sensed, and the site is a natural metaphor (Martin 1994).

The visitors of *Cryptopology* appeared reluctant to share direct thoughts right after their exit. It was however observed that the space at the exit point (foyer of the gallery) served as a mediatory reflection space in between the world and the artwork. Some visitors took time to mentally digest and revisit the experience often remaining silent or gazing towards the exit, with very few leaving the Crypt immediately to head towards the churchyard and the city. Chorotopical art as inscribed in cultural heritage sites may create experiences that are subjective, intimate and fragile. They depend on participation, which is a matter of anticipation, readiness and choice as well as background familiarity with the site. One may choose the way they mentally and physically engage with space and this will define the aftermath of their experience. One of the multiple journeys to follow in *Cryptopology* empirically narrated unfolds as follows:

I enter the Crypt the same way I enter home; with a feeling of longing. I turn the curtain aside and the passage unfolds dark and wide, ready and moving, beautiful and fragile, material but made of no substance. I hear my boots echoing on the Crypt floor; a floor made of a thousand layers of mud, a millefeuille of earth and dust, so thick that the bricks are hidden, nearly not there. I am guiding myself in a space that guides me and leaves me unguided at the same time.

Light beams as columns touch the vaulted ceiling of the Crypt but hold no load, no forces, almost fighting a gravity that does not belong to them. The columns mark my way and frame my steps. I pass them and I pass a threshold. I am in front of them and behind them. I walk in uncertainty beyond the light. I see nothing. A cloud of mist surrounds me and only the light beams remain to remind me of where I am. No entrance and no exit in my visual field. Distances are immeasurable. I turn.

I feel like I define my journey but spaces absorb me. My footsteps fade as a buzzing noise covers them. I fight with uncertainty but a blow on my left rescues me and I hear water dripping. Space is not still; it is alive and moving. Water penetrates; I penetrate. I pass the cool field of air and I am drawn by two openings; two rooms. I enter. It is warm. I approach. I am bathed in warmth and light. I stay. I am dry and I sweat. I go. My face is tingled by coldness and my nostrils fill with humid air and a substance I cannot recall. I enter. I breathe. I take in. The more I stay the more I sense and feel. Time is immeasurable. I walk out and detect a sound, another sound. Here. There. Everywhere. There is more space.

I see a beam. There is depth. I hear depth. Space is immeasurable. I reach the end and turn back. A plane of light cuts the space in two. The spaces in front of me and behind me are gone; disappeared; dissolved. Blind, I walk away towards the other light, very dim gradually brighter. The air absorbs me and I turn to a passage. I see more. More than I thought. I have been here before but it feels different. I keep going...Space is immeasurable. The light beams remind me of where I came from and where I am going. The mist is lighter. I see the exit and walk out. Everything is lighter. Everything is measurable again. I need time.

The conception, development and finalization of *Cryptopology* were processes of reflection and continuous alterations. The first phase of the project focused on site mapping and analysis, a method inherently used in architectural design processes. A site visit and a provisional plan drawing marked the inauguration of the project six months before exhibition. The first notations made on plan created an initial conceptual mapping for the intervention focusing on the spatial effects to be produced. A study of the geometry and topological order of the site led to propositions on alterations of the site temperature and airflow, as well as the control of light. At this stage empirical observations were limited and propositions were based on the photographic material from the first site visit and the information contained on the site plan.

The proposal approval was followed by a stage of reconsiderations and improvements, conceptually as well as in terms of technological support. The level and nature of intervention afforded by the Grade I listed building that would host *Cryptopology* almost defined the progression and completion of the project. The services and architectural components of the original site encouraged particular interventions or the contrary. The positioning of sound sources, for instance, to achieve a 3D sound effect was such that two main requirements were fulfilled: the power sources were in close proximity in order for no cable wires to interrupt the main passages unless carefully protected, and the surfaces of the site surrounding the sound sources would be sound reflecting instead of sound absorbing.

Studio testing focused on the technical specifications as well as the calibration of the effects produced by certain installations and mechanisms. Directed airflow was extensively tested using different fan alignments and airflow speeds with the intention to identify the most desirable installation method with the site in mind. The creation of environments of different temperature level followed the same pattern of testing with different heating and cooling apparatuses examined in the studio. This process was repetitive and perhaps slightly speculative because it took place off-site. However, it initiated a series of insightful observations regarding the pragmatic development of a chorotopical art project as most of the tactics decided in studio did not fulfil the expectations in situ, especially the methods and mechanisms related to non-substance interventions, such as sound and temperature.

The following stage was a second round of in situ, this time pre-realization, documentation and testing. Although the strategies for creating the sensory stimuli remained, their application and relative positioning changed drastically. The moments of reflection were exactly the moments when nothing was taken for granted when engineering solutions and devising methods. The mapping of the installation transformed many times before reaching its final form. The relative positioning of the mechanisms producing the stimuli changed successively until the desired atmosphere was shaped. The site and its architectural elements, from fundamental structural components to minor details, contributed to critical decisions taken concerning where and how each mechanism operated.

The sound sources, which were programmed to play the same sound piece, were moved around in site to test sound reflection and absorption and in the end remained hidden in pockets creating virtual extensions of a space. Whilst the first sound source was a hi-fi system to play on loop mode a recorded sound piece, the second sound source was a sound amplifier that connected to an MP3 player and transformed the surface it sat on into a speaker. When put in a wooden barrel found on site it instantly amplified the sound piece almost competing with the volume of the hi-fi system. The soundscape created embraced the atmosphere of the Crypt and mediated the internal time and rhythms of the space, simulating a strangely tuned spatial metronome. The impression was so strong that the visitors frequently attempted to explore the space touching the wall at the very back.

Light was the last element to be tested in situ during the development stage of *Cryptopology*. The light intervention in *Cryptopology* welcomed the visitors in the main passage, indicating three more corridors to explore. When in between the light gates, the visitors had no indication of spatial boundaries other than the light beams that enveloped them in a cloud of thick fog. The space absorbed and guided (Fig. 6.5). It served as an immediate visual introduction; a threshold to a synthesis of sensory stimuli, which—in order to be perceived—demanded that the subject is already partly immersed in space. The technology used together with the site materiality defined the effect of the light installation as a synthesis of different elements. Four LED bars threw narrow and sharp beams of bright white light on the vaulted ceiling of the central passage in the Crypt. Resting on the uneven floor in pairs, the lights divided the long passage framing immaterial gates that became fully visible under thick mist. The light intervention responded to the physicality of the site, and gently altered the site rhythm and interior articulation.

In *Cryptopology* the ramifications that the poetics and agenda of the cultural heritage site impose on the artistic outcome are enlightening. It has become apparent that chorotopical art is the spatial practice that creatively embraces the challenges of an architectural envelope that may be

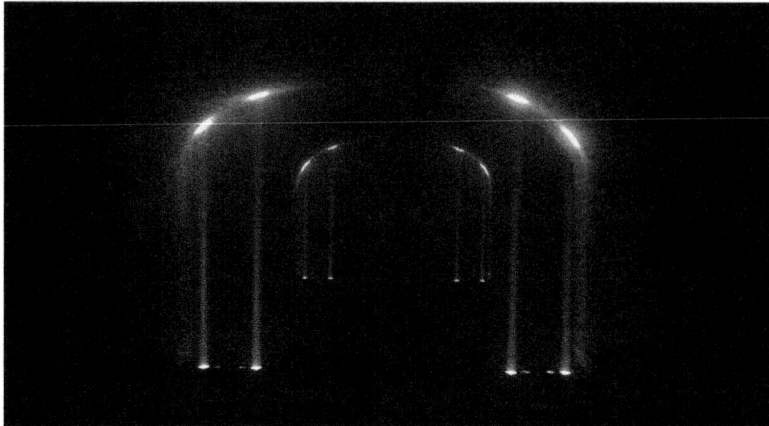

Fig. 6.5 Liana Psarologaki (2014) *Cryptopology*, St Pancras Church Crypt London, light installation view

protected, restored and preserved in time as a place of heritage and culture. It may amplify important spatial qualities of historical architecture that have yet to regain their dominance in space or surpass the hypersignification of the place of cultural heritage as a destination per se.

6.4   Conclusion

This chapter attempted to introduce the importance of site as a culturally defined place in the making of a newly defined practice framed as chorotopical art. It presented two case studies of heritage sites that have transformed temporally receiving artistic intervention and offers a critical review of artistic output produced in the context of a doctoral research project that aimed to frame the ontology of site-reliant spatial practices that merge art and architecture under the creation of space. The chapter contributes to the current philosophical debate on the poetics of atmospheres and the ongoing discourse on contemporary art becoming architecturally dependent. It demonstrated that cultural heritage as architecture may very much define the parameters of artistic creation as the latter escapes the white cube of the gallery. It is also important to note that the contribution of the chapter's investigation may entail intriguing interdisciplinary extensions.

Perhaps the most anticipated extension for this project is the active involvement of the receptive visitors in the documentation and post-production and their contribution to the research input in quantitative and qualitative data. The recording of the visitors' feelings, thoughts and reflections during and upon experience would potentially lead to the reformulation and adjustments to practice perhaps utterly changing the perception of the maker of her own creation. Visitors' verbal responses and reactions as well as the affects evoked were often unexpected and thought-provoking, only asserting that empirical reading of a space can be so intimate that brings some to screams of fear or distress and others to tears of bliss and tranquillity. Scientists agree that behaviour can be patterned only in the context of actions related to habit, making the recording of responses to a spatial experience disrupting the habitual, of perhaps little scientific value. The receptive visitors' responses may contribute scientifically to the development and the expansion of the investigation in the domain of neuroscience and neuroaesthetics.

Much of neuroscience research on the arts has been looking at the traditional artwork as object focusing on the perception of painting and sculpture, reluctant to embrace any new genre of contemporary art that is ontologically spatial if not "architecturalized" (Osborne 2013, 141). This investigation entails the possibility of approaching chorotopical art from the standpoint of neuroscience and neuroaesthetics, to investigate and record the immanence of spaces as recorded via the neurons activity in the brain of the receptive visitor. The methodological schemes developed in the context of this investigation will involve the creative production of technologically mediated artwork and the formulation of critically explored philosophical ideas as well as practical engagement in creating new spaces in existing places. Focusing on theories of ontology rather than phenomenology, the investigation attempted to frame a new site-reliant spatial practice that is architecturally and culturally informed.

NOTES

1. The work draws from the author's PhD Thesis entitled "Beyond the Physical Threshold: Enfolding the Ontology of Immersive Experience" submitted for the University of Brighton in 2015.
2. The theoretical concepts in this chapter were presented in the 3rd International Conference on Defence Sites: Heritage and Future Alicante 4–6 May 2016 Alicante, Spain, and briefly examined in the essay

"Transforming fortresses into artworks: two cultural sites become spaces of topological immersion", *Defence Sites III: Heritage and Future WIT Transactions on the Built Environment* 158: 117–26.

3. The work examined in this section was presented in the 10th Arts in Society International Conference, Imperial College London 22–14 July 2015 and reviewed in the essay "A Theory on the Ontology of Site-Reliant Immersive Environments", *The International Journal of Arts Theory and History* 11 (3): 1–10.

REFERENCES

Bishop, Claire. 2005. *Installation Art a Critical History*. London: Tate Publishing.

Deleuze, Gilles. 1993. *The Fold: Leibniz and the Baroque*. London: Athlone Press.

Doel, Marcus A. 2000. Un-glunking Geography: Spatial Science After Dr Seuss and Gilles Deleuze. In *Thinking Space*, ed. Michael Crag and Nigel Thrift, 117–135. London: Routledge.

Eisenman, Peter. 2007. *Written into the Void: Selected Writings 1990–2004*. Yale: Yale University Press.

Fernie, Jes. 2006. *Two Minds: Artists and Architects in Collaboration*. London: Black Dog Publishing.

Krauss, Rosalind. 1979. Sculpture in the Expanded Field. *October* 8 (Spring): 30–44.

Kwon, Miwon. 2004. *One Place After Another: Site-Specific Art and Locational Identity*. London: MIT Press.

Martin, Elizabeth. 1994. y-Condition. In *Architecture as Music: Pamphlet Architecture*, 16–25. New York: Princeton Architectural Press.

Massumi, Brian. 1992. *A User's Guide to Capitalism and Schitzophrenia: Deviations from Deleuze and Guattari*. London: MIT Press.

———. 2002. *Parables for the Virtual: Movement, Affect, Sensation*. Durham: Duke University Press.

Osborne, Peter. 2013. *Anywhere or Not at All: The Philosophy of Contemporary Art*. London: Verso Books.

Osbourne, Peter. 2014. *Installation: The Vanishing Mediator*. Lecture at the Royal College of Art, Battersea, London, 30 May.

Psarologaki, Liana. 2013. "Hydor." Site Specific Installation at Canterbury Cathedral Cathedral Festival, 18–20 October.

———. 2016a. A Theory on the Ontology of Site-Reliant Immersive Environments. *The International Journal of Arts Theory and History* 11 (3): 1–10.

———. 2016b. Transforming Fortresses into Artworks: Two Cultural Sites Become Spaces of Topological Immersion. *Defence Sites III: Heritage and Future WIT Transactions on the Built Environment* 158: 117–126.

Rodaway, Paul. 1994. *Sensuous Geographies: Body, Sense and Place*. London: Routledge.

Ursprung, Philip. 2011. Anarchitecture: Gordon Matta-Clark and the Legacy of the 1970s. In *Pioneers of the Downtown Scene, New York 1970s*, ed. Laurie Anderson, Trisha Brown, and Gordon Matta-Clark, 133–141. London: Prestel.

Vidler, Anthony. 2000. Skin and Bones: Folded Forms from Leibniz to Lynn. In *Warped Space. Art, Architecture and Anxiety in Modern Culture*, ed. Anthony Vidler, 219–234. Cambridge, MA: MIT Press.

Vischer, Robert, Harry Francis Mallgrave, and Eleftherios Ikonomou. 1994. *Empathy, Form, and Space: Problems in German Aesthetics, 1873–1893*. Los Angeles: Getty Center for the History of Art and the Humanities.

CHAPTER 7

(Ukulele) Strings of Knowledge: Tactile and Digital Interactivity with Archives and Ethnography

Rachel M. Ward and Kate Hennessy

7.1 Introduction

When anthropologist Clifford Geertz presented the concept of "thick description" in 1973, anthropologists were prompted to turn inward and reflect on their own methods of interpretation. Whereas a "thin" description is purely factual and superficial, a "thick" description reflexively explores nuances, commentaries, interpretations and multifarious, layered cultural meaning. Since that time, anthropologists have been working towards creating new, robust ways of describing culture, mostly through visual, auditory, and textual representation. This discussion will focus on the creation of what we might consider "thicker" description via methods such as sensorial and embodied (physical and tactile) approaches within the disciplines of sensory, visual, and digital anthropology.

Sensory anthropology focuses on felt and experiential approaches to writing about culture. In *Sensuous Scholarship* (1997) and *The Taste of Ethnographic Things* (1989), Paul Stoller suggests that anthropologists

R. M. Ward (✉) • K. Hennessy
Simon Fraser University, Surrey, BC, Canada

© The Author(s) 2018
S. Whatley et al. (eds.), *Digital Echoes*,
https://doi.org/10.1007/978-3-319-73817-8_7

125

should write about the sensorial experience of fieldwork: sights, sounds, smells and flavors. Another anthropologist, Sarah Pink suggests mediums other than text (an important point that I will address below) for conveying sensory experience:

> Novel forms of ethnographic writing...as well as filmmaking...and the appropriation of techniques from arts practices might secure means of communicating academically framed representations of the sensory embodied experiences of one group of people and/or ethnographers themselves to (potentially diverse) target audiences. (2009, 24)

Following this line of reasoning, Nakamura explores what happens when sensory anthropologists "move beyond a discipline of words—that is, to the visual, aural, and otherwise supratextual" (2013, 134). She examines the ways in which the mediums used in the history of anthropology reflect the concurrent changes in visual technologies, whereby "photography was developed in 1839, sound recording in 1877, motion film in 1895, talkies in 1927, and portable synchronous sound in 1962" (ibid.). The adoption of these technologies by anthropologists led to the creation of a new sub-discipline of applied research in what became known as "visual anthropology." This approach focused mainly on the creation and theoretical analysis of ethnographic films. In combining the tenets of sensory anthropology with the production of ethnographic films, a new style emerged, such as the films being produced by Harvard's Sensory Ethnography Lab (SEL).

Sensory ethnographic film represents a "thicker" description than written text, although video and audio equipment are only able to capture meaning from two of the five sense categories. In this vein, "although camera and editing technology has advanced since then, ethnographic films have only used the same basic senses of vision and hearing" (Nakamura 2013, 134). New digital technologies have the potential to incorporate multiple sense categories—visual, auditory, and haptic (touch)—but "traditionally, most anthropologists do not receive computer science training in current anthropology curricula" (Underberg and Zorn 2013, 6–7). This lack of familiarity has dual repercussions as "anthropologists themselves may be the best prepared to understand the impact of digital media on culture and to use their expertise in ethnographic methods to influence the use and even design of new technologies" (ibid., 7).

But what happens when anthropologists *are* trained in computer science? Hennessy et al. (2015) (also author of this chapter) present examples of new media ethnographies from anthropologists trained in computer science and HCI (human–computer interaction) design and question the implications of utilizing new technologies in the field of anthropology:

> What happens when ethnographic works are made with electronic media or when they are interactive? Does the use of digital research tools disrupt the making of ethnographies or does it trigger the emergence of new possibilities for ethnographers? Are some methodologies better suited to addressing the new ontological conditions of emerging digital-material research tools? (p. 1)

New digital technologies are changing the ways in which reality and lived experience can be conveyed, particularly through haptic and interactive platforms. Whitehead and Wesch (2012) explore "how the occluded worlds of digital culture, and also those of hidden and marginalized persons, can be better integrated into anthropological thinking and how the ethnography of both the 'unhuman' and the 'digital' leads to exciting possibilities for reconfiguring the notion of what is human" (p. 1). In other words, rather than viewing technology as a demarcation between the human and non-human, it may bring us closer to understanding what humanity can mean from a cross-cultural context.

In terms of sensory integration, virtual imaging technologies are revolutionizing the way we experience places, people, and objects. Many projects are now using scanning devices to create virtual 3D replicas of objects in museum collections (e.g., Hollinger et al. 2013). Bearman and Trant (1999) explain that online platforms and "virtual spaces are emerging in which visitors can apprehend the sights, sounds and ultimately the feel of cultural artefacts, and interact with each other and with experts as they come to understand and appreciate that culture" (24). Exhibiting museum collections online in an embodied, non-academic way also opens up opportunities for accessibility and connectivity between institutions, origin communities, and the public (Hennessy et al. 2013).

This integration of sensory experience can be taken one step further by bringing the virtual from the laptop into the museum as a physical and interactive haptic-platform (Brewster 2001). Muntean et al. (2015) developed an interactive digital table for visitors at the Museum of Anthropology (MoA) in Vancouver to provide the "opportunity for incorporating tangible technology within the museum space to tell the greater stories of Musqueam history" (p. 4). This exhibition, *Belongings*, is a "tangible interface to explore intangible cultural heritage"—the tabletop uses replicas of excavated cultural objects (e.g., a harpoon, Coke can, and car keys) to access information about the history and contemporary community of Musqueam people in British Columbia (pp. 1, 5).

Ethnographic Terminalia is an art collective that exhibits a gallery show alongside the annual American Anthropological Association (AAA) conference (co-author Hennessy is one of the members of the Ethnographic Terminalia Collective). They are "grounded in the commitment to pushing the boundaries of anthropological scholarship and contemporary art through interdisciplinary exhibitions" (*Ethnographic Terminalia* website). Their exhibitions highlight "'non-traditional' engagements of the senses and space (physical and conceptual) in the representation of 'ethnographic' [...] encounters" (Boyer 2011, 94). The importance of this innovative approach is summed up by anthropologist Dominic Boyer, who says this anthropology-meets-art exhibition is "one of the most important and innovative commentaries on the representation of anthropological knowledge to have appeared in the long history of the American Anthropological Association (AAA)" (ibid.). In sum, new spaces, mediums, and technologies are providing novel, creative ways to convey intangible cultural heritage (ICH), or the immaterial aspects of culture such as music, ceremonies, dance, and even sense-experience. This comes at a crucial time when curators are struggling to find novel ways of representing intangible cultural heritage in public museums (Kurin 2004).

This chapter focuses on two case studies that utilize a material object (a ukulele) in order to access information about archives and intangible cultural heritage. Using this object as the "contact zone" between visitors and information has practical and theoretical significance since "knowledge may be said to be embodied in objects". Srinivasan et al. (2009) explain "a necessary condition for the generation of knowledge is engagement with objects [...] engagement involves more than perception and cognition; it involves purposiveness and interpretation" (p. 7).

Importantly, by making objects the "contact zone," they also allow us to consider new ways to make information and archives more accessible to public interest (as well as multiple age categories). This comes at an important time when modes of archiving and access are becoming outdated in a new technology-oriented era:

> Like museums, libraries are institutions whose staff have long been concerned to provide effective public access to information about cultural resources, and many of the standards that systematize library practices today date back to the nineteenth century. (Chan, 2007 and Miksa, 1998; as quoted in ibid., 12)

In the following sections, we explore two anthropology art installations that Ward, Dodge, and Fernandes created that utilize an approach of tangible-interactive ethnography to individually address two categories of contemporary issues facing anthropologists:

1. How can intangible cultural heritage (ICH), particularly the sensory experience of culture be conveyed and preserved? How can ICH be an "embodied way of knowing"? How can we exhibit it in this way?
2. What are some methods museum curators can use to "democratize" the archive (in terms of public access)? What type of exhibitions could be accessible to youth, adults, non-English speaking, and non-literate adults? What techniques can be used to increase public interest in the vast resources of museum and institutional archives?

Ukulele: An Interactive Biography (2015) addresses the first set of questions by demonstrating how sensory experience and emotion can be conveyed through an interactive, object-oriented experience. The technology is based on *auditory* readings from the ukulele, coded to generate video content.

Liliuokalani: Archival Experimentations (2015) playfully explores the second category of inquiry by creating a novel way of interacting with historical photographs from a museum collection through tangible interaction. The technology is based on *conductivity* readings from the ukulele strings, coded to elicit the archival photographs.

Each project utilizes the same object (a ukulele) as a site of public interaction and source of knowledge. The first project reveals (1) the *immaterial* (feelings and senses) and the second project (*Liliuokalani*) showcases (2) the *material* (archives in an institutional collection). Together, they represent an experiment in utilizing new forms of technology to tell stories about culture.

Finally, both projects utilize the same object (a ukulele) as a site of public interaction and source of knowledge. In this way, the ukulele, "as a piece of tangible cultural heritage, is a gateway to a number of intangible, yet critically connected, practices: the telling of a story, a prayer, the process of research, the history of the exhibition, [and] the relation to other objects" (Srinivasan et al. 2009, 5).

7.1.1   Case Studies: Background

The inspiration for this research began in 2013–14 while filming a documentary short that explores an emerging social movement related to DIY subcultures, "radical environmentalism", and anarchist youth through the lens of old-time mountain music (Ward et al. 2014). This piece combines interviews and archival materials to tell the interrelated stories of four groups of geographically and socio-economically separated musicians in urban areas and in rural Appalachia. The experience of filming and editing this project led to certain methodological-musings related to the relevancy of linear film in conveying musicians' lived experiences. Playing music, inherently, is a tactile and embodied way of knowing. The instrument itself is a source of physical knowledge: the way the instrument is held, tuned, cared for, displayed, damaged and, ultimately, discarded. Through questioning the ways in which these felt modes of experience could be translated to non-linear mediums, it led to the ideation that the physical instrument could be used as a platform through which to tell an ethnographic story.

As an alternative to written text or video, we developed a concept for which one of the musician's instruments, a ukulele, could serve as an interface for a non-linear, interactive ethnography. The ukulele was borrowed from one of the musicians featured in the film, as a utilitarian piece of utilitarian *living* heritage. In other words, it was significant to utilize a "secondhand" piece of material culture in telling a story about intangible cultural heritage. This is based on contemporary concerns surrounding the "fragmentation" of material and non-material culture within institutional contexts. Revisiting a point from the introduction by Muntean et al. (2015, 362):

> museums are struggling to find ways to bring representations of intangible cultural heritage into the museum space (Kurin 2004). Continuity of intangible forms of knowledge, languages, and traditions is in tension with their historical fragmentation, just as the prioritization of objects as the focus of museum collections has contributed to the fragmentation of tangible and intangible heritage.

By using a musician's own instrument as a platform for telling a story, it playfully addresses themes of sensory interaction and the making of *social* relationships between people and objects (in addition to the theoretical importance of "objects as interface" explored in Chap. 1). For instance, in

Ukulele a "non-human kinship" is represented visually as a bond between a musician and his or her material belongings. Shared empathy, arguably, serves as the foundational tenants of sensory anthropology (as a shared experience of feelings) in the same manner similar to the lived experience of "kinship." By evoking a collective empathy (between the object, owner, and audience) through an application of sensory anthropology methodologies, this serves as the theoretical basis for rationalizing a kinship between a human person and a non-human "object."

Another impetus for the instrument-as-ethnographic-platform is based on the implication of everyday utilitarian objects as important sites of knowledge. Like Degnen (2009) who explores non-human kinship through development of a reciprocal relationship with plants, these projects advocate an exploration of "everyday forms of knowledge" in sites such as gardens. Degnen (2009, 165) describes her work as serving to:

> complicate several sets of anthropological understandings: of Western notions of body as mechanized in direct opposition with non-Western notions of body as part of the natural cosmos; of the ascendency of Western naturalist ontology when instead it appears that this is more uneven and less uniform than commonly assumed; and how connections between people and plants are not necessarily metaphorical but are instead reciprocal and social.

As detailed in the Introduction to this chapter, the desire to utilize a musician's instrument as a platform for telling a story about intangible heritage evolved into two art installations, *Ukulele: An Interactive Biography* and *Liliuokalani: Archival Experimentations,* showcased in April and August 2015. *Ukulele* explores the musician-instrument life cycles as symbiotic and reciprocal through the combination of original sensory film, auditory readings, and Max MSP software. *Liliuokalani* represents the artistic-experimental manipulation of archival materials, tactile-conductive readings of string touches, and Processing software. Both installations playfully explore the concept of immersing the viewer-reader-participant in the ethnography by taking on a role of "musician" by physically playing the instrument to interact with sensory-visual materials. In this way, these projects represent various aspects of interaction as they relate to ethnographic storytelling, documentary, and accessing archives of information in non-linear and experimental ways.

7.2   Interactive Anthropology (Technical Overview): Two Projects

Ukulele: An Interactive Biography
Rachel M. Ward and Carey Dodge
Public Exhibition: April 16, 2015
School of Interactive Arts + Technology (Vancouver, Canada)

Ukulele is an interactive, sensory biography about the life cycle of one instrument and its owner, Shannon. It is an exercise in non-linear, interactive narrative in which the story of the ukulele's life (such as "kinship" with its owner and eventual abandonment) is revealed by physically playing the instrument (see Fig. 7.1). By plucking the strings, it generates sensory visual memories—from the point of view of the instrument—where each note (G, C, E, A) corresponds to one stage of the ukulele's life cycle: conception (instrument construction), birth (purchase), life (with the owner), and senescence (eventual abandonment). Fifty-five videos and an original soundtrack were recorded to represent the instrument's various "life stages." By focusing on themes of inanimate kinship, transpersonal narrative, and embodiment, this interactive story conveys a visual non-human biography as based on "imagination" and "memory" (Pink 2009) and explores the potential of interactive sensory-digital narrative as a new tool in ethnographic research.

The ukulele's "biography" is told through Max MSP patch, created in partnership with Carey Dodge (School of Interactive Art and Technology, Simon Fraser University), where each string corresponds to one of four video folders: construction, birth, life, or death (see Fig. 7.2). A contact microphone on the ukulele picks up the sound, which is then converted to a number. The numbers 440, 392, 329, and 261 correspond to the G, C, E, and A string frequencies (in Hertz). When the programmed Max MSP software patch recognizes one of the frequency numbers, it activates one of four video folders. The four moving images are then projected in quadrants on the screen (see Fig. 7.1). When a string is plucked it causes the corresponding quadrant to grow and shrink. Plucking the string repeatedly causes the video to expand and retract in a manner similar to the oscillation of the string itself (Fig. 7.1).

The ukulele's "life story" begins with the string that generates the lowest frequency—'G'—and increases in scale sequentially as the ukulele metaphorically "ages." In this way, the 'G' string represents the instrument's conception, time before it was "born" or, in this case, physically

Fig. 7.1 Participants were invited to enter the enclosed installation space and play the ukulele to experience the ethnographic story in a non-linear manner. Each string corresponds to one video quadrant on the screen and each quadrant correlates to one video folder that contains video clips corresponding to one stage of the instrument's "life cycle." Plucking the strings repeatedly causes the corresponding quadrant to expand and retract in a manner similar to the oscillation of the string itself. Photographs: Rachel M. Ward

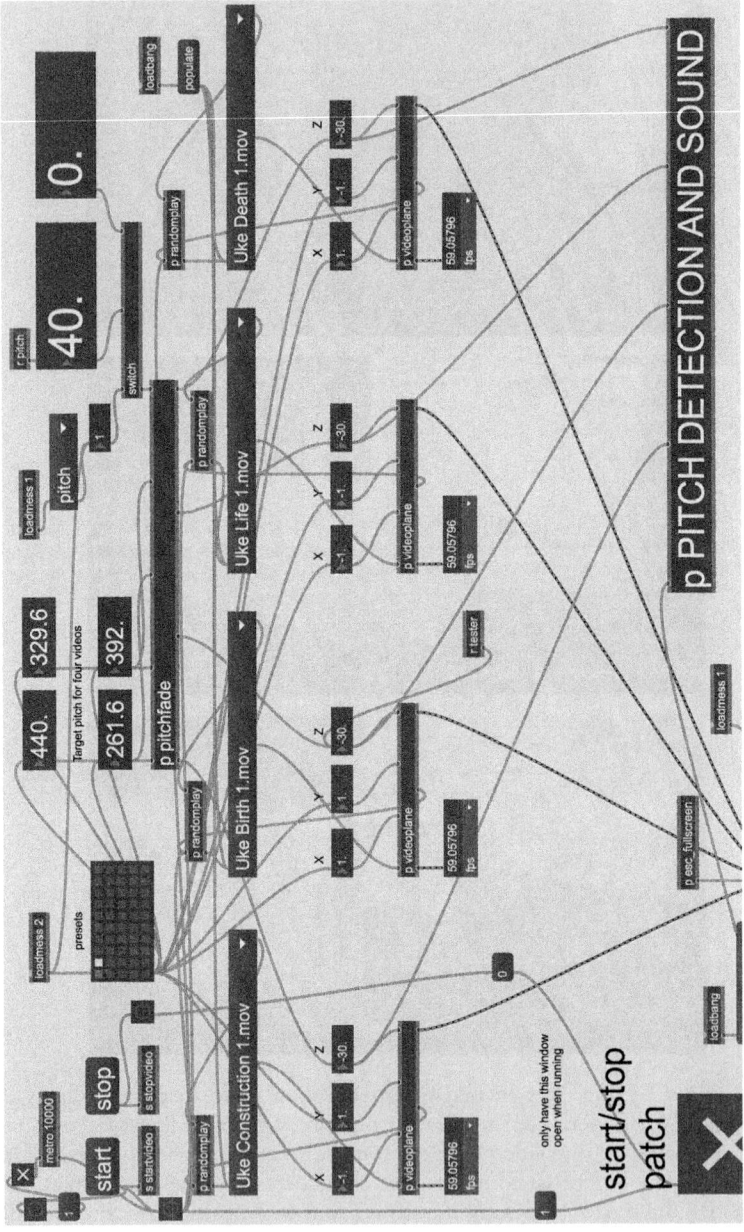

Fig. 7.2   Max MSP patch that detects string plucks based on frequency levels, activating video output

constructed. The content for this sequence was filmed at a woodworker's studio near White Rock, British Columbia. It includes shots of tools, equipment, and materials.

The 'C' string represents the ukulele's metaphorical "birth," that is, when it came into being as a part of the owner's life. This sequence was filmed in a local instrument shop. The shots show a woman—the eventual owner—browsing the store's selection of ukuleles and, ultimately, picking out one and purchasing it.

The 'E' string represents the ukulele's "life" with its owner. This sequence was filmed in a way that represented the ukulele's own perspective and in a manner that would elicit a feeling of kinship between the instrument and its owner. There are many shots of the musician, Shannon, cradling the ukulele in an attempt to visually elicit emotion and feeling, as well as a connection between the viewer and the ukulele itself. In this way, the 'E' string sequence of life represents the theoretical concept of non-human "kinship."

The 'A' string represents senescence (aging) and the ukulele's metaphorical death. It includes shots of decaying wood and trees as a visual representation of the ukulele's physical materials and their eventual return to the earth. By including shots of the trees, it was intended to demonstrate death as a reincarnation, rather than an abrupt and linear end (see Fig. 7.3). This sequence also includes some very pivotal scenes that are central to the development of the ukulele's narrative. It shows the house that the ukulele "lived in" with its owner, now in a state of dilapidation and disrepair. One key sequence that unlocks the plot for the viewer: the owner is shown pulling away from the house in a van. Sadly, the ukulele is left behind in the decaying house. This "abandonment" by the owner is the end of the ukulele's life or, in other words, its metaphorical "death."

Each string also corresponds to one song, composed by Shannon, the musician featured in the videos. Without interaction, the four songs play together continuously at a low ambient level. When a string is plucked, the volume level of the corresponding song is raised. For instance, if the 'A' string is plucked repeatedly, the song "Trouble"—which represents the ukulele's death—will get continually get louder until Shannon is singing at full volume. By utilizing the music that Shannon writes and performs, it incorporates a level of emotional engagement with the instrument, musician, and ethnographic story.

The tangible space of the installation was designed to promote engagement with the piece in a relaxed and physically uninhibited manner. Two

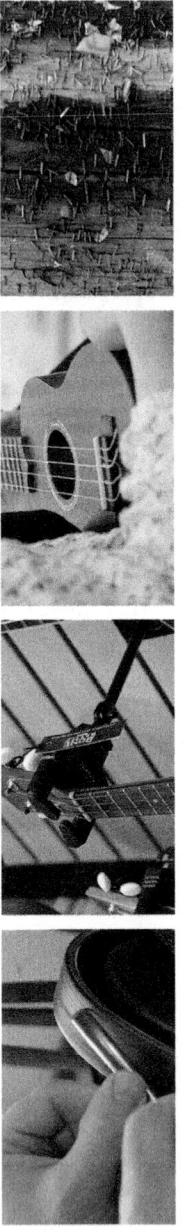

Fig. 7.3 Example clips from each of the four video folders representing the instruments "life cycle" in the form of "conception" (construction), "birth" (purchase), "life" ("kinship" with the owner), and "death" (decaying wood and "abandonment")

cushions were placed in front of a large monitor and black velvet curtains enclosed the space. The participants were invited to recline and play the instrument and experience the narrative at their own pace. The project trailer (5 minutes), which explains the content and filming process, was played on loop outside of the installation. While people were waiting to enter the exhibit, they were invited to have a seat with headphones on to learn more about the creation process and meaning of the piece.

Liliuokalani: Archival Experimentations
Rachel M. Ward and Tim Fernandes
Public Exhibition: August 6, 2015
Centre for Digital Media (Vancouver, Canada)

Like *Ukulele: an interactive biography*, this art installation represents an experiment in interactive biography and participatory transmedia story-telling. Although rather than telling a "biography" through original documentary content, this story is told through public archival media. Queen Liliuokalani was an ideal biographical subject for the piece as the last reigning monarch of Hawaii, a celebrated musician and prominent historical figure with a vast media archive that documents her life (1838–17). Importantly, for the purposes of this piece, she had authored original ukulele songs, published her own autobiographical memoirs, and is accessibly featured in historical, public access archival materials. Symbolically, the ukulele is the national instrument of Hawaii and was a significant part of Liliuokalani's life, particularly during her term of incarceration when her monarchy was overthrown (Liliuokalani 1898).

Like the previous installation, the strings on the ukulele generate video sequences that tell Liliuokalani's life story. For this exhibition, the plastic ukulele strings were replaced with ones constructed from conductive metal so that they reacted to physical touch. This is in contrast to the first project where the data input was coded from auditory readings from the instrument. To pick up on tactile readings, the ukulele was rigged with a "Makey Makey" kit that connected electrodes on the metal strings to a computer running Processing software. Each time a string was plucked, it activated what was read as one of four key presses in the software program. Rather than Max MSP (used in the *Ukulele* installation), this installation utilized Processing software. The code, created in partnership with Timothy Fernandes (Centre for Digital Media, Vancouver), was created based on the logic of string plucks being generated to alphanumeric code that corresponded to video clips that represented various stages of her life story, as told through her memoirs. The videos that were generated based on the string plucks were projected onto a large wall in front of the seated participant (see Fig. 7.5).

Within the media content, Liliuokalani's life story is divided into sixteen clips, detailing her birth, youth, reign, eventual overthrow, and imprisonment—in the process of making Hawaii the "50th State of the Union." Her personal narrative is representative of the historical chronicle of Hawaii and the shift in power from autonomy to subjugation, as well as the overarching story of the Hawaiian people more broadly. Each of the sixteen video segments serves as a standalone visual poem, each containing a single archival photo and sentence from her auto-biographical memoir (see Fig. 7.4), first published in 1898. In doing so, the installation aims to highlight Liliuokalani's own voice.

Archival images of Liliuokalani were collected from the Hawaiian Governmental Archives open-access online repository ("Photograph Collection"). Within this small image collection, the "publicly supported institution Hawaii State Archives does not charge permission fees for use of images and cannot give or deny permission to publish or otherwise distribute images in its collections" ("Photograph Collection"). Utilizing these images, we paired the content of Liliuokalani's written memoirs (similar in style to dated journal entries) to align with the years of the images published in the archives. The historic photographs were stylistically modified and animated using Final Cut Pro X software. Each resulting ten-second video was overlaid with an animated text sequence that represents one sentence from her biography. Each sentence corresponds to one of sixteen "eras" in her life story.

The installation was showcased in August 2015 in Vancouver, Canada. Visitors were invited to pluck the ukulele strings—rigged to sense touch via conductivity—in order to generate the visual poems (see Fig. 7.6). The biography can be "plucked" in any order and experienced in a non-linear manner—or, her biography can be viewed in chronological order. In order to "unlock the chronology," participants must play sixteen notes from sheet music, provided. This sixteen-note "melody" represents the song "Aloha Oe" or "Farewell to Thee" (see Fig. 7.6). Written by Liliuokalani during the time she was detained as a political prisoner, this song now serves as an important cultural symbol of Hawaii.

From a methodological perspective, it was important that the piece could be played in a non-linear manner, though it was also imperative that participants had the opportunity to experience the biography in chrono-

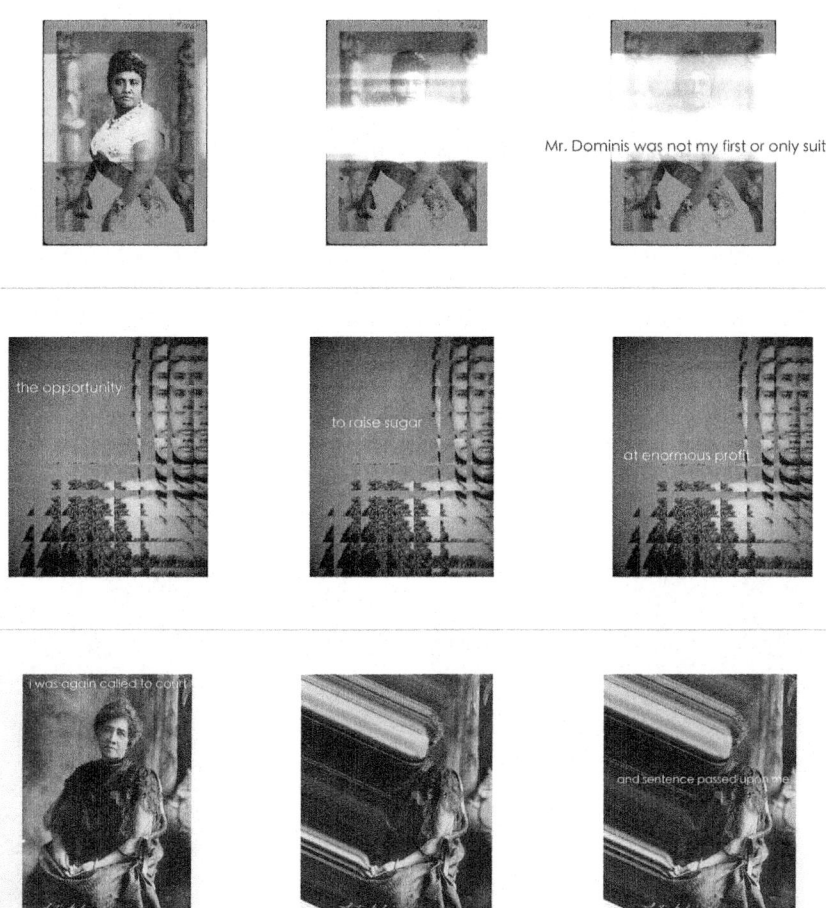

Fig. 7.4 Three examples of the sixteen "visual poems," that depict one era (chapter) of Liliuokalani's life (as based explicitly on the content of her memoirs). Each "video poem" is about ten seconds long and represents an experimental modification of archival photos using Final Cut Pro software. Images: Hawaiian Governmental Archives

logical order as Liliuokalani experienced and recorded it in her memoirs. By inviting participants to play a song she wrote during her final "chapter" (imprisonment), "Aloha 'Oe," it added another layer of metaphor and meaning to the *felt* experience of ethnographic empathy. (In other words, this song has additional implications that align with the colonial experience of Hawaii. Although it was written during the time Liliuokalani was detained in her palace, it became a commercially popular song throughout the United States.

From a perspective of academic praxis, *Liliuokaliani* stands contra to linear, academic documentary modes of presenting historical photographs and archival material. It endeavours to convey the archive in an experimental, poetic, and non-linear fashion. This conceptual piece represents an experiment in the surface wanderings over art, history, anthropology, interactivity, and digital media in an attempt to locate the nebulous space where the five modalities intersect. From an anthropological perspective, it serves as an important example of ethnography that is based on archives and memoirs as a way to convey one individual's lived experience with as little interpretation as possible. Moreover, it serves as an example of ways in which cultural information can be made public and accessible to a wide variety of age groups in institutional contexts (Figs. 7.5 and 7.6).

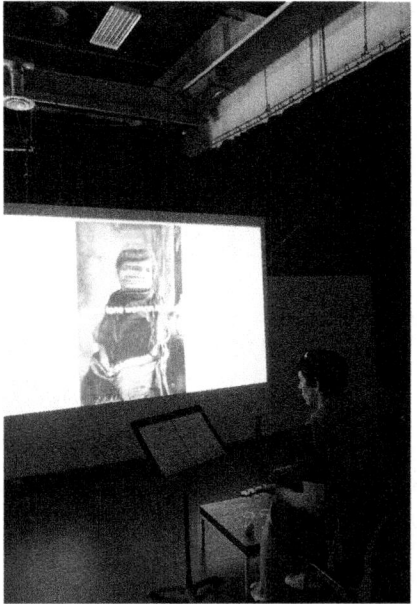 

Fig. 7.5   Visitors interacting with the installation. Photograph: Rachel M. Ward

aloha óe

"Farewell to Thee"
composed by Liliuokalani
[during her imprisonment]

G
is the top string

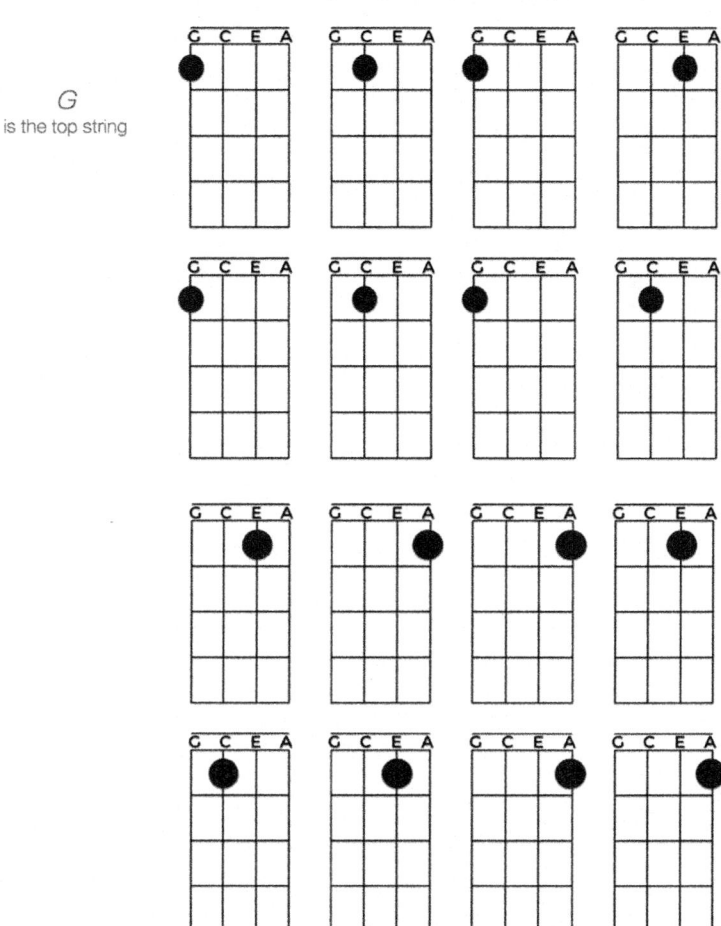

Fig. 7.6 Liliuokalani's biographical narrative could be explored in a non-linear or fashion or in chronological order by playing a song she composed "Aloha Oe." This song sheet was posted in the installation. Each note corresponds to one video that represents a different sentence (life stage) from her memoirs. Created by Rachel M. Ward

7.3   Discussion

7.3.1   Sensory Approaches to Interactivity

Tactile-embodied ethnographic art installations could represent a "quaternary engagement" or joint collaboration between interlocutor, anthropologist, "the senses", and audience. In consideration of a "quaternary engagement" in terms of the two projects described above, it demonstrates that the juxtaposition of sensory anthropology, digital media, and installation art is a fruitful partnership, as many of these types of "imaginative" (Pink 2009) engagements that may transcend articulation through the written word. By utilizing other sense categories, the ethnographer can construct a meaningful, vibrant world that is directly relevant to the experience of the individual (or in this case of the first project, "inanimate kinship"), in a manner similar to Geertz's (1973) notion of "thick description" (consider Feld 2012). These projects purposefully experiment with interactive-digital mediums as a physical-tactile exploration of sensory anthropology in order to increase the participants' understanding of felt ethnographic experience.

A "quaternary engagement" through sensory filmmaking (consider the work of Castaing-Taylor 2009; Castaing-Taylor and Paravel 2012 as part of the Harvard Sensory Ethnography Lab) and interactive digital media could be a useful approach. Sarah Pink (2009, 23) elaborates:

> one of the goals of the sensory ethnographer is to seek to know places in other people's worlds that are similar to the places and ways of knowing of those others. In attempting to achieve this, she or he would aim to come closer to understanding how those people experience, remember and imagine.

This leaves us to ponder the question: In what ways can the field of anthropology utilize new digital technologies for conveying ethnographic information? By exploring new mediums of digital interaction, video, and sound, how can the media-producing anthropologist better incorporate a collaborator's personal contribution, such as his or her voice, artwork, songs, and stories? A cooperation of this sort is a meaningful gesture by the discipline as whole, which has a history of encapsulating and compartmentalizing the beliefs of the "other" (see Ignace et al. 1993, 321), often in a medium that is inaccessible to the interlocutor or culture from which they came from (either due to language differences or illiteracy).

Although film is an important aspect of the sensory-digital-interactive approach, a focus on the visual should not necessarily prevail and "there are a number of anthropologists (Howes 1988; Seeger 1981; Stoller 1989) who have criticized the dominance of the visual in contemporary anthropology and have argued for the development of an anthropology of the senses" (Classen 1990, 723; see also Nakamura 2013). But what type of medium is suitable for this so-called "anthropology of the senses"? In line with Sarah Pink (2006, 2009), "the future of visual anthropology" may lie at an intersection of both visual and sensory anthropology, as founded in a basis of embodiment and experience. Pink (2006, 41) provides the impetus for this approach: A consideration of experience is relevant for two reasons, first, because how we conceive experience and sensory experience has implications for how we think we can use visual methodologies to research and represent them; second, because more generally a sensory as opposed to a visual approach to anthropology challenges the centrality that the idea of a visual anthropology gives the visual by suggesting it is resituated in relation to other elements of sensory experience.

This intersection between visual and sensory anthropology could conceive a theoretical offspring in the form of sensory film and interactivity. Sensory film has the ability to manifest a certain empathy between the audience and the image, be that emotional empathy or sensorial empathy (for instance, see Hahn 2007), whereby both instigate a form of embodied reaction. As argued by Pink (2009), this type of empathetic embodiment finds its very foundations in sensory ethnography. When considered in tangent with the applied methodologies of visual anthropology, one can see the powerful effect this may have in "evolutionizing" ethnography to become a participatory event between informant, anthropologist, and "the senses." By incorporating interactivity, this notion could be deemed a "quaternary collaboration" (interlocutor, anthropologist, "the senses," and audience) as premised on notions of visual and sensory anthropology and could serve to supplement certain lacunas (of empathy, imagination, and experience) left by a Western model of ethnography as demarcated by socially-created strictures of cross-cultural sensory engagement.

Some anthropologists are currently working towards the incorporation of interactivity through ethnographic art displays. As discussed in the Introduction to this chapter, *Ethnographic Terminalia* is a collective that is "working in capacity to develop generative ethnographies that do not subordinate the sensorium to the expository and theoretical text or monograph"

(Boyer 2011, 94). Through interactive installations, the public can learn about culture and ethnographic narratives through experimental and artistic displays. In this manner, "the appropriation of techniques from arts practices might secure means of communicating academically framed representations of the sensory embodied experiences of one group of people and/or ethnographers themselves to (potentially diverse) target audiences" (Pink 2009, 24). In this way, the interactive ("playable") biographies *Ukulele* and *Liliuokalani* are an experiment in the making of a public, embodied, sensory, and interactive method of conveying ethnographic research data.

7.3.2   Implications for ICH

The impetus for the *Ukulele* and *Liliuokalani* installations builds on scholarship exploring the implications of the UNESCO Convention for the Safeguarding of Intangible Cultural Heritage (2003) and recent developments in the field of interactive documentaries. This research focuses on the question: how do interactive ethnographies create access to collections and help (or hinder) safeguarding intangible cultural heritage? Although there is significant research in the realm of digital cultural preservation (e.g., Alivizatou 2011; Anderson and Christen 2013; Boast 2011; Geismar 2013; Hennessy 2010; Kreps 2009; Kurin 2004; Parry 2007), there is a gap in the literature that explores the use of new interactive and digital documentary methods as tools in the dissemination and preservation of culture. As a platform that is becoming integral to our understanding of the documentary as a genre, interactive documentaries utilize "action and choice, immersion and enacted perception as ways to construct the real, rather than represent it" (Aston and Gaudenzi 2012, 125). A number of recent articles explore the theoretical impact of interactive documentaries (Coover 2012; Foster and Evans 2015; Gifreu-Castells 2014; Hennessy et al. 2015; Hight et al. 2014; Mikelli 2014; Nash 2014; Freixa and Soler-Adillon 2014), which testify to the immediacy and contemporary relevance of this new medium. Importantly, Dvorko (2014) proposes the use of "interactive documentary" as a new form of cultural heritage mediation.

Interactive documentary forms unite theory and praxis as a visual representation of trans-disciplinary research related to globalization, intangible cultural heritage, and participant production as a research method (see Lassiter 2005; Markham 2005; Pink 2013). The two installations utilize "music as a tool of discovery to question value systems—not just the differences between genres or subjects, but how the divides themselves are constructed and negotiated" (Leyshon et al. 1998, 5). At the local level, these projects have the potential to serve as a digital resource focused on local needs by focusing on the "value of meaningful community participation in efforts to safeguard their digital cultural heritage" (Hennessy 2012, 43). As a public digital archive, such interactive projects might contribute to "democratizing access to archives" (Huvila 2008), and reinforcing the development of *interactive anthropology* as an emerging field of scholarship.

7.4   Conclusion

Ukulele: An Interactive Biography and *Liliuokalani: Archival Experimentations* are anthropological art installations that represent playful experimentations with new forms of digital and interactive ethnography. By utilizing a musical instrument as the "contact zone" between viewer and personal (*Ukulele*) and institutional (*Liliuokalani*) knowledge, it allows for an embodied, tactile, and interactive learning experience—and may serve to address the questions we posed at the beginning of this chapter regarding how to best convey, preserve, and exhibit intangible cultural heritage (ICH) in an accessible way. Specifically, the installation *Ukulele* focuses on themes of non-human kinship between the instrument and the owner, incorporates original video footage and soundtrack, and relies on auditory signals to activate code that generates the multimedia installation experience. In this way, it serves an example methodology for representing ICH as sensory experience, emotions, and feelings of kinship through an interactive exhibition.

Whereas *Ukulele* brings the *immaterial* to light, *Liliuokalani*, is founded in the purely *material* experience of photographic archives. It allows viewers to strum the ukulele—now coded to sense conductivity rather than sound—to reinterpret the autobiography of the Hawaiian Queen Liliuokalani. It represents an alternative method to reconnect the public with archives of cultural heritage as a form of civic engagement and as a platform for publicly accessible education materials. Together, *Ukulele* and *Liliuokalani* demonstrate the potential for tangible-interactive anthropological art installations to facilitate access to archival collections across age, regions, and socioeconomic backgrounds in the goal of conveying cultural experience and safeguarding intangible cultural heritage. Importantly, the participatory nature of this research-creation process demonstrates the potential for collaboration with local communities, museum archives, and international institutions of cultural heritage, as a form of a cooperative, public, reflexive, and dynamic repository for the collaborative generation and preservation of culture.

REFERENCES

Alivizatou, Marilena. 2011. Intangible Heritage and Erasure: Rethinking Cultural Preservation and Contemporary Museum Practice. *International Journal of Cultural Property* 18 (01): 37–60.

Anderson, Jane, and Kim Christen. 2013. 'Chuck a Copyright on It': Dilemmas of Digital Return and the Possibilities for Traditional Knowledge Licenses and Labels. *Museum Anthropology* 7 (1–2): 105–126.

Aston, Judith, and Sandra Gaudenzi. 2012. Interactive Documentary: Setting the Field. *Studies in Documentary Film* 6 (2): 125–139.

Bearman, D., and J. Trant. 1999. Interactivity Comes of Age: Museums and the World Wide Web. *Museum International* 51 (4): 20–24.

Boast, Robin. 2011. Neocolonial Collaboration: Museum as Contact Zone Revisited. *Museum Anthropology* 34 (1): 56–70.

Boyer, D. 2011. A Gallery of Prototypes: Ethnographic Terminalia 2010, Curated by Craig Campbell, Fiona P. McDonald, Maria Brodine, Kate Hennessy, Trudi Lynn Smith, Stephanie Takaragawa. *Visual Anthropology Review* 27 (1): 94–96.

Brewster, S.A. 2001. Impact of Haptic 'Touching' Technology on Cultural Applications. In *Digital Applications for Cultural Heritage Institutions*, ed. James Hemsley, Vito Cappellini, and Gerd Stanke. London: Routledge.

Castaing-Taylor, Lucien. 2009. *Sweetgrass*. New York: Harvard Sensory Ethnography Lab.

Castaing-Taylor, Lucien, and Verena Paravel. 2012. *Leviathan*. New York: Cinema Guild.

Classen, Constance. 1990. Sweet Colors, Fragrant Songs: Sensory Models of the Andes and the Amazon. *American Ethnologist* 17 (4): 722–735.

Coover, Roderick. 2012. Visual Research and the New Documentary. *Studies in Documentary Film* 6 (2): 203–215.

Degnen, Catherine. 2009. On Vegetable Love: Gardening, Plants, and People in the North of England. *Journal of the Royal Anthropological Institute* 15: 151–167.

Dvorko, Nina. 2014. Interactive Documentary and Its Potential for Cultural Heritage Mediation [Working Paper].

Ethnographic Terminalia. n.d. Accessed May 2, 2016. http://ethnographicterminalia.org/.

Feld, Steven. 2012. *Sound and Sentiment: Birds, Weeping, Poetics, and Song in Kaluli Expression*. Durham: Duke University Press.

Foster, Stephen, and Mike Evans. 2015. The Prince George Métis Elders Documentary Project: Matching Product with Process in New Forms of Documentary. In *Reverse Shots: Indigenous Film and Media in an International Context*, ed. Wendy Gay Pearson and Susan Knabe, 221. Waterloo: Wilfrid Laurier University Press.

Freixa, Pere, and Joan Soler-Adillon. 2014. Snow Fall and a Short History of the Highrise: Two Approaches to Interactive Communication Design by the *New York Times*. *Textual & Visual Media* (7): 63–83.

Geertz, Clifford. 1973. *The Interpretation of Cultures: Selected Essays*. New York: Basic Books.

Geismar, Haidy. 2013. Defining the Digital. *Museum Anthropology Review* 7 (1–2): 254–263.

Gifreu-Castells, Arnau. 2014. Mapping Trends in Interactive Non-Fiction Through the Lenses of Interactive Documentary. In *International Conference on Interactive Digital Storytelling*, 156–163. Cham: Springer.

Hahn, Tomie. 2007. *Sensational Knowledge: Embodying Culture Through Japanese Dance*. Middleton: Wesleyan University Press.

Hennessy, Kate. 2010. *Repatriation, Digital Technology, and Culture in a Northern Athapaskan Community*. PhD thesis, Department of Anthropology, University of British Columbia.

———. 2012. Cultural Heritage on the Web: Applied Digital Visual Anthropology and Local Cultural Property Rights Discourse. *International Journal of Cultural Property* 19 (03): 345–369.

Hennessy, Kate, Natasha Lyons, Stephen Loring, Charles Arnold, Mervin Joe, Albert Elias, and James Pokiak. 2013. The Inuvialuit Living History Project: Digital Return as the Forging of Relationships Between Institutions, People, and Data. *Museum Anthropology Review* 7 (1–2): 44–73.

Hennessy, Kate, Claude Fortin, Aynur Kadir, Reese Muntean, and Rachel Ward. 2015. Producing New Media Ethnographies with a Multi-sited Approach. *Proceedings of the 21st International Symposium on Electronic Art*.

Hight, Craig, Kate Nash, and Catherine Summerhayes. 2014. *New Documentary Ecologies*. New York: Palgrave Macmillan.

Hollinger, R. Eric, Edwell John Jr., Harold Jacobs, Lora Moran-Collins, Carolyn Thome, Jonathan Zastrow, Adam Metallo, Günter Waibel, and Vince Rossi. 2013. Tlingit-Smithsonian Collaborations with 3D Digitization of Cultural Objects. *Museum Anthropology Review* 7 (1–2): 201–253.

Howes, David. 1988. On the Odour of the Soul: Spatial Representation and Olfactory Classification in Eastern Indonesia and Western Melanesia. *Bijdragen tot de Taal-, Land-en Volkenkunde 1ste Afl* 144: 84–113.

Huvila, Isto. 2008. Participatory Archive: Towards Decentralised Curation, Radical User Orientation, and Broader Contextualisation of Records Management. *Archival Science* 8 (1): 15–36.

Ignace, Ron, George Speck, and Renee Taylor (Interviewed by N. Dyck). 1993. Some Native Perspectives on Anthropology and Public Policy. In *Anthropology, Public Policy and Native Peoples in Canada*, edited by N. Dyck and J. B. Waldram, 166–191. Montreal: McGill-Queen's University Press.

Kreps, Christina. 2009. Indigenous Curation, Museums, and Intangible Cultural Heritage. In *Intangible Heritage*, ed. LauraJane Smith and Natsuko Akagwa, 193–208. London: Routledge.

Kurin, Richard. 2004. Safeguarding Intangible Cultural Heritage in the 2003 UNESCO Convention: A Critical Appraisal. *Museum International* 56 (1–2): 66–77.

Lassiter, L.E. 2005. *The Chicago Guide to Collaborative Ethnography*. Chicago: University of Chicago Press.

Liliuokalani (Queen). 1898. *Hawaii's Story by Hawaii's Queen*. Boston: Lee and Shepard. Accessed June 15, 2017. http://digital.library.upenn.edu/women/liliuokalani/hawaii/hawaii.html.

Leyshon, Andrew, David Matless, and George Revill, eds. 1998. *The Place of Music*. The Guildford Press: New York.

Markham, Annette N. 2005. The Methods, Politics, and Ethics of Representation in Online Ethnography. In *The Sage Handbook of Qualitative Research*, ed. K. Denzin and Y.S. Lincoln, 3rd ed., 793–820. Thousand Oaks: Sage.

Mikelli, Danai. 2014. Introducing Interactive Documentary in the Context of Critical Media Education. *Networking Knowledge* 8 (1): 1–12.

Muntean, Reese, Kate Hennessy, Alissa Antle, Susan Rowley, Jordan Wilson, Brendan Matkin, Rachael Eckersley, Perry Tan, and Ron Wakkary. 2015. ʔeləẁḱ^w Belongings: A Tangible Interface for Intangible Cultural Heritage. *Proceedings of Electronic Visualization and the Arts (EVA)*, 360–366. London, June.

Nakamura, Karen. 2013. Making Sense of Sensory Ethnography: The Sensual and the Multisensory. *American Anthropologist* 115 (1): 132–135.

Nash, Kate. 2014. Strategies of Interaction, Questions of Meaning: An Audience Study of the NFBs Bear 71. *Studies in Documentary Film* (October): 1–14.

Parry, Ross. 2007. *Recoding the Museum: Digital Heritage and the Technologies of Change*. Oxford: Routledge.

"Photograph Collection." State of Hawaii: Department of Accounting and General Services, n.d. Web. 19 June 2017. http://ags.hawaii.gov/archives/about-us/photograph-collection/.

Pink, Sarah. 2006. *The Future of Visual Anthropology: Engaging the Senses*. London: Routledge.

———. 2009. Principles for Sensory Ethnography: Perception, Place, Knowing, Memory and Imagination. In *Doing Sensory Ethnography*. London: Sage.

———. 2013. *Doing Visual Ethnography*. London: Sage.

Seeger, Anthony. 1981. *Nature and Society in Central Brazil: The Suya Indians of Mato Grosso*. Cambridge: Harvard University Press.

Srinivasan, Ramesh, Robin Boast, Jonathan Furner, and Katherine M. Becvar. 2009. Digital Museums and Diverse Cultural Knowledges: Moving Past the Traditional Catalog. *The Information Society* 25 (4): 265–278.

Stoller, Paul. 1989. *The Taste of Ethnographic Things: The Senses in Anthropology.* Philadelphia: University of Pennsylvania Press.

Underberg, Natalie M., and Elayne Zorn. 2013. *Digital Ethnography: Anthropology, Narrative, and New Media.* Austin: University of Texas Press.

Ward, Rachel (Dir.), Chris Mason, Sarah Whitelocke, Elanor Balser, and Marilyn Caldrone. 2014. *Appalachian Punks: A Resurgence of Tradition.* Documentary. 14 min. http://www.vimeo.com/rachelward/punks.

Whitehead, Neil L., and Michael Wesch. 2012. *Human No More: Digital Subjectivities, Unhuman Subjects, and the End of Anthropology.* Boulder: University Press of Colorado.

CHAPTER 8

Open State: Event Spaces of Infinite Perspective

Adam Benjamin and Mathew Emmett

8.1   INTRODUCTION

Adam Benjamin and Mathew Emmett have been exploring intercultural performative space within contemporary dance. The impetus for *Open State* has grown from an interdisciplinary practice that interrogates the spatial quality of sound, constructed from the interpretation of Japanese speech patterns as a medium for transmission, communication and community. Benjamin and Emmett propose a participatory process that explores language as a medium for art making that is both spatially distributed, accessible and collective.

Just as the production of *Open State* demands the formation of new collaborations and Anglo-Japanese communities, the performance elicits the formation of a shared language enabling a new performative culture to emerge linking Plymouth in the UK to Tokyo in Japan. By engaging these concepts as a means of uniting cultures, *Open State* utilized the mutable relationship between voice, space, identity and community. The work focuses on the spatialization and performative dimension of the human voice.

A. Benjamin (✉) • M. Emmett
Plymouth University, Plymouth, UK

151

As well as being an instrument in its own right, the human voice acts as a cultural identifier (Cooper 1991). Composed of pitch, tone and tempo, the voice combines these dynamics to create a unique sound. Voice quality is specific to the individual and can be differentiated by diction, rate of speech, intonation and volume. Many physiological factors influence the human voice: the shape and thickness of the vocal chords, the length of the throat, the shape of mouth and lips. Geographic factors also influence the way we speak as do race, religion, familial and individual idiosyncrasies, yet despite these multiple differences we are for the most part united by our use of voice as our primary means of communication. The 'most' here is significant as not all of those who participated in the project were able to understand each other, and this for a variety of reasons.

The outcomes of the project quite literally expanded the reach of the voice as a medium to bridge distances that were defined both by disability and geography.

8.2   Main Text

The cultural heritage of this project resides within an historic exchange that took place between England and Japan 400 years ago when the British envoy ship *The Clove* made a round trip from Plymouth to the port of Hirado, establishing the first formal trade and cultural links between the two countries. The event was celebrated nationally in 2013 and in Plymouth (and Plymouth University) in 2014 to coincide with *The Clove*'s return to Sutton Harbor, a stone's throw from where the university now stands. *Open State* carries forward the festival's aims of 'exchange, collaboration and discovery' by creating a platform for Anglo-Japanese artistic innovation.

8.3   Exchange

Though separated by ten thousand leagues of clouds and waves, our territories are as it were close to each other.
Tokugawa Ieyasu, letter to King James I, October 1613.

Benjamin's links to Asia date back two decades to his first visit to Tokyo in 1996. He was one of the first foreign artists to introduce integrated dance to Japan and has been building on that initiative with workshops, residencies and performances over the intervening years. His first invitation to work in Tokyo came from community arts practitioner Yuko Ijichi, who witnessed his work in London. A week later Benjamin received a fax with an invitation to teach in Tokyo. Twenty years on aided by new technologies, that first 'paper' exchange has, through the work of Emmett, progressed to more complex dialogues in which 'the cloud' and 'waves' feature as a means of joining artists in the two countries

8.4   COLLABORATION

Open State is layered throughout with collaboration. In terms of its cultural inheritance the project is the culmination of twenty years of shared practice that has resulted in the founding of the first integrated dance company in Japan: Integrated Dance Company-Kyo, for whom Benjamin continues to act as mentor. There is the collaboration on the new work *Open State* between dance artists and lighting designers in Japan, and Benjamin as choreographer. Most vital to this chapter is the collaboration between Benjamin and Emmett on the innovative use of sound and spatialization technologies and how the construction and implementation of those technologies affected the creation of the piece itself.

8.5   THE INDIVIDUAL VOICE

The nascent or incubation period described by authors such as Dodds et al. (2003); Ritter and Dijksterhuis (2014), prior to the creative act or the formulation of a new idea, often takes place internally, a period of rumination pursued in solitude. For the choreographer this may be a time when ideas, images and voices can emerge and in which the attended interactions with dancers in real time can, in some ways, be prepared for. A choreographer may not be grappling with a clearly defined problem, rather, an array of interlinked elements, which includes bodies moving in space, sound, light, duration, audience and environment. These need to come into a resonant pattern in order to create a coherent, integrated whole that might be considered a performative event.

Unlike those 'aha' moments documented in the writing on creativity (Darwin aboard the *Beagle* being a classic example), where a solution to a previously attempted problem arises unprompted from the unconscious, postmodern choreographers are more likely to be engaged in an unfolding process in which 'live' elements are repeatedly calibrated and re-ordered. This is particularly so in collaborative practice, where choices are being sifted and re-adjusted to meet with the interjections and offerings of the other artists (other viewpoints). If the choreography in and of itself represents a future 'problem' (or series of problems) the choreographer is often processing and preparing for this encounter long before any actual meeting takes place in the studio.

Over the past few decades contemporary dance has moved towards collaborative models of making, in which dancers serve as 'dance artists' contributing ideas and movement, rather than the 'classical' model of mute bodies on which the choreographer scribes his or her ideas (Butcher and Melrose 2005). Integrated dance has emphasized the importance of this contributory status, as an individual disabled dancer may be far more knowledgeable about their body and what it can do than an invited choreographer. Despite this collaborative shift in methodology, the nascent phase of the choreographic process is often remote from the dancers—no more so than when those dancers happen to be on another continent.

The process pursued in the making of *Open State* attempted to extend the collaboration forwards in time, allowing the choreographer to engage dance artists in creative exchange weeks before they met in the studio, opening up the possibility of multiple dialogues, and mitigating against the solipsism of traditional choreographic practice.

8.6   IMPROVISATION 1

Saturday 9 May 2015 11.30 [19.30 Tokyo]
Plymouth University, House Studio[1]

In the first instance, three members of the Integrated Dance Company-Kyo, in Tokyo, watched dancers in the UK improvising at Plymouth University. While our primary intention was to capture their commentary on the improvisations (i.e., to record the Japanese voices), there was an immediate interplay between their voices and how these were incorporated and responded to by the improvising dancers (Fig. 8.1).

Over a period of an hour a number of short improvisations were run and as dancers on both sides relaxed, the quality of the interactions changed, both through responses to sound and through direct interplay between dancers sharing both the physical and virtual spaces in the two countries. While this kind of exploration has been more fully explored elsewhere (Popat 2005; Bailey et al. 2009), these recordings sessions became intriguing, interactive, performative events in their own right, opening possibilities for further exploration that might shape future projects. Perhaps most significantly, the recording of the Japanese commentary was akin to the Droste effect, where the interrelationships created a

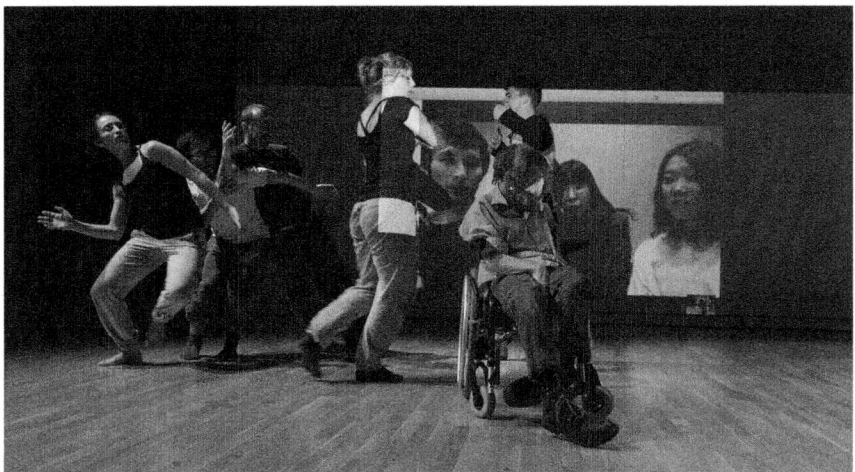

Fig. 8.1 Sophie Colthurst, Saurav Rai, Adam Benjamin, Ellen Hunn, Nathan Matthews and Kevin French improvising in The House Studio, Plymouth, watched by Seiichiro Kondo, Maho Amakata and Asumi Masuda. Saturday 9 May, 2015 11.30 [19.30 Tokyo]

feedback loop of sound instancing that travelled back and forth between the observed and the observer.

The voice material was treated in a variety of ways by Emmett to produce a series of sound scores. While usually it is the choreographers' 'internal voice' that guides the work, in this instance the recordings of the dancers' voices furnished inspiration on a number of levels. Benjamin reunited the Japanese dancers with their own voices in the rehearsal process in Tokyo, sometimes in recognizable form, sometimes in forms that had been created from the data extracted from the recordings. This passage of voices across continents, and this passage of time between the early research and the studio rehearsals allowed a 'slow burn' of ideas and discussions to take place prior to the five-week making period in Tokyo.

8.7   Multiple Voices

On many occasions during the rehearsals the dancers found themselves listening to their own voices. These moments always led to smiles of recognition and outbursts of conversation as the Skype session was recalled;

Fig. 8.2   Performance of *Open State*. White Studio, Tokyo Arts Centre 2015

a reminder of the dancers in the UK, the possibilities of developing further conversations and that the work was 'ours', and therefore collective, and not tied solely to one person/author. The use of recorded voice led to further explorations of spoken word in rehearsal, and the piece eventually contained text that came from, and was spoken by, the dancers themselves (notably Maho Amakata, Yoko Izumi and Tomomi Kosano) although all the dancers eventually used their voice at some point in the piece and text was also projected in both Japanese and English at various points in the performance in an event that pushed simultaneously at the barriers of dance and language (Fig. 8.2).

8.8   Compositional Potentials: The Human Voice

Speech is one of the most complex of motor tasks, transforming thought through muscular activity into sound waves, which, distilled, present unique personality. Breathing fills the lungs with air that passes up the trachea causing the vocal chords to vibrate. This vibrational movement creates the first layer of speech, the second coming from the resonating chambers of the mouth, nose and throat. The third layer of sound emanates from the movement of the tongue, lips and teeth that combine to create the final characteristics of the voice, better known as intonation.

Intonation is the dynamic variation of pitch within sentences. We modulate pitch to articulate and differentiate meaning by changing the rate of vibrations to raise or lower the tone. This dynamic layer of sound gives the voice a musical dimension; certain sounds are emphasized within words by stepping or gliding through notes to create vocalization patterns. These sound clusters form patterns, and these patterns form language.

By playing with modulation patterns a referencing structure is established that renders tone, cadence and rhythm as a plastic medium open for interpretation. By studying these phonetically generated soundscapes, *Open State* reveals the structure of the voice as a medium for choreographic exploration.

8.9   COMPOSITIONAL POTENTIALS: VOICE CONNECTIONS

The *Open State* sound score established a sonic relationship between the Japanese voice and the creative processes of the choreographer. For this work Emmett recorded hundreds of Japanese sounds to discover common patterns and phonetic forms that would normally be inaudible in terms of time, pitch and intensity (Fig. 8.3).

Once the recording had been achieved, the unedited audio was digitally enhanced to increase the volume of the voice. This process signified the beginning of the sound treatment followed by the spectrograph analysis that generated a series of numerical data values for pitch, timing and intensity. For this work Broz analysed Emmett's sound recordings in Praat, a software tool commonly used by linguists to analyse the phonetics of speech. A script was written to record the intensity of the sound signal and the frequency of sounds within the human vocal range from sound recordings of the dancers' commentary (Fig. 8.4).

The purpose of this processing was to extract fundamental acoustic characteristics of the speech that could be visualized, analysed and used as raw material for new sounds inspired by the speakers' verbal commentary. The analysis of the speech was confined to an acoustic rather than a semantic level. This analysis can be applied regardless of language to reveal the sound patterns of a particular commentary.

A Praat script was written to record the intensity of the audio signal and the frequency of sounds within the human vocal range from the audio files

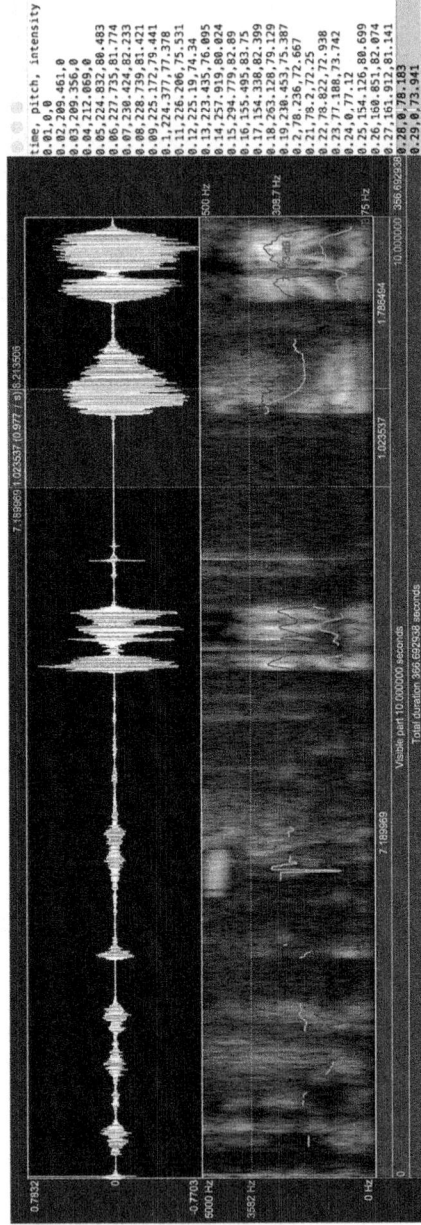

Fig. 8.3 Digital spectralization of the human voice. Dr Mathew Emmett

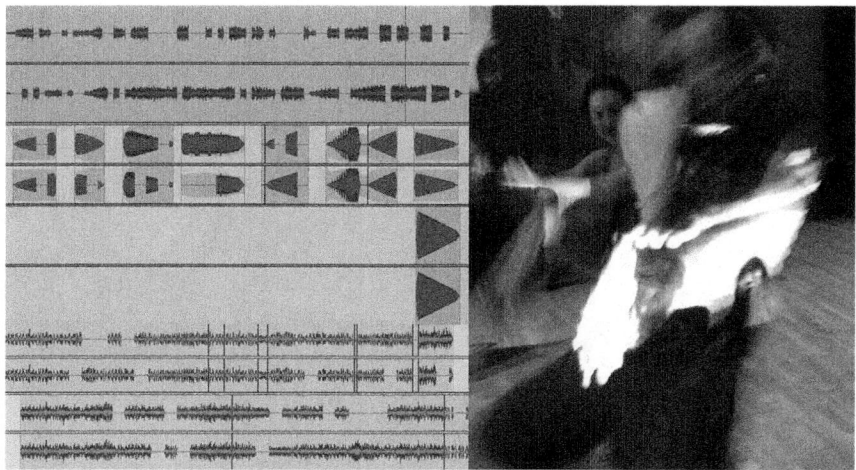

Fig. 8.4   Composition of micro-tonalities. Dr Mathew Emmett

of dancer commentary. A range of pitch from 75 to 300 Hertz was chosen, as this range encompasses the fundamental frequencies of adult male and female voices. The intensity and frequency values of sounds within this frequency range in the audio file are saved to a text file at a sampling rate of 100 Hz. This numeric data about the frequency and intensity of the dancers' voices could then be used as input data to compose new sounds based on the qualities of their speech (Fig. 8.5).

This data was put into tabular form, creating a numerical data set that transformed accent, syntax and breathing patterns into an indexed set of related values. Using Pure Data, an audio patch was constructed to synthesize musical sounds from these numeric arrays. Pure Data (PD) was used as the composition tool throughout *Open State*. PD is a visual programming language similar to MaxMSP, originally created by Miller Puckette in the 1990s. PD is used for generating electronic music and interactive multimedia works by digitally synthesizing audio and sound effects. PD is "open source", it's very versatile, and it enables work in "real-time", therefore offering incredible functionality to computer sound composition. The system is based upon conditional logic, which simply describes a decision-making process based upon input/output arguments; the concept of patching is central to PD, as a patch contains and organizes these arguments in codified form. PD references the world of modular synthesizers

Fig. 8.5 Algorithmic soundscape score. Dr Mathew Emmett. Maho Amakata in Tokyo dances with Ellen Hunn in Plymouth

whereby each module performs a certain task, the first task usually being that of the oscillator that generates sound from an oscillating source. PD contains boxes called 'objects', which have 'inlets' and 'outlets' linked together via lines or 'wires'. These 'objects' can contain arguments that pass into the patch to control the sound output which is then 'wired' to a digital analogue converter (DAC) which uses digital signal processing (DSP) to make sound. *Open State* used Pure Data as a sound composition tool by patching a sine wave oscillator to the table array comprised of the voice analysis. Thus, the music for *Open State* was generated algorithmically from 'data specific' values. This spectral approach (formulated through computer-based sound analysis) revealed a deep, perspectival sonic world, rich in frequencies, transitory rhythms, tempo and dynamics. These sounds formed the tonality base for musical thought and structure.

8.10   PURE DATA: CHOREOGRAPHER'S NOTES

'My initial response to 'pure data' was one of mild panic. The sound score was very digital and computerized, not at all within the musical range that I would normally work as a choreographer. It would be fair to say that it struck me as 'soulless' and problematic. I was thrown into doubt as to whether I could actually use it, and it was with considerable trepidation that I took it into the studio to try out with a trio that I was working on with Shunpei, Seiichiro and Tomomi. To my surprise the score not only threw an entirely new light on the piece, but gave me considerable insight into how I might progress the work and what kinds of detail I could now focus on. The 'pure data' sound score led me to a very different way of working with the body and a newly elucidated physical language that seemed to work particularly for Seiichiro's very unique quality of movement. Rather surprisingly, the music provided a bridge between his movement and the two non-disabled dancers by encouraging me to be more anatomically focused and precise in the feedback and suggestions I offered in the shaping of movement' (Fig. 8.6).

By using PD *Open State* explored the overtones, subharmonics and resultant tones from the spectral analysis to highlight the sounds not normally registered when listening to the human voice. These were treated in

Fig. 8.6   Tomomi Kosano, Seiichiro Kondo and Shunpei Mitsuhashi in trio to *PureData4*

three primary ways including stretching (time varying frequency), overlay (composed of a combination of scalar values) and the pure un-manipulated form. Each became a phenomenological trigger with a cumulative effect of immersion, where the underlying idea would allow a world of acoustic communication to reveal a complex and entrancing connection to the frequency trace of the Japanese voice through extended duration. Further, the manipulated sounds were polyphonic and spatially distributed, being composed of a combination of scalar values whilst specified to move in the environment to articulate a complex trajectory in both frequency and dynamics.

The example of slowing down the voice introduced a microscopic effect. By manipulating time, the effect is to magnify the breath and extend its volume both in duration and granular detail. These sounds were strangely alluring and reminiscent of La Monte Young's minimal compositions and phase shifting. And as a direct consequence of the interlocking rhythmic patterns, together with the creation of uninterrupted textures, a sound world involving psychoacoustics emerged, suggesting a more internal element to the sound spectrum.

8.11   Pulled Apart Duo: Choreographer's Notes

'Shunpei Mitsuhashi and Asumi Masuda had been working on their own on a contact based duet. They were industrious, and while I was occupied working with the other dancers, soon produced a lot of material. However without an 'outside eye' the duet they created felt to me, overly compact, and didn't seem to engage or allow me a way in as a viewer. Mat had been talking about 'pulling apart voices and opening spaces within sounds' and reluctant to discard the material Shunpei and Asumi had very conscientiously worked on, I applied the same principle to the duet. I separated the two dancers spatially and began to pare down their movement into simple, discrete elements, allowing a more sculptural quality to emerge. Each moment of the duet began to be refined and spaces that were sometimes poetic, sometimes painful opened up between them, giving far greater valence to those moments when the dancers came near to each other. When we brought the sound of the 'pulled apart' voices to this there was an immediate resonance and rightness of fit. The sound seemed to echo around the spaces between their bodies and support them in their moments of isolation, giving me the courage to further reduce the material. As a result, far less seemed to be happening physically, but far more seemed to be happening psychologically and emotionally.'

8.12   PULLED APART CHOREOGRAPHER

'The two examples above were those moments where the collaborative process paid huge dividends. It soon became apparent that the piece needed more melodic qualities across its forty minutes duration if it was to have dynamic variation and be accessible to an audience largely unfamiliar with integrated dance (or with specturalized voice). I was hugely relieved that Mat was open to a variety of approaches to the scoring of the project and not at all parochial in his outlook. I started listening to music by John Matthias with who I had collaborated on previous projects. Yet initially his music seemed to be too great a leap to be useable alongside Mat's material. There were details however within certain tracks that I was strongly attracted to and so with John's permission I began to edit and loop extracts from tracks such as *Burning Mouth* and *Rotate* which I then tried out with a number of different passages of movement. One of these was another trio I had been working on, this time with Shunpei, Asumi and Maho, that was based on a revolving structure and which seemed appropriate to try with Matthias' track *Rotate*. Although there was a clear thematic, structural correspondence in the composition of both music and choreography, the combination of movement and music seemed to 'overstate' the lyricism, leaving the whole rather too 'sweet'—it was so close a fit and yet ended up as a disappointing and rather frustrating experiment. This trialling of John's material initially resulted in several other near misses.'

'It was at this point that I began to look more closely at the vocal materials we had amassed throughout the process, including the original voice recordings of the Japanese dancers when they had watched the UK improvisations and began to experiment with layers of sound, returning to some of the looped, edited sections that had nearly, but not quite worked. Adding Mats treated voice to these instrumental tracks opened them up in a rather wonderful way. For example, introducing Mat's treated voice lent a haunting sense of unease to *Rotate* giving the choreography a new edge by shifting it away from a simple lyrical accompaniment.'

'Having identified this unexpected confluence between the work of the two composers I was able (with permission from both) to explore further mixes. Thus the looped guitar intro to Matthias' *Burning Mouth* was mixed with slowed down voices in a section in which the dancers, all seated, shift across the stage in silhouette. Their "found movement" sequences were reflected and augmented through the introduction of the treated voices and the guitar lick lent a necessary rhythmic pulse to the silhouetted action. Within this simple choreographic sequence, at least ten contributions can be distinguished. The base "found movement" from the six dancers, the placing and timing of that movement (Benjamin), the recorded voice itself, plus Mat's treatment of that voice, plus John's guitar, plus Asako's lighting.'

8.13   Multiple Voices: Aha, Aha

The work was to be premiered in The White Studio in the Tokyo Arts Centre. This is an impressive exhibition space with a huge white back wall that curls around the upstage perimeter. We were able to visit the space early in the rehearsal period to discuss access and technical arrangements, but would not be able to use the space itself until production—the day before the premier. With no wing spaces, no back stage or crossover area and very little by way of rigging possibilities, it was evident that the space itself would have a profound impact on how *Open State* was to be shaped and lit, and indeed how the materials created would be 'offered up' to the stage during the rather brief production period. A priori knowledge of the venue had determined the open-ended title, which was required by funders and publicists long before the making of the piece. In many ways the space determined the overall structure: the decision to seat the dancer when not moving, around the edge of the stage; the decision to interact with the audience; the decision to use the simplest of lighting states, were all prompted by the architecture of the White Studio. Thus while most of the sections were firmly set by the time we came to Tokyo Arts Centre, much of the transitional material was evolved in response to the space itself, slightly nerve-wracking for the dancers, but a process that we had talked through and prepared for. This artistic brinkmanship allowed us to remain creative and open to ideas and possibilities right up to the final hour. For example, we had illuminated the space by using a projector with a frosted gel, to create a Rothko'esque block of light on the back wall. Towards the end of the piece we needed to remove the gel so that words from Matthias' song, *Burning Mouth* could be projected in English and Japanese (see Fig. 8.2) in partial accompaniment to the lyrics, and in recognition that the text being used needed to be made available to a non-hearing audience (text used elsewhere in the piece was available in programme notes, as a ubiquitous prompt sheet available to all.) A combination of thematic and technical issues meant that the removing of the gel couldn't be achieved in a blackout. The projector had to remain on and the gel had to be removed and there seemed no elegant way of achieving this. The solution came from Seiichiro raising his arms, as if lifting a window. Somehow the fragility of his body was transformed into a moment of strength, that seemed to capture something about his inner world, as this one solitary gesture transformed the light in the entire space.

8.14 Conclusions

Open State developed a spectral approach to acoustic composition by concentrating exclusively on one small sequence of the voice, and by magnifying these notes, an entire universe of overtones filled the environment—recalling the liminal state of being immersed within the breath. By foregrounding the timbre and envelope of these sounds, the music was designed to increase the dancers' integration of space and movement with the sound environment. Amplifying the lower registers of the recorded voice created a meditative experience in combination with the performance. Here the tuning of the sound atomized and opened up the voice and directed the attention to the spectral sum of overtones and texture, which included the transitory aspects and subtle harmonic intonations only made evident through manipulation. A duality of identity and non-identity emerged, creating micro-tonalities—where a single tone is both an individual entity but also the conveying medium for the whole, creating a complete field that invites the listener to go beyond sonic boundaries.

Just as specturalization opened up the minutest aspects of voice (a voice that might have held no meaning), so Seiichiro's gesture, amplified through its relationship to light, revealed something hidden within. Moments such as these were testimony to an exchange and an interrogation of assumed limits that resulted in shared understanding that crossed cultural barriers.

This invitation, to 'go beyond' is at the heart of integrated work, and the discovery that any voice or sound can be opened in this way to provide choreographic inspiration means that even a performer without speech, but who can utter a sound might underscore an entire work. *Open State* points toward further dialogue between disabled and non-disabled artists, across cultures and across continents and to a continued journey of discovery. *Open State* thus declines the desire to draw any lines of separation; rather it encourages a contemplation of sonic relationships and what it means to have a voice.

In 2017 *Kyo Company* travelled to the UK and performed *Open State* in The House at Plymouth University, making possible a 'real time' connection between the dancers and musicians who had first encountered each other in the same building, by video link, two years previously.

Acknowledgements We would like to thank Dr Frank Broz, Integrated Dance Company-Kyo Dance artists: Maho Amakata, Yoko Izumi, Seiichiro Kondo, Tomomi Kosano, Asumi Masuda, Shunpei Mitsuhashi, Takiko Iwabuchi (Artistic Director) Yuko Ijichi (Director of MUSE Company), Mikari Suzuki (translator and studio assistant), Tamami Benjamin (translation of texts), Asako Miura (lighting), Norimasa Ushikawa (sound engineer), John Matthias for additional music and the UK dancers: Sophie Colthurst, Kevin French, Ellen Hunn, Klara Lucznik, Nathan Matthews and Saurav Rai.

NOTE

1. A second improvisation took place in the Saison Studio, Tokyo 19.30, 30 June 2015, watched on Skype by dancers in Plymouth (12.30 GMT), whose voices and commentary were recorded for future work.

REFERENCES

Bailey, Helen, et al. 2009 Dancing on the Grid: Using e-Science Tools to Extend Choreographic Research. *Philosophical Transactions of the Royal Society A* 367: 2793–2806. https://doi.org/10.1098/rsta.2009.0048. http://rsta.royalsocietypublishing.org/on. Accessed 7 November 2015.

Butcher, Rosemary, and Susan Melrose. 2005. *Choreography, Collisions and Collaborations.* Enfield: Middlesex University Press.

Cooper, Joanne. 1991. *Telling Our Own Stories: The Reading and Writing of Journals or Diaries.* In *Stories Lives Tell: Narrative and Dialogue in Education,* ed. Carol Witherell and Nel Noddings. New York: Teachers College Press.

Dodds Rebecca, D., Thomas B. Ward, and Steven M. Smith. 2003. *Incubation in Problem Solving and Creativity.* In *The Creativity Research Handbook,* ed. Mark A. Runco, vol. 3. New York: Hampton Press.

Popat, Sita. 2005. *Invisible Connections: Dance, Choreography and Internet Communities.* London: Routledge.

Ritter, Simone, and Ap Dijksterhuis. 2014. Creativity: The Unconscious Foundations of the Incubation Period. *Frontiers in Human Neuroscience* 8: 215.

PART III

Preserving the Intangible: New Tools and Documentation Strategies

CHAPTER 9

Demystifying or Destroying? Cultural Heritage and Tradition in Playing the Tabla, and Developing the Electronic Tabla and Digital Notation System

Jerri Daboo

9.1 INTRODUCTION

Issues of cultural heritage and tradition contain complex and often contradictory discourses and debates which increase when encountering the process of digitization and preservation. Performance forms in particular can embody these contradictions, as performers and performance-makers struggle with the pressures of making work that is both new, and yet also preserving a connection to a past tradition and heritage. This is thrown further into focus when examining performance from a culture that is considered to be 'other', particularly if from a perceived 'minority' culture, which interrogates how identity is formed and performed in those cultures and traditions, and questions who has the right to determine how that form is preserved and adapted in a new context. This is very much a product of the modern era, and this chapter examines these issues through

J. Daboo (✉)
University of Exeter, Exeter, UK

© The Author(s) 2018
S. Whatley et al. (eds.), *Digital Echoes*,
https://doi.org/10.1007/978-3-319-73817-8_9

169

a specific case study of an approach to playing and learning an Indian instrument in the UK, and what happens when digitization of both the instrument and notation for playing and learning are introduced. Debates around lineage, transmission, authenticity and the tension between preservation and lived heritage become manifest not as an intangible philosophical discourse, but as a very real and tangible encounter in the process of the project.

Questions of cultural heritage, whether tangible or intangible, have a particular inflection when examining performance in diasporic contexts, particularly in relation to the sense of home/homeland and identity. For sociologist Avtar Brah:

> Home is a mythic place of desire in the diasporic imagination. In this sense it is a place of no return. ...On the other hand, home is also about the lived experience of a locality. ...When does a location *become* home? What is the difference between 'feeling at home' and staking claim to a place as one's own? Is it quite possible to feel at home in a place and, yet, the experience of social exclusions may inhibit public proclamation of the place as home. ... Identity is a multi-faceted and context-specific construct. ...[It] is neither fixed nor singular; rather it is a constantly changing relational multiplicity. (Brah 1996, 193)

Cultural heritage becomes part of the means by which the diasporic community creates a sense of identity and 'feeling at home', often in relation to tangible and intangible cultural forms from the 'homeland' that has been left behind. This leads to a particular cultural space in the diaspora that establishes complex and sometimes contradictory relationships to memory and belonging. Forms of performance that have migrated over from the 'homeland' as intangible cultural heritage can also become a site of contestation in this context, particularly when faced with changes to the 'tradition' of the performance form through adaptation or digitization in the new 'home' of the diaspora.

This chapter examines these issues through a project I undertook with British South Asian musician and composer Kuljit Bhamra, who is also a renowned tabla player. The project was supported by a grant from Research and Enterprise in Arts and Creative Technology (REACT), funded by the Arts and Humanities Research Council in 2014, and aimed to create a prototype for an electronic and digital version of the tabla drums, along with further developing the notation system and teaching method that

Fig. 9.1 Kuljit Bhamra playing the tabla drums. Photograph: Jerri Daboo

Bhamra has been working on for six years. The tablas are a form of North Indian drums normally consisting of a set of two drums: a lower bass sounding drum and a higher pitched drum (see Fig. 9.1). They are a foundation instrument in much classical and popular South Asian music, mainly taught through the *guru–shishya parampara*, or guru–disciple tradition, where a student is affiliated to a guru in a particular *gharana*, which is a school or house, often associated with a family lineage and place, which has a distinctive style of performance, such as the *Delhi Gharana, Banares Gharana, Lucknow Gharana* and so on.

Bhamra's aim with developing the electronic instrument is to 'demystify' the tabla and make it accessible to learn and play in a wider context, as well as to enable more composers to write music for it. Bhamra has played extensively with Western musicians in classical and jazz music, as well as performing in theatre and film productions. It was through working with Western musicians that he encountered the need for a form of precise notation for the tabla to be able to perform with other instruments in music which requires playing to a particular beat and rhythmic pattern, often to a click-track, which traditional tabla players find very difficult. In addition, when teaching schoolchildren in the UK to play tabla, he discovered that not only is the guru system of teaching not appropriate or possible, but also that schools found it difficult to buy and look after sets of tabla,which are very delicate. Furthermore, the Western orchestral percussionists he worked with expressed a desire to learn and play tabla in order to incorporate this into their repertoire of percussion instruments, but felt restricted from doing so due to not knowing where to buy a 'good quality' set, and how to learn to play fast and complicated patterns. Composers that Bhamra has worked with also declared they would like to write for the tabla, but find it too 'foreign' or inaccessible to know how to include it in their work.

To address these issues, Bhamra began to develop a notation system for the tabla that he designed using the digital notation software programme Sibelius. In this way, the tabla could be composed for as part of an ensemble of instruments and incorporated into a Western musical score by the composer through the digital notation programme. Bhamra has been using this system with composition students on the Sound and Music Summer School at the Purcell School of Music in London for several years, and as a result there is now a growing number of musical compositions which include tabla. More recently, Bhamra has been involved with orchestrating for and performing in the Indian percussion section for the stage musical version of the film *Bend It Like Beckham* (2015), and composer Howard Goodall has used the notation for the tabla in his score for the musical. Bhamra expanded the design of his notation system to include other Indian instruments that were also played in the show, such as *Dhol*, *Dholak* and *Matki*.

Producing the electronic version of the tabla aims to address the problem of the lack of accessibility of buying and looking after the drums. Having an electronic version which mimics the experience of playing the actual tabla makes a robust and more easily available way to learn and play the instrument. The prototype, developed by industrial designer company Rogue Product in association with Bhamra, includes USB and MIDI ports in order to allow for digital connectivity and interaction with a computer and amplifier, and can be plugged directly into a computer to access the notation system via Sibelius or other notation software. This allows for a greater ease in composition and playing the notation by giving the composer the option of inputting his score by playing the electronic tabla as an interface. Bhamra is also connecting this to his system of teaching tabla to make this more straightforward and as accessible as possible, bypassing the need for the *guru–shishya* tradition. The electronic tabla was carefully constructed with sensitive placement of sensors to be as close to the actual experience of playing the drums as possible, which no other drum machine does. This means that someone can learn to play the electronic version and transfer straight to playing the actual drums, which we proved during the testing stage of the prototype (Fig. 9.2). In this way the electronic instrument, the notation system and the teaching method are closely interconnected components in the overall project. Above all, it is

Fig. 9.2 The electronic tabla prototype, next to the actual tabla drums. Photograph: Jerri Daboo

Bhamra's desire to 'demystify' not just the tabla, but also Indian music as a whole, that was the driving force behind the project. This idea of 'demystifying' in his terms, leads to complex questions of tradition, authenticity, lineage and heritage that became very apparent during the focus groups we conducted as part of the project with South Asian tabla players and Western orchestral percussionists, and it is these contestations surrounding issues of tangible and intangible cultural heritage that will be the focus for the chapter.

9.2   MUSIC AS CULTURAL HERITAGE: TRADITION, PRESERVATION, CONSERVATION

In the wake of expanding migration after the Second World War from the Indian subcontinent and Indian communities from the Caribbean, and later on Asians from East Africa, Indian music increasingly began to be played in the pockets of the UK where these migrants settled, forming diasporic communities. There were concerts held at places such as the Commonwealth Institute as well as venues within the diasporic localities, often for special events such as Independence Day and celebrating religious festivals. In addition, music was needed to be played at community events including weddings and *mehfils* (gatherings or parties), as well as in the religious institutions for the purposes of worship. Initially, this was part of the desire of the migrated communities to find a way to be 'at home' in the place that was away from home, often encountering difficulties and hostilities with life in the UK, coping with racism and prejudicial employment and immigration laws. Music was a way of holding on to the life that had been left behind, and so became part of the nostalgic memory landscape in the diaspora, as well as preserving a cultural heritage whilst integrating into a new cultural context, in order not to lose the sense of identity that is bound up with cultural performance and artefacts. This became even more important when their children began to grow up and go to school, with a fear that they would be 'contaminated' by British culture, and lose touch with their own heritage and identity. Part of a response to this was to send children to learn Indian music and dance at classes that were set up in religious institutions and schools. Through this, parents hoped to ensure their children grew up with a strong sense of tradition and identity of 'where they came from', as well as instilling the religious and moral values and discipline inherent in learning and playing music.

The tabla was one of the most popular instruments that migrated over to the UK as part of this shift in the cultural landscape, and boys in particular were sent to learn to play the instrument as part of their education in their cultural heritage, and to instil a sense of located identity and being part of a community. Through this, the tabla became part of both intangible and tangible cultural heritage. The learning and playing of the music is part of the intangible heritage of South Asian communities, whilst the object of the instrument itself became a tangible heritage of something that was brought over from the 'homeland', and was often seen on display in the household, along with other musical instruments, as a physical reminder of that other home. Cultural geographer Divya Tolia-Kelly has examined ideas of memory and 're-memory', a term developed from Toni Morrison's *Beloved* (1987), in relation to artefacts in South Asian homes in Britain. She explains that re-memory 'is a resource for the sustenance of a sense of self that temporarily connects to social heritage, genealogy, and acts as a resource for identification with place' (Tolia-Kelly 2004, 316). Her research looks at memory through visual and material culture, questioning how objects that were brought over from the 'homeland' give a sense of identification with that past in the newly located context of the diaspora, and that memories 'activated through these cultures in the home are considered as essential in discourses of heritage, which are significant for the South Asian diasporas' (Tolia-Kelly 2004, 314). This has a socio-political dimension in being part of the means to shape identity in a post-colonial diasporic context:

> Re-memory bridges notions of transnationalism, with the effects on individual and collective consciousness that informs new identities and new processes of identification. These flows across continents inscribe re-memories that allow for the post-colonial memories of migration to be figured through processes of identifying with a social heritage and sense of enfranchisement to various lands and collective memories of the journey. Precipitates of re-memory allow us to view, imagine and connect with this dynamic post-colonial consciousness, dialectically formed through memories of these other worlds and pasts, as they are figured within Britain. (Tolia-Kelly 2004, 327)

The visibility of the object of the tabla, as one of the artefacts brought over from the homeland, acts as a system of re-memory to create a sense of individual and community identification through memory and the seeing of the object in the present location of the new home. As interest in playing the tabla has increased, so has the visibility of the instrument-as-object itself, not just within the home, but also in commercial contexts in music shops. Bina Musicals in Southall is one of the foremost Indian music shops in the country. Its founder, Kuldeep Sura, started selling Indian instruments in the UK in 1975 when he realized there was a demand for these instruments and their care and repair amongst diasporic communities, and the shop itself opened in 1983. Sura's son, Manu, who now runs the shop, explains that although there are some tabla-makers in the UK, he imports all his tablas from India, which he attributes to economic reasons: 'Everything still comes from India, because the labour is much cheaper there and there are very skilled craftsmen in India and the material is cheaper also. If you produce the same kind of item here, it's not that it can't be done here, but the cost price would be higher' (Sura 2011).[1] This is leading to particular socio-economic circumstances in communities of makers of the instrument in India as part of a transnational flow of capital and cultural heritage between the homeland and the diaspora (see Roda 2015, on the ecology of the global tabla industry). However, the fact that the physical instrument is from India gives it an added cultural and economic value as an object 'from the homeland', creating a re-memory for South Asians, and an exoticization of an 'authentic', 'ethnic' instrument for Western musicians. Shops like Bina offer a visible space for the imported cultural heritage objects which can interrupt the mainstream Western musical heritage, whilst also reinforcing the traditional values from the 'homeland' (Fig. 9.3).

The idea of holding on to a tradition, and that tradition becoming the embodiment of a cultural heritage, is reflected in the attempts of policy-makers to define intangible cultural heritage. This leads to contested ideas of preservation and adaptation, as well as contradictory notions of culture as a way to exhibit both unity and diversity in wider geographical contexts. The European Union's policy on culture states that 'even when it has its roots in a particular country or region, culture is a shared heritage—one the **EU aims to preserve** and help make **accessible to others**' (http://www.libergdc.eu/culture, accessed 3/12/2015, bold in original). Similarly, the more recent ASEAN union of countries in South East Asia discusses the importance of preserving cultural heritage, as well as seeing its potential to create connections across people in different national locations, as it aims to '[p]romote the conservation and preservation of ASEAN cultural heritage; to ensure its continuity; to enhance awareness and understanding of the people and the unique history of the region; and

Fig. 9.3 Bina Musicals in Southall with shelves of tablas, along with *dhols* and other percussion instruments, as well as harmoniums. Photograph: Jerri Daboo

the cultural similarities and differences between and among ASEAN Member States, as well as to protect the distinctiveness of ASEAN cultural heritage as a whole' (ASEAN 2009, 88). UNESCO, which has been officially acknowledging and registering intangible cultural heritage since 2008, has also grappled with the complex issues surrounding questions of preservation of traditions. In the UNESCO report *World Heritage and Cultural Diversity*, Marie-Theres Albert asks the following set of questions:

How can intangible heritage and cultural expressions be protected in dynamically changing cultures without hampering cultural innovation—the dynamic potential of all cultures?

What is the sense in safeguarding intangible heritage, and when does support and protection of lifestyles turn into making a museum out of people's lives?

Where is the line between the protection of culture and its transformation into an exotic object?

How can traditions be conserved and passed on without becoming static? What needs to be done to prevent the safeguarding of intangible cultural goods from becoming counterproductive to the development of diverse practices and cultural innovation? (Albert 2010, 17)

This highlights the problematic process of 'preserving' a tradition, which implies that tradition can exist as a fixed and unchanging object, rather than acknowledging that tradition is something that is instead multiple, in process, emergent and relational. The apparent desire to preserve and conserve an intangible heritage 'tradition' as if it were a static object in a museum could be perceived as an act of neo-liberalism which can prevent the natural flow of growth and change in a living cultural performance form. This is particularly the case with culture and performance amongst migratory communities in post-colonial contexts, where issues of power, appropriation and representation are highly pertinent. Culture and cultural objects, both tangible and intangible, are markers of identity, so losing these or having them remain invisible can be equated with losing identity, or that identity being suppressed. However, the fixing of a form of performance as a 'tradition' which is 'authentic' to a culture can deny the process of change and adaptation that is inherent in the nature of the history of that form, and also that adaptation is itself a process of diasporic communities. At what point in the process does a form of music become 'authentic'? What makes it authentic, and who is deciding this? The tabla as an instrument has evolved into its current form over time, and approaches to techniques of playing and the type of music performed have similarly changed and adapted at different times in various locations. So, at what point could it be said that a particular form of the instrument or way of teaching and playing it are 'authentic' and should be preserved?

It is not just outside forces that can be imposing fixed ideas of 'tradition' and 'authenticity' on a performance form, but this can also come from within factions of the community itself. This was mentioned earlier in relation to the first generation of South Asians in Britain wanting to maintain and preserve certain forms of cultural practices in order to establish a strong sense of individual and shared community identity. However, the second and succeeding generations have often challenged this idea of 'tradition' being fixed, and have wanted to change and adapt the music and its performance to suit their own different approaches and contexts. This can lead to a confrontation between generations over cultural heritage and 'authenticity'. Kuljit Bhamra is not only a tabla player, but also a renowned music producer, and was one of the pioneers of the 'British sound' of *bhangra* that began in the 1980s, which modernized the 'folk' form of *bhangra* music from the Punjab into a style of music incorporating Western instruments, beats and technology to suit the second generation. Some elders felt that this was 'contaminating' the 'traditional' and 'pure' form of *bhangra*, and a sign of the 'contamination' of the younger generation by the West, reflected in moral behaviour as well. As Katrak explains:

> The elders object to a modernized *bhangra* because they wish to preserve a traditional style of *bhangra*. They regard fusion attempts as betraying their cultural values. They want their *bhangra* sounds 'unpolluted' by 'Western influences,' and as pristine as their memories of this music and dance when they themselves may have participated in them in their native India. [...] For the elders, the new sounds and movements betray their culture and memories. (Katrak 2002, 78–9, 81–2)

This tension between 'tradition' and 'modernization', between preserving the 'old ways' and embracing new ones to allow for transformation, is at the heart of the examination of cultural heritage. The context of a diasporic community highlights this tension, as the pull between homeland and home, and first and second generations, can result in those attempting to revision a cultural tradition being seen as either pioneers or betrayers of their culture. The act of preservation or conservation as expressed by the EU and ASEAN policies often preserves the most conservative forms, and restricts the flow of natural growth and adaptation of both the performance form, and the community itself. As Naidoo suggests, 'the liberal face of a heritage project can meet the reactionary face of a community and little progress is made' (Naidoo 2005, 45), so to repeat Albert's question: 'What needs to be done to prevent the safeguarding of intangible cultural goods from becoming counterproductive to the development of diverse practices and cultural innovation?' (Albert 2010, 17).

9.3   Teaching, Notating and Composing: Adapting or Destroying?

This issue of holding on to a particular form of a traditional approach to music was also expressed by some of the tabla players in the focus groups for the REACT project, who were troubled by the changes to learning and playing the instrument that would result from the use of the digital notation system and related teaching method which we explored during the project. The resulting dialogue with Western percussionists highlighted this concern and conflict between 'authentic' approaches to performance, and the effect of adapting this process through digitization and the distancing from the original cultural context to make the instrument more accessible to a wider audience. The tabla players were not as concerned with the creation of the electronic form of the instrument as they were with the changes to the understanding of playing with the inherent spiritual values that would be affected through the new notation and teaching system. In this way, it was the intangible cultural heritage that had more value for them than the tangible. This may have been because the electronic instrument is not intended to replace the actual drums, and also that it can offer new potentials for performing through the MIDI and USB connectivity, as well as automatic tuning. However, it was the surrounding cultural issues of how it is taught and the experience of playing that were the most contested areas in relation to preserving the tradition of the instrument and the music.

There were three focus groups conducted as part of the overall REACT project between September and December 2014 (referred to below as Focus Groups A, B and C). The groups consisted of between eight and ten participants, usually an equal split between South Asian tabla players, some of whom had worked with Bhamra on his notation system or performing with him in the stage musical *Bombay Dreams* (2002), and Western orchestral percussionists who are at an early stage of their career, and want to learn to play the tabla out of interest and to add to their repertoire of instruments for future employment potential. Bhamra and I led the discussions in the three sessions, focusing on ways of teaching, playing and notating for the instrument, as well as Bhamra leading some practical exploration of these issues through everyone playing the tabla using his notation system.

One key point that emerged, most particularly in the first session, was of Bhamra's desire to 'demystify' the teaching of the tabla in relation to the *guru–shishya parampara* mentioned previously. This system of teaching involves a student affiliating themselves to a guru through a special ritual ceremony. The bond is more than that of a teacher showing a technique of playing, but rather is an act of transmission at a spiritual level where the student becomes part of the family or lineage of the guru in their *gharana*. As Gurdeep John Singh Khabra explains, this involves a close union between a learner and their teacher. As well as involving a transmission of musical knowledge, this system of learning emphasises a significant bond between master and pupil. Young musicians will encounter several ceremonial rites of passage of a particular lineage of musicians, and often the name of the teacher will hold currency within musical circles. [This] stems from the desire to maintain accuracy in the transmission of musical knowledge. As there are so few written resources, accurate transmission becomes crucial, and therefore a well-reputed teacher is highly desirable. (Khabra 2012, 149)

A classical tabla player in the focus group, N,[2] explained that for him a guru is 'someone who leads you from the darkness into the light' (Focus Group A). In this way, learning the instrument is only part of the process, as the student must also develop themselves as a person, show respect to the guru, understand the spiritual aspects inherent in the music, and follow prescribed forms of behaviour: 'To learn tabla initially is something that is not taking up an instrument and learning it. There's a whole system behind it where there's a way of respecting one another, respecting the instrument, respecting the tradition' (N, in Focus Group A). He said that he was shocked when he saw the informal way that Western musicians treat their instruments, and that respect to the teacher in the Indian tradition includes touching their feet when you greet them. The Western percussionists expressed that these aspects of the traditional form of the *guru–shishya* approach alienate them from feeling able to learn to play the tabla, as it is very unfamiliar to them, and they do not want to attach themselves to an individual or *gharana* in this way. Bhamra in particular feels that the guru tradition is what inhibits a greater number of people from choosing to play the tabla, and that this approach is not necessarily appropriate in the UK. However, both N and another tabla player, S, felt strongly that the guru tradition is vital to becoming a 'proper' tabla player, and that an understanding of the philosophical and spiritual intricacies present in the music, as well as the ritual forms of learning and playing, cannot be ignored. A Western percussionist might be able to learn the technicalities of playing the instrument, but this would not make them a 'tabla player', in their view. This is what the term 'classical' means in relation to Indian music: that a performer has been trained in this system of teaching; whereas 'classical' in the Western context tends to refer to a range of musical genres. In Indian classical music, emphasis is on solo performance, technical flair and expertise in improvising on an orally disseminated repertoire of themes, scales, motifs and rhythms. The performers are trained to become 'composer and creator' of their own pieces. However, in Western classical music, generally musicians are trained to read and accurately perform a piece which has been written by another composer.

The Western percussionists said that another feature of the traditional way of learning tabla that they find difficult is the length of time that a student would be expected to train in the *guru–shishya* system. The tabla players explained that a common experience might be that a guru would expect a student to spend six months playing and perfecting just one note. This approach leads to a very deep learning experience and engagement with the instrument and the music; however, it also results in a very long period of training. For the highly-skilled Western percussionists, the idea of spending such a long time learning to play the basics is problematic, as they have the ability and are trained to pick up playing different instruments and forms of music very quickly. They acknowledge that this does not make them experts in the instrument, nor lead to a full awareness of all the cultural aspects of the music, but they are able to play it in a way that may be sufficient for the particular needs of a composition. Bhamra's approach to teaching the tabla offers a much faster route than that of the traditional gurus, by notating the talas (rhythmic patterns) and variations in a way that the musicians can read and play. In addition, Bhamra breaks down the physical process of playing each sound of the drum, exploring which part of the hand or finger hits which area of the drum. This is not the usual process in the guru system, where the student would be expected to imitate the playing of their guru, with virtually no specific verbal instruction or feedback. Bhamra demonstrated his approach during a concert at Queen Elizabeth Hall as part of the Darbar Festival in 2009. In preparation, he spent only an hour teaching four orchestral percussion students from the Royal Academy of Music the finger positions for the various note-heads in his notation system. With only one rehearsal, they performed a piece written by him for five tablas entitled *Quinte-te*. When experiencing Bhamra's way of investigating how to play each note in the focus group session, tabla player M stated that he had found it very useful: 'When I first started learning, that would have been a really helpful thing to do, getting the hand positions, that wasn't something we were taught' (Focus Group B). He acknowledged how fast the Western percussionists were able to pick up the basics through this form of learning, however he also felt that this was just one part of the process, and that the experiences that he had when training with his guru had resulted in a depth of learning

Fig. 9.4 Kuljit Bhamra teaching the tabla to Western percussionists. Photograph: Ammy Phull

that was also very valuable. This also emphasized what we decided was potentially the difference between someone who could play the tabla, and a 'tabla player' who had undergone the classical training (Fig. 9.4).

There have been alternative approaches to the *guru–shishya* system in India and diaspora contexts, often within educational institutions, which have sought to create a system of learning that is more similar to a Western approach based on grades and exams, leading to qualifications. One key figure in this is tabla player Frances Shepherd, originally from Guiana, who established a syllabus for teaching forms of Indian music and dance which is used in both India and the UK. Even though this may be a shift away from the highly traditional form of learning with a guru, the idea of preserving 'tradition' is still very important for her:

> No matter what happens we must not dilute the tradition. So with all our veneer of openness etc. we still are very conservative when it comes to the actual teaching of the strokes and the music etc. Because I think the philosophy is that you'll be able to do anything, you can break the rules, you can be innovative, but you need to have the strong base being taught to the students because they're all different, they have all different talents and skills or interests, but the one thing that binds them together is the solid tradition. (Shepherd 2011)

Shepherd herself studied with a guru, Pandit Sharda Sahai, but her students can choose to follow either the traditional guru system, or the syllabus system. She said that this tends to be about a fifty-fifty split (Shepherd 2011). Another renowned tabla teacher in the UK, Gurmit Singh Virdee, taught many students in Southall and Leicester. His son, Sandeep, explains how his father tried to make the learning of the tabla more accessible for young people in the British diaspora:

> He wasn't like a lot of the teachers who would want you to sort of still follow the typical *guru–shishya* programme. So he broke that stranglehold and he made it accessible, and he almost designed it in a way that he could spoon-feed you into learning the tabla art in a very quick way. And the classes used to have on average 50 students. [...] So a simple thing like 2 syllables, *gege tetay*, he would actually write it down. And *gege* was g-e and g-e again, and *tetay* he would write t-e-t-a-y. So you could actually just look at it and see, oh, he was saying *gege tetay*. And he would just sort of mark it down so he had a time score on it. So he developed this to a really fine art. (Virdee 2011)

Although this shows that Virdee was attempting to break down the system of teaching and developed a way of writing the rhythmic patterns, he was still using the *bhols* or sounds used in teaching, for example *dha, nah, teh*, and so on. There have been other attempts at creating a notation system, but similarly these tend to be based in writing down the *bhols* (see Kippen 2002; Widdess 1994 for examples). Bhamra believes that the use of *bhols* is another factor that can prohibit people from wanting to learn to play the tabla, as the sounds are unfamiliar, can be difficult to pronounce, and sometimes do not bear a relation to the actual sounds of the drum. His notation system in Sibelius uses a Western form of notation based in crotchets and quavers etc., with particular symbols that represent specific finger-strike positions on the drums. We experimented with this notation system during the focus groups. What was very noticeable was that the Western musicians were able to pick up complex patterns very quickly through reading the notation. This astonished the tabla players present: B said that one of the patterns was played accurately on the tabla by the percussionists in a matter of minutes, whereas it had taken him several months to learn it with his guru (Focus Group C). However, speed of learning is not necessarily a marker of quality, so even if the notation and teaching system allows for a faster route into learning the basics, it was agreed that working with a teacher and a longer in-depth experience of learning is necessary to move to a more advanced level of playing.

The use of notation on paper also caused concern amongst some of the tabla players. This is partly due to Indian music being passed on orally, and also that the idea of a composition is very different, with much more emphasis on the performer themselves 'composing' the music through improvisation in performance. As A explained: 'The difference between Western classical music and Indian classical music is that in Indian music 50 per cent is structured or composed, and the rest is free, for improvisation' (Focus Group A). This led A in particular to feel that the notes on the piece of paper would cause a barrier for him to experience playing the music. He could not accept that the intangible cultural heritage present within the music itself could be 'captured' in the notation on a sheet of paper. To him, this was a betrayal of the very nature of the music and the experience of playing it. However, Western percussionist J suggested that this was maybe due to A's unfamiliarity with the language of the notation, and the use of a score is just the first introduction to a piece of music. As he says, the notation is just the means to document and share the music, and that it is a way in, rather than the end point: 'If I give you a piece of music notation, I'm not giving you the music' (Focus Group A), implying that there still needs to be a process of understanding and embodying the music itself in order to be able to express it.

Notation, and therefore 'created written repertoire', can be seen to act as an intervention into the intangible cultural heritage of an oral form, and potentially runs the risk of 'fixing' it into a tradition or way of playing due to it being written down, rather than transmitted in person. However Bhamra's notation system also offers the potential for Western composers to begin to write for tabla in a meaningful way. He has often been asked to play for film and television scores, as well as classical compositions, where the composer has simply indicated that they want the sound of the tabla, but left it for the performer to decide exactly what to play. Bhamra gives the example of playing the tabla part in John Tavener's final major composition *Flood of Beauty* in 2014, shortly after the composer's death. Tavener did not know how to write for the tabla, or have a form of notation for it, so instead Bhamra was faced with a score which indicated when the tabla should be played, but instead of musical notes, had phrases including: 'magical—sparkling like a crystal...shining forth of the divine feminine, ecstatically beaming down to earth...thunderous, then rapt with cosmic beauty...with divine play (Indian style)...like flowing nectar...like the rising sun—gradually opening like the lotus'. This, for Bhamra, explains why he feels the need to 'demystify' the tabla, as phrases such as these embody an exoticization of the instrument and Indian music generally, which has been seen in popular and classical music, often as part of an imperialist or orientalist view of 'mystical India'. Composers such as John Cage, Steve Reich, Philip Glass, Olivier Messiaen and George Crumb have been influenced by Indian music and attempted to include it in their work, but often without an understanding of how to write for each specific instrument. Instead, they want the sounds to be part of an imaginative musical landscape or atmosphere. Bhamra however feels that with his notation system linked into Sibelius, and through the accessibility of the electronic tabla plugged into this, composers will have a greater understanding of the technicalities and possibilities of the tabla, and be able to write specific compositions for the instrument which can then be performed by percussionists, whether they have been trained in the guru system or through other approaches. This will result in a repertoire of music for the tabla that integrates it into the musical mainstream, whilst maintaining the integrity of its nature. In this way, the tabla can become another instrument, rather than 'other'.

The REACT project raised many complex questions about cultural heritage, tradition, digitization and adaptation. These questions and concerns are not ones that can necessarily be answered or solved, but the focus groups showed that the discussion and sharing was a starting point to find ways to address the issues in a respectful and open manner. However, they also showed that these questions are not ideological abstracts, but rather tangible forces at play in the lives of the performers, as they are having to engage with practical ways to address Albert's question: 'How can traditions be conserved and passed on without becoming static?' (Albert 2010, 17). Bhamra is continuing to develop the electronic tabla, notation and teaching system in association with both tabla players and orchestral percussionists, and believes that through this, the tabla will be made accessible to a wider audience and range of people. He has published his approach to teaching using the notation system in a series of three books, which is allowing for this wider engagement with learning and playing the drums (Fig. 9.5).

Bhamra feels that this approach to learning the tabla can be done without loss of cultural integrity in the performance and playing of instruments, but may challenge the traditional views about the instrument and

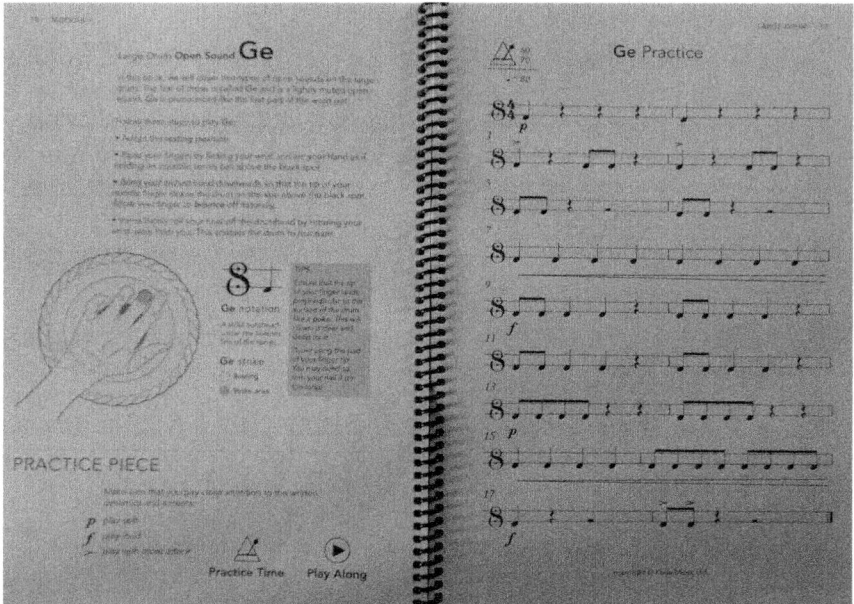

Fig. 9.5 Example of the notation system and teaching method from Module 1 of *Read and Play Indian Tabla Drums* (Bhamra 2017). See www.keda.co.uk for further details. Photograph: Jerri Daboo

the music. However, he states that 'simply keeping a tradition alive is actually suffocating it' (Focus Group A). For diasporic communities negotiating their position between homeland and being at home, the importance of cultural heritage is fundamental to their sense of identity. Yet if a tradition is fixed and held onto for the sake of the preservation of the memory of the homeland, then this can deny the fluid process of change and adaptability that is inherent in the experience of migration, as well as performance.

Acknowledgements With special thanks and acknowledgement to Kuljit Bhamra for his collaboration on the project, and assistance with writing this chapter.

NOTES

1. This interview, and some others used in this chapter, were conducted as part of the AHRC-funded 'Southall Story' project run by Jerri Daboo, which undertook an extensive cultural history of the diasporic town of Southall.
2. I have elected to use initials for the participants of the focus groups, however they all gave their signed informed consent to the discussions from the sessions being used.

REFERENCES

Albert, Marie-Theres. 2010. World Heritage and Cultural Diversity: What Do They Have in Common? In *World Heritage and Cultural Diversity*, eds. Offenhäußer, Zimmerli and Albert, UNESCO. Accessed 3 December 2015. https://www.unesco.de/fileadmin/medien/Dokumente/Bibliothek/world_heritage_and_cultural_diversity.pdf.

ASEAN. 2009. *Roadmap for an ASEAN Community, 2009–2015*. Jakarta: ASEAN Secretariat.

Bhamra, Kuljit. 2017. *Read and Play Indian Tabla Drums*. London: Keda Music.

Brah, Avtar. 1996. *Cartographies of Diaspora: Contesting Identities*. London: Routledge.

Chadha, Gurinder. 2002. *Bend it Like Beckham*. Redbus Film Distribution.

Katrak, Ketu H. 2002. Changing Traditions: South Asian Americans and Cultural/Communal Politics. *The Massachusetts Review* 43 (1): 75–88.

Khabra, Gurdeep John Singh. 2012. Music of the Sikh Diaspora: Devotional Sounds, Musical Memory and Cultural Identity. *Sikh Formations* 8 (2): 147–170.

Kippen, James. 2002. Wajid Revisited: A Reassessment of Robert Gottlieb's "Tabla" Study, and a New Transcription of the Solo of Wajid Hussain Khan of Lucknow. *Asian Music* 33 (2): 111–166.

Morrison, Toni. 1987. *Beloved*. New York: Alfred A. Knopf.

Naidoo, Roshi. 2005. Never Mind the Buzzwords: "Race", Heritage and the Liberal Agenda. In *The Politics of Heritage: The Legacies of 'Race'*, ed. Jo Littler and Roshi Naidoo, 26–48. London: Routledge.

Roda, P. Allen. 2015. Ecology of the Global Tabla Industry. *Ethmusicology* 59 (2): 315–336.

Shepherd, Frances. 2011. Interview with Jerri Daboo for the 'Southall Story' Project, June 11.

Sura, Manu, 2011. Interview with Jerri Daboo for the 'Southall Story' Project, June 12.

Tolia-Kelly, Divya. 2004. Locating Processes of Identification: Studying the Precipitates of the Re-Memory Through Artefacts in the British Asian Home. *Transactions of the Institute of British Geographers, New Series* 29 (3): 314–329.

Virdee, Sandeep. 2011. Interview with Jerri Daboo for the 'Southall Story' Project, June 24.

Widdess, Richard. 1994. Involving the Performers in Transcription and Analysis: A Collaborative Approach to Dhrupad. *Ethnomusicology* 38 (1): 59–79.

CHAPTER 10

Digital Environments for Intercultural Content: A Case Study on the Asian Shakespeare Intercultural Archive

Alvin Eng Hui Lim

The Asian Shakespeare Intercultural Archive is a collaborative archive created by two major Shakespeare projects together with individual scholars, practitioners, and translators: "Relocating Intercultural Theatre" (Singapore Ministry of Education Academic Research Fund Tier 2 and National University of Singapore) and "A Web Archive of Asian Shakespeare Productions" (JSPS Kaken/Gunma-Nagoya City Universities, Japan).

10.1 INTRODUCTION: DIGITALIZING INTERCULTURAL CONTENT

Cultural content is becoming increasingly digitalized, resulting in existing and new challenges to archiving dance and performance-based cultural heritage. Evanescent and embodied performances may be recorded on

---

This chapter is dedicated to the late founding member of the archive, Professor KOBAYASHI Kaori.

A. E. H. Lim (✉)
Department of English Language and Literature, National University of Singapore, Singapore, Singapore

S. Whatley et al. (eds.), *Digital Echoes*,
https://doi.org/10.1007/978-3-319-73817-8_10

191

video but each recording only offers a single iteration of a corpus, a repertoire, or a production run. Digital archives such as the *Routledge Performance Archive* and MIT's *Global Shakespeares* are collecting and showcasing more recordings of theatre and performance events. There is now a need to carefully consider an archive's use of the digital medium, especially since one of the key intentions of doing so is to preserve the performance event as a historical record. As Sarah Bay-Cheng notes, "recent documentation and digital technologies have complicated this seemingly straightforward historicizing procedure [from history-as-record to history-as-event] by altering the processes by which we locate the available documents, how we reconstruct the event from historical evidence, and the very characteristics of the documents themselves" (2012, 27). Although Bay-Cheng focuses on the ramifications of digital media on theatre and performance historiography, her observations are relevant to the archivist's work that must take into account the ephemerality of performance and the mediation of digital technology. Performance scholars such as Peggy Phelan and Diana Taylor expressed their concerns about digital technology over a decade ago. Taylor (2003), for example, writes that "Now, on the brink of a digital revolution that threatens to displace writing, the body again seems poised to 'disappear' in a virtual space that eludes embodiment" (16). A decade of being influenced and surrounded by digital processes have made Internet users learn to access and even expect cultural content to be mediated and performed through digital media. As a point of departure from earlier scholarship on performance and digital technology, Bay-Cheng argues that:

> [O]ur notions of theatre, dance, and performance history [are] influenced by digital processes of recording, storing, writing, retrieving, and performing historical documents of performance...When we re-enact, record and circulate these performances through digital media, we participate in a kind of mediated exchange that takes on all of the hallmarks of theatrical performance, including careful attention to scripts, costumes, and audience response. (Bay-Cheng 2012, 32)

This chapter closely inspects the design processes and protocols that determine the development of the Asian Shakespeare Intercultural Archive (A|S|I|A) website (Yong et al. 2015).[1] When A|S|I|A "reenacts, records and circulates," to cite Bay-Cheng, Shakespeare adaptations in Asia through digital media, I realize that the archival practice necessarily takes on all the "hallmarks of theatrical performance". The ensuing analysis will provide insights into the nature of the digital archiving of performance. A|S|I|A is a digital platform with a pioneering multilingual interface that displays and re-presents a culturally diverse spectrum of theatre productions for a wider audience. On this platform, the video performance now engages its unknown audience long after the performance event. Yet, it also produces its own event, prolonged on a new digital stage, as long as the servers remained connected. New and old audiences are engaged with when a performance goes digital. Digital interfaces restage and digitally circulate theatre productions and in that sense, A|S|I|A's website takes on all of " the hallmarks of theatrical performance". However, it is one that has its own unique complexities in its conception, production, and reception that are unlike from theatre.

Since 2009, A|S|I|A has archived audiovisual recordings, scripts, and production materials of some of the key intercultural productions of East and Southeast Asia. Till now, the archive continues to face questions and challenges of presenting cultural records as digital content, and of facilitating user engagement with those archived materials. For the first two years, legal solutions and conceptual framings were sought and examined in order to best establish a digital environment where a wide and diverse spectrum of cultural content could be displayed and reproduced online. When the digital environment of the pilot edition was set up in May 2010 to host the materials, new questions on spectatorship, user behaviour in virtual spaces, and the ramifications of using digital tools to mediate user-engagements arose. As the archived materials are now used in teaching and research worldwide, most recently in a partnership with Wellesley College to provide content for their WellesleyX Massive Open Online Course (MOOC), the archive team is increasingly conscious of issues of literacy (both language and technological literacies). We also saw the need to provide users with the socio-historical, cultural, and theatrical contexts of a theatre production, and to have the technical capability to host and make available the bandwidth for the recent influx of users.

Notions of ownership, representation, and interculturality are inevitably tested when cultural productions that are translations and creative interpretations of Shakespeare's text and Asian performance forms are hosted in a single repository that online audiences from around the world have access to. Thus, the video player of the online archive has now become a complex site of intercultural reproduction and reception. It is a playback machine with scripts in multiple languages (mostly English,

Mandarin, Japanese, and Korean) and a notepad that shows notes made by editors, translators, and users (both student and teacher), which deepen the experience of watching intercultural productions. Intercultural productions are, to begin with, an assemblage of perspectives, translations, and cultural entanglements.

The experience of watching digital recordings of intercultural theatre performances, however, highlights the debates on the digital archiving of cultural heritage and reproduction. More significantly, the case study of A|S|I|A exemplifies what Mike Featherstone (2000) identifies as the problem of "archiving cultures" as the question becomes "what one dare leave out". For Featherstone:

> Rather than see the archive as a specific place in which we deposit records, documents, photographs, film, video and all the minutiae on which culture is inscribed, should the walls of the archive be extended and placed around the everyday world? If everything can potentially be of significance should not part of the archive fever be to record and document everything, as it could one day be useful? The problem then becomes, not what to put into the archive, but what one dare leave out. (170)

Featherstone questions whether the expansion of culture can "be subjected to a meaningful ordering" when we are "faced by the 'digitalization of culture', which promises enormous gains in speed and mobility of access to information" (166). He is concerned that the increased availability of and ease of access to cultural sources may cause the details and complexity of the archived to be left out. For him, this question leads us to related problems of "closure, of drawing boundaries around a work, both in conception and executions" (166). While Featherstone's primary example is the hypertext and hyperlinks that allow users of archives to jump from one page to another, the issue of "reintermediation", as he calls it, is equally crucial to A|S|I|A's own concern with context framing and the mapping of intercultural intermediaries. One of the challenges of making available culturally specific contents, in the form of digital videos and electronic texts, is that those cultural sources may be taken out of their contexts. As archivists providing an environment for those materials to persist, we may have to provide them with a new context. The A|S|I|A website performs its intercultural content with a unique interculturality—one that echoes the actual and multiple contexts in which those

Shakespearean adaptations are (already) or were found in. I consider it an echoing because the presentation of the intercultural is shown in a few limited but nuanced features and functions. Yet, it is precisely these features and functions that show how the production and reception of digital archives of performance are intricately intertwined. This chapter aims to explore the intermediary roles that the A|S|I|A archive performs and considers the implications the archive has on the theory and practice of intercultural interpretation, translation, and research on intercultural theatre and Shakespeare in Asia.

First, one of the ways a "new" context emerges is through the website's multilinguality. The most critical component of the web archive is found in the language translation of the production scripts. The A|S|I|A digital platform is a parallel language website and participates in its own intercultural production. Mostly translated into English, Mandarin, Japanese, and Korean, the productions collected in the archive have expanded their scope of cultural reception. Viewers encounter both the live performance and the text. Collectively they may be grouped under a cultural heritage, but their mediums of performance are different. The historical context of a written text, especially when it has been published as a standard translation, might differ from the text used in a live performance. Being translated also means that a script extends to both the heritage of the source language and the target language.

Second, the videos are themselves records of the intercultural process of various Asian theatre companies or are part of a heritage of adapting Shakespeare's plays in the respective countries. Thus, each production found in the archive is the result of a long process of intercultural interactions between art forms, theatre conventions, languages, and translations. This means that the productions collected in the archive cannot be understood as definitive of the supposed represented cultures and performance traditions, though they lend themselves to such a reading, especially when they invoke traditional forms in their performances.

In addition, the contents are assembled online in a single repository, with Shakespeare being the common denominator and point of reference. However, the productions are, to begin with, the result of intercultural negotiation, reinterpretation, or conflict, sometimes resulting in a privileging of one's own culture over the other. The website can only provide a partial showcase of those intercultural processes. The decision to provide multilingual content is an attempt to reflect this complex cultural negotiation. A monolingual platform, on the other hand, may force a kind of audience engagement that subsumes those foreign Shakespeare adaptations into the cultural economy of English Shakespeare.

This "partiality" of cultures is further complicated by the fact that a video recording is a reiteration of a production run. It may reiterate the cultural significance of adapting Shakespeare's text to a local version, or by placing one recording alongside another, it prompts a comparison between two separate encounters between Shakespeare and an artistic practice. Therefore, any display of this single performance has been re-contextualized such that any subsequent viewing of it expands the significance of that performance instance in relation to many others found on the website and beyond.

Third, digital content also tends to flatten out the experience of watching an intercultural performance because a video recording can dominate the ocular senses and reiterate a spectacle of an Asian foreign identity, that is, as a visual spectacle instead of a whole continuum and process of cultural interactions, including its aural and linguistic negotiations. More explicitly, when these recordings are housed in a virtual site instead of a geographical site, the performances are taken out of their spatial context, which have their own particular demographics and histories. A digitally streamed performance can be reconfigured as a visual frame of contact, two-dimensionally framing one's viewing experience.

To counter this tendency, A|S|I|A designed the video interface to assign a large portion of the screen to the scripts and translations of the original script. The script in each language is displayed in blocks of text. With each toggling of the language buttons the user can select the desired language. While the viewing is still done on a flat screen, the experience is expanded by the possibility of having multiple frames of languages and commentaries.

At this stage of the archive's development, I will evaluate the processes involved in archiving and presenting those multimedia contents in order to make observations about the experience of watching cultural productions digitally. The above three critical components that restage intercultural theatre productions online, as embodied in the scripts, video, and digital content, will be critically examined. The three aspects inform the project team's commitment to provide access in the most culturally sensitive manner. More crucially, the interface displays cultures in particular ways that draw attention to specific aspects of artistic production, whilst leaving others out.

10.2 Multilingual Interface: Digital Production and Access to Intercultural Content

The interface of a digital archive is the focal and meeting point for the archivist and the user. It is where the archivist arranges the materials and presents them to users and viewers. It is also where a user has the first contact with the materials, albeit digital, and creates the first impression of them. Hence, the interface has always been the priority in the archive's development. More crucially, the interface contextualizes any given performance recording. More than housing the streaming video, the interface situates the user in a digital environment where the original context of the production is mapped onto a new setting. Recognizing the significant role that an interface plays, the A|S|I|A team and designers had to customize a video player on which an intercultural production re-performs its meanings and contexts. One key feature of the video player is, as mentioned, providing translations for the user to access the foreign production (Fig. 10.1).

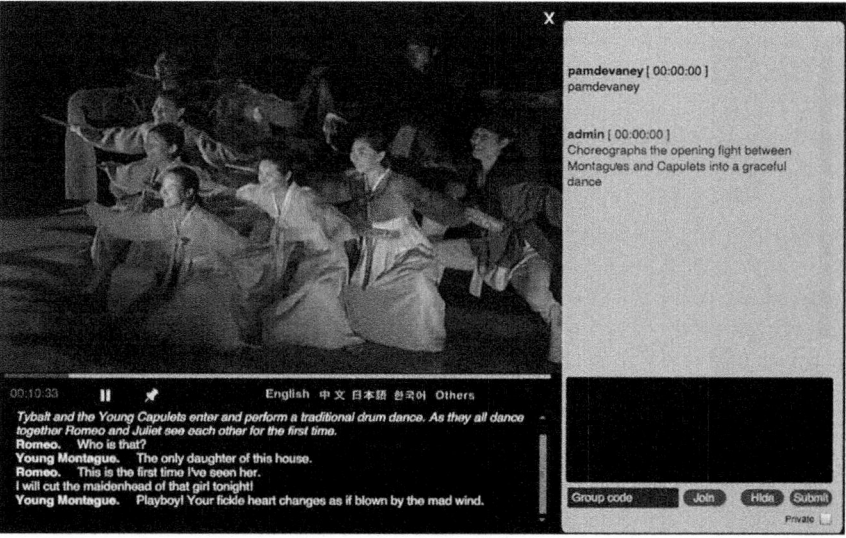

Fig. 10.1 Screenshot of A|S|I|A video playback of *Romeo and Juliet* (2005), Mokwha Repertory Theatre, directed by OH Tae-suk. Dance scene when Romeo and Juliet meet for the first time. Courtesy of Asian Shakespeare Intercultural Archive

When we started developing the multilingual platform, we immediately faced a ton of language related issues. In 2008, software programming was mostly done in alphanumeric (Latin letters and Arabic digits) and remains so for many software developers. One of the first issues we focussed on was the appearance of East Asian scripts in intelligible fonts on different browsers. One related technical requirement was to provide three versions of the same database,[2] and display scripts in three languages (English, Mandarin, and Japanese). While we could design a database schema for organizing the information and data surrounding any given production every data entry was translated into two more languages. What this also effectively meant was that any textual work was always multiplied threefold, and later four times when the Korean language was added to the mix. In that sense, the automation and digital organization of data was always coupled with a labour-intensive process that involved translators and data editors who created data in the performance language of any given production. The coding was done in English-based programming language but the platform had to accommodate the display of foreign fonts. It may now seem like a straightforward function on our latest Internet browsers but when we first started, older browsers could not automatically display those codes and scripts and they would appear as gibberish.

The issue of language translation highlights the work of intermediaries that frame and contextualize the new (digital) encounter with the cultural production. The common process is always a combination of machine or technical mediation, and the tedious human creation and processing of data. I focus on the site for video display because it best illustrates the tensions between machine and human processes. For example, behind the fully automated display of scripts and videos and a set of algorithms that process the playback of a video is the labour of sub-editors working behind the scenes to format scripts and generate data before the upload of these contents. The A|S|I|A team introduces a set of processes to limit human and machine error and to create digital content:

1. check the original script against video;
2. format video to desired video quality and streaming format;
3. time code the script to match the video;
4. create and provide translation and editorial notes for viewer.

While the video recording is the documentation of one iteration of a full production, the scripts that A|S|I|A receives from theatre companies are sometimes a different version of the production script. A performance recording may often differ greatly from the production script for an array of reasons. Theatre companies, directors, or actors make revisions to the script, which include cuts and additions either because of onstage improvisations or when a production is being restaged and adjustments are made. A video recording captures the singular event but it may not recover the long process of script revisions. A production script is thus not necessarily the performance script. A check of the script against the video is needed to ensure that the translation at least follows the sequence presented on stage as a recording. If they are gaps in the script, the spoken word on video will be transcribed.

Scripts are time-coded in blocks of eight lines and by native speakers of the language spoken in the production. All scripts have to be formatted as a quadrilingual document so that any sub-editor can quickly identify the corresponding lines in the different languages. Every block of text is arranged in English, Mandarin, Japanese, Korean and/or the original language:

Romeo.   Who is that?

罗密欧。   她是谁?
ロミオ。   あれは誰だ?
로미오.   저 애 누구지?

Young Montague.   The only daughter of this house.

太古家男壮丁。   这家的独生女儿。
モンタギュー家の若者。   この家の一人娘です。
로미오 패.   이 댁 외동딸. 몰랐냐.

Romeo.   This is the first time I've seen her.   I will cut the maidenhead of that girl tonight!

罗密欧。   我第一次遇到这位姑娘。
　　　　　　　今晚我要摘取这女孩的初爱!
ロミオ。   初めて見た。
　　　　　　　あの子の純潔を今夜切り取ってやろう。
로미오.   첨 보네.
　　　　　　내 오늘 저 지지배 꼭지를 잘라 놀 거야![3]

In theory, the text can be copied to the software to create those individual blocks of text in one language to be displayed on screen. Every block of text displays one script. As long as a sub-editor follows one language, he or she can copy the text in any language to the word processor. In practice, however, extra sub-editorial checks must be done to ensure that there are no discrepancies. This is where a final check, after the scripts have been uploaded to the server and displayed by the video player, has to be done by a native speaker. In any case, some blocks are not always equivalent—for example, a single line in the English verse may not be the same in Japanese as the syntax may differ. Sub-editors are told to break the scripts up into blocks but some leeway is given even if the last line of the block of text in, for example, English does not correspond to the last line in Japanese in its meaning.

The above example highlights the virtual crossings between two or more cultural forms, resituated digitally in a customized space. This issue of breaking text into blocks and the framing of multilinguality is most pronounced when the website archives and presents multilingual productions such as those directed by Ong Keng Sen: *Lear* (1998), *Search Hamlet* (2002) and *Lear Dreaming* (2012). In the next section, I elaborate on the process of video player customization, echoing the intercultural negotiation when a playwright or artist translates or adapts a text to another and restages it within his or her own process and range of artistic practice. Not all video screens perform the same complex process that is found in stage productions of *Lear* (1998) but they all perform the remediation of a cultural production. They re-perform the cultural production with its own theatrical context.

10.3   Video Archiving Practices for Remediating the Intercultural

The video playback of multilingual productions such as *Lear* (see Fig. 10.2) echoes the dramaturgy of having artists of different cultures and languages brought together in the stage production. Bharucha (2001) may have heavily criticized *Lear* for its particular juxtaposition of spoken languages and "self-orientalism" tendencies in relation to the characters and status of the language in the Southeast Asian region. Nevertheless, the video playback of *Lear* also revisits the ethics of cultural inclusion and exclusion, where a monolingual presentation would have been more detrimental to *Lear*'s renewed reception on A|S|I|A. At the very least, the video player engages the text at the production's most curious positionality: the curating of languages, cultural traditions, and perspectives on a highly mediated

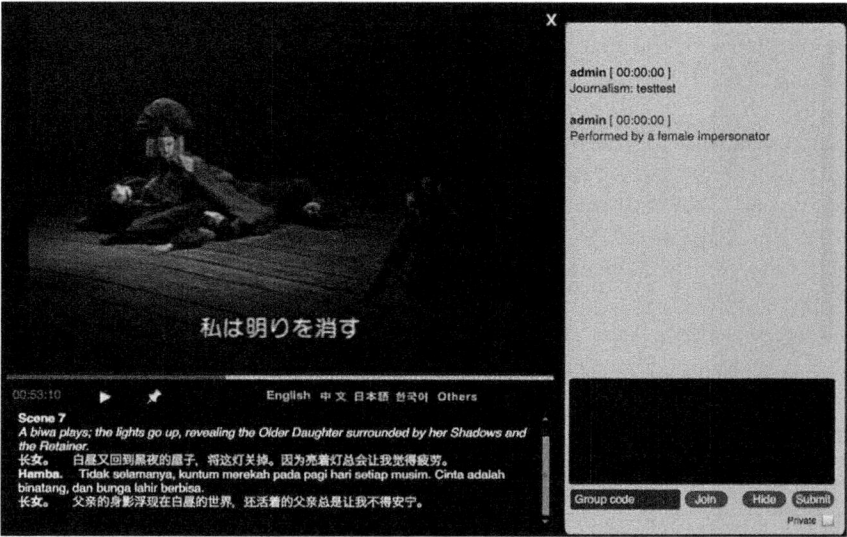

Fig. 10.2 Display of multilingual scripts alongside the video recording. Screenshot of video player playback of Japan Foundation's *Lear* (1997) courtesy of Asian Shakespeare Intercultural Archive

stage. The hallmarks of the theatre production are still echoed by the presence of a multilingual text alongside its multi-panel display. The dramaturgical composition of the website, or the web design, frames the viewing experience. Within the digital medium, a production does not exist in isolation but must interact with other frames of experience.

Nothing exemplifies this intermediation of theatre production and digital reproduction, technology, and human labour, than the main site of the archive's performance: the video player. The video player has gone through several rounds of coding to suit the unique requirements of the website. It is the only instance on the website where the languages are displayed alongside each other or easily switchable when the language buttons are "pressed". Unlike other video players you see online, the first specification we gave to the web design company was to create a player that could support several languages and display lines of text alongside the video.

However, it is not simply a video platform for the screening of video recordings. Compared with subtitles superimposed onto the screen (such as for film) where the text serves the function of providing an immediate translation of what is being spoken line by line, the separate window places an emphasis of the text being apart from the performance and yet it also supports the performance. This displayed text reiterates its particular cultural heritage, translation context, and the translation standards of the target language. Sometimes the translations are standard translations (such as Yushi Odashima's Japanese translations of Shakespeare's plays, or Zhu Shenghao's Chinese translations) that theatre companies used as the basis for their adaptations. Keeping the scripts separate highlights the relationship between the performance and the text, but it also manifests the translation's own trajectory—from source text to translation, and from translation to being a definitive translation referred to or preferred by directors and playwrights.

More crucially, such a framing of the text with the video highlights quite starkly the differences between the embodied and visceral performance and the textual and structural aspects of the performance, that is, the acts, scenes, role names, and stage directions. The video player clearly frames and demarcates the components of performance, and teases out the different components of an intercultural production. It also quickly allows a user to identify Shakespeare's role names and its attributions to actors who may not be easily recognizable if one does not understand the cultural codes mapped onto Shakespeare's story world. What we initially thought of was to display individual scripts as economically as possible, while not relegating the text to being a supplement to the recording. The current result is an interface (see Fig. 10.3) that manifests aspects of intercultural production and its complexities.

The text-blocks below the video screen work as a panel. Each panel can be described as a translated version of the performance but it stands on its own to provide an entry point or point of access for the viewer. Such a panelling frames the experience and the attempt is to have them all relate to each other in meaningful and interactive ways.

The video acquired by the archive may sometimes come with "hard subtitles", line-by-line subtitles that have been superimposed onto the video. More commonly, the video is often a digitally rendered copy of a DVD copy or videotape if the recording is of an older production. The "original" copies are digitally formatted in streaming formats so as to implement the display of scripts specifically timed to the video, and to stream the video with maximum security and prevent the illegal downloading of the videos.

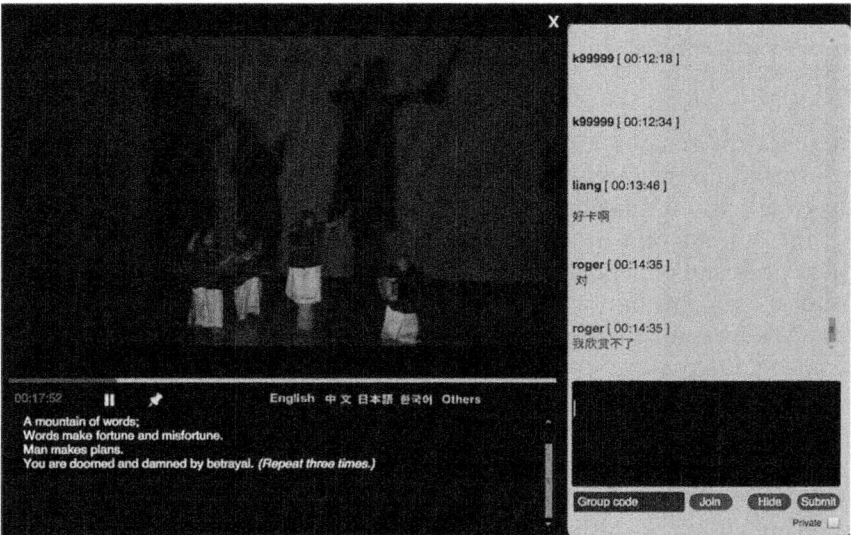

Fig. 10.3 *Lear Dreaming* (2012), TheatreWorks, directed by Ong Keng Sen. Screenshot of video recording courtesy of Asian Shakespeare Intercultural Archive

The team attempts to provide cultural accessibility, which is seen at the level of the screen performance. As mentioned, the recording follows the format of the theatre company's or copyright owner's own copy. While the archive cannot change the given version or reiteration of the production, with its given spoken language performed on stage, which may or may not be the user's language, A|S|I|A gives the document its renewed context to perform.

Clicking on different language buttons performs the switch between scripts. As the pre-set soundtrack of the performance is heard, a user may choose a language that is the same as the speech or song, or read the translation to understand what the spoken text means. The spoken vis-à-vis the written is a display of tendencies; one may be privileged over the other, depending on one's language familiarity and competence. For bilinguals or those who know more than one of the languages, the experience is thus different when there is a choice of whether to focus on the spoken or the written, or both. The comprehension of the performance oscillates between the video screen and the text-blocks. Either way, the text and video are working alongside each other to anchor the performance encounter, even as the engagement with it may vary from user to user. It is this variation that the A|S|I|A has to be wary about because the common practice is to display subtitles line by line. The viewing experience on A|S|I|A challenges the viewer to read a block of text while he or she watches the recording. The viewing may not be smooth for users who resist shifting their vision to and fro between the two panels. Thus, both types of script display have their pros and cons. Nevertheless, the analysis of the current version of the A|S|I|A video player highlights how one's behaviour and preference in watching online videos is determined by software trends and one's encounter with existing conventions. There may not be a best way to display video simply because each user accesses online content differently. Nonetheless, the choice to display video and text as separate but integrated panels highlights the cultural translations that occur when adapting Shakespeare to a new text and performance.

The video player also comes with a "notepad" function, which appears at the side of the video player. This is where a user can leave notes, either as private notes for future reference or as notes publicly readable once the video reaches the time code where the note has been placed. It is also where translation editors can add their own notes and commentaries on the translations. We initially conceived it as a space for commentaries and editor's notes and did not expect it to be used as a chat room. Referring to Fig. 10.3, you will see the Chinese text on display: "liang" complains that the streaming is not smooth, which "roger" agrees with, but it seems that he later makes a comment, as a reply to "liang" "欣赏不了 [I cannot appreciate it]." This has two possible meanings—the user "roger" either cannot appreciate the performance because of the mixing of performance forms so that he finds the performance difficult to understand or he cannot appreciate the performance simply because the video was not streaming well. We have since increased our streaming bandwidth and the streaming is much better now but that instance (the notes are still on display) created a mediated reception of the performance as the video is playing for these users.

The inclusion of a notepad was also a later development but we soon realized its immense potential as a panel for educational use. We have tested it with several institutions such as Wellesley College. A group function (called "Group code") has been used to facilitate group discussions in a classroom setting. The group function is a program that allows only members of a group who submit a shared code to access any notes made by them. When the group code is entered into the entry bar, the set of

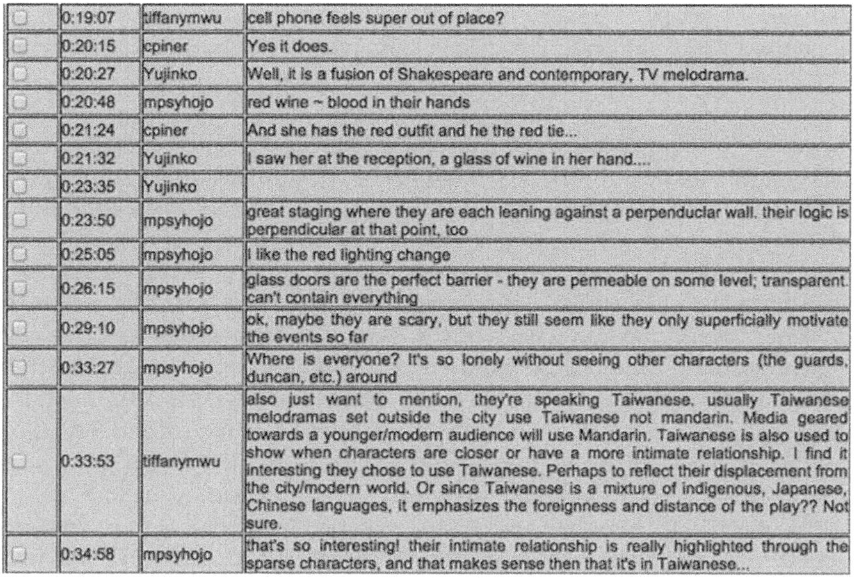

	0:19:07	tiffanymwu	cell phone feels super out of place?
	0:20:15	cpiner	Yes it does.
	0:20:27	Yujinko	Well, it is a fusion of Shakespeare and contemporary, TV melodrama.
	0:20:48	mpsyhojo	red wine ~ blood in their hands
	0:21:24	cpiner	And she has the red outfit and he the red tie...
	0:21:32	Yujinko	I saw her at the reception, a glass of wine in her hand....
	0:23:35	Yujinko	
	0:23:50	mpsyhojo	great staging where they are each leaning against a perpenduclar wall. their logic is perpendicular at that point, too
	0:25:05	mpsyhojo	I like the red lighting change
	0:26:15	mpsyhojo	glass doors are the perfect barrier - they are permeable on some level; transparent. can't contain everything
	0:29:10	mpsyhojo	ok, maybe they are scary, but they still seem like they only superficially motivate the events so far
	0:33:27	mpsyhojo	Where is everyone? It's so lonely without seeing other characters (the guards, duncan, etc.) around
	0:33:53	tiffanymwu	also just want to mention, they're speaking Taiwanese. usually Taiwanese melodramas set outside the city use Taiwanese not mandarin. Media geared towards a younger/modern audience will use Mandarin. Taiwanese is also used to show when characters are closer or have a more intimate relationship. I find it interesting they chose to use Taiwanese. Perhaps to reflect their displacement from the city/modern world. Or since Taiwanese is a mixture of indigenous, Japanese, Chinese languages, it emphasizes the foreignness and distance of the play?? Not sure.
	0:34:58	mpsyhojo	that's so interesting! their intimate relationship is really highlighted through the sparse characters, and that makes sense then that it's in Taiwanese...

Fig. 10.4 Screenshot of the notes from a group of students discussing the production of Tainaner Ensemble's *Macbeth* (2007). Courtesy of Asian Shakespeare Intercultural Archive

notes will be displayed and the user will be able to submit notes private to the group. The most telling aspect of the group discussion is the cultural positionality that users take on when a production is in a language that they are familiar with; or when his or her cultural background gives the user some cultural authority to comment on particular aspects of the cultural forms (Fig. 10.4).

One such group setting is the online discussion of the Taiwanese theatre company, Tainaner Ensemble's *Macbeth* (2007). The group conversation saw a clear distinction between an insider (user "tiffanywu"), presumably a Taiwanese and the other students who may not have the cultural knowledge or linguistic competence (the performance is in Taiwanese). The user "tiffanywu" performs the informed audience and begins to provide the context and explanations for the other students. We speculated that this form of reception would occur but this is one instance where a correspondence happens alongside a performance, albeit a digital recording. Written reception, feedback, and insider knowledge are only generated post-performance but in this case, the written response can be generated while viewing. This panel, in particular, can also potentially be a site for the exchange of ideas, perspectives, and positionalities within a digital environment. While the correspondence is not live, the ongoing "conversation" introduces the possibility of prolonging the reception of a cultural production where discussion on it forms a spectrum of perspectives. Though the example of "liang" reminded us that not all people have the same streaming speeds, it is still a valid reception after the performance. This highlighted the disparities among Internet users—not all can afford the fastest broadband connections and the availability of the archive does not necessitate a universal access. The Internet is not global, yet.

Recognizing the differences in entry points for the users, the A|S|I|A technical team is now developing a new functionality. It aims to integrate the production metadata, that is, the contextual information and details of any given archived production—production details, art forms, points of reference and reception—into the video player. Providing hyperlinks on the search results interface and on the notepad can create a cross-linkage between the two pages. From the data search results page (which is a map of data), a particular point in a performance can be quickly viewed by clicking on a playback icon. Upon clicking it, the video player appears and shows a segment that the data entry refers to. From the video player, an editorial note can be created to display the data entry and conversely a hyperlink can transfer the user to the data map.

For example, if an editor makes a reference to a significant staging strategy, such as the distinctive use of Beijing Opera in the production of *Lear* (1998), a click will technically open up the video player and the video will begin at almost the exact point when there is such an instance in the performance video. I believe that we would not be so insistent on this feature if not for the experience of how people used the notepad. These individual panels contribute to the performative context of the video player and frame the reception of the video.

The interface may not be a theatre performance's stage but building this environment also requires a tedious amount of trouble-shooting, customization and conceptualization. While this may not be the only way to frame and showcase the intercultural content, it provides a basis for users to appreciate the complexity of an intercultural Shakespeare production via a cross-panel framework. The interface inevitably becomes the renewed stage wherein the intercultural re-emerges as a point of consideration, contestation, or simply a historical record of how Shakespeare's plays were adapted in a relatively short period of time. After all, A|S|I|A's existence is entirely dependent on the availability of pre-existing copies of the performance recordings, often in DVDs. This is telling of theatre's increasing sense of responsibility to archive, albeit a phenomenon determined by technological evolution. It also points to the gaps in the archive, where productions before the 1990s are increasingly difficult to find. A|S|I|A has to be aware of its role as an intercultural intermediary that showcases a particular set of people, time periods, cultures, recordings, translations, and metadata. The web archive recontextualizes and groups them as intercultural productions co-performing on a particular digital environment.

10.4   A|S|I|A as an Intercultural Digital Environment

How does A|S|I|A perform as an intercultural intermediary? Beginning with this question requires a definition of "intercultural" because the cultures and performances that are mapped onto the A|S|I|A online platform are often intercultural in their assemblage. The term "intercultural" (theatre) has been heavily contested as a broad term for twentieth-century international theatre. Much of my own perspective on the use of the term is a reaction to Min Tian's (2008) critique of scholarly responses that seemed to theorize and define the intercultural as a utopian project. This "project" was first put forward by Erika Fischer-Lichte, who writes that contemporary intercultural theatre has a role in "the creation of a world culture in which different cultures not only take part, but also respect the unique characteristics of each culture and allow each culture its authority" (Fischer-Lichte 1996, 38; see also Pavis 1992, 5–6). For Min Tian, Patrice Pavis' seminal book, *The Intercultural Performance Reader*, is largely "affirmative of the theory and practice of Western intercultural theatre" and that "[d]issenting voices of 'another point of view' are negated by the structure of the book", which is filled with the aesthetic visions of directors and practitioners such as Robert Wilson, Eugenio Barba, and Jerzy Grotowsky. It took Rustom Bharucha's critique of Western intercultural theatre to point out the "ahistorical approach" and "universal assumptions" inherent in those Western practitioners and theorists (see Bharucha 1993, 1996). Nevertheless, Min takes issue with Bharucha's counter-discourse, in that Bharucha's call for "a genuine exchange" (1996) is "at odds with the premises of his critique of Euro-American intercultural theatre, which stress the importance of social, political, and economic determinants" (Min 2008, 5). Min's argument is that "it is the differences in cultural, social, ideological, political, economical and ethnic dimensions that serve as a common denominator determining the mechanism of intercultural exchange" (5). More importantly, he argues that "[s]o long as such differences exist, we cannot avoid the Other being perceived differently, displaced, and re-placed from different, centralized, and re-centralized perspectives" (5).

These long-drawn out discourses and critiques of Western and non-Western versions of intercultural theatre underpin the complex situation that A|S|I|A faces. It is in such a climate of reception and production that the archive has to engage with the "Other". Those re-centralized perspectives are brought together under a single four-word umbrella: Asian Shakespeare Intercultural Archive. Min Tian's treatise on the Chinese-Western poetics of displacement has to be recalibrated in light of more recent developments. There are now three online video archives of Asian Shakespeare intercultural productions: the *Taiwan Shakespeare Database*, MIT *Global Shakespeares*, and *A|S|I|A*. A digital archive offers an absolute mediation of the other audience, displaced as it were from the cultural specificity of the initial intercultural exchange. The differences now exist in a re-centralized virtual location, accentuated when there is an unknown audience perceiving the contents. The contents are filtered through an interface. The interface frames the reception, but the exchange between the archive and the audience may next inform how video interfaces will develop in the future.

A|S|I|A's interculturality redefined here is in fact a gathering of languages, voices, and spectacles, where the technical meets the aesthetical, cultural, social, ideological, political, economical, and ethnic dimensions embodied in the original production. These aspects can be easily veiled or ignored if there were no context by which they could be later retrieved. The digital environment, as it is used, acts as the other intermediary and highlights the complexities of reception. Reception is expanded because of the scope of viewership the World Wide Web predicates. Reception does not only refer to the number of hits and views but the potential of having a user accessed those online materials with little or no clue as to what a particular production performs or represents; conversely, a user who is extremely familiar with a cultural form may take issue with the way the site reproduces the experience of the live event, and how it is co-opted into the digital environment. Cultural heritage, in that sense, is reimagined online on a site capable of evoking multiple cultural contexts and sites. By introducing to the reader the processes and aspects of multilingual production in the earlier sections of the chapter, the aim was to examine how the interface evokes those multiplicities. Though it is a particular approach to archiving performance, it does highlight the implications of providing multilingual access to a set of theatre productions, especially those produced domestically. A|S|I|A began with the motivation to provide the means to do comparative research across countries and languages but I would like to suggest that it goes beyond that. It provides a way to think of interculturality in a digital way, where spatial and temporal constraints are reduced (such as not needing to fly across the globe to watch a live performance in order to write an academic report on it) through technological shifts and hyperlinks. To make this digital environment possible, then, it requires a support system, often seen in the most sophisticated theatre communities, where critical care is involved in making a creative environment.

A|S|I|A presents the possible practices that can be used to engage intercultural materials and highlights key elements of their production and reception. This is, however, not the only means to do so. As much as theatre is responsible in recontextualizing the everyday, is part of a cultural heritage, and reimagines human experience in its own unique and artistic manner, digital theatres have the other potential to prolong these processes in its own reproduction. At the same time, digital theatres produce their own contexts and events, echoing the preceding live performances and expanding the possible exchanges with new audiences, and thus produce a new reception of the archived production. The interface of A|S|I|A is one of many other possibilities but it is a negotiated result of the technological vis-à-vis the intercultural, which is in A|S|I|A's case most exemplified by the interaction and translation of languages and cultural forms, and the people involved in translating, editing, designing, and working on the scripts and the website. As such, any new digital environment for intercultural content must take into account the cultural specificities of its cultural sources and have a heightened sensitivity to the copyright owners and stakeholders, and a clear sense of its audience and usage.

The best practices of archiving live performance were not well-developed or documented back in 2008 when A|S|I|A was first launched. In other words, A|S|I|A practices and protocols were not developed with the best performance archiving practices in mind. We had to troubleshoot and design our own interface for intercultural viewing. Now we are beginning to see new portals and platforms such as the Digital Theatre in the UK host theatre productions in digital formats. I am keen to see how the practice of digital archiving of performance will continue to develop but one area for improvement that our practice and experience in A|S|I|A are showing us is that the archiving of Asian Shakespeare performance need not be subsumed under a monocultural and two-dimensional framework, that is as a flat screen and viewing experience. It inevitably must go beyond being a screen reproduction of the performance event. We still have a long way to go in defining what this multilingual and multidimensional or even "inter-lingual" environment will look and sound like. Nevertheless, providing multilinguality on digital archives is one possible way to contextualize intercultural content, which goes beyond providing a translation for the content. Instead, it can invite intercultural exchange through the recognition of cultural differences. Having designed an interface for hosting intercultural productions, we must continue to evaluate its functions, effects, and to suggest improvements to it. This is one instance where an ongoing practice (understood as troubleshooting) leads us to shape the interdisciplinary field of digital archiving, theatre, and performance, and we ought to consolidate those practices and refine the best practices to the field of performance archiving.

NOTES

1. The online archive is available at http://a-s-i-a-web.org.
2. The database here refers to the detailed information about the performance event. The information is grouped according to four main categories of data: (1) *Production*; (2) *Reception*; (3) *Art/Forms*; (4) *Points of Reference*. As the website states, "data is collected and written on the live performance event, not on the video-recording of it collected in the archive" (*A|S|I|A Web*, "Database"). Thus, the database also contributes to providing a context for the production, where the scope of the data is also "knowledge about one instance of historically and culturally embedded practices". For a more detailed elaboration on the categories and how information is grouped, please go to http://a-s-i-a-web.org/en/database.php.
3. English, Mandarin, and Japanese translations of the Korean production script of Mokwha Repertory Theatre's *Romeo and Juliet* (2005). Theatre company's translation by Kim Ah-Jeong and Paul Matthews of the production script by Oh Tae-Suk, both script and video kindly donated to A|S|I|A by Mokwha Repertory Company. Edited by Hwang Ha Young and Yong Li Lan.

References

Bay-Cheng, Sarah. 2012. Theater Is Media: Some Principles for a Digital Historiography of Performance. *Theatre* 42 (2): 27–41. Accessed 2 October 2015. https://doi.org/10.1215/01610775-1507775.

Bharucha, Rustom. 1993. *Theatre and the World: Performance and the Politics of Culture*. London: Routledge.

———. 1996. Somebody's Other: Disorientations in the Cultural Politics of Our Times. In *The Intercultural Performance Reader*, ed. Patrice Pavis, 196–212. London: Routledge.

———. 2001. Consumed in Singapore: The Intercultural Spectacle of Lear. *Theater* 31 (1): 107–127.

Featherstone, Mike. 2000. Archiving Cultures. *British Journal of Sociology* 51 (1): 161–184.

Fischer-Lichte, Erika. 1996. Interculturalism in Contemporary Theatre. In *The Intercultural Performance Reader*, ed. Patrice Pavis, 27–40. London: Routledge.

Pavis, Patrice. 1992. *Theatre at the Crossroads of Culture*. London and New York: Routledge.

Taylor, Diana. 2003. Acts of Transfer. In *The Archive and the Repertoire: Performing Cultural Memory in the Americas*. Durham: Duke University Press.

Tian, Min. 2008. *The Poetics of Difference and Displacement: Twentieth-Century Chinese-Western Intercultural Theatre*. Hong Kong: Hong Kong University Press.

Yong, Li Lan, Eng Hui Alvin Lim, Ken Takiguchi, Chee Keng Lee, Hyon-u Lee, Ha-young Hwang, Michiko Suematsu, and Kaori Kobayashi. 2015. *Asian Shakespeare Intercultural Archive (A|S|I|A)*. 2nd ed. National University of Singapore. In English, Chinese, Japanese. Accessed 1 October 2015. http://a-s-i-a-web.org.

CHAPTER 11

Mediating and Visualizing Paxton's Material for the Spine

Rebecca Stancliffe

11.1 Introduction

An ephemeral medium that is difficult to grasp, live dance evades cultural heritage, as it does not exist as a tangible object. Throughout history, technologies such as movement notation, film, and video, have been employed to record choreographic works, methods that stabilize or fix particular aspects of the live and allowing for their repeated study. These approaches also participate in the persistence and legitimization of selected dance practices and, therefore, provide the conditions for a tangible cultural heritage. The aforementioned technologies often concretize the *actual* content of dance, or that which can be seen to exist within the body (see Preston-Dunlop 1981, 1998) over *virtual* content, spatial illusions that can be perceived by the directed or trained analytic eye but do not actually exist. In privileging visually received information, or that which can be objectively known, the knowledge gained through the other senses is often not prioritized. This is a concern if the moving body is understood as a rich repository of knowledge and multi-sensorial information. This is not to say that the body is a passive container but that foregrounding the intelligence of the moving body can

R. Stancliffe (✉)
Coventry University, Coventry, UK

S. Whatley et al. (eds.), *Digital Echoes,*
https://doi.org/10.1007/978-3-319-73817-8_11

prove difficult through existing technologies without sensitivity to the knowledge arising in and through the experience of movement, and thus pose predetermined limitations on what can be known and discovered about movement or choreographic practice.

With the turn of the century, publications emerged that adopt computational approaches to documentation, including annotation and data visualization, to draw attention to information that might otherwise remain hidden to those not intimately involved in the dance-making process.[1] *Material for the Spine* (2008), created by Contredanse[2] in collaboration with American choreographer and movement practitioner Steve Paxton (1939–), is one such publication. Computational methods offer the potential to challenge and expand what features of movement practices are articulated and transmitted and, through a mixed media approach, can alter what is and can be known about movement. Furthermore, the collaborative practices essential to the development of these publications, including *Material for the Spine*, bring together knowledge-bases, methodologies, and interests from different research fields. This results in analytic processes that transcend traditional boundaries of documentation, moving beyond the surface representation of form, rendering different kinds of dance knowledge accessible to heterogeneous audiences and, arguably, helping to raise the cultural status of dance.

Following an introduction to Paxton's movement practice, this chapter examines how movement and artistic philosophies are more successfully mediated through video annotation and data visualization than would have been possible using traditional modes of documentation. Selected excerpts of *Material for the Spine* are described and analysed to examine how different movement concepts are articulated and transmitted. Discussion will consider how these approaches to analysis and documentation can encourage multi-sensory engagement for the collaborators involved in the process and DVD-ROM users alike. This, it is argued, has positive implications for how non-verbal phenomena may be seen, analysed, interpreted, and understood, and how intangible dance heritage is represented in and through tangible time-based objects. By using techniques that interrogate and expand what is known about movement and its representation, I position *Material for the Spine* as a unique contribution to cultural heritage.

11.2   PAXTON AND CONTACT IMPROVISATION

A founding member of the Judson Dance Theatre[3] and The Grand Union,[4] Paxton was a driving force behind the emergence of Contact Improvisation (CI) in New York in 1972. Paxton describes CI as an "improvised dance form that is based on the communication between two moving bodies that are in physical contact" (in *Contact Quarterly* 2014). In 1975, the dancers working with Paxton rejected trademarking CI in favour of sharing the form throughout the world (Bither in Walker Art Center 2015) which, with the publication of the first *Contact Quarterly* journal in 1978, helped it to develop as an open form and collective practice. Senior curator of Performing Arts at the Walker Arts Centre Philip Bither suggests that CI "upended standard hierarchies in dance by privileging body awareness and physical reflexes over pre-planned constructed movements of most other forms of dance composition" (in Walker Art Center 2015). Practiced worldwide and intended to be open to all, this ethos led to diversity in CI practice and coalescence with other forms of somatic practice, encouraging movement exploration from a range of starting points.

In an effort to "understand what exactly improvisation is", Paxton studied its naturally arising and emergent movements and spent "a lot of time teaching the beginning forms over and over again [...] in agonising minute detail with great rigour and clarity" (Paxton in Walker Art Center 2015). A "syllabus of basic forms" emerged, referred to as *Material for the Spine*, designed for solo exploration and focused on the articulation and flexibility of the spine, and releasing excess muscular tension of the body. This syllabus, according to Scott Smith, a practitioner of *Material for the Spine*, invites the mover to "explore subtle or gross initiations of movement" (in Morrissey 2011), and provides a limited structure and guidance for basic technical forms. However, the improvisational side of CI, Paxton felt, could not be taught but is something that dancers have to teach themselves (in Walker Art Center 2015). Paxton describes *Material for the Spine* as a "spine, head, and pelvis centred experience, which is explicit in design but asks the practitioner to design the necessary sensations of movement for its manifestation" (2008). It strives to develop movement intelligence and heightened bodily awareness by directing the mover's attention away from form and toward the sensations of the body. At the same time, the syllabus creates practical skills to ensure safety when responding to the stimuli and experience of movement improvisation with other movers.

Accessing the subtle details of Paxton's movement practice requires a perception developed over time through the close reading and analysis of the body combined with physical engagement and reflection. In other words, an engagement with the inner and outer structures of movement experience from both a mover's and observer's perspective. Baptiste Andrien and Florence Corin, collaborators in the creation and development of the DVD-ROM *Material for the Spine,* were able to find a clarity and understanding of movement through the daily practice and immersion of Paxton's work that transcended a purely mechanical execution, leading to the development of a common understanding of movement experience as a basis for researching how it may be documented (Andrien et al. 2015). This engagement, combined with their understanding of graphic work and three-dimensional processing of information, was fundamental to the successful illumination of Paxton's movement and artistic philosophies, in particular drawing out the hidden or difficult to access features of his practice.

Form and embodiment are essential in many contemporary movement practices, however, a dichotomy between the two is commonly constructed in documentation and traditionally the shape and form of pre-planned constructed movements are objectified. Articulating embodied corporeal experience is a challenge that is embraced in *Material for the Spine* which navigates the dichotomy between form and sensation and presents not only the actual form of movement and its virtual content,[5] but also the deeper structures that give rise to these. *Material for the Spine* will now be positioned as a pedagogical tool, the analytic approaches used to foreground the relationship between form and sensation will then be discussed. Reference will be made to the use of annotation to illuminate spatial trajectories and movement projections, the visualization of Motion Capture (MoCap) data to mediate sensorial experience, and the use of visual metaphors created through the juxtaposition of moving images.

11.3   A Pedagogical Tool

Paxton suggests that students "arrive at Contact Improvisation with a habitual way of moving" which means that a significant aspect of his practice deals with recognizing these habitual movement patterns and learning to release the correlative excess muscular tension that the body may carry (in Morrissey 2011). This is a common feature of many movement and somatic practices which use a mixture of studio-based pedagogical methods including both guided and independent movement exploration, visual demonstration, proprioception, hands-on physical feedback, and verbal feedback. These methods support the mover's independent body-research and encourages an understanding of body–mind connectivity, and the interrelation of the sensorial systems. As will be described, this methodology is at the heart of *Material for the Spine.*

Material for the Spine is a DVD-ROM comprised of a series of audio-visual essays which are organized according to the categories "Form" and "Sensation and Senses". Nevertheless, the exercises documented in these essays are interrelated; the ability to attend to the sensation of the body is important for realizing the form of prescribed movement exercises and vice versa. A selection of the exercises that focus on form feature graphical annotations that make the spatial components of movement explicit, and exercises that direct attention to the sensations of movement use animation and visual metaphors to facilitate an imaginetic stance. Compliant and open-minded students, Paxton explains, will attempt to access the interconnectivity of form and sensation leading them to become more aware of the possibilities of improvisation, while less compliant or beginning students "should be encouraged toward perfecting the movements, as a way of deepening the dialogue between what they tend to do and what the system suggests" (in Morrissey 2011). As a pedagogical tool, therefore, *Material for the Spine* supports learning at different levels and provides ways into the syllabus for different learning preferences and styles. This has the potential to encourage engagement from individuals with wide-ranging skill sets and knowledge-bases, not only those with prior experience in dance.

Most of the essays in *Material for the Spine* use video footage which provides a visual reference for the shape and form of movement. To augment what the DVD-ROM user and viewer of the material can access, inventive approaches to staging movement material emphasis the spatial and sensorial facets of filmed movement. In some, the film footage is layered with annotations in the form of graphical lines to illuminate otherwise hidden features of movement. MoCap is used as an alternative method for recording movement and the creative visualization of resulting data helps to reveal the inner skeletal structures of the body not usually visually accessible. Combined, these approaches provide the space and freedom for the user's own exploration and offers a more democratic approach to engaging with movement practice than has traditionally been possible. I now describe and analyse these approaches in turn, starting with editorial choices in the filming and staging of movement, followed by discussion of annotation that emphasizes the dynamic shaping of movement forms, and finally the use of skeletal animations deriving from MoCap data and the use of visual metaphors to bring attention to the sensorial experience of moving.

11.4   Bringing the Light of Consciousness to the Dark Side of the Body

A 360-degree spatial orientation of the body is an essential feature of CI, for mover and spectator alike. This is unlike more traditional Western dance practices such as classical ballet and modern dance that determine a "front", sometimes determined by the formality of the proscenium arch, which often directs the spatial orientation of movement and performative focus towards a seated audience. In *Material for the Spine,* approaches towards representing space subtly encourages a three dimensional awareness of orientation through juxtaposing different camera angles including horizontal, vertical, and birds-eye view perspectives. These perspectives are interactive and allow the user to alter their visual perspective according to what details invite their attention. It is conceivable that documentary projects in the future may invite further autonomy on the user's behalf and enable perspectives to be selected in a similar way that *Google Earth* users can navigate images online.

Moving away from the visual and towards the experience of movement, a mover's spatial disorientation commonly manifests through the actions of "spinning, flinging the body about" and shifts of weight in relation to other bodies (Paxton 1975, 41). This, according to dance scholar Ann Cooper Albright, challenges the body to "reroute old habits" (1989, 42). In *Material for the Spine,* movement exercises such as "Puzzles" aim to develop the movement awareness that arises from such experiences, specifically how the visual and vestibular systems of the mover alternate in moments of disorientation in supporting the spine during movement (Paxton 2008). In contrast to "Puzzles" where the user must engage physically to deepen their understanding, essays such as "Spherical Space" attempt to represent, replicate, and induce the experience of disorientation through filming techniques, which means that meaning emerges from an observational rather than movement perspective. "Spherical Space" provides valuable contextualization for the viewer and acts as a vehicle for Paxton to share his early experience of, and reflections about, using the centre of gravity in relation to other moving bodies. Paxton's experience led to a belief that the co-ordination of the body in space is merely, or actually, an artificial and imagined construct (Paxton 2008). The combination of an infinity mirror and a fish eye lens in "Spherical Space" makes it difficult to discern how body parts relate to one another, or even which part of the body in view. It is also not possible to identify clear spatial directions, up and down, or the effect of gravity, which disorientates the viewer's eye and the reading of the material. Significantly, and in the spirit of *Material for the Spine* and CI, the viewer must develop their own understanding of the information presented and how it relates to their own experience of moving.

A straightforward yet clever illumination of three-dimensional space comes from the use of a glass floor under which there is space to accommodate a camera in order to film movement exercises from underneath the body. Observing movement from such an unusual perspective is a significant contribution to the documentation of dance as it enables visual access to effect of gravity on the body, the distribution of weight, and subsequent "deformation of the skin" (Paxton 2008). The awareness of the body's sensations and use of weight becomes second nature for skilled improvisers, which correlates to competency in shape and co-ordination of movement (Novack 1988, 125). Filming from underneath a glass floor provides a quite literal window into Paxton's practice, how it relates to sensation, and the relationship between the form of the body and the effect of weight and gravity. "Undulation: Initiated by the Pelvis" is a particularly clear example where staging provides visual access to key movement details. In this essay, the initiations and movements that originate in the pelvis resonate through the spine and alters the distribution of the weight across the feet. The effect of gravity, visible through the changing fluid impressions of the feet seen from underneath the glass floor, effectively communicates how even the subtlest change in one part of the body influences the whole. This is not always a straightforward concept to communicate, yet here it is visually reinforced. The glass floor enables a simple yet effective multi-directional perspective of movement that literally supports Paxton's intention to bring "the light of consciousness to the dark side of the body, that is, the side not much self-seen" (Paxton 2008, Paxton in Morrissey 2011).

11.5   ILLUMINATING SPATIAL FORMS
THROUGH ANNOTATION

For Paxton, maintaining and improving shape while developing movement co-ordination are fundamental goals for the mover (2008) and half of the contents of *Material for the Spine* is dedicated to this exploration. The dynamic interplay between spatial intentions and bodily co-ordination, which I refer to as shaping, is essential to the successful execution of many of Paxton's movement exercises. Yet, identifying these details through observation alone requires experience in "reading" the body, a skill that is developed over many years of training. Furthermore, an understanding of the projection of energy beyond the physical limits of the body, which is implicit in many of Paxton's exercises, requires greater attention still because they have an imagined rather than actual existence. While video provides access to the surface representation of movement's external form, this alone is insufficient for understanding the subtlety of movement and the patterning and sequencing fundamental to working with the forms presented.

In the early stages of research for *Material for the Spine,* MoCap was used to abstract positional data from sensor markers placed at key points on the dancer's body. While MoCap effectively leaves the kinetic signature of the dancer intact, the researchers realized that it provided insufficient data to effectively transmit the subtleties of spinal articulation (Andrien et al. 2015). This was primarily because the points on the spine from which data was collected was far less than the thirty-three vertebrae that make up the spinal column and would result in a general rather than detailed account of movement. While MoCap proved useful for the skeletal animations that are discussed later, an alternate strategy of embedding video footage with annotations was adopted.

Digitally drawn lines are layered over video footage to illuminate the dynamic and intended use of space in a selection of movement exercises. In many cases, these temporal forms illuminate the three-dimensional properties of movement and, significantly, direct the user's attention to information that might otherwise have been difficult to access. A clear example of video annotation can be seen in "Helix Roll: Led by the Hands", which is a variation of a primary movement pattern, the helix, evident in Paxton's practice but also in everyday activities such as walking. The spatial intention of this form is key to the successful execution of this difficult roll, which involves creating and maintaining a double helix formation through the co-ordinated coiling of the two sides of the body. This exercise is filmed from two perspectives at ground level; from the top of the body to the feet providing access to the vertical axis of the body in motion, and horizontally to allow the simultaneous shaping of the upper and lower body to be seen. At the beginning of the essay, only the video footage is presented. This alone is valuable as it shows the dancer's struggle and work to maintain this difficult roll and reinforces the complexity of the movement pattern. Annotations then gradually appear over the top of the moving image and directs the viewer's focus towards the spatial intentions and projection of energy necessary to complete the desired form. These annotations are slender temporal lines and become more explicit as the image of the moving body disappears from view, abstracting and foregrounding the coiling body halves that are working to shape the motion. Soon, only the abstract lines of motion remain, orphaned from the context of the moving body to which they relate, and this three-dimensional virtual sculpture embodies the continuity and temporality of the body in motion. Reportedly, Paxton was excited by this approach, feeling that it elucidated his research about the "abstraction of lines of motion"[6] and enabled a clear visual mediation of the imagined and intended use of space without reducing or translating these concepts into other forms.

As well as the shaping of the body, annotations are also used to reveal virtual content. Paxton's use of *Qi*, is a concept adopted from Aikido that relates to the use and projection of energy beyond the physical boundaries of the body,[7] is a fundamental concept not only in dance but also in everyday life. In the DVD-ROM, through the everyday action of pointing, Paxton describes this projection of energy, or *Qi*, as implicitly understood and unconsciously used. He observes that children learn to point towards an object they desire from a young age, an unconscious action that is more efficient (and sometimes more socially appropriate) than touching the object itself (in Walker Art Center 2015). In "Pointing: Relation to Scapula", annotation layers the video footage to reveal the physical action of pointing as originating in the pelvis before moving through the arm and to the tip of the fingers.[8] Severing movement from the bony landmarks of the body, in this case the pelvis and the base of the skull, results in an empty and unconvincing gesture disconnected from movement intention. Illuminating the physical connections of the body, therefore, appears integral to understanding this concept and is particularly important because it challenges the common assumption that the arms start at the shoulder crease and reveals them to be deeply connected to the core. A series of graphical annotations guide the viewer through the pointing action initiated sequentially by the five digits of the hand, which demonstrates how initiations resonate differently in the movement of the scapula. These annotations not only identify what is happening within the body but also draw attention to the projection of energy as reaching far beyond the physical boundary of the body and toward an intended object. In this example, annotation helps to visualize the integration between movement form and intention and for *Qi* to be understood, which would otherwise be difficult for the untrained eye.

Paxton initially expressed resistance to the documentation of his practice fearing that "the medium (graphic or digital) would take over the physical". However, he became exited by the abstraction and illumination of movement concepts, in particular the annotation lines of motion, which was a development of his initial idea of drawing this onto glass.[9] The collaborative research and development of *Material for the Spine* facilitated access to, and transmission of, embodied knowledge. This arguably helps to bridge the gap between analogue and digital modes of documentation, without reducing the dance record to an account of form alone.

11.6   MEDIATING SENSATIONS

Paxton explains that studies had shown that the number of bodily senses available to humans had been estimated at twenty-five, a far more interesting number than the five taught at school (1987, 16). Furthermore, the analysis of experience, he explains, is typically fragmented between the senses; we talk about something we see or something we hear, but in fact experience is related to an integrated system of sensory perception (Paxton 1987, 17). For this reason, Paxton believes that the mind could be referred to as mixed media in composition, and that perception should be considered "a rather powerful conceptual tool with which one could cause change in experienced reality" (1987, 18). Subsequently, it is possible to understand how choices in the analysis, description, and representation of bodily knowledge can significantly influence understanding and engagement. Thus greater diversity in appealing to the senses may help to support a richer and multi-dimensional experience for viewers with a wide range of viewing experience.

Paxton refers to the sensations of the body as the "palette of the dancer" and can be developed and stored with the body, ready and available for release and liberation in performance (2008). The spectrum and sophistication of this palette can be developed through the structured exercises in Paxton's syllabus that guide the mover through a given form whilst encouraging attention to the sensations of movement. Repetition is essential for the fine-tuning of perception and development of heightened sensorial awareness. It is also considered necessary for ensuring safety when practicing CI where "thinking is too slow" and dancers must rely on muscle memory to respond to moments of contact with other dancers and to guide momentum away from potential hazards when falling (Paxton in Walker Art Center 2015). As Paxton explains, too much tension in the body overpowers the subtlety of movement, while a relaxed state is "almost right, but flaccid is wrong" (in Walker Art Center 2015). Training the sensations of the body enables the dancer to respond intuitively to the now of movement whilst adopting the necessary tensibility of the musculature.

The difficulty in "trying to describe the corporeal" and working with the immediacy of the senses of the moving body led Paxton to shift his early teaching towards developing interiorization techniques (Paxton 2003 175–6 and 182–3). In other words, he designed imagery to influence the mover's sensorial experience beyond the capabilities of language representation. Paxton incorporates ideokinetic imagery (the use of visual and tactile imagery) to support the visualization of movement concepts, thereby working to develop somatic awareness in movement combined with minimal muscular effort. In an effort to transmit this approach, a selection of exercises in *Material for the Spine* use a combintation of animation and visual metaphors, which is an important contribution to the resource.

An understanding of movement execution can be supported if details relating to the initiation and articulation of various body parts are clear. An understanding of the skeletal and mechanical structure of the body is, therefore, advantageous. In movement therapies and somatic practices this is facilitated through various methods including drawings, imagery, or props such as a three-dimensional replica skeleton. A replica skeleton stripped of organs, muscles, connective tissue, and skin enables visual access to the shape, size, and location of individual bones, the manual manipulation of which can provide an understanding of joint mobility and function, which can augment and inspire an expanded repertoire or range of movement. The possibility to explore a three-dimensional skeletal structure that is not the mover's own serves as a reminder of the volume of the body, which is essential in CI. "Ischia to Heels" maps MoCap data onto to an animated skeleton to invite the contemplation of bodily connections that one does not normally have visual access to. While MoCap was deemed insufficient for capturing the subtleties of movement initiations and sequencing particular to movement form, the captured data provides a valuable representation of the body, and point of reference for movers. In "Ischia to Heels", the animated skeleton is lying on its back with the soles of the feet together is shown exploring the relationship between the left and right ischium (one of three bones that fuse to form the pelvis) and the left and right heels in response to Paxton's verbal instruction. This simple visual demonstration appears to be all that is required to, firstly, identify the location of the ischia and, secondly, portray the simplicity of movement generated by the exploration. This stripped down skeletal frame draws attention to key movement concepts and communicates how a small movement can resonate through the entire body.[10]

Whilst some concepts are communicated through annotation (form) or data visualization (the structure of the body), the correlation between intention and sensorial experience is not so easily quantified and, in some exercises, visual metaphors support the user to attend to their sensory experience in movement. In *Material for the Spine,* visual metaphors are presented through a series (and, at times, the accumulation) of moving images. Some of these bear no relation to the body so the viewer must contemplate the meaning of the images and what they offer. "The Flat and the Round" is one such example. It features half a lemon, "the flat" and a whole lemon, "the round" and, from vertical, the flat and the round lemon each fall to the floor. The flat lands abruptly, while the round slowly rocks to stillness. The motion of the round suggests that when falling to the floor the redirection of energy is essential for movement efficiency and safety. As there is no verbal commentary or textual indication to guide the viewer, curiosity and imagination is essential in order to relate the visual metaphor of the falling lemons to the bodily experience of falling. In a CI class this information can be demonstrated, verbally explained, and physically corrected, but "The Flat and the Round" puts the onus on movement exploration by appealing to the mover's imagination. Arguably, visual metaphors demand greater investment from the viewer than annotation and data visualisation and this is correlative to the gradual process of recognizing and responding to habitual movement patterns that influence responsiveness in the now of moving.

"Gravity Falls" brings together visual metaphors, the glass floor, and the animation of MoCap data to allude to the experience of falling. To begin, water falling and hitting the ground can be seen and heard. The viewer has time to contemplate the speed and weight of the droplets falling and to make the connection between this image and the essay title. The image of the water is then replaced by a dancer who, filmed from underneath the glass floor, performs a similar falling action. The comparative mass of dancer means that the weight and speed of the falling is explicit, and the dancer's vocal exhalation signifies the importance of the breath in supporting the descent. An animated skeleton then replaces the physical body. Descending in slow motion, the speed and weight of the fall in response to gravity is no longer emphasized, instead the clarity in the organization and sequencing of movement in falling is highlighted. Paxton suggests that "our bodies are completely attuned to the gravitic effect—that the rate a body falls is abundantly obvious to our own bodies" (Paxton 1987, 16), so the fact that this skeleton does not fall in real-time in this example is of little consequence. The sequencing of these images allows the user to accumulate different details of movement that, when combined, reveals the complexity and sophisticated simplicity of the body falling safely to the ground.

11.7   EVALUATION

Material for the Spine articulates and transmits aspects of Paxton's movement practice and ongoing movement research relating to his movement syllabus of the same name. The DVD-ROM format makes it possible to widely disseminate Paxton's practice and provides any interested person, irrespective of experience and geographical location, with the opportunity to learn about and benefit from his work. Significantly, *Material for the Spine* offers a democratic approach to movement learning that allows users to find their own way through the information presented, which is not only valuable for Paxton's practice but has positive affordances for the documentation of dance in general. Engagement with the information presented is possible at different levels of experience and is supported by clear direction in viewing. The shaping of the body and spatial projection of energy is illuminated through graphical annotations, the mapping and animation of MoCap data provides visual access to the hidden skeletal structure of the body, and visual metaphors stimulate the mover's imagination. This creative and analytic mediation creates a valuable pedagogical tool. *Material for the Spine* alludes to the necessity of repetition and continued investment as a primary movement goal rather than the intention to reach a perfected physical form. Though presented as isolated concepts, the interrelation of form and sensation and senses is a significant aspect of Paxton's practice and while this is not made explicit, a conscientious, curious, and motivated user will be able to make these connections working from the DVD-ROM alone.

Initally, Paxton was resistant to creating a publication that might transmit and fix his practice through a medium other than the physical body (Andrien 2015).[11] Andrien and Corin shared Paxton's concern for transmitting a practice that is rooted in and communicated through the body and felt it paradoxical to create a document about sensory experiences that one does not have visual access to (Andrien et al. 2015). Paxton's involvement in the process was fundamental in shaping the resource, although *Material for the Spine* is a perspective on Paxton's practice through the the lens of Andrien and Corin who draw upon their experience in computational processes and data visualization (Andrien et al. 2015). The publication was possible only through the collaborative process that entailed a commitment from Andrien and Corin honouring Paxton's work, which led to a rich understanding and dialogue that informed their research and ensured that the design, presentation, and mediation of movement concepts were true to Paxton's work. Though clear about the value of documenting and studying Paxton's practice, Andrien remains sceptical of the publication's potential; he is concerned about the process of experience and feedback for the user.[12] Despite interacting with such a publication, Andrien acknowledges that the trajectory of a user's knowledge is likely to remain unchanged. He writes, "I look at Steve's DVD and I go in the studio [... t]he DVD stays what it is and I have my own path", identifying a gap between *Material for the Spine* and studio practice despite the collaborator's best intentions.[13] Nevertheless, although the flow of information from publication to user is unidirectional, *Material for the Spine* demands curiosity and exploration for the successful and in-depth engagement with movement ideologies. The use of annotation and data visualization goes some way to lessen the gap between the representation of movement experiences, virtual content, and moving forms. For this reason, the DVD-ROM presents a unique and sophisticated contribution to the cultural heritage of dance.

11.8   CONCLUSION

This chapter has presented a descriptive analysis of selected excerpts of *Material for the Spine* that feature creative and analytic methods for articulating and transmitting Paxton's movement practice. It has shown that graphical annotations can make spatial intentions and properties of movement more explicit, which provides a concrete focus for working with virtual content. Animations created through mapping MoCap data were used to unlock the skeletal structure of the body, an approach that directs the viewer's attention to details of initiation and movement sequencing, which supports the examination of spatial forms, and vice versa. Finally, visual metaphors entice the imagination, helping to attend to and access the sensation and experience of the body. Presented in isolation for the purpose of documenting the *Material for the Spine* syllabus, these techniques combined have great potential for the transmission of other dance practices. Embracing an approach that foregrounds the corporeality of the body and the multi-faceted experience of the body and incorporating both form and sensation of movement has great significance and allows the knowledge arising from movement practices and creative practice to be studied, examined, and discussed today and by future generations. *Material for the Spine* is an important publication to acknowledge in the discussion of contemporary dance documentation, as it sets a precedent for augmenting video to reveal the inner structures of movement and experience.

NOTES

1. Recent publications that examine movement practices using computational methods include *Improvisational Technologies* (Forsythe 1999), *Synchronous Objects* (Forsythe and OSU 2009) and *Using the Sky* (Hay and Motion Bank 2013).
2. "Founded in 1984 by the Belgian dancer and choreographer, Patricia Kuypers, Contredanse has, since its inception, taken on the mission of supporting choreographic creation. It wishes to provide tools and resources for choreographers and dancers in order to enable them to link their studio work to an analysis of the philosophy of movement, body, composition, and history of their discipline" (Contredanse n.d.).
3. Judson Dance Theatre, whose founding members included Paxton, Deborah Hay, and Yvonne Rainer, was a collective of artists who were instrumental in the development of postmodern dance and performed at the Judson Memorial Church in Greenwich Village, New York between 1962 and 1964.

4. Described as "the wonderful collective, comedic, and anarchic group [...
who] improvised all of their works" (Bither in Walker Art Centre 2014),
the Grand Union was an improvisational collective that emerged from
Yvonne Rainer's *Continuous Project: Altered Daily* (1969–70) and involved,
amongst others, artists including Trisha Brown, David Gordon, and
Douglas Dunn.

5. In this chapter, virtual content is used in the choreological sense, which
refers to the knowledge arising from the intrinsic study of movement.
Dance scholar Valerie Preston-Dunlop describes virtual forms as illusions
"made visible by the performance given to it by the dancer and/or by the
relationships and dynamics structured by the choreographer" (1981, 30).

6. Baptiste Andrien, email message to author, 15 October 2015.

7. Paxton explains that although *Material for the Spine* first derived from
studying the way contact improvisers used their spines, he was also influenced by the Japanese martial art form Aikido. Aikido seeks to redirects the
energy of an attacker or opponent without inflicting harm.

8. In Aikido gestures of the arm start from the pelvis and through *Qi*, which
has not been translated, follows the underside muscles of the arm and out
into space through the ring and little finger (Paxton in Walker Art Center
2015).

9. Andrien Baptiste, email to author, 15 October 2015.

10. "Napping" is another exercise that uses the animated skeleton to successfully communicate the fluidity and scale of movement that occurs even
when the body is resting and allows the viewer to contemplate how big
even perceptively small movements can be.

11. It took twenty years from when Paxton was first asked to create a document of his material for the spine until something was created
(Andrien 2015). Reportedly, Paxton also feared that such a short process,
initially estimated at two years of research and development (though taking
five years in the end) would provide insufficient commitment to the work
he had been researching for twenty years (Andrien et al. 2015).

12. Andrein Baptiste, email to author, 15 October 2015.

13. Andrein Baptiste, email to author, 15 October 2015. Contredanse is currently working with Lisa Nelson's *Tuning Scores,* seeking to minimize this
gap by developing a publication that enables the user to play with video
content changing its linearity by pausing, reversing, and looping sections
of video footage. As Andrien explains, "you see what you do or I'd better
say you see what you saw. So the material is reflecting your own experience
rather that someone else's that you have to meet" (email to author). This
project challenges traditional approaches to movement representation and
the mediation of movement ideologies.

REFERENCES

Albright, Ann Cooper. 1989. Writing the Moving Body: Nancy Stark Smith and the Hieroglyphs. *Frontiers: A Journal of Women Studies* 10 (3): 36–51.

Andrien, Baptiste. 2015. *Contredanse.* Keynote presented at the 20th/21st Century Performer Training Working Group: Remediated Training, University of Leeds, 13 May.

Andrien, Baptise, Corin Florence, and Scott deLahunta. 2015. *Choreographic Objects: Contredanse and the Publication of Dance Ideas.* Curated session presented at the Conference for Dance and Somatic Practices, Coventry University, 11 July.

Contact Quarterly. 2014. About Contact Improvisation. Accessed 2 October 2015. http://www.contactquarterly.com/contact-improvisation/about/.

Contredanse. n.d. Contredanse. Accessed 3 October 2015. http://www.contredanse.org/contredanseV4/templates/index.php?path=contredanse/contredanse.php.

Forsythe, William. 1999. *Improvisational Technologies: A Tool for the Analytic Dance Eye.* Karlsruhe: ZKM Zentrum for Kunst and Medietechnologie. CD-ROM.

Forsythe, William, and Ohio State University. 2009. Synchronous Objects for One Flat Thing, Reproduced. Accessed 5 January 2015. http://synchronousobjects.osu.edu.

Hay, Deborah, and Motion Bank. 2013. Using the Sky. Accessed 26 February 2018. http://scores.motionbank.org/dh/#/set/sets.

Morrissey, Charlie. 2011.Spinal Trialogue: Charlie Morrissey, Steve Paxton, Scott Smith Email Dialogue. Accessed 30 September 2015. http://www.charliemorrissey.com/writing/spinal-trialogue-charlie-morrissey-steve-paxton-scott-smith-email-dialogue/.

Novack, Cynthia J. 1988. Contact Improvisation: A Photo Essay and Summary Movement Analysis. *TDR* 32 (4): 120–134.

Paxton, Steve. 1975. Contact Improvisation. *The Drama Review* 19 (1): 40–42.

———. 1987. Improvisation Is.... *Contact Quarterly* 12 (2): 15–19.

———. 2003. Drafting Interior Techniques. In *Taken by Surprise: A Dance Improvisation Reader*, ed. Ann Cooper Albright and David Gere, 175–183. Middletown, CT: Wesleyan University Press.

———. 2008. *Material for the Spine: A Movement Study.* Brussels: Contredanse. DVD-ROM.

Preston-Dunlop, Valerie. 1981. *The Nature of the Embodiment of Choreutic Units in Contemporary Choreography*. PhD Diss., The Laban Centre for Movement and Dance.

———. 1998. *Looking at Dances: A Choreological Perspective on Choreography*. London: Verve Publishing.

Walker Art Center. 2015. Steve Paxton Talking Dance. Accessed 16 October 2015. https://www.youtube.com/watch?v=_82Od5NM4LI.

CHAPTER 12

In/Tangible: The Duality of Video Documentation in Dance

Heather Young Reed

12.1 INTRODUCTION

With the rapid advancement of technology, traditional modes of documenting dances through written notation systems continue to be on the wane. As video equipment, computer applications and globalized online communities have become more readily accessible, many dance companies and individual practitioners have eagerly embraced technology as a mode of preserving their choreographic works. This trend has caused a considerable shift in the practice of dance documentation, and as a result, video has come to be considered a widely accepted mode of dance preservation. Rehearsals and performances are recorded in order to attempt to capture something of the choreographic process and notoriously ephemeral fragments of live performance. However, other than a growing library of resources, that will eventually have to be transferred to some other medium in the threatening wake of inevitable obsolescence, what value do these video records provide? This chapter interrogates this issue through a discussion that illuminates the functionality of digital documentation, and foregrounds the practical uses of video records within the wider topic of digital preservation. Specific examples are drawn from a case study that

H. Young Reed (✉)
University of Lincoln, Lincoln, UK

© The Author(s) 2018
S. Whatley et al. (eds.), *Digital Echoes,*
https://doi.org/10.1007/978-3-319-73817-8_12

analyses the ways in which *Synchronous Objects* acted as a documentary tool in a restaging of William Forsythe's *One Flat Thing, reproduced* (2000) at The Juilliard School in 2013. The video and graphic animations that are made available through the site provided a valuable set of visual cues to the students who were learning the dance. However, it also provided the stager with visual references through which to re-activate his kinaesthetic memory of the work.

Video records are undeniably useful modes of preservation; they provide valuable resources that enable the development of dance studies, analysis and criticism. However, as complete archival records, they are enigmatically problematic. Video recordings, like written notation systems, attempt to fix the ephemeral and encapsulate dances in a format that does not allow for the fluidity and plurality that is often characteristic of dance, and contemporary choreography in particular. I suggest that in addition to providing a comprehensive set of visual cues, video records also serve the equally valuable function of activating kinaesthetic memories. The act of watching a video of a dance performance brings to life a corporeal experience that has actually been inscribed into the embodied memory of the performer, resulting in a living archival site as opposed to a static one.

12.2   DANCE PRESERVATION

The preservation of cultural heritage remains a topic of global concern as attentions turn to the ever-developing phenomenon of digitization. Within the field of performing arts, and specifically dance, discussions about conserving the legacy of choreographic works have consistently been riddled with a number of philosophical issues relating to the tangibility of live performance. Comparisons are often made between dance and other performing arts such as music and theatre. For example, in 1992 at the *Dance ReConstructed* Conference held at Rutgers University, Stuart Hodes asserted the following: "the designs, in theatre and music, are preserved as text in scripts and scores. Dance designs, throughout the centuries, have been preserved almost entirely in memory" (Hodes 1992, 97). Similarly, Helen Thomas explains, "dance, unlike other arts, does not leave a record of its existence in the form of a tangible object, like a painting, a script or a musical score" (Thomas 2003, 121), and Douglas Rosenberg describes dance as "the most ephemeral of the art forms" (Rosenberg 2012, 176). References to the ephemerality and elusiveness of dance are commonly found across the body of dance and performance studies literature, with scholars such as Maxine Sheets-Johnstone (1979), Peggy Phelan (1993) and Marcia Siegel (1972) all commenting on the inability of live performance to be fixed to a certain time and space. The following oft-cited statement by Siegel serves as a seminal reference to the ephemeral nature of dance:

> Dance exists at a perpetual vanishing point. At the moment of its creation it is gone. All of a dancer's years of training in the studio, all the choreographer's planning, the rehearsals, the coordination of designers, composers, and technicians, the raising of money and the gathering together of an audience, all these are only a preparation for an event that disappears in the very act of materializing. No other art is so hard to catch, so impossible to hold. (Siegel 1972, 1)

There is, however, a contrasting school of thought represented by scholars such as Sally Ann Ness (2008), Tomie Hahn (2007) and Diana Taylor (2003) who suggest that gestural movement becomes inscribed into a dancer's body through corporeal experience, thereby creating an embodied record of a dance's existence. Subsequently, dance historians and practitioners have continuously grappled with the challenges of how to document and preserve adequate records of dance.

Though historically, the practice of preserving and transmitting dances has relied heavily on oral traditions, the advent of Beauchamp-Feuillet notation at the end of the seventeenth century marked a shift towards a reliance on written notation that persisted through the twentieth century, and has resulted in the development and codification of numerous dance notation systems. In the latter part of the twentieth century, technological advancements provided opportunities to challenge the tradition of the written score, and practitioners began to experiment with film, video, motion capture and graphic animation as alternative modes of documenting dances. Though there are certainly merits to written scores, video recordings and graphic animations in the documentation of dances, there remains a curious dichotomy between the ephemerality of live performance and the ability to fix a record of it in the form of a tangible artefact.

12.3   IN/TANGIBILITY

The notion of tangibility, as it pertains to dance preservation, continues to be a topic of debate amongst practitioners, dance notators and historians. Many artists are adamant that they do not want their choreographic works to be documented for the purpose of preservation and analysis, arguing that the process objectifies the work as a finished product. For example, in an interview with Selma Jeanne Cohen George Balanchine was famously quoted as saying "they don't have to be preserved. Why should they be? I think ballet is NOW. It's about people who are NOW. Not about what will be" (Cohen 1992, 192). When asked if he was concerned about the eventual loss of his ballets, Balanchine answered:

> Absolutely not concerned. Besides, there will be different people then. The art of dancing will disappear—or maybe it will be done with acrobats. Who knows what they're going to do? But I don't want my ballets preserved as museum pieces for people to go and laugh at what used to be. *Absolutely not.* (Ibid.)

William Forsythe shares similar views about the preservation of his works. As dramaturge Heidi Gilpin explains, "Forsythe is not interested in the survival of his work as an object; that would fetishize the work as a finished, categorizable, reproducible object" (Spier 2011, 123). Other choreographers such as Paul Taylor, Merce Cunningham and Canadian dance artist Peggy Baker have embraced the practice of documenting their work through extensive archiving projects, recognizing the fact that such a practice will allow for their works, and their legacy, to endure long after they are gone. Dance notators such, as those based at the Dance Notation Bureau in New York City, have built entire careers on the belief that documented choreographic scores are integral to the preservation and continual development of dance history, because they ensure that there are records to be analysed by future generations of historians.

Despite the widespread recognition that written scores, video recordings and other modes of dance documentation produce invaluable records that contribute to the preservation of cultural heritage, there remains a porous relationship between artefact and experience that must be considered. Performance studies scholar Diana Taylor investigates issues relating to the performativity and transferability of embodied memory in her book *The Archive and the Repertoire* (2003). At the root of her argument is the supposition that cultural memory is constructed by a repertoire of performed and experienced events. She articulates the fundamental difference between archival records and embodied experiences and suggests that while the archive has historically been linked to notions of permanence, the repertoire is a more fluid concept. Contrasting the traditionalist view that has privileged the written word Taylor argues, "the repertoire, on the other hand, enacts embodied memory: performances, gestures, orality, movement, dance, singing—in short, all those acts usually thought of as ephemeral, nonreproducible knowledge" (Taylor 2003, 20). Taylor's notion of the binary between archive and repertoire can be used to explain the complexities presented by using video as a mode of preserving cultural heritage through dance. As a documentary method, video recordings serve a dual purpose; they capture a version of the dance that can be preserved, archived and viewed repeatedly, whilst also acting as a visual cueing system that enables a dancer to re-enact embodied memories from his or her repertoire of experience. In this way, the video recording can simultaneously be archive and repertoire, artefact and experiential impetus, tangible and intangible.

As Taylor suggests, "now, on the brink of a digital revolution that both utilizes and threatens to displace writing, the body again seems poised to disappear in a virtual space that eludes embodiment" (Taylor 2003, 16). It is based on this notion that I suggest a reconsideration of video and digital technologies as they relate to dance preservation discourse. By foregrounding the practical applications of video records, and their role in the process of bringing past works back to life, we can attempt to re-prioritize the role of embodiment in discussions about preserving cultural heritage. Digital documents distance choreographic works from corporeal experience by fixing them as objectifiable records. However, they are also capable of illuminating embodiment, by producing at once a tangible artefact that provides a record for future analysis, and a memory aid that enacts kinaesthetic memories from the past.

12.4   Video as a Memory Aid

The process of recollecting physical memories that have been inscribed into a dancer's body relies upon the translation of cues to corporeal reality. These cues can be aural, tactile or visual, or indeed may involve an assimilated web of various combinations of all three, and the translation can occur in any number of ways. I posit that the most effective way to recall and share pre-inscribed choreographic information is through a combination of video recordings and coaching from an individual who has an embodied experience of the work in question. Based on observations gathered through the following case study, I have discovered that even though video records cannot be considered complete documented versions of a work, they serve the invaluable purpose of assisting the retrieval and recollection of one's embodied knowledge of it. The records that are produced through traditional modes of dance notation and video documentation provide clues as to the nature of a work such as the general choreographic design, temporal qualities and spatial pathways. They do not, however, always ensure that information pertaining to intention, dramaturgical concepts and improvisational directives are adequately recorded. It is for this reason that the practice of preserving and sharing dances has come to rely primarily on oral and physical traditions.

Dancer Stuart Hodes addressed this issue at the *Dance ReConstructed* conference by suggesting the following: "dance is ruled by an ancient paradigm, that of oral history; its works are preserved by being passed directly from one dancer to another" (97). In the paper that is now published in the 1992 conference proceedings Hodes draws upon his own experiences of learning Ted Shawn's *O Brother Sun and Sister Moon* (1931) from a film of Shawn, a video of another dancer's performance and coaching from first generation dancer Barton Meeker. According to Hodes, film and video engages with what he refers to as "kinetic history", a process that he describes as "one dancer learning from another, whether that other is alive or an image" (Hodes 1992, 97). Integral to Hodes' argument is the notion that film and video are capable of capturing the kinetic history of a dance, thus allowing it to be preserved as a moving record. However, he also recognizes the limitations of video and argues, "that with a mechanical medium, video in particular, loss can be faster than with living memory" (ibid.). This is because unintentional mistakes, performer interpretation and issues with filming angles often result in the preservation of a version of the work that is not entirely accurate. Of course, inaccuracies and subjective interpretation are likely to occur throughout the process of live transmission as well, however the ability to have a reciprocal dialogue with someone who has firsthand experience of the work can often help to clarify these issues.

Unlike Hodes, I do not suggest that video is entirely capable of capturing and preserving the kinetic history of a dance. I do agree that video's capacity to record moving images is useful, and sometimes invaluable to the process of reconstructing and restaging dances, but I struggle to accept the notion that kinetic history can be divisible from kinetic experience, and as Hodes suggests, preserved in the form of a video recording. Instead I suggest that video is capable of recording visual cues that, when seen, activate a memory of a kinetic experience. The visual cues then act as a trigger for that embodied memory to be recalled, but it is only the re-embodiment of that memory in the present moment that enables the memory to be re-activated. The following case study interrogates this concept through an analysis of the ways in which video and kinaesthetic memory intersected in a 2013 restaging of *One Flat Thing, reproduced* at the Juilliard School.

12.5   RESTAGING WILLIAM FORSYTHE'S *ONE FLAT THING, REPRODUCED*

Every year the dance students at Juilliard work with a member of one of the twentieth century's most prominent dance companies to learn pieces of iconic repertory, which are then performed in a public concert. In 2013 works by Paul Taylor and Murray Louis were featured alongside William Forsythe's *One Flat Thing, reproduced* (*OFTr*). Even though *OFTr* had been restaged twice before coming to Juilliard, this occasion marked the first time the piece was staged by only one member of the Forsythe Company. In the past, restagings had relied on as many as nine company members working together to recreate the intricate choreography. However, in this instance ballet master Christopher Roman assumed the daunting task on his own. Out of necessity Roman was forced to allow the web-based digital resource *Synchronous Objects* a more prominent role in the restaging process than he would have liked. Although despite the multiple ways in which *Synchronous Objects* was used throughout the restaging process at Juilliard its primary function was to provide a record of the dance to which Roman could refer.

Roman was a member of the Ballett Frankfurt and then the Forsythe Company for more than sixteen years, and was involved with the original creation of *OFTr*. To restage *OFTr* at Juilliard, Roman was equipped with a variety of tools, including his own written score of the dance and the selection of visual representations of the work that are available through *Synchronous Objects*. In addition, Roman brought with him a hard drive, which housed a vast library of videos from the Forsythe Company archives and included footage of the movement material being generated, as well as rehearsals and numerous performances of *OFTr*. Of course, not to be overlooked is Roman's personal experience as a participant in the creation of the work and his own kinaesthetic repertoire of dancing in over one hundred performances of *OFTr*.

The visual information made available through *Synchronous Objects* functioned as digital cues that activated Roman's own embodied memories of both making and performing the dance. Both Tomie Hahn and Stuart Hodes refer to the role of video in the activation of embodied memory and suggest that this is its most useful purpose in the practice of dance preservation. Of the use of video in the teaching practice of *nihon buyo* Hahn explains, "for the most part, media are permitted within the pedagogical system primarily as a device for extending memory, as a memory aid" (Hahn 2007, 135). Similarly, Hodes suggests, "video and film remember dances for us to extend the movement analogue of oral history" (Hodes 1992, 97). In this way, *Synchronous Objects* assisted in the retrieval of Roman's repertoire of experience with *OFTr*, and his kinaesthetic history (as inscribed through the process of embodied inscription and recalled by way of visual cues) provided an additional mode through which to facilitate the transmission of choreographic information to the students at Juilliard.

12.6   THE DIGITAL DOCUMENTATION

Synchronous Objects (2009) was developed by an interdisciplinary group of researchers at Ohio State University, led by a creative team that included William Forsythe, Maria Palazzi and Norah Zuniga Shaw. Forsythe Company dancers Christopher Roman, Jill Johnson and Elizabeth Waterhouse were appointed as additional research collaborators on the project. *Synchronous Objects* provides a selection of tools through which to conduct thorough analyses of the intricacies embedded within the organizational structure of *OFTr*. On the surface, *Synchronous Objects* appears to be an interactive website that allows for one to explore the choreographic structure of *OFTr*. However, as you begin to navigate around the site, it soon becomes evident that that there is much more embedded within the site than initially meets the eye. In actuality, what *Synchronous Objects* offers is a glimpse into the depths of Forsythe's choreographic mind. It operates as a portal through which to transcend into a revolutionary way of thinking about movement, one that considers the multiplicity of manifestations that choreography can undertake. In an essay written by Forsythe, he articulates this very point, "to reduce choreography to a single definition is not to understand the most crucial of its mechanisms: to resist and reform previous conceptions of its definition" (Forsythe 2011, 90). Underpinned by this statement, *Synchronous Objects* provides a point of departure from which to explore the possibility suggested by Forsythe, that choreography can be divisible from the human body and represented in alternative ways to divide and reinstate, when necessary, the relationship between technology and the body.

The introductory section of the website is divided into three primary sections labelled "the dance", "the data", and "the objects". By choosing one of these headings you are re-directed to a short essay explaining the details of each of the three sub-categories. The dance section outlines the organizational elements that make up the choreographic architecture of *OFTr*, and extrapolates on the highly methodical network of strategies that provide the framework of the piece. The intricate ways in which the movement material, cues and alignments operate within the dance, were decoded by the *Synchronous Objects* research team and organized into two separate data sets, which they labelled "Spatial Data" and "Attribute Data". Drawn primarily from video recordings of the company perform-ing *OFTr*, the spatial data was generated by mapping the locations of each dancer as they moved around the performance space. The attribute data is based on the dancers' experiential accounts of the ways in which the move-ment material, cues and alignments interacted throughout the work. Each data set provides quantifiable information about the spatial, visual and temporal aspects that form the choreographic structure of *OFTr*. This information was then analysed, translated and repurposed by academics in various other departments at Ohio State University resulting in the various "Objects" that are available to view on the *Synchronous Objects* website.

Although *Synchronous Objects* is a valuable resource for the analysis of choreographic structure, it is not capable of providing a complete record of *OFTr* for the purposes of documenting, preserving and restaging the work. In fact this was never the intention of the project, as Creative Director Norah Zuniga Shaw explains:

> We weren't concerned with documenting or reconstructing the dance for the stage, nor were we concerned with purely scientific questions. Instead we worked with the Forsythe Company to unearth the choreographic building blocks of *OFTr*, quantify them, and repurpose this information visually and qualitatively.[1]

Despite the fact that *Synchronous Objects* was not specifically designed to act as a record for the preservation of *OFTr*, this has inadvertently become a secondary effect of the project. The video representation of the work and the computer animated score both function as archival materials, which have preserved many of the dance's spatial, temporal and visual qualities. The process of restaging *OFTr* at Juilliard relied heavily upon the use of *Synchronous Objects* and as a result, its effectiveness as a mode of documentation has been brought into question.

When discussing the use of *Synchronous Objects* as a restaging tool in relation to this case study, there are two key considerations. The first of these is the fact that the role of the stager, which had previously been shared by multiple people, was limited to one individual with extensive knowledge of the work. In past instances of restaging *OFTr* stagers had the opportunity to offer plurality through the corroboration of their collective memories that allowed them to work together to demonstrate certain choreographic elements. In this case, without aid from his colleagues Roman was challenged to experiment with different ways of transmitting information about the theme of interdependency that is integral to the dance. *Synchronous Objects* afforded Roman the ability to share vital information about the work, and in particular about relationships that are integral to the operation of the dance, which would have otherwise been extremely difficult to explain. Roman was able to identify and clearly explain the internal cueing system and hook-ups as they occur throughout the dance through the visual animations in *Synchronous Objects*.

The second consideration is the students' proficiency in navigating the technological aids that were made available to them. The studio housed two viewing stations that were readily accessible to the dancers throughout the entire rehearsal process. Each viewing station consisted of a large flat screen that displayed *Synchronous Objects* through a live Internet connection. Users were able to navigate through all of the applications that are available on the website, and were invited to make use of the viewing station at any point throughout the rehearsal. Students also had access to *Synchronous Objects* outside of the rehearsal studio on their personal devices, and could view the dance and any of the website's components at any time. To augment the two existing viewing stations students often brought their personal tablets, phones and laptop computers to rehearsals, meaning that many of the students had a mobile version of *Synchronous Objects* that they could refer to anywhere in the space. This multiplicity of viewing sites and increased access to the visual components of the dance made for a dramatic increase in productivity while the movement material was being learned, but also provided a unique set of challenges.

12.7   LEARNING FROM VIDEO: ARCHIVE VS. REPERTOIRE

In the case of *OFTr* the primary choreographic structure of the dance is based on the principle of counterpoint, which Forsythe describes as "a field of action in which the intermittent and irregular coincidence of attributes between organizational elements produces an ordered interplay".[2] These attributes to which Forsythe refers are otherwise termed as "movement material", "modalities", "cueing" and "alignments", and it is the complex interaction of these strands that propels the momentum of the work. The movement material comprises twenty-five structured phrases, which the dancers refer to as "themes". These themes are repeated and reconfigured throughout the duration of the work, and are considered to be set material, meaning that they do not change between iterations of the work. The term "modalities" is used to identify movement patterns that link themes together and act as modes of locomotion that allow the dancers to travel throughout the space. The terms "cues" and "alignments" are used to refer to specific moments when dancers either indicate to each other when to move next, or when they find synchronicity in the trajectory line of their movements. A number of improvisational tasks are also interspersed throughout the piece, whereby the dancers make impromptu choices in response to predetermined directives. Although much of the movement material is set, the temporal aspect of the dance is constantly fluctuating in response to a selection of improvised moments. Choreographic tasks as allocated by Forsythe (or the assigned stager) are applied to the original thematic material, resulting in variations of the theme that differ in ways such as temporal quality and directional flow.

The specific timing of when the dancers perform certain movements or enter into a theme or hook-up by way of an alignment is determined by the dance's intricate cueing system, which Forsythe refers to as "an internal clock". The sequential ordering of the choreographic structure is entirely reliant upon the dancers' adherence to the cueing system. Cues can present themselves as either visual or aural and as a result, the dancers are required to be in a constant state of heightened awareness so as not to miss a cue, as doing so can throw off the pace of the entire dance. Similarly, a keen sense of focus is required of the dancers in order for them to match up during the choreographed moments known as alignments. Embedded strategically within the work are hundreds of moments where two or more dancers link up in a manner that Forsythe describes as "short instances of synchronization between dancers in which their actions share some, but not necessarily all, attributes".[3] These structural elements are imperative to the integrity of the dance, as it is only the functional relationship between each of these components that renders the work identifiable in ontological terms. Operating in isolation from one another would not be possible as the occurrence of alignments and repetition of themes are both reliant upon the dance's internal cueing system. The result is an illusion of chaos, a group of frantic bodies on stage manoeuvring around a sea of tables in a manner that appears to have no sense of structure or order. In actuality, the work is intricately ordered to ensure that the alignments occur when they are supposed to and the dancers' internal cues continue to fuel the momentum of the piece.

At first glance *OFTr* reads as an intricately complex work, and many of the students commented on their initial fears about learning the dance. One student said, "every time we were ready to move onto a new section of the video I would watch it and think what are they doing? I'll never figure it out",[4] and another explained, "you would watch the piece on the website and it just looks like a mountain".[5] The students' reactions to the overwhelming density of the piece was matched by Juilliard faculty member and former Cunningham dancer Banu Ogan (the school's appointed rehearsal director for *OFTr*) who shared the following comments:

> I was so fascinated by how complex the *Synchronous Objects* looks, the dance looks so complex and I thought I couldn't even begin to deconstruct it. As they were learning their individual parts it was hard for me to even find phrases or grounding points in the phrase. It is such a different movement style than I'm used to.[6]

Admittedly, without being aware of the internal cues that govern the piece, it is easy to be deceived by the speed and apparent disorder that seem to render the piece un-learnable. In reality though, there is a remarkably clear structure that is expertly constructed to give the illusion of uncontrolled chaos. In order to alleviate some of the apprehension that emerged after the first viewing of the dance, Roman proceeded to explain the various components of the work that are illuminated in *Synchronous Objects*. He described the four key elements of the work: themes, cues, alignments and modalities and showed the students how they could view each of these components on the digital score through the website.

For the most part, the video was used to give a general overview of the specific section of the piece that was being worked on and to point out the cues and alignments of which the dancers needed to be aware. On the second day of rehearsals the group was divided into two separate casts of seventeen dancers each, and were assigned to a role based on their likeness (in some way) to one of the Forsythe Company's original cast members. Roman expressed that despite the multiple versions of the work that exist "in his head" for this particular re-staging he would be teaching *OFTr* as it appears in the video on *Synchronous Objects* and each dancer was assigned a character from the video to watch. Throughout the rest of the first week the students continued to learn the movement material at an astounding rate, and Roman fell into a routine of constructing and piecing together the choreography. The group would gather around the television set and watch a short section of the dance, often two or three times with Roman pointing out the various cues and alignments that occurred during that particular section. It is worth noting that the annotation feature on *Synchronous Objects*, which highlights the cues and alignments, proved to be particularly useful here. Once the group had an idea of how the section was to operate mechanically they would move to the tables and practice embodying the material.

At this stage, Roman rarely worked with the group as a whole; instead he worked with small groups on the construction of the relationships that occur between the dancers and the tables. He worked with both casts at the same time, ensuring that both sets of dancers had an equal amount of time working with the tables. As Roman was busy working with another group the students were able to work together to learn what they could from the video on *Synchronous Objects*. Of course, there were instances where neither the video nor the digital score were able to provide clear answers, at which point the students would patiently wait for Roman to answer their queries. This well-organized system of watching the video, talking the dancers through the mechanics of the scene, physically demonstrating the movement themes, and then helping them to construct the material on the tables proved to be a highly effective framework through which to conduct the rehearsals. By the end of the first week the group had learned and constructed about half the piece.

The second week of rehearsals continued along the same efficient course as the first. As Roman and the students became more familiar with their newly established working process they gained momentum, and by the end of the tenth rehearsal they had finished piecing together the entire choreographic structure. The process continued to rely heavily on the video to get an overall idea about the mechanics and use of space, augmented by Roman's demonstrations and verbal cues to translate what they had seen into practice. Interestingly, at no point throughout this part of the process did Roman or the dancers refer to the written score, and rarely were the scoring applications on *Synchronous Objects* used as the dance was constructed.

On numerous occasions, Roman identified mistakes that had been performed during the recorded version of *OFTr* that is shown on *Synchronous Objects*. His extensive knowledge of the work allowed him to be able to identify mistakes and inconsistencies within the video that might otherwise be overlooked. I often noted him saying things like "that's what that was supposed to be, but it didn't work" and "if you saw it otherwise on the video it's wrong" (Field Notes, 02/08/2013). This tended to occur earlier in the rehearsal process, as the students were learning the movement material, leaving Roman ample time to "fix" the learned mistakes. However, that it occurred at all highlights one of the primary challenges that video recordings present. Hahn identifies the same issue shared with her by a dancer in her study: "what is problematic about learning dances from these tapes is that if performers in Japan have made mistakes during the performance, we have no way of knowing" (Hahn 2007, 143). It is precisely for this reason that the presence of someone who has a lived experience of the work is integral to the restaging process. As Roman remarks:

> That's the problem with all this modern technology sometimes. It's great and it gets the job done, its just that the humanity, what goes into the construction of these things sometimes gets lost for a time, and then you have to find a way of getting it back.[7]

The way that Roman got it back was through immersing himself deep into the restaging process, and by utilizing his physical presence in the space to transmit his embodied knowledge of the work through verbal, tactile and kinaesthetic cues. He was reminded of the choreography through watching the video, and the students were able to develop an overall sense of the work in the same manner. However, when it came to actually transmitting the material, this was achieved through Roman's ability to re-embody the steps and verbally articulate specific directions to the students, even when those directions differed from what appeared on the video.

12.8   CONCLUSION

Video documentation provides records that simultaneously preserve choreographic works and enact physical memories. Their widespread use as a mode of dance documentation is undeniably valuable, but we must not forget that they are in and of themselves something other than that which they represent. They show a version of a work as it was performed in one place at one time, and should not be accepted as a complete archival record of that work. Instead, what video records provide is an opportunity to revisit, and be reminded of, a repertoire of embodied experiences, whereby the video itself is not the objectifiable account of a work, but rather a conduit through which to recollect kinaesthetic memories.

Through observations gathered at Juilliard, it became clear that the video recordings, digital scores and graphic animations on *Synchronous Objects* did not, on their own, provide sufficient enough records to be able to restage *OFTr* with the accuracy that was required. Instead, these records enabled Roman to access his own kinaesthetic memories of making and performing the work through an interrelated set of cues. The video served as both memory aid and teaching tool as it displayed the overall choreographic structure of the work. However, to restage the dance with the intended motivational, performative and dramaturgical qualities required Roman to interpret the fixed record based on his extensive knowledge of the work's broader context. Roman used the video to recall his own bodily memories of performing the work; however he also occasionally made the decision to substitute the record, as it appeared on the video, when he knew the dancers in the video had made mistakes.

Video recordings leave behind traces of evidence that take the shape of digital echoes; versions of the work that are reminiscent of, and referential to, the performance as it was in one instance, whilst also distancing the work from its "original" version through the passing of time. If we are to consider the practice of dance documentation and its role within the preservation of cultural heritage, we must think about the ways in which tangible artefacts serve multiple roles. Not only do they sit on shelves in libraries, store rooms and museum galleries, but they also act as conduits through which to enact physical memories of a lived experience. In this way digital records have the capacity to both preserve the past whilst simultaneously reinventing the future.

Notes

1. Norah Zuringa Shaw, "The Data," *Synchronous Objects* March 2009, http://synchronousobjects.osu.edu.
2. William Forsythe, "The Dance," *Synchronous Objects* March 2009, http://synchronousobjects.osu.edu.
3. Ibid.
4. Anonymous (Juilliard Dance Student) in discussion with the author, March 2013.
5. Anonymous (Juilliard Dance Student) in discussion with the author, March 2013.
6. Banu Ogan (Juilliard Faculty Member) in discussion with the author, March 2013.
7. Christopher Roman (Forsythe Company Dancer and Ballet Master) in discussion with the author, March 2013.

References

Baker, Peggy. Choreographer's Trust. Accessed 12 June 2013. http://peggybakerdance.com/choreographers-trust.

Cohen, Selma Jeanne. 1992. *Dance as a Theatre Art: Source Readings in Dance History from 1581 to the Present*. Hightstown, NJ: Princeton Book Company Publishers.

Forsythe, William. 2000. *One Flat Thing, reproduced*. The Forsythe Company, Frankfurt. Performance.

———. 2009. The Dance. *Synchronous Objects*. Accessed 22 March 2013. http://synchronousobjects.osu.edu.

———. 2011. Choreographic Objects. In *William Forsythe and the Practice of Choreography*, ed. Steven Spier, 90–92. London: Routledge.

Gilpin, Heidi. 2011. Aberations of Gravity. In *William Forsythe and the Practice of Choreography*, ed. Steven Spier, 112–127. London: Routledge.

Hahn, Tomie. 2007. *Sensational Knowledge: Embodying Culture Through Japanese Dance*. Middletown, CT: Wesleyan University Press.

Hodes, Stuart. 1992. *Dance Preservation and the Oral History Paradigm*. Presentation at Dance Reconstructed: A Conference on Modern Dance Art Past, Present, and Future. New Brunswick, NJ, 16–17 October.

Ness, Sally Ann. 2008. The Inscription of Gesture: Inward Migrations in Dance. In *Migrations of Gesture*, ed. Carrie Noland and Sally Ann Ness, 1–30. Minneapolis, MN: University of Minnesota Press.

Phelan, Peggy. 1993. *Unmarked: The Politics of Performance*. London: Routledge.

Rosenberg, Douglas. 2012. *Screendance: Inscribing the Ephemeral Image*. New York: Oxford University Press.

Shawn, Ted. 1931. *O Brother Sun and Sister Moon*. Denishawn Company. Performance.

Sheets-Johnstone, Maxine. 1979. *The Phenomenology of Dance*. 2nd ed. London: Dance Books Ltd.

Siegel, Marcia. 1972. *At the Vanishing Point: A Critic Looks at Dance*. New York: Saturday Review Press.

Taylor, Diana. 2003. *The Archive and the Repertoire*. Durham, NC: Duke University Press.

Thomas, Helen. 2003. *The Body, Dance, and Cultural Theory*. New York, NY: Palgrave Macmillan.

Young, Heather. 2013. Field Notes, 2 February–29 March.

Zuniga Shaw, Norah. 2009. The Data. *Synchronous Objects*. Accessed 22 March 2013. http://synchronousobjects.osu.edu.

CHAPTER 13

Kapturing Kung Fu: Future Proofing the Hong Kong Martial Arts Living Archive

Hing Chao, Matt Delbridge, Sarah Kenderdine,
Lydia Nicholson, and Jeffrey Shaw

13.1 INTRODUCTION

There are intangible cultural heritage benefits associated with the capture, documentation and preservation of Kung Fu practices in Hong Kong. The School of Creative Media, City University Hong Kong, and the International Guoshu Association, are collaborating on the development of the Hong Kong Martial Arts Living Archive (HKMALA). This revolu-

H. Chao
International Guoshu Association, Hong Kong, China

M. Delbridge (✉)
Victorian College of the Arts, University of Melbourne, Southbank, VIC, Australia

City University Hong Kong, Kowloon Tong, Hong Kong

S. Kenderdine
École polytechnique fédérale de Lausanne, Lausanne, Switzerland

L. Nicholson
University of Tasmania, Hobart, TAS, Australia

J. Shaw
City University of Hong Kong, Kowloon Tong, Hong Kong

© The Author(s) 2018
S. Whatley et al. (eds.), *Digital Echoes,*
https://doi.org/10.1007/978-3-319-73817-8_13

tionary archive encompasses an analysis of a comprehensive digital strategy of archiving and annotating Hong Kong's diverse and rich Kung Fu styles and traditions using state-of-the art motion capture data. By using high-definition and high-speed capture sequences, the activity of preservative annotation is transformed. The HKMALA challenges the established tradition of transference and record, to include motion data to visualize speed, torque, torsion and force (or momentum and acceleration). Framing the HKMALA as a cultural heritage project significantly shifts focus from annotation to preservation, enabling the provision of benchmarking in the use of extensive analytic tools for future generations. This approach enables a revitalized method of capture and subsequent transference never before undertaken within this discipline. When traditional organizations like the International Guoshu Association embrace tools of Digital Humanities research, they become part of a broader community of intangible cultural heritage archival projects. This active association furthers the documentation and preservation of heritage internationally, enabling a richer strategy for future research and preservation projects.

13.2   PROJECT BACKGROUND

Chinese martial arts have a long history dating to the beginning of Chinese civilization. In origin these martial arts were methods of combat and self-defence, but since at least the Zhou dynasty they have acquired a humanistic dimension, becoming instruments for education and 'the rites'. Confucian pedagogy defines a gentleman's education in terms of the 'Six Arts'—rites, music, archery, charioteering, literature and mathematics—which cover the gamut of intellectual and moral training in ancient China. Within this scheme martial arts are represented not only by archery and charioteering but also the rites and music. In ancient China the archery rite was one of the most important Confucian rituals, and dance (*wu* 舞) was often used synonymously with martial arts (*wu* 武). From an early period in Chinese history, martial arts were considered an essential part of a colloquial whole-person education and continued to develop in tandem with other aspects of Chinese culture until modern times. For this reason, literature (文) and martial arts (武) were considered the twin pillars of Chinese civilization. Under this idealized scheme a Confucian gentleman embodies both literary and martial qualities as encapsulated in the sayings, '文武雙全' ('possessing both literary and martial qualities'), '文武兼修' ('well cultivated in literature and martial arts') and '文通武備' ('thoroughly versed in literature and possessing martial preparedness').

According to the *Book of Rites* (200 BC), a thorough humanistic revaluation of Chinese martial arts took place after Emperor Wuwang of Zhou defeated the preceding Shang dynasty, and made the practice of archery and swordsmanship an essential way to cultivate correct moral values.[1] In time, civilian Chinese martial arts absorbed and became embodiments for Chinese philosophical thinking; intersecting with Buddhism, Taoism, neo-Confucianism, Islam and heterodox creeds, to give birth to multiple, complex expressions where the body became a multi-layered text for diverse cultural discourses.

While Chinese martial arts or 'Kung Fu' are frequently thought of as a singular style in the West, Chinese martial arts are extremely diverse and may best be understood in terms of regional systems. Within each system are a plethora of empty-hand and weapon practices, and a bewildering range of styles and schools. The formation and development of regional styles are framed by administrative as well as geographical boundaries shaped by socio-political dynamics at the time, which might either be of a local or national character.

Within this context Hong Kong emerged as a regional hub for South Chinese martial arts in the first half of the twentieth century, as its role as a major port and trading centre under colonial Britain attracted migrants from Guangdong province. Hong Kong became a gateway for Western ideas and institutions to enter China and vice versa. Its existing network and connection to Guangdong through trade, lineage ties and well-established migration routes facilitated a wholesale transfer of martial arts knowledge, human resources and institutions from the turbulent years of the mid Republic onwards.

Republic China sought to construct a new national identity through reform and modernization of traditional culture, which led to the 'Guoxue' 國學 (literally, 'National Studies') movement. Nationalism also fuelled reform in traditional martial arts, which gathered momentum after 1928— when the Central Guoshu Institute was established to promote Guoshu as a national physical education and sports system. This provided an opportunity for martial artists seeking upward social movement, with many flocking to urban centres. The metropolis of Canton, one of the first Chinese cities to industrialize during the 1920s and 1930s, attracted rural labourers across Guangdong province (and beyond), and its prosperity also drew in accomplished martial artists.

In 1929 the first National Guoshu Examination was held at Nanjing. Among those in attendance was Li Guangji 李廣濟, the governor of

Guangdong. Much impressed by what was witnessed, he immediately invited Wan Laisheng 萬賴聲, a young martial art master who distinguished himself at the examination, together with several other 'Guoshu' masters, to set up the Guangdong and Guangxi Guoshu Institute. Li Guangji only stayed in power for a short period of time before being overthrown by Chen Jitang 陳濟棠, who replaced him as military governor of Guangdong. The provincial Guoshu branch did not endure beyond Li's term, but Chen Jitang became a patron of the martial arts and took the Guoshu masters under his wing, while also recruiting local martial artists. Hung Kuen master Lam Sai Wing 林世榮, Shaolin master Gu Ruzhang 顧汝章, Lam Yiu Gwai 林耀桂 of the Dragon Style, Cheung Lai Chun 張禮泉 of Pak Mei, and others congregated under Chen Jitang, working as personal bodyguards and martial art instructors to his army. This group of martial artists eventually became the backbone for Hong Kong's martial arts community as many of them moved to Hong Kong after Chen Jitang lost his position.

Arguably the most influential martial artist during this time was Lam Sai Wing, whose reformed style of Hung Kuen became the most well-known martial art school in Guangdong. Lam Sai Wing was an instructor at Chen Jitang's Army, and also gave private instruction to Chen Jitang's family. During this time it is said that Lam Sai Wing was invited by the Hong Kong Meat Association to open a school. He continued to travel between Canton and Hong Kong in the 1920s and 1930s before eventually making a permanent move to Hong Kong. Lam Sai Wing's influence was largely behind the emergence of the Wong Fei Hung film phenomenon, which dominated Kung Fu cinema from the 1960s through to the end of the century, with a franchise of over seventy films. Lam Sai Wing was survived by his nephew and adopted son, Master Lam Cho, who inherited and continued his teachings. Lam Family Hung Kuen is now one of the most influential Chinese martial arts styles in the world and Hong Kong remains its spiritual centre.

After 1949, Hong Kong became a safe haven for refugees throughout China. Its population swelled from around 100,000 to over 2 million in the years after the war. Among the new arrivals were martial artists from different provinces, not only Guangdong but also Fujian, Zhejiang, Hebei, Shandong and elsewhere, bringing with them knowledge of a wide range of styles. These included Fujian Yongchun White Crane, Liuhebafa, various styles of Taijiquan (particularly the Yang family and Wu family styles), Pigua, Praying Mantis, Xingyiquan, Bagua and many others. As

Mainland China was closed to the West for the next few decades, Hong Kong became the most important bridge for East–West cultural exchange. Since the 1970s Hong Kong has continued to export a large volume of Kung Fu films in the wake of Bruce Lee, and continues to be a major supplier of these incredibly popular movies. It is not an exaggeration to say that global perception of Chinese martial arts was, and continues to be, largely filtered through Hong Kong. Equally important, as Mainland China experienced the catastrophic purge of the Cultural Revolution from 1966 to 1976, with a devastating impact on all forms of traditional culture including the martial arts, Hong Kong remained a safe haven for all forms of traditional cultural practices.

Since the 1990s, there has been a gradual decline in public interest and community participation in martial arts in Hong Kong This is due to a combination of factors including: rapid urban development; population increases; import of foreign cultures and pastimes; and importantly that Chinese martial arts have remained largely un-institutionalized. The significance of Hong Kong's martial arts legacy cannot be overstated, as many martial arts, lost in Mainland China (particularly from the Guangdong province), are still preserved in Hong Kong. Equally, this intangible cultural heritage has become fragile as fewer young people participate in the martial arts. A number of traditional styles are already in danger of being lost due to a lack of young practitioners and the aging master population. The only viable solution is a modern documentation strategy able to preserve this tradition before lost for all time.

13.3   Intangible Digital Cultural Heritage Documentation Using Motion Capture

The need for the preservation of intangible cultural heritage was first recognized by UNESCO in 1972 and has been gaining particular momentum since 2001 when nineteen international 'Masterpieces' of intangible cultural heritage were identified. This has been explored fully in Richard Kurin's detailed critical appraisal of UNESCO's 2003 Convention on the *Safeguarding of Intangible Cultural Heritage*, outlining some of the limits and challenges of intangible cultural heritage (ICH) preservation (Kurin 2004). Yola de Lusenet provides a similar critical reading of UNESCO's *Charter on the Preservation of Digital Heritage*, highlighting how digital heritage and ICH can sometimes blur into one another (de Lusenet

2007). For consideration of ICH in a particularly Chinese context Helen Rees discusses the shift in attitude towards ICH in China from a twentieth-century climate of occasional active destruction to a twenty-first century approach of major preservation (Rees 2012) and Zhang Liu describes the cross-cultural nuances of the concept of 'intangible' cultural heritage in China—intangible translating more accurately as 'spiritual' (Liu 2015).

As part of situating the HKMALA in an ICH and digital heritage context, it's necessary to locate the beginnings of this project within a brief history of movement notation and documentation. In *Writing for the Body: Notation, Reconstruction, and Reinvention in Dance* (2011) Mark Franko explores the history of dance notation and documentation, charting shifts from: written coded steps; to non-word tracking systems; to images of dancers and a focus on a dancer's body rather than their technique or movement through space; to the development of Labanotation; the use of video; and finally the advent of the digital, placing motion capture at the forefront of the dance documentation timeline. In doing so he highlights the fundamental difference between 'what might have happened'—the movement according to the choreographer's choices—as opposed to 'what did happen'—how the dancer performed in that particular performance.

Other contemporary projects documenting 'what might have happened'—in a notation context—can be seen in Eugenia Kim's research into ChoreoSave, a digital documentation tool for emerging choreographers, and El Raheb and Ionnidis' Labanotation Based Ontology for dance databases (Kim 2011; El Raheb and Ioannidis 2012). El Raheb and Ionnidis' work highlights the difficulty of classifying and cataloguing movements in a database context, which presents as a constant challenge throughout much of the work that contextualizes this project outside of martial arts. Contemporary work documenting 'what did happen' can be seen in Pietrobruno's analysis of UNESCO's use of YouTube in preserving ICH—an example of an informal archive, based on classification and cataloguing of existing content rather than developing content specifically for the project (Pietrobruno 2013). There are also a number of official texts by institutions on current best practice for documentation and preservation of dance (Smigel 2006; Schmitz 2015). These progressive movements in the capture and subsequent enabling of dance analysis provide the most logical frame to place around similar problematics associated with the capturing of Kung Fu.

There is a limited amount of existing (Western) scholarship about the documentation of Kung Fu. Acavedo (2015) and Judkins (2014) stress the importance of teacher–student transmission in Kung Fu, in that it is (much like dance) not traditionally taught through notation or documentation. However, in his analysis of the appropriateness of the term Kung Fu Judkins does describe a variety of documentation materials, particularly in the context of dissemination outside of China. These documentation materials are primarily for the purpose of transmission, rather than preservation, and Kennedy and Guo explore in more detail the practice of martial arts notation for training purposes in their analysis of historical Chinese martial arts training manuals (Kennedy and Guo 2008). A variety of critics and practitioners have also written about the documentation of martial arts in film and television, however this is usually in the context of entertainment and technological advancements in film-making, rather than as an archival process (North 2005; Yip 2014).

Motion capture technologies are playing an increasingly natural role in ICH preservation. Historically it is used widely in humanoid robotics research (Zhao et al. 2004; Ou et al. 2015), sports medicine (Schwartz et al. 2012), film-making (Gadassik 2010; Whissel 2010), video games (Pronost et al. 2008; Deng et al. 2011) and now contemporary dance and performance-making (Birringer 2002; deLahunta 2002; Delbridge 2015; Dils 2002; Ebenreuter 2005; Barber 2015). Given the capacity to enable the capture of movement using an 'omniscient frame' generated by the capacity of a motion capture system's camera array to 'see within a volume, to capture not just the height and width of the 2D frame, but to capture depth (via movement) as well' (Delbridge 2015), it is the perfect solution for an unbiased record of Kung Fu.

Early martial arts motion capture involved highly restrictive wearable sensors with limited data capturing capabilities. Whilst the data captured in these early projects was somewhat useful to evaluate the gaps in skill between novices and masters, it lacked precision and detail and was not initially considered in an ICH preservation context. In Thailand, a 2009 motion capture project for Muay Thai postures was developed into short animations for ICH educational and showcasing purposes. A subsequent 2011 project, using the same system and marker set, contributed to the development of a Nintendo Wii game based on Thai Sword Dancing (Phunsa et al. 2009; Kovavisaruch and Wisanmongkol 2011). The latter project was framed in the spirit of ICH preservation, but with the major aim of encouraging revival and new audiences who might be interested in learning Thai Sword Dancing.

Other similar international motion capture projects are informing strategy development for the capture and preservation of the Kung Fu data. These cover Folk Dancing, Chinese Opera, and ArtiMuse (a project that captures hand gestures central to music and handicrafts). The folk dance project comes from the University of Cyprus' Computer Graphics and Virtual Reality Lab where researchers are using motion capture to archive and document Cypriot folk dance. Unlike Kung Fu (and other forms of ICH), Cypriot folk dances are always engaged within social contexts and taught informally with a great degree of variation between regions and individual style. This means that the specifics of capturing them differ significantly to the HKMALA. As the project has progressed a strand of Laban Movement Analysis (LMA) has been added as a documentation tool alongside the motion capture. Whilst motion capture documents the 'geometry' of the dance, it is clear that it is unable to capture the 'nuance'—the emotion, intention or interaction with the environment by the performer (Aristidou et al. 2014a, b, c). This point is of particular significance when related back to the necessary nuance required in the capture of Kung Fu. Using LMA allows an assessment of the motion-captured dances in terms of Body, Effort, Shape and Space. Including LMA notation is similarly used for guiding cues in the training game—for example alerting students how to make changes to a particular sense of *Effort* which might improve technique, rather than giving targeted feedback on angle or technical movement (Aristidou et al. 2014a, b, c). Motion capture doesn't capture the dance itself, just one aspect of its documentation, which highlights the importance of situating the data within a rich database of other media—video, audio, photographs, drawings and text in order to create an accessible folk dance archive which can be used for future research (Aristidou et al. 2014a, b, c). Similar recommendations are made by Mallik et al. (2011) in developing an ICH archive (albeit without purpose captured motion data) for classical Indian dance, drawing on traditional texts and images as well as audio, video and photographs.

ArtiMuse is a multidisciplinary project exploring gesture recognition methodologies in musical and handicrafts interactions. It seeks to identify, record, analyse, model and recognize these gestural skills for their preservation (Manitsaris et al. 2014). The project uses a human–computer interface called 'Art Orasis' for gesture capture, modelling and recognition, based on data capture from wireless inertial sensors. A sample case study focuses on the capture of pottery experts at work from the Macedonian Region of Northern Greece and Côte d'Azur in France. This project is a prototype for a long-term collection strategy, recording and classifying wheel throwing pottery gestures. Future directions include increasing precision of finger movements, finding ways to record finger pressure on clay, and developing systems to assist with the knowledge transmission of these gestures. In the interrogation of associated projects and literature this was the only one to specifically discuss pressure, which plays an important role in the HKMALA.

Zhou and Mudur (2006) have conducted explorations into Chinese Opera, or *Kunqu*—one of UNESCO's first ICH 'masterpieces,' using motion capture of contemporary opera performers and 3D scans of faces to create virtual opera performances, synched with archival audio of opera masters. This concept of a virtual ICH experience is also explored by Li et al. (2013) who used motion capture to recreate the Yamahoko Parade in the Kyoto Gion Festival for a real-time virtual reality user experience, and Yang et al. (2006) who recreated an ancient Chinese palace and court dance scene. Delbridge and Tompkins (2012), similarly use motion capture in an ICH research-focused context—as opposed to a re-enactment context—exploring a virtualized Rose Theatre from Elizabethan England and the process of performing early modern theatre. These strategies are now being applied to an Australian colonial context.

13.4   ACHIEVEMENT OF THE HKMALA TO DATE

Though still in its early stages, to date the HKMALA has captured over 120 sets of empty-hand and weapon sequences, known as '*taolu*套路', representing nineteen martial art styles documented so far. '*Taolu* 套路' are pre-arranged movement sequences used for learning, practicing and performing traditional martial arts. Before the twentieth century the practice of Chinese martial arts was often conducted in secret, and it was quite rare for martial artists to commit their knowledge to writing, so movement sets/routines were created as mnemonic aids for practice. Importantly therefore, *taolu* may be considered the primary 'text' for Chinese martial arts, and the learning process consists in first memorizing the 'text', which is then subject to detailed exegesis to explain the nuance of movements and their applications (Fig. 13.1).

China has maintained a tradition of documenting martial arts in the form of written manuals for over two thousand years. The earliest martial arts literature appeared in the Han dynasty, during which time specialized treatises on swordsmanship, archery and empty-hand combat were composed.

Fig. 13.1   Master Li Tin Loi Performing Sai (鐵尺). Photograph: Chao, Hing

A rich literary tradition meant that a sophisticated technical language was developed early to describe and annotate the martial arts. Later, textual descriptions were accompanied by illustrations. Sometimes the manuals also include diagrams, which show the pattern of footwork to guide practitioners through routine performance. The illustrated manual became the norm by the Ming dynasty. The advent of photography did not replace the illustrated manual as the primary medium to document martial arts, but simply replaced hand-drawn illustrations with photographs. The arrival of motion pictures around the same time provided an alternative, and more accurate medium to record martial arts, but significantly, it did not replace the manual, which continues to be the most widespread (and popular) means for documentation. Significantly, none of these conventional tools are able to represent precise movement in three-dimensional space.

Motion capture is poised to transform how Chinese martial arts are documented and, eventually, how they are taught. For the first time in history, we now have a tool that is able to precisely capture intricate movement for prosperity but also subsequently translate and revisualize this to the screen. It was not until recently that the technology has reached the point of sophistication and accuracy able to meet the technical demands of capturing this vital form. In 2009 the International Guoshu Association had its first trial with motion capture, at the time using facilities at Cyberport in Hong Kong. The motion capture equipment available in Hong Kong at the time was unable to capture (and replay) Chinese martial arts' high-speed movements, due to insufficient image resolution, the frame rate of the cameras, and inefficiencies with suit and markers. Worse still, the technology available in Hong Kong at that time was simply unable to sufficiently record the nuanced joint movements of the hands.

These issues are resolved by contemporary optical motion capture systems. The speed of movement is no longer an issue for cameras that capture motion at a rate of 120 frames per second, while the quality of the data is such that they can be displayed also in real-time and at life-size. Even the issue of capturing complex hand movements, which was the major stumbling block in previous experiments, is now overcome (at least in respect of capture). However, challenges using motion capture persist and, even though current available infrastructures like the 24-camera Motion Analysis system at the motion capture lab at City University of Hong Kong is sufficient for data capture, there are many areas we seek and welcome improvement.

The difficulties encountered so far for the HKMALA capture cycles are not uncommon to other (similar) projects. Research done by Li et al. (2009) using markerless motion capture technology to explore the cataloguing and classification of 3D gestures into a database library, identified ongoing issues with the accuracy and efficacy of the data captured. Key issues in the use of motion capture seem to be recurrent (throughout practice and associated literature in the field). These problematics are not dissimilar to the early stages of capturing data for the HKMALA and include: the difficulty of translating high dimensional data to low dimensional latent space; modulating gesture variability; the benefits of using biomedical constraints as 'rules'; the process of syncing and evaluating captured data with existing library data; and the difficulty of choosing appropriate capture technology to suit the project—in the case of Li, Horain, et al., the struggle was with depth ambiguities from using only a single camera, but with the HKMALA the most serious problem is to do with the effective capturing of hands and the movement of fingers.

Hand movements have so far presented the most serious problems in terms of equipment, templating and necessary accuracy. At the commencement of the project in 2013, capture gloves available were unable to meet our requirement so we used markers instead (eighteen on each hand). While this setup enabled us to document hand movements fairly accurately, during the data capture process the joints and hands sometimes overlay with each other. When multiple markers intersect this generates considerable 'noise' in the data which can only be cleaned manually. The manual clean-up is exceptionally labour intensive, such that one minute of data requires up to several hours of dedicated personnel to clean (depending on complexity). At present, we are seeking a technical solution and have been experimenting with new motion capture gloves and the ability to co-capture hand gesture in a separate (but synched) data stream.

A final problematic (yet to be resolved), is that the technology we use is unable to capture human textures: expression, skin movement and other nuances. This means motion capture is unable to replace more conventional means of documentation altogether. While it offers accurate 3D motion data it diminishes aspects integral to the identity of the martial artists, and the performance itself. For this reason, we aim to use synched high-definition video capture as a parallel tool for documentation co-located within the archive.

13.5   CONCLUSION

The HKMALA is an ambitious project that builds capacity and expertise in the use of techniques and technologies traditionally based in film production and animation to facilitate cultural heritage preservation. In doing so it makes a lasting, necessary and meaningful contribution to a reassessment of the conditions for intangible cultural heritage preservation. The HKMALA future proofs the important place Kung Fu occupies in Chinese identity and permits us to reconsider many aspects of original Kung Fu practices whose purpose has altered radically since first constructed, and whose traditions face the risk of being lost. Internationally, the use of motion capture technology is currently undergoing a significant turn, generating unforeseen cultural heritage experiences in the form of open environments and interactive cultural experiences. It is anticipated, even at the early stages of this project, that it will preserve the tradition and generate significant opportunities for the scholarship and practice of Kung Fu into the future.

NOTE

1. 《禮記:樂記》.

REFERENCES

Acavedo, Juan. 2015. *The Craft and Geometry of Martial Arts*. London: Prince's School of Traditional Arts.

Aristidou, Andreas, Efstathios Stavrakis, and Yiorgas Chrysanthou. 2014a. Cypriot Intangible Cultural Heritage: Digitizing Folk Dances. *Cyprus Computer Society Journal* 25: 42–49.

———. 2014b. *LMA-Based Motion Retrieval for Folk Dance Cultural Heritage*. 5th International Conference, EuroMed Limassol. Cyprus: Springer International Publishing.

———. 2014c. *Motion Analysis for Folk Dance Evaluation*. 12th EUROGRAPHICS Workshop on Graphics and Cultural Heritage. Germany.

Barber, Tiffany. 2015. Ghostcatching and After Ghostcatching: Dances in the Dark. *Dance Research Journal* 25 (1): 44–67.

Birringer, Johannes. 2002. Dance and Media Technologies. *PAJ: A Journal of Performance and Art* 24 (1): 84–93.

de Lusenet, Yola. 2007. Tending the Garden or Harvesting the Fields: Digital Preservation and the UNESCO Charter on the Preservation of the Digital Heritage. *Library Trends* 56 (1): 164–182.

deLahunta, Scott. 2002. Virtual Reality and Performance. *PAJ: A Journal of Performance and Art* 24 (1): 105–114.

Delbridge, Matt. 2015. *Motion Capture in Performance: An Introduction*. Basingstoke: Palgrave Macmillan.

Delbridge, Matt, and Joanne Tompkins. 2012. Reproduction, Mediation, and Experience: Virtual Reality, Motion Capture and Early Modern Theatre. In *Space-Event-Agency-Experience*, ed. Riku Roihankorpi and Teemu Paavolainen. Tampere: Centre for Practise as Research in Theatre, University of Tampere.

Deng, Liqun, Howard Leung, Naijie Gu, and Yang Yang. 2011. Real-Time Mocap Dance Recognition for an Interactive Dancing Game. *Computer Animation and Virtual Worlds* 22 (2–3): 229–237.

Dils, Ann. 2002. The Ghost in the Machine: Merce Cunningham and Bill T. Jones. *PAJ: A Journal of Performance and Art* 24 (1): 94–104.

Ebenreuter, Natalie. 2005. Dance Movement: A Focus on the Technology. *IEEE Computer Graphics and Applications* 25 (6): 80–83.

El Raheb, Katerina, and Yannis Ioannidis. 2012. A Labanotation Based Ontology for Representing Dance Movement. In *Gesture and Sign Language in Human-Computer Interaction and Embodied Communication*, ed. Eleni Efthimiou, Georgios Kouroupetroglou, and Fotinea Stavroula-Evita. Berlin: Springer.

Franko, Mark. 2011. Writing for the Body: Notation, Reconstruction, and Reinvention in Dance. *Common Knowledge* 17 (2): 321–334.

Gadassik, Alla. 2010. Ghosts in the Machine: The Body in Digital Animation. In *Popular Ghosts: The Haunted Spaces of Everyday Culture*, ed. Esther Peeren and Maria del Pilar Blanco. New York: Bloomsbury Publishing.

Judkins, Ben. 2014. Inventing Kung Fu. *JOMEC Journal* 5: 1–23.

Kennedy, Brian, and Elizabeth Guo. 2008. *Chinese Martial Arts Training Manuals: A Historical Survey*. California: Blue Snake Books.

Kim, Eugenia. 2011. ChoreoSave: A Digital Dance Preservation System Prototype. *Proceedings of the American Society for Information Science and Technology* 48 (1): 1–10.

Kovavisaruch, La-or, and Juthatip Wisanmongkol. 2011. Conserving and Promoting Thai Sword Dancing Traditions with Motion Capture and Nintendo Wii. In *Portland International Center for Management of Engineering and Technology (PICMET)*. Portland.

Kurin, Richard. 2004. Safeguarding Intangible Cultural Heritage in the 2003 UNESCO Convention: A Critical Appraisal. *Museum International* 56 (1–2): 66–77.

Li, Liang, Woong Choi, Kozaburo Hachimura, Takanobu Nishiura, and Keiji Yano. 2013. Presentation of Japanese Cultural Event Using Virtual Reality. In *Computer Vision—ACCV 2012 Workshops*, ed. Il-Jong Park and Junmo Kim. Berlin: Springer.

Li, Zhenbo, Patrick Horain, and Andre-Marie Pez. 2009. Statistical Gesture Models for 3D Motion Capture from a Library of Gestures with Variants. In *Gesture in Embodied Communication and Human-Computer Ineraction: 8th International Gesture Workshop*, ed. Stefan Kopp and Ipke Wachsmuth. Bielefield: Springer.

Liu, Zhuang. 2015. Indigenising Intangible Cultural Heritage: Comparison and Interpretation of the Concept of ICH in China. *International Journal of Intangible Heritage* 10: 126–134.

Mallik, Anupama, Santanu Chaudhury, and Hiranmay Ghosh. 2011. Nrityakosha: Preserving the Intangible Heritage of Indian Classical Dance. *Journal on Computing and Cultural Heritage (JOCCH)* 4 (3): 1–24.

Manitsaris, Sotiris, Alina Glushkova, Frederic Bevilacqua, and Fabien Moutarde. 2014. Capture, Modeling, and Recognition of Expert Technical Gestures in Wheel-Throwing Art of Pottery. *Journal on Computing and Cultural Heritage (JOCCH)* 7 (2): 1–17.

North, Dan. 2005. Virtual Actors, Spectacle and Special Effects: Kung Fu Meets all that CGI Bullshit. In *The Matrix Trilogy: Cyberpunk Reloaded*, ed. Stacy Gillis. London: Wallflower Press.

Ou, Yongsheng, Jianbing Hu, Zhiyang Wang, Yigun Fu, Xinyu Wu, and Wiaoyun Li. 2015. A Real-Time Human Imitation System Using Kinect. *International Journal of Social Robotics* 7 (5): 587–600.

Phunsa, Suwichai, Nawuttagorn Potisarn, and Suwich Tirakoat. 2009. *Edutainment: Thai Art of Self-Defense and Boxing by Motion Capture Technique.* International Conference on Computer Modeling and Simulation (ICCMS). Macau: IEEE.

Pietrobruno, Sheenagh. 2013. YouTube and the Social Archiving of Intangible Heritage. *New Media & Society* 15 (8): 1259–1276.

Pronost, Nicolas, Franck Multon, Qilel Li, Weidong Geng, Richard Kulpa, and Georges Dumont. 2008. *Interactive Animation of Virtual Characters: Application to Virtual King-Fu Fighting.* International Conference on Cyberworlds. Hangzhou: IEEE.

Rees, Helen. 2012. Intangible Cultural Heritage in China Today: Policy and Practice in the Early Twenty-First Century. In *Music as Intangible Cultural Heritage: Policy Ideology, and Practice in the Preservation of East Asian Traditions*, ed. Keith Howard. Burlington and Farnham: Ashgate.

Schmitz, Dawn. 2015. A White Paper for the Dance Heritage Coalition. In *The Dance Preservation and Digitization Project: The Technology Summit and Beyond*. North Carolina: J. Murrey Atkins Library Special Collections, the University of North Carolina.

Schwartz, Cedric, Amandine Hazee, Vincent Denoël, Olivier Bruls, Jean-Louis Croisier, and Benedicte Forthomme. 2012. *Shoulder Injury Prevention in Sports Using 3D Motion Capture.* 11th Belgian Day on Biomedical Engineering. Brussels: National Committee on Biomedical Engineering.

Smigel, Libby. 2006. *Documenting Dance: A Practical Guide.* Washington: The Dance Heritage Coalition.

Whissel, Kristen. 2010. The Digital Multitude. *Cinema Journal* 49 (4): 90–110.

Yang, Cheng, Dongmei Peng, and Shouqian Sun. 2006. *Creating a Virtual Activity for the Intangible Culture Heritage.* 16th International Conference on Artificial Reality and Telexistence. Washington: IEEE.

Yip, Man-Fung. 2014. In the Realm of the Senses: Sensory Realism, Speed, and Hong Kong Martial Arts Cinema. *Cinema Journal* 53 (4): 76–97.

Zhao, Xiaojun, Qiang Huang, Zhaoqin Peng, and Kejie Li. 2004. *Kinematics Mapping and Similarity Evaluation of Humanoid Motion Based on Human Motion Capture*. Intelligent Robots and Systems (IROS 2004). Sendai: IEEE.

Zhou, Hao, and S.P. Mudur. 2006. On the Use of 3D Scanner for Chinese Opera Documentation. In *Interactive Technologies and Sociotechnical Systems*, ed. Hongbin Zha, Zhigeng Pan, Hal Thwaites, Alonzo C. Addison, and Maurizio Forte. Berlin: Springer.

PART IV

Authorship, Ownership and Legal Aspects

Presenting the Intangible: Curating the Intangible Cultural Heritage in the Museum Practice—Legal Aspects

Teodora Konach

14.1 INTRODUCTION

Intangible cultural heritage (ICH) as a living memory and experience transmitted through ages ensures the constant reproduction of cultural identity of communities, groups and nations in the context of sustainable development and intercultural dialogue.

The UNESCO Convention for the Safeguarding of the Intangible Cultural Heritage of 2003 recognizes expressions of intangible cultural heritage as a basic factor in the protection of cultural continuity. Since the adoption of this central international document, intangible cultural heritage has been safeguarded on three different levels: international, regional and national.

Intangible cultural heritage (henceforth ICH) is a group-oriented and tradition-based creation that expresses the cultural identity of a given community or group. Recently, advanced technological processes and widespread online accessibility have facilitated the commercial exploitation of traditional culture and knowledge on a scale that is unprecedented.

T. Konach (✉)
Jagiellonian University, Kraków, Poland

© The Author(s) 2018
S. Whatley et al. (eds.), *Digital Echoes*,
https://doi.org/10.1007/978-3-319-73817-8_14

At a time when all intangible assets have become a global resource—the *terra nullius* of the twenty-first century (Johnson 2001)—some general issues emerge at the crossroads of intellectual property rights, communities' empowerment, international cultural heritage safeguarding and national cultural policies, all of which are related to the questions of human dignity and cultural continuity. The ongoing cultural and technological globalization has been recognized as an international threat to the cultural diversity of many nations. Equally problematic is the commercialization of the intangible cultural heritage of local communities in many, including European, countries (Brown 2005). This often involves the use of low quality materials in comparison to traditionally produced crafts and can be seen as a cultural threat to communities whose value those artefacts express (Aikawa 2004; Skounti 2009).

In current literature heritage is perceived as providing a special sense of belonging, but also it reflects the complexities of how communities define and negotiate their identity, symbols and memory (Agnew 1987). Strategies for heritage preservation and safeguarding pertain simultaneously to the regulation and negotiation of the multiplicity of meaning in the past and to the mediation and arbitration of the cultural and social politics of identity and belonging (Augé and Colleyn 2006). Since the adoption of the UNESCO 2003 Convention, intangible cultural heritage has been the subject of a significant academic debate. Traditional heritage was also further problematized in the context of the ownership of cultural property (Brown 2005). These discussions have been broadened consequently to include the rights of local communities to control, protect and share their own notions of ICH in their own ways (Anderson 2006; Atalay 2006). However, the vulnerable social capacity of local communities in many countries, including European ones, works against the sustainability of intangible culture.

Engaging with intangible culture in heritage institutions raises the issue of participatory museology (Karp et al. 1992), and evokes ideas of cultural inclusion and dialogue (Kreps 2003; Butler 2006; Smith 2006). It also provides a framework for rethinking contemporary museum work and the relation between tangible and intangible heritage (Kurin 2004; Kreps 2003). The model of a museum of living history hints a new exclusivity inherent of the power of self-representation, as groups that had historically been marginalized are now actively involved in museum work (Zimmerman 2000).

The new role of local communities, as holders of ICH expressions, may be a difficult task considering their vulnerable social capacity and could work against the sustainability of intangible culture. Museums, in comparison, have a long and established tradition of protection, curation and interpretation of tangible works from the past and may serve as an example for the safeguarding processes of expressions of ICH.

The current rate of technological globalization has strengthened the discussions concerning legal protection of ICH. At the international level, the foremost initiative is the World Intellectual Property Organization Model Provisions for National Laws on the Protection of Expressions of Folklore Against Illicit Exploitation and Other Prejudicial Actions of 1982, and the 2003 UNESCO Convention for the Safeguarding of the Intangible Cultural Heritage. The Convention has established new administrative rules for identification and protection of ICH and set the conceptual framework of the reflections on this heritage. The 2003 Convention has introduced the requirement that countries take into consideration the interaction between societal development and cultural processes, seen as a result of their members' activities (Boylan 1992) which is an undoubtable merit of this document. However, many countries, also in Europe, struggle in defining mechanism of cooperation with local communities when dealing with ICH issues. From the very beginning, reflections have pertained to the potential application of intellectual property law to forms of intangible culture. This may be justified on account of the similarities between ICH and other works protected under copyright law. However, intangible heritage generally does not fulfil the requirements for copyright protection. Safeguarding intangible cultural heritage under general national legislations and international arrangements is complicated by the inability to fit it in the statutory criteria of individual ownership, originality and fixation. Suggestions for improving this unsatisfactory law regime have ranged from the complementary use of laws and policies that do not deal specifically with intangible culture, such as moral rights, domain public, unfair competition laws and trade secrets to the creation of *sui generis* regulations.

The article aims to retrace the state of research in the field of ICH protection and curation in heritage institutions with special attention given to the nature and structure of ICH and the relations with the ICH holders and owners–local communities.

First, the article examines recent developments in intellectual property law regarding the safeguarding of ICH and will assess the extent to which ICH can be protected, if possible, under general intellectual property law. In this part, the implication of a complementary use of existing laws that do not deal specifically with ICH will be analysed. The paper discusses each of these models in turn and explains why there is ongoing ambivalence surrounding the protection of intangible cultural heritage. The following part analyses risks of misuse and incompatibility associated with the ICH preservation by heritage institutions. The final conclusion proposes a tentative way forward, suggesting some effective policies and mechanisms in the field of intellectual property law that are founded on cultural institutions' practice and procedures.

14.2   INTELLECTUAL PROPERTY AND INTANGIBLE CULTURAL HERITAGE

For more than four decades, UNESCO and WIPO have drawn up documents that reflect the concept of creating the conditions for development through cultural heritage in both its tangible and intangible forms. The issues of protecting folklore was addressed for the first time during an international forum in 1973 by the representatives of Bolivia (Blake 2003). They proposed a project of an additional protocol to the Universal Copyright Convention of 1952 which would extend the subject of protection to also include folklore. The direct effect of this initiative was the creation of the Tunis Model Law on Copyright for the Developing Countries, as a joint document between UNESCO and WIPO. The next step was a publication of the Model Provisions for National Laws on the Protection of Expressions of Folklore Against Illicit Exploitation and Other Prejudicial Actions in 1982. They were accepted a year later at a joint session of the Executive Committee of the Berne Convention and Intergovernmental Copyright Committee in Geneva. The Model Provisions were considered as a preliminary document before the creation of a binding international Convention on intangible cultural heritage and folklore. However, the Convention was never accepted due to the objections made by the developed countries (Blake 2003).

A holistic approach to heritage was established by the regulations of UNESCO 1972 Convention concerning the Protection of the World Cultural and Natural Heritage. The conceptualization of the term *natural heritage* was used as a model solution for defining the essence of intangible heritage as the variety of living heritage of humanity and the most important manifestation of cultural diversity. The past decades have seen a concentrated effort to broaden the category of *cultural heritage* (van Präet 2004). The term *intangible cultural heritage* was first introduced by the

UNESCO Convention for the Safeguarding of the Intangible Cultural Heritage of 2003. The Convention is the first international legal document that has created the legal, administrative and financial framework for the safeguarding of ICH.

The intangible cultural heritage has frequently been ignored when global standards on intellectual property were being set, making it difficult—but not impossible—to fit traditional works and knowledge of local communities all over the world into the conventional framework for intellectual property protection. The oldest act of international intellectual property law, the Berne Convention for the Protection of Literary and Artistic Works of 1886 did not make reference to folklore or other expressions of folk art, craftsmanship and knowledge. The Convention's Revision in 1967 added a provision of potentially useful application to traditional art and heritage (enables member states to create institutions in charge of works where the identity of author is unknown), however to date no state has notified the international institutions about the creation of any such competent bodies. Folklore, and the traditional heritage was excluded from the conventional intellectual property protection and this situation has not changed considerably during the twentieth century since there is no binding international arrangement protecting works of folklore.

More recently, scholars have tended to focus on features of copyright law that do not accommodate intangible cultural heritage expressions and argue that copyright regimes should be changed (von Lewinski 2008; Hilty 2009; Wendland 2009; Torsen and Anderson 2012).

One of the main issues of copyright protection which should be reconsidered in relation to traditional culture and knowledge is the establishment of mechanisms of protection available for collectively-produced creative works and a different model applicable to traditional works. The concept of intellectual property law is mostly related to tangible artefacts perceived as author's "property". Copyright systems in Europe were founded as individual rights to protect one's work against illicit or abusive dissemination and exploitation. The concept of art and heritage as a property is rather foreign to the traditional works and knowledge, often collectively held, and reflecting the social and inter-generational aspects of traditional culture (Telesetsky 2008).

One could suggest five main forms of intellectual property protection that might be useful for the safeguarding of ICH: copyright, patents, geographical indications, unfair competition legislation and trademarks. The most appropriate forms of intellectual property law in relation the expressions of

ICH of local communities appear to be the following: *the copyright system, patents and geographical indications.*

14.2.1   Copyright

The fundamental problem with contemporary copyright models of protection is the emphasis on private property—author's rights—rather than safeguarding the communities' identity. Both the continental system of *droit d'auteur* and the copyright model require authors to be identified in order to grant their work protection. In turn, intangible cultural heritage rather evokes the rights of communities rather than individual artists. Therefore, the existing models of copyright protection can be applied to limited expressions of ICH. Furthermore, ICH protection under the copyright systems is complicated by the inability to fit folklore into the statutory criteria of ownership, originality, duration, fixation and inventiveness (Janke 2009).

14.2.2   Patents

According to the regulations of Trade Related Aspects of Intellectual Property Agreement (TRIPS), the requirements for granting patents are the novelty and nondisclosure of a patentable invention (Art. 27[i]). This can be applicable to certain expressions of ICH, especially for craft activities. However, under copyright, the subject of patent application has to be the creation of an individual artist. Also the "novelty" of the invention required for the patent application is not in line with the inter-generation and communal nature of ICH.

14.2.3   Geographical Indications

The use of geographical indications could be a useful tool for the safeguarding of ICH amongst the practitioners. Geographical indications grant collective rights, with minimum levels of innovation required, to all producers in a given area or geographic region who fabricate certain type of items with a particular quality. In this instance, the right is related to the product and not assigned to the individual owner. Protection is granted to a "name" that is attached to a specific community—the bearers of the know-how. Geographic indications safeguard a product of which the quality, reputation and other essential characteristics are determined by its place of origin (Otieno-Odedek 2005; Kono 2009b).

Nevertheless, under the TRIPS agreement geographical indications are limited to production of wines and spirits and the protection is restricted to the principles guarding against unfair competition (Art. 23).

To fulfil the existing legal gap in the intellectual property law regimes, the World Intellectual Property Organization Intergovernmental Committee (WIPO IGC) has suggested several actions for the safeguarding of ICH. Amongst them are the creation of governmental authorities for implementing the UNESCO Convention, national strategies and inventories, and negotiating written agreements with local communities concerned.

14.3   UNESCO CONVENTION FOR THE SAFEGUARDING OF THE INTANGIBLE CULTURAL HERITAGE

The UNESCO Convention for the Safeguarding of the Intangible Cultural Heritage adopted on 17 October 2003 during the 32nd Session of the General Conference of UNESCO has established a new legal and administrative framework for the identification, preservation and promotion of intangible cultural heritage. The creation of this international document, the most significant legal act concerning intangible culture on a global scale, is perceived as the turning point in the process of promoting intangible cultural heritage (Nas 2002). The Convention of 2003 is based on the existing documents of international law concerning cultural and natural heritage, especially the UNESCO Convention concerning the Protection of the World Cultural and Natural Heritage of 1972.

In accordance with the resolutions of the 2003 Convention, it is possible to define intangible heritage as all elements and forms of spiritual and social culture which are transferred through generations of a community, or a group, or by individuals, providing them with a sense of continuity and identity (Art. 2). However, the definition of the ICH proposed in the text of the Convention is very broad and descriptive. Article 2(1) puts emphasis on some of the main features of the expression of ICH: "transmitted through generation to generation, is constantly created and recreated by communities and groups in response to their environment, their interaction with nature and their history, and provides them with a sense of identity and continuity, thus promoting respect for cultural diversity and human creativity". Moreover, Article 2(2) of the 2003 Convention includes a non-exhaustive list of the domains in which intangible cultural heritage is manifested, namely: oral traditions, performing arts, social practices, rituals and festive events, knowledge and practices concerning nature and the universe, and traditional craftsmanship. In this definition we can observe an attempt to include also certain tangible objects such as the works of craftsmanship or musical instruments, as well as traditional tools, since they are strictly linked to intangible culture.

The very general wording and not very precise terminology and definitions are one of the main characteristics of the 2003 UNESCO Convention (Kono 2009a). This lack of precision in the text of the Convention may be explained by the fact that this document offers a framework for the safeguarding processes and leaves many issues open for the implementation by contracting States. Particularly, the 2003 Convention lacks specific rules on ownership of intangible cultural heritage, its commercial exploitation and the very tangible benefits that may derive from its safeguarding (Kearney 2009, 209–16).

Under the established conventional system, member states have significant discretion mainly from the perspective of the position of local communities—the ICH bearers. In the thought of the Convention, the basic responsibility of the contracting states is to "identify and define" the elements of ICH present in their territories and to protect them (Art. 11(b)). In the process of safeguarding intangible cultural heritage, the Convention also envisioned the necessity of ensuring local communities wide access to creating descriptions of given objects if needed. In practice, however, under the provisions of the 2003 Convention, a very selective protection is offered to certain expressions of ICH—since the determination of those forms which are worthy of safeguarding is strictly connected to those elements included in the national inventories established by state authorities and the international Representative List of the Intangible Cultural Heritage of Humanity and the List of Intangible Cultural Heritage in Need of Urgent Safeguarding created in the UNESCO frame (Marrie 2009).

Nevertheless, even if the characterization of the expressions of intangible cultural heritage remains problematic, it is undisputed that ICH as defined in the Convention and its manifestations may also be the subject matter of commercial activities. ICH, and in particular, certain forms of traditional culture and knowledge could be significant economic assets of the communities or groups who create, practice, develop and custody them. The Operational Directives for the Implementation of the 2003

Convention acknowledge that those commercial activities may not only generate income for the communities concerned, groups or individual practitioners, but also enhance the awareness of the value of traditional art and knowledge. The Operational Directives also stress the danger of the misappropriation of forms of traditional culture in commercial exploitation.

14.4 Museums and Intangible Cultural Heritage

According to the regulations of the UNESCO Convention of 2003, intangible cultural heritage is manifested in the following domains: oral traditions and expressions, performing arts, social practices, festive events, rituals, knowledge and practices concerning the nature of the universe and traditional craftsmanship. Such works and artefacts could be subject to multiple uses in cultural institutions, especially in museums, as performances, recordings, adaptations, and so on. Moreover, elements of ICH are valuable tools in interpreting or re-interpreting the tangible artefacts in museums' institutional collections. The living character of ICH is the proper perspective and context for tangible artefacts, presenting and re-animating them in an appropriate way, by taking into consideration the societal and historic rationales for their creation. The interplay between heritage and self-identification issues plays an important role in the new museology concepts. According to Corsane's and Holleman's statement (1993, 121), only the "holistic" paradigm of museology provides a strong identification of the importance of cultural assets, communities and place, in both tangible and intangible contexts. In sum, integrating ICH into heritage institutions' practice brings into question the understanding of the role and mission of cultural institutions and museums. The recent shift in the definition of "museum" is in line with the global development of the categories of cultural heritage—ICOM has already started to broaden museums' goals by replacing the "material evidence" with "tangible and intangible heritage" in the 2005 ICOM statute draft.

Museums have on many occasions committed themselves to the protection of ICH as a part of their institutional mandate. Nevertheless, the first step in the integration of traditional culture and knowledge into the heritage institutions practise is the understanding of the very nature of ICH (Pinna 2003).

Since traditional culture is a living memory of communities, groups and nations, it forms the very essence of their identity and continuity. ICH safeguarding requires the acknowledgement and recognition of practices that take place within the communities and definitely outside the museum's walls.

Expressions of ICH are often used in the processes of the digitization of museums' assets. Works used for these processes are usually granted protection under intellectual property law, especially copyright or related works and databases. However, this is unlikely to work for ICH for the following reasons: inability to meet the individual creation act and individual ownership, originality, duration, fixation and novelty criteria. For those reasons, presenting and safeguarding ICH in museums raises numerous intellectual property concerns regarding the ownership of intangible heritage and its appropriate use (Wendland 2009; Torsen and Anderson 2012).

Nowadays, institutions and cultural institutions are going digital. All around the world, cultural heritage institutions have embraced the use of digital technologies with alacrity, since to digitize an institutional collection is less demanding of space, is more accessible, and collections are "interactive" and can be used for interactive displays without harming the original artefacts. In addition, the only limiting factors for those multiple benefits of the digitization processes are financial constraints.

During the processes of digitization, many cultural institutions claim ownership of copyright to both the digital images of the artefacts from their collections and in the databases of those images. However, few cultural institutions take into account intellectual property issues related to the digitization of their collections. A typical museum collection includes artefacts that are considered to be in the public domain, and as such, are excluded from the copyright protection. If we reconsider the expressions of ICH, however, it is not obvious that they can be a part of public domain threshold. As mentioned before, traditional culture and knowledge are not covered by the conventional intellectual property systems and were never protected within them, but now they seem to have entered the domain public in copyright terms.

Aside from copyright considerations there is a growing awareness of several ethical and cultural concerns around reproducing and re-interpreting the ICH, mostly in national museums or other heritage institutions. Under the UNESCO 2003 Convention, member states are obliged to identify and safeguard the expressions of ICH present in their territory, but they are not necessarily compelled to cooperate with the local communities or groups—the holders of traditional heritage. The creation of national inventories and the management of cultural heritage in national and regional cultural institutions might pose a threat that the ICH of communities may be used to convey a political message (Hazucha 2009).

Furthermore, there is a certain ambivalence surrounding the presentation of digital images of intangible cultural heritage items in online databases. The architecture of a database may reflect the communication policy of cultural or heritage institutions. This model may not be reconcilable with the custody transmission and governance of traditional works and knowledge by communities which is and was of a more communal and cooperative nature. Here, the question is not only the assertion of copyright but also a broader, ethical perspective in the online governance of the ICH.

14.5   CONCLUSION

The process of identifying and preserving intangible cultural heritage may be called "the phase of patrimonialization". The introduction of international criteria due to the needs of international law regulations and international organizations leads to the determination of a certain hierarchy in managing and safeguarding expression of cultural heritage. This process is strictly related to choice making and involves the presence of evaluating restriction (Santova 2015). Curating ICH in museum also assumes cooperation between different actors: curators, practitioners, national experts, communities concerned, and so on. If communities are going to play a major role in safeguarding intangible culture then a new approach is required, one that demands community empowerment.

The use of expressions of traditional culture, which have been excluded from the intellectual property protection until present, calls for the establishment of a policy concerning the management of ICH in heritage institutions. Cooperation between cultural institutions and local communities or groups is needed since there are not many binding national or international documents concerning the safeguarding, curation and promotion of intangible heritage. Museums are institutions with great potential for the curation and protection of traditional culture and knowledge forms and they could also contribute to the social and economic empowerment of local communities. Local communities in turn, should be encouraged to cooperate with heritage institutions for the appropriate transmission of their ICH threshold.

However, the historic development of heritage institutions was parallel with the development of the Western model of the scientific knowledge system. The integration of traditional culture and knowledge is challenging in relation to the established museums' classification (history, fine art, natural history, ethnography) and the category of collections, terminology, conservation, and so on.

Furthermore, museums are still committed mainly to the preservation of artefacts. Engaging with some forms of ICH could change this situation, because expressions of traditional culture are not only the evidence of the past, they are also living practices associated with communal values. Museums, in turn, with the help of modern technologies "preserve" those ICH elements without tangible representation by transforming them into digital items. However, diminishing the dynamic characteristics of ICH is a real threat to its transmission and safeguarding. An effective ICH integration strategy will involve the use of ICH elements to enhance community participation and new cultural expressions that connect the past and have relevance in the present.

Finally, heritage institutions are never places of neutral status—the curation, interpretation and even the protection of artefacts reflect the processes of negotiating, judgement and choice of what and how to safeguard their collections, since *heritage does not exist, it is created* (Skounti 2010, 15). Heritage institutions' professional standards and collection management, as well as their ethic codes should not only reflect the new developments, but also introduce the universal approach to the ICH safeguarding with special attention given to the experiences of the practitioners and the participation of the local communities or groups concerned. Museums should explore the way in which ICH might be related to the existing institutional collections and harness the interpretation of them for the visitor and the communities the museum serves.

REFERENCES

Agnew, John A. 1987. *Place and Politics: The Geographical Mediation of State and Society*. London: Allen & Unwin.

Aikawa, Noriko. 2004. An Historical Overview of the Preparation of the UNESCO International Convention for the Safeguarding for the Intangible Cultural Heritage. *Museum International* 56 (1–2): 137–149.

Anderson, Benedict. 2006. *Imagined Communities: Reflections on the Origin and Spread of Nationalism*. Verso: London.

Atalay, Sonya. 2006. Indigenous Archaeology as Decolonizing Practice. *American Indian Quarterly* 30 (3&4): 280–310.

Augé, Marc, and Jean-Paul Colleyn. 2006. *The World of the Anthropologist*. Oxford and New York: Berg.

Blake, Janet. 2003. On Developing a New International Convention for Safeguarding Intangible Cultural Heritage. *Art Antiquity and Law* 8 (4): 381–411.

Boylan, Patrick. 1992. Ecomuseums and the New Museology: Some Definitions. *Museums Journal* 92 (4): 29–30.

Brown, Michael F. 2005. Heritage Trouble: Recent Work on the Protection of Intangible Cultural Property. *International Journal of Cultural Property* 12: 40–61.

Butler, Judith. 2006. *Gender Trouble: Feminism and the Subversion of Identity.* New York and London: Routledge Classics.

Corsane, Gerard, and Wouter Holleman. 1993. Ecomuseums: A Brief Evaluation. In *Museums and the Environment*, ed. Robert De Jong, 111–125. Pretoria: South Africa Museums Association.

Hazucha, Branislav. 2009. Community as a Holder of Intangible Cultural Heritage (A Broader Public Policy Perspective). In *Intangible Cultural Heritage and Intellectual Property (Communities, Cultural Diversity and Sustainable Development)*, ed. Toshiyuki Kono, 223–224. Antwerp: Intersentia.

Hilty, Reto M. 2009. Rationales for Legal Protection of Intangible Goods and Cultural Heritage. *International Review of Intellectual Property and Competition Law* 40 (8): 883–911.

Janke, Terri. 2009. Indigenous Intangible Cultural Heritage and Ownership of Copyright. In *Intangible Cultural Heritage and Intellectual Property (Communities, Cultural Diversity and Sustainable Development)*, ed. Toshiyuki Kono. Antwerp: Intersentia.

Johnson, Vivien. 2001. *Getting Over Terra Nullius.* Paper presented at the Australian Registrars Committee Conference, Melbourne, Australia, 2006. Accessed July 2016. http://www.eniar.org/news/art13.html.

Karp, Ivan, Christine Mullen Kreamer, and Steven Levine. 1992. *Museum and Communities: The Politics and Public Culture.* Washington, DC: Smithsonian Institution Press.

Kearney, Amanda. 2009. Intangible Cultural Heritage (Global Awareness and Local Interest). In *Intangible Cultural Heritage*, ed. Laurajane Smith and Noriko Akagawa, 209–225. London: Routledge.

Kono, Toshiyuki. 2009a. Convention for the Safeguarding of Intangible Cultural Heritage (Unresolved Issues and Unanswered Questions). In *Intangible Cultural Heritage and Intellectual Property (Communities, Cultural Diversity and Sustainable Development)*, ed. Toshiyuki Kono, 3–42. Antwerp: Intersentia.

———. 2009b. Geographical Indication and Intangible Cultural Heritage. In *Le indicazioni di qualità degli alimenti*, ed. Benedetta Ubertazzi and Esther Muñiz Espada, 298–299. Milan: Giuffrè Editore.

Kreps, Christina. 2003. *Liberation Culture: Cross-Cultural Perspectives in Museums, Curation and Heritage Preservation.* London: Routledge.

Kurin, Richard. 2004. Safeguarding Intangible Cultural Heritage in the 2003 UNESCO Convention: A Critical Appraisal. *Museum International* 56 (1–2): 66–77.

von Lewinski, Silke, ed. 2008. *Indigenous Heritage and Intellectual Property (Genetic Resources, Traditional Knowledge and Folklore)*. 2nd ed. The Hague: Wolters Kluwer.

Marrie, Henrietta. 2009. The UNESCO Convention for the Safeguarding of the Intangible Cultural Heritage and the Protection and Maintenance of the Intangible Cultural Heritage of Indigenous Peoples. In *Intangible Cultural Heritage*, ed. Laurajane Smith and Noriko Akagawa, 169–192. London: Routledge.

Nas, Peter J.M. 2002. Masterpieces of Oral and Intangible Culture: Reflections on the UNESCO World Heritage List. *Current Anthropology* 43 (1): 139–148.

Otieno-Odedek, James. 2005. *The Way Ahead-What Future for Geographical Indications?* Paper presented at the Worldwide Symposium on Geographical Indications, Jointly Organized by the Ministry of Productive Activities of Italy and WIPO, Parma, Italy, 27–29 June.

Pinna, Giovanni. 2003. Intangible Heritage and Museums. International Museum Day 2004 Museums and Intangible Culture. *ICOM News* 56 (4): 3.

van Präet, Michel. 2004. Natural Heritage: Three Perspectives on Intangible Cultural Heritage. *ICOM News* 57 (1): 11.

Santova, Mila. 2015. Development of National Inventories and Cultural Policies: The Bulgarian Perspective. *The IOV Journal of Intangible Cultural Heritage* 1: 34–49.

Skounti, Ahmed. 2009. The Authentic Illusion: Humanity's Intangible Cultural Heritage, the Moroccan Experience. In *Intangible Heritage*, ed. Laurajane Smith and Noriko Akagawa. London: Routledge.

———. 2010. De la patrimonialisation. Comment et quand les choses deviennent-elles des patrimoines. *Hesperis-Tamuda* XLV: 19–43.

Smith, Laurajane. 2006. *Uses of Heritage*. London: Routledge.

Telesetsky, Anastasia. 2008. Traditional Knowledge: Protecting Communal Rights Through a Sui Generis System. In *Le patrimoine culturel de l'humanité/The Cultural Heritage of Mankind*, ed. James A.R. Nafziger and Tullio Scovazzi. Leiden and Boston: Martinus Nijhoff.

Torsen, Molly, and Jane Anderson. 2012. Intellectual Property and the Safeguarding of Traditional Cultures (Legal Issues and Practical Options for Museums, Library and Archives). *WIPO*: 67–82.

Wendland, Wend B. 2009. Managing Intellectual Property Options When Documenting, Recording and Digitizing Intangible Cultural Heritage. In *Intangible Cultural Heritage and Intellectual Property (Communities, Cultural Diversity and Sustainable Development)*, ed. Toshiyuki Kono, 77–100. Antwerp: Intersentia.

Zimmerman, Larry J. 2000. Regaining Our Nerve: Ethics, Values, and the Transformation of Archaeology. In *Ethics in American Archaeology: Challenges for the 1990s*, ed. Mark J. Lynott and Alison Wylie, 64–67. Washington, DC: Society for American Archaeology.

International Instruments

Agreement on Trade-Related Aspects of Intellectual Property Rights, 15 April 1994, Marrakesh Agreement Establishing the World Trade Organization, Annex 1C, 33 ILM 1197. 1994.

Bern Convention for the Protection of Literary and Artistic Works of 1886.

Tunis Model Law on Copyright for the Developing Countries. 1976. http://portal.unesco.org/culture/en/files/31318/11866635053tunis_model_law_en.web.pdf/tunis_model_law_en-web.pdf.

UNESCO. 1972. Convention Concerning the Protection of the World Cultural and Natural Heritage, Paris.

———. 2003. Convention for the Safeguarding of the Intangible Cultural Heritage, Paris.

WIPO Model Provisions for National Laws on the Protection of Expressions of Folklore Against Illicit Exploitation and Other Prejudicial Actions. 1982. www.wipo.int/tk/en/documents/pdf/1982-folklore-model-provisions.pdf.

WIPO/GRTKF/IC/4/4—Technical Co-Operation on the Legal Protection of Expression of Folklore Operational Directives for the Implementation of the UNESCO Convention for the Safeguarding of the Intangible Cultural Heritage of 2003, Adopted by the General Assembly of the States Parties to the Convention at Its Second Ordinary Session in 2008 and Amended at Its Third Session in 2010.

CHAPTER 15

Artworks-Spawning-Artworks: Trans-Disciplinary Approaches to Artistic Spin-Offs and Evolution in the Dance and Digital Context

Jordan Beth Vincent, Caitlin Vincent, Kim Vincs, Scott deLahunta, and John McCormick

15.1 INTRODUCTION

The notion of 'artwork-spawning-artwork' refers to the process by which one artwork inspires or generates a subsequent 'generation' of artwork and particularly, where the spawn finds its iteration in a different genre or format than its parent source. This is related, in a sense, to the notion of a 'spin-off'—perhaps best understood in the context of popular film and television. From *The Simpsons* to *Frasier*, popular television programming

J. B. Vincent (✉) • C. Vincent
Deakin Motion.Lab, Deakin University, Burwood, VIC, Australia

K. Vincs • J. McCormick
Swinburne University of Technology, Melbourne, VIC, Australia

S. deLahunta
Coventry University, Coventry, UK

© The Author(s) 2018
S. Whatley et al. (eds.), *Digital Echoes*,
https://doi.org/10.1007/978-3-319-73817-8_15

has long been populated by spin-offs, some of which outlive and even out-rate their original sources to the point that they no longer carry a signifi-cant association with their artistic parents. In this commercial broadcast media, the spinning-off of a new work is generally viewed as a positive outcome of original artistic creation, in which the notion of the 'primary source' can be dispersed across multiple iterations and forms without any perceived artistic damage. In other words, the parent and the spin-off can exist simultaneously and autonomously, even when sharing the same pub-lished format. This form of commercial spawning can arguably be seen as simply another method for maximizing the financial return on a specific 'property' or 'franchise'.

Internet memes present a similarly positive view of a functioning spin-off. Driven by user participation and the inherent adaptability of digital imagery, each Internet meme exists as an independent statement of embodied action, interpretation, and visibility, one that ultimately reflects a specific social, political, or cultural context even as it retains its reference to the 'original.' Through this process of recycling an art product into something new (and often something humorous or satirical), Internet memes constitute a 'secondary order of production and publication, that establishes the visibility of the work', albeit with potentially different cul-tural connotations than were initially conceived (Barrett 2004. See also Dawkins 1976). However, we draw a distinction between 'spin-off' and 'artistic spawn' based on the ontology and form of the artwork. A spin-off implies a 'child' artwork that exists in the same genre or format as the par-ent source. The process of 'spawning,' as we wish to explore it in this chapter, differs in that it refers to a cross-genre or cross-platform shift across generations. The insertion of a platform shift is fundamentally related to the concept of trans-media storytelling, in which a single story or concept is explored via different media, and a narrative may 'jump' from one form to another (see trans-media dance work, *The Crack Up*, Vincs et al. 2014). In the world of dance and other embodied performance genres, such trans-medial spawning can provide both cultural longevity and an extension of influence over time in ways that potentially address some of the inherent difficulties in preserving ephemeral artistic practices.

Artistic spawns can be understood as secondary or subsequent means of publishing a primary source in a way that extends the artistic lifespan of the original idea, character, theme, or world. As such, these spawns comprise a natural step in an original artwork's evolution into something new, something rediscovered, or something newly relevant. In essence, an artistic spawn exists as two simultaneous artistic forms: first, as an autonomous and self-contained work that may benefit from, but does not rely on, an understanding of its unique lineage; and second, as the embodiment of a specific history, origin, and inspiration that can *only* be defined by its 'parent' source. In the world of television programming and Internet memes, this dichotomy is largely superficial: while one television show may spin-off into another, both works maintain their artistic independence as a result of the shared genre that allows them to be compared side-by-side. Consider, for example, the *Star Trek* television franchise: both *Star Trek: Voyager* (1995–2001) and *Star Trek: Deep Space Nine* (1993–1999) were spin-offs from the original 1960s series and were released two years apart, yet both occupied the same narrative time period and overlapped for four seasons, which specifically encouraged shared plot developments, as well as side-by-side comparisons from its viewers (Pearson and Davies 2014).

However, in embodied artistic genres such as dance, a field that has been historically defined by its ephemerality, the inherent tension between an artistic spawn and its parent source is complicated by questions of individual ownership, authenticity, and artistic legacy. This speaks as much to the nature of embodied artforms and their natural resistance to archiving and preservation, as it does to the process of artistic spawning.

Artistic spawns and spin-offs, as secondary (or tertiary) modes of publishing a primary source, extend the artistic lifespan of an original idea and facilitate an artistic evolution, regardless of whether the relationship from 'parent' to 'spawn' is hidden or immediately recognizable. This paper explores the notion of 'artwork-spawning-artwork' in dance and digital technology, and specifically examines individual works that extend the lifespans of dance across different genres through variable forms of transmission. These works offer new perspectives on the generational relationship between artworks, but also lead to a re-evaluation of the practice and process of art-making itself. As our notion of what constitutes dance and digital technology expands to incorporate new technologies, methods, and even unintentional glitches, cross-discipline collaborations invite new interpretations of what constitutes a primary source within a networked, creative, and embodied environment. By examining the process of 'spawning' in terms of embodied artforms and digital outcomes, we can consider how this process might extend the life cycles of embodied genres and ultimately allow for new modes of dissemination, publication, and accessibility to primary sources.

15.2   Spawning Embodied Works

Artistic spawns enrich the landscape of art creation and enable conceptual evolution alongside the existence of a specific history, origin, and inspiration. They allow an art object to exist apart from the 'original' and, although an understanding of one generation of artwork may benefit from an understanding of its unique lineage, the spawned art is in no way diminished by the distance from its artistic ancestor. Within the framework of 'artwork-spawning-artwork,' an original artwork can theoretically co-exist alongside myriad artistic spawns or find an evolutionary iteration in a completely different genre, format, or media than first conceived. This is art as *artefact*, a term which draws on the archeological definition of an object that is historical, discovered, and embedded in a past historical context. In this context, art that spawns art from choreographic to digital objects or from digital objects to choreographic may not necessarily be commercial (as with broadcast media) or purely socio-cultural (in the Internet meme sense), but rather draws on the critical perspective of performance and digital art practice. Here, the tradition of artistic practice is something shared and dispersed in that an artistic work acknowledges the influence of the master as part of the process of learning a 'craft' before the apprentice finds his or her own voice. But the notion of spawns as artistic artefacts also draws on the definition of 'artefact' from the world of digital creative arts, where the term refers to something created as a result of a process, with unforeseen future results. The action of art spawning across different forms of media draws upon this idea, particularly the potential to create a kind of link between past and future articulations of an artistic idea that strengthens—rather than dilutes—the originating idea (Banks 2011; see also Lepecki 2010). The balance between looking backwards (preservation) and looking forwards (evolution and rebirth) underpins this negotiation and informs our understanding of artwork-spawning-artwork.

In embodied artforms, such as contemporary dance, the live performance (or 'a' live performance) is generally viewed as the primary source; additional remountings of the work, as well as filmed versions of the performance, are often considered to be secondary source documents: records of an original rather than the original itself. Despite the role of notation systems and digital publishing platforms (such as those developed by Motion Bank as online, or other annotated scores), the notion of 'The Primary Source' for a dance work is very difficult to pin down. For scholars and academic authors, published commentary and analysis of a live dance performance—most often found in the traditional media of written text—are what form the permanent trace of the primary source over time.

With non-ephemeral art objects and spawns, the lifespan and longevity of a 'parent' source can be generally assumed. In dance, however, the lifespan of the 'parent' source is ultimately unstable. For example, Sally Gardner's (2014) use of Laurence Louppe's writings on the 'afterlife' of dance works describes:

> ...[an] endless chain of reciprocal emissions, transmissions, receptions, and exchanges of times, gestures, steps, affects, sweat, breathing, and historical and political particles. Under this transformative system of excorporations and incorporations, the afterlife of dance works gains a new objectivity, bypassing melancholia as its main affect, its main drive or nostalgic impulse. (Gardner 2014, 39–40)

Similarly, Andre Lepecki (2010) refers to 'a haunting' as something that captures the ephemerality of an embodied knowledge. His comment runs parallel to Gardner's translation of Louppe's suggestion that dance, 'relative to many other "objects", is unstable—perhaps alluding to the more hidden or slower instability of all objects—and its "itself givenness" is contingent and temporal' (Gardner 2014, 232). As a result, 'many literary and visual artworks have been remade or freely "adapted" or quoted without losing their "identities", or they have been able to be deconstructed and their authorship subverted while their identities or the actual "originals" can remain intact' (Gardner 2014, 230). However, due to sheer biological forces and the impossibility of preserving exact physical choreography across multiple generations of dancers, a dance work simply cannot achieve the kind of fixed status that Louppe recognizes in literary and visual art works. This inherent instability underpins certain anxieties about the ownership and creative authenticity of dance, as well as concerns about the preservation of choreographic legacies.

15.3   Ownership and Spawning: Negotiating Artistic Influence and Plagiarism

Fundamental to a discussion of artistic spawns is the recognition and acknowledgement of the significant role of the primary or 'parent' source. In order for art to be acknowledged as either an 'artistic spawn' or 'spin-off,' logic dictates that it must emerge from *something else*, whether it is a visual, textual, conceptual, or philosophical artefact, a combination of all four, or a derivation of some other external source. As such, the fidelity of the 'parent' or original is a necessary construction in order to map the spawning relationship, albeit one that may be complicated by the many threads of influence, lineage, and inspiration within artists and the art they create. Dance has neither a universal nor easily accessible notation system, and, as such, no consistent basis to determine the 'canonical' version of a work. Instead, the primary mode of transmission is via human performance, expressed through (as) a series of specific performances by specific dancers who have specific artistic and aesthetic qualities. As such, dance works unavoidably change and even disappear as they are passed from one generation of dancers to the next. As a result, when an artform such as dance privileges and relies on embodiment, these notions of 'life-span', 'spin-offs', and 'spawns' become particularly complex. What happens when the creation of a new artefact means the unavoidable destruction of the one that came before?

The instability of embodied dance performances as 'parent' sources naturally leads to anxiety about the dilution of authenticity over succeeding generations of artistic spawns. Lepecki discusses the 'will to archive' in contemporary dance, or the 'capacity to identify in a past work still non-exhausted creative fields of "impalpable possibilities"' (Lepecki 2010, 31). Unlike an Internet meme or a broadcast television spin-off, in which both the parent and the spawn may co-exist even as they are battered by varying interpretations, transitions, and cultural constructs, the parent artwork in dance is sufficiently fragile to be fundamentally affected and even modified by its external evolutions. This was a particular concern for seminal American postmodern choreographer, Yvonne Rainer, who wrote about her personal shift in thinking in terms of authenticity and the 'transmission' of dance from one body to the next, commenting;

> For the first decade of *Trio A's* existence I was teaching it to anyone who wanted to learn it—skilled and unskilled, trained and untrained, professional and amateur—and gave tacit permission to anyone who wanted to teach it to do so. I envisioned myself as a postmodern dance evangelist bringing movement to the masses, watching with Will Rogerslike benignity the slow, inevitable evisceration of my elitist creation. Well, I finally met a *Trio A* I didn't like. It was fourth or fifth generation, and I couldn't believe my eyes. It was all but unrecognizable. (Rainer 2009, 16)

In her essay, Rainer mourns the fact that the early versions of her piece were never properly documented on film (the piece was recorded on video in 1978, several years after Rainer had stopped performing it). As Rainer writes, 'The difference between the two performances—one in my memory, muscles, and photos, the other on the screen—is immense' (Rainer 2009, 16). *Trio A* was once considered to be a beacon example of 'open source' (deLahunta 2003) dance performance and practice, in stark contrast to the kind of control and adherence to authenticity and reconstruction demonstrated by organizations such as the George Balanchine Trust, which carefully and judiciously presides over each and every performance of the late choreographer's extensive body of work, 'preserve[ing] the artistic integrity of the works by providing Balanchine-trained répétiteurs to stage his ballets for qualified companies and by requiring periodic reviews of the productions' (The Balanchine Foundation 2002).

Rainer permitted the formal notation of her work through Labanotation in 2004 and nominated a handful of 'custodians', or individually-selected dancers to pass on the work to new bodies. Above all, Rainer was very much aware that elements of her work were at risk of being 'lost in translation' (Gardner 2014, 233). Her textual emphasis on 'transmitting' the work rather than 'transferring' or 'translating' it (see Gardner 2014) is particularly significant to our understanding of the way an embodied artwork may become diluted as it travels further from an originating source that is embedded within both the body of the original creator and the moment of the work's creation. In this example, *Trio A* (both the 1966 version by Rainer and more contemporary reconstructions of the work) resists categorization as either 'parent' source or 'spawn'. Whereas a transference might signal a change in ownership, Rainer's choice to use the phrase 'transmitters' emphasizes the source of the work, its parental and primary status, and perhaps suggests that *Trio A* can only truly exist as a primary source within Rainer's physical body from 1966, long since changed and aged.

The transmission of a work from one performing body to the next could be seen as an unavoidable loss or weakening of an inherent embodied knowledge. One might question the extent to which an absent primary source for *Trio A* contributes to the idea that re-versions of the work may negatively affect its fidelity. It is also significant to note that we do not think of *Trio A* as a spawn-source in the mode of Internet 'memes,' nor does Rainer herself, judging from her desire to 'set the record as straight as possible and forget, at least for the moment, scruples and caveats about fetishization and immortality' (Rainer 2009, 17). Perhaps the difference lies in Rainer's ability to retain artistic control of *Trio A*, as opposed to the kind of artistic spawnings that multiply across digital media and exist beyond a single creator's artistic grasp (see *The Economist* 2015, for a discussion of 'The Streisand Effect'). Yet, regardless of the number of 'spawns' of Rainer's original work, the majority of *Trio A*'s performative spin-offs are still embodied and are therefore just as unstable, temporal, and fragile as their 1966 'parent'.

In recent years, there has been a spate of accusations of dance plagiarism and 'appropriation', particularly in cases when dance has 'spawned' artwork in other high-profile genres, such as digital and commercial media, particularly music videos (Sutton 2015). For example, in 2011, American pop singer Beyoncé was prominently accused of plagiarizing the movements and filmic framing of Belgian choreographer Anna Teresa De Keersmaeker's *Achterland* and *Rosas danst Rosas* for her music video, *Countdown* (McKinley 2011). According to reports in *The New York Times*, the co-director of the video, Adria Petty, 'brought Beyoncé a number of references … most were German modern dance' to inspire the creation of the music video (McKinley 2011). While De Keersmaeker referred to the imitation as 'plagiarism' and 'stealing', Beyoncé casually credited the choreographer alongside a string of other influences, remarking, 'I've always been fascinated by the way contemporary art uses different elements and references to produce something unique' (McKinley 2011). In other words, whereas Beyoncé and her team perceived *Countdown* as an homage to De Keersmaeker's work—similar to the process in which a music producer might sample riffs from existing tracks—De Keersmaeker herself viewed it as something more akin to artistic theft. This is perhaps an extreme case in that the similarities between the works were glaringly apparent. However, it begs the question: how much imitation equates to plagiarism in an embodied context? Moreover, should the creator of the 'primary' source retain any rights over the spawns that have emerged in other genres through the efforts of other individual artists? This example points to the specific cultural differences in the creation of contemporary pop music and the creation of some contemporary dance, not least because Beyoncé elected to frame De Keersmaeker's work in a very different commercial and cultural context than the one it was created in three decades ago. Perhaps, the issue is not only one of permission and acknowledgement, but concern that a commercialized spin-off may result in monetary gain for the author of the 'spawn', rather than the author of the parent source.

As the De Keersmaeker/Beyoncé example also demonstrates, the development of digital media has facilitated a method of spawning artwork that does not rely on the traditional process of developing, sharing, and transferring an artistic lineage. No relationship exists between De Keersmaeker and Beyoncé beyond the 'look' of their works: there was no formal transference of knowledge or skill as would have occurred in a more traditional passing on or transmission of the dance work as a part of repertoire, through remounting or reconstruction. Eventually, and perhaps in response to her experience negotiating plagiarism in regards to her own work, De Keersmaeker created the *Re:Rosas* project (http://www.rosasdanstrosas.be/en-home/). This online repository provides a pedagogical breakdown of De Keersmaeker's choreography and encourages dancers to record their own versions of *Rosas danst Rosas* and digitally publish it to the site. Now, numerous versions of *Rosas* have been filmed all over the world in public spaces, as well as in living rooms and theatres. The act of imitation, or even, perhaps, of artistic plagiarism, has now been recontextualized through its interaction with digital media, but also in its re-framing as part of an open-source attitude. In other words, both De Keersmaeker and Beyoncé can be seen as facilitating a kind of 'spawning' process that has given *Rosas* new life in a digital context. However, one key difference between Beyoncé's work and the works that have emerged through the *Re:Rosas* project is the role played by De Keersmaeker herself: a 'primary source' creator providing formal 'permission' for the reinterpretation of her work, as well as establishing a digital venue that permanently highlights the lineage between 'parent' and 'spawn'.

In the article 'The Value of Dance: Notes on Dance and Copyright', Madeline Ritter and Rupert Vogel (2012) use this example to investigate the shortfalls of copyright law in terms of dance. Ritter is not alone in her discussion of 'what can be owned' in terms of gesture, movement, and ideas, and this particular area of interest is underlined by real-world examples of artistic works that have been lost completely due to gaps in our understanding of how movement might be understood as an artistic primary source, or how a work of choreography, a body of work, or a technique might be understood as artistic primary sources of their own.

There is a shifting line between artistic inspiration and artistic plagiarism that is embedded in the very act of making art, but the De Keersmaeker/Beyoncé incident highlights the challenge of crediting and copyrighting material within an art form that was once live, embodied, and grounded in human movement. The rise of video documentation and dissemination has unquestionably helped artists to access greater audiences, but it has also created an opportunity for artworks and ideas to be 'claimed' by others. The notion that dance can even *be* plagiarized is a relatively new concept, with choreographers throughout the twentieth century presenting their own versions of significant and historical dance works without necessarily acknowledging the relationship of the 'new' work to an 'original' source. Classical ballets that are created 'after Petipa', for example, embody this uncomfortable understanding of dance ownership. However, recent high-profile cases (such as the 2002 Supreme Court judgement about Martha Graham's dance works and the relationship of Graham and her works to her dance company) have demonstrated that unresolved issues of ownership and copyright can result in significant damage to the artform, the art, and the artist (Dunning 2002).

Lepecki also raises this concern in his discussion of Richard Move, an artist who 'drag[ged] Martha back from the dead' through his re-enactments of Graham's works and persona. Lepecki frames Move's work as a 'haunting', recognizing Move's 'will to archive' as both a potent creative inspiration and a key to keeping Graham's own legacy alive in the midst of the acrimonious legal battle over the ownership of her works (Lepecki 2010, 42). In his early days performing as 'Martha', Move 'received from the Graham Company lawyers a "Cease and Desist" letter accusing him of copyright infringement and misleading the public' (Lepecki 2010, 42). This is an ironic twist: before an author's death, it was the repertoire (which Diana Taylor famously 'opposed to the supposed stable objects in the archive' as all that 'enacts embodied memory' [Taylor 2003, 20]) that had been 'frozen, controlled, and disciplined' (Lepecki 2010, 42). Significantly, a decade later, Move's 'Martha spawns' were fully embraced by the Martha Graham Dance Company, with Move invited to create an original work inspired by *Lamentation*, one of Graham's most seminal pieces (Seibert 2015).

Another crucial consideration in our understanding of 'artwork-spawning-artwork' in embodied forms is the question of legacy: the ways in which the 'parent' source and the 'spawn' author collaborate (or not), as well as the recognition of the transmission process from one generation of the lineage to the next. We might hypothesize that the more a 'spawned' artwork acknowledges its parental source, whether through actual artistic collaboration or through a simple reference in a performance programme, the more stability it ultimately provides both to itself and to the original source. In practice, a number of dance companies are currently grappling with this issue of artistic legacy, striving both to preserve dance works as authentic historical documents and to utilize the potential of such historical documents to spawn new works. The acknowledgement that an artwork can be more than just a stand-alone 'product', but actually be mobilized for inspiration into new forms, is something that is being explored by several significant arts companies. Beginning in 2007, the Martha Graham Dance Company launched a project called the 'Lamentation Variations', in which a number of contemporary choreographers including Move, Kyle Abraham, Liz Gerring, and Sonya Tayeh were commissioned to create new works in response to Graham's 1930 solo. The scope of the 'Lamentation Variations' expanded Graham's original idea into different dance genres (tap, urban dance, etc.), fostering artistic spawns that could 'use the Graham legacy as a springboard' and 'take the legacy to a different place' (Seibert 2015). This project is particularly telling in light of the company's fraught history with Graham's legacy after her death in 1992. Nevertheless, when we look at the Graham Company's recent repertoire, it is clear that the administration leadership actively acknowledged the necessity of evolving beyond a mere historical archive (crucial though it may be not to lose Graham's significant repertoire and influence on modern dance). The company has recognized an artistic obligation to allow and facilitate the spawning of Graham's seminal artworks, and, with each new variation of 'Lamentation' that is commissioned and performed, we are introduced to a new facet of the original through the germs of inspiration that are highlighted by each contemporary artist.

Towards the end of the twentieth century, an awareness of the complexities of preserving embodied legacies has largely informed the artistic and administrative choices of several living choreographers, including Merce Cunningham, Pina Bausch, and most recently, Paul Taylor (Harss 2015). Central to the conversations about 'legacy building' and artistic preservation is a recognition of the inadequacy of traditional notation methods for dance (including 2D film and Labanotation), as well as a nascent understanding that choreographic thinking and practice might find new life and foster new artistic spawns by leveraging the capacity of digital technology, such as Motion Bank. As dance transverses the pathways from embodied to the digital and back again, cross-disciplinary spawns might counter the challenges of decaying and changing bodies, and what that has long meant for capturing live performance as a primary source document (see Groves et al. 2007).

15.4   THE IMPACT OF DIGITAL PROCESSES

Motion Bank, a four-year project of the Forsythe Company in Germany, specifically explored the potential of artistic spawns that are created by the fusion of dance and digital technology, with choreographic data becoming the point of inspiration for creative coding (deLahunta and Hennermann 2013).[1] The Synchronous Objects website (http://synchronousobjects. osu.edu/), for example, includes numerous examples of artistic 'spawns' in which the dance data is translated into digital media in the form of data visualizations and design. When Motion Bank was conceived, its goal of sharing choreographic processes and ideas through the use of computer-aided documentation and design was never meant to be a work of archivation or preservation, or even to produce new artworks. The original intention of the initiative was predicated entirely on the basis of documenting and analysing extant processes and products of dance making; the opportunity to develop a responsive artwork arose during the investigation of the practice. However, in the process of exploring the meaning of dance practice, a number of interesting 'spawns' have been developed, and these, in turn, have been able to foster rich interdisciplinary collaborations.

One prominent kind of artistic output that has emerged from Motion Bank are 'responsive artworks, or artworks that are directly inspired by the data or the practice of artists. For example, 3D digital visual artist Amin Weber created a response to postmodern dance choreographer Deborah Hay's written score for her solo, *No Time to Fly*.[2] Both of these outputs (among others) were published together on the Motion Bank website, highlighting and encouraging the connections between the works (www. motionbank.org). Weber's work is an example of an artistic creation in which an embodied choreographic product directly spawned a digital artwork. Weber's animation has itself inspired new choreographic outcomes, a process of spawning that has created a multi-generational lifespan for Hay's work (and now Weber's work), alongside and integrated with the 'original' source (Hay 2010). The processes of computer-aided documentation and design related to communicating choreographic practice that inspired Weber's animation has also inspired new choreography by Deborah Hay in the form of a work commissioned by the Cullberg Ballet in Stockholm, further demonstrating a multi-sensory experience that, while based on the original dance work, could be engaged either as an adjunct to the original or as an independent experience.[3] Through the translation of dance to data and then to art, Hay's original choreography has found a form more resistant to decay that its ephemeral primary source state and in this way, the life of the choreographic work has expanded beyond the scope of the originating body and time of creation, while simultaneously establishing a new artistic lifespan through digital media.

As intellectual and inspirational starting points, other datasets from Motion Bank have been used by creative coders at the Choreographic Coding Labs in 2013 and 2015 to generate new artwork in digital domains, and, as with Weber's artwork, digital processes present an exciting opportunity for digital artworks to 'spawn' choreographic ones. For example, researcher John McCormick and choreographer Steph Hutchison (Queensland University of Technology) have also explored ways in which dance and digital technology can enable the process of artistic spawning by constructing digital surrounds and artificially intelligent systems to create choreographic outputs. In McCormick and Hutchison's *Emergence*, a digital performing agent (or Artificially Intelligent neural network) learned to dance and recognize Hutchison's physical movement in order for the two to perform together in a semi-improvisational setting (McCormick et al. 2014). The performing agent was also able to dance independently of Hutchison, using a style and vocabulary of movement that was derived from Hutchison's original choreography. Through this process, the digital performer's dance, along with its visual representation, became a newly spawned generation of Hutchison's original choreography. This cycle repeated again during the performance as Hutchison found choreographic inspiration in her improvisational interactions with the digital performer, in particular when the digital was not represented as a recognizable humanoid. In the dance work *Recognition*, another collaboration between McCormick and Hutchison, the digital agent was represented as a morphing collection of blobs that prompted a particular style of buoyant dancing from Hutchison that changed rapidly in levels and in which body parts retained the primary focus. This new movement vocabulary in turn spawned the work *Meta*, an artistic iteration that further developed the movement inspired by the digital performer (Hutchison et al. 2015). The Dance Haptics project, undertaken at Deakin Motion.Lab and the Centre for Intelligent Systems Research (now called the Institute for Intelligent Systems Research and Innovation) at Deakin University, represents another example of 'spawning'—in this case from an embodied form (performance) to a set of haptic-driven digital interfaces that enabled blind and visually-impaired audience members to experience a customized version of the work in a non-visual form (Hossny et al. 2015). The resulting work employed two haptic-driven digital artforms: first, a haptic 'cushion' that relayed vibration patterns to the audience member based on elements of motion capture movement data from the original dance; and second, a small robot that 'performed' the dancers' movement while the user held the robot's hands. This shift from one genre to another—in this case, from visual experience to haptic experience—can be seen as a positive utilization of untapped potential in the original artwork.

Through the development cycles of these new performance works but also as a result of this interdisciplinary research, dance is actively spawning and being spawned, from human to digital performer and from the digital to the human. While the notion of 'original' or 'primary' is still acknowledged in this context, these successful collaborations suggest that the life-cycle of ephemeral artwork can be extended as a direct result of utilizing new forms that have both creative potential and a natural resistance to decay. This also lessens the distinctions between art genres, with 'dance' now potentially existing not only in the human body, but in the format of digital media and in the language of coded and networked arts. Ultimately, in the case of embodied art, with its inherent complications of ownership, authenticity, and legacy, these digital artefacts offer a way to 'stabilize' the artistic lifespan of ephemeral parent sources, as well as foster new avenues for artistic exploration (Gardner 2014, 232).

15.5   Conclusion

Our discussions of artwork-spawning-artwork, as well as some of the challenges that arise from this process in embodied artforms, are by no means exhaustive and do not specifically address issues regarding intangible cultural heritage. Framing artistic spawning as a mechanism that allows the transposition of one artwork into another form or media is ontologically complex, as ultimately, no art exists in a vacuum. However, we see enormous potential for artists and researchers to explore the longevity of dance, as an embodied artform, in a digital domain. In the age of digital technology, with its capacity for widespread and user-driven dissemination, artistic spawns are increasing, both in number and in visibility. While digital media has made the process of 'spawning' more obvious, it has also allowed for opportunities to reflect on the authenticity, originality, and many other facets that make up an artistic product, including the ideas, inspiration, and legacy of the originating artists and their creative processes.

Moreover, the notion of something spawning from an original can be seen within the context of a fundamental and arguably necessary relationship between generations of artworks. As one artwork makes space for the one that follows, the notion of 'original' or 'parent' unavoidably fades into a larger understanding of an overall artistic landscape: each artistic spawn becomes creatively generative and ultimately enriches this landscape, rather than being diminished by any distance from the primary source. When original artefacts are able to co-exist alongside their artistic spawns without suffering any negative effects to their own fidelity or authenticity, the process of 'spawning' can be recognized, acknowledged, and even celebrated.

We argue that the concept of artwork 'spawning' artwork, with its implicitly dual nature as causally dependent yet ontologically independent, provides a means of extending the influence and exposure of dance ideas and dance practices far beyond the limitations imposed by dance's original performative contexts. While the cost of this development is inevitably the increasing distance between an original work and a spawned work, the potential benefit is a new degree of longevity and influence for the embodied artform, as well as the cultivation of dialogue in the knowledge systems within and outside dance. On balance, we argue that the risk is justified, though one that demands vigilant acknowledgement of original sources and artists and a concerted effort to ensure that such attribution is not abandoned as artworks spawn artworks in an ever-evolving lineage of creative innovation.

Acknowledgments Thanks to Steph Hutchison, Peter Divers, Richard Burt, Deanne Czarnecki, Jordan Kaye, Thomas Ingram, Kieren Wallace, Deakin Motion. Lab, and Motion Bank.

Notes

1. Making this connection between choreographic data and new digital forms is made explicit through the activity of the Choreographic Coding Labs, an outcome of the first phase of Motion Bank (2010–2013). See: http://choreographiccoding.org/.
2. Amin Weber's Digital Adaptation of Deborah Hay's score *No Time to Fly* is available here: http://scores.motionbank.org/dh/#/set/digital-adaptation-of-no-time-to-fly.
3. The commissioned work, *Figure a Sea*, premiered with twenty-one dancers in Stockholm on 24 September 2015.

REFERENCES

Banks, David. 2011. On Performative Internet Memes: Planking, Owling & Stocking. *Cyborgology*, 21 September. http://thesocietypages.org/cyborgology/2011/09/21/on-performative-internet-memes-planking-owling-stocking/.

Barrett, Estelle. 2004. What Does It Meme? The Exegesis as Valorisation and Validation of Creative Arts Research. *TEXT*: 3. School of Arts, Griffith University, 4 April. http://www.textjournal.com.au/speciss/issue3/barrett.htm.

Dawkins, Richard. 1976. *The Selfish Gene*. Oxford: Oxford University Press.

deLahunta, Scott. 2003. Open Source Choreography? In *Code: The Language of Our Time*, ed. Katalog zur Ars Electronica, 304–310. Ostfildern-Ruit: Hatje Cantz.

deLahunta, Scott, and Célestine Hennermann. 2013. *Motion Bank: Starting Points and Aspirations*. Frankfurt, DE: Motion Bank/The Forsythe Company.

Dunning, Jennifer. 2002. Martha Graham Wins Rights to the Dances. *New York Times*, 24 August.

Gardner, Sally. 2014. What Is a Transmitter? *Choreographic Practices* 5 (2): 229–240.

Groves, Rebecca, Norah Zuniga Shaw, and Scott deLahunta. 2007. Talking About Scores: William Forsythe's Vision for a New Form of 'Dance Literature'. In *Knowledge in Motion: Perspectives of Artistic and Scientific Research in Dance*, ed. Sabine Gehm, Pirkko Husemann, and Katharine von Wilcke. Bielefeld/Piscataway, NJ: Transcript/Distributed in North America by Transaction Publishers, c2007.

Harss, Marina. 2015. What Is the Future for Modern-Dance Companies? *The New Yorker*, 14 February. http://www.newyorker.com/culture/cultural-comment/future-modern-dance-companies-paul-taylor.

Hay, Deborah. 2010. *No Time to Fly* (Solo Dance Score). http://x.motionbank.org/nttf_score/nttf_score.pdf.

Hossny, M., S. Nahavandi, M. Fielding, D. Creighton, J. McCormick, K. Vincs, J.B. Vincent, and S. Hutchison. 2015. *Haptically-Enabled Dance Visualisation Framework for Deafblind-Folded Audience and Artists*. IEEE International Conference on Systems, Man, and Cybernetics, Hong Kong, 9–12 October.

Hutchison, Steph, John McCormick, and Kim Vincs. 2015. *META: Notes from a Dancer from Inside a Duet with an AI Agent*. International Symposium of Electronic Art, ISEA 2015, Vancouver, Canada.

Lepecki, Andre. 2010. The Body as Archive: Will to Re-Enact and the Afterlives of Dances. *Dance Research Journal* 42 (2): 28–48.

McCormick, John, Kim Vincs, Saeid Nahavandi, Douglas Creighton, and Steph Hutchison. 2014. *Teaching a Digital Performing Agent: Artificial Neural Network and Hidden Markov Model for Recognising and Performing Dance*

Movement. Proceedings of the 2014 International Workshop on Movement and Computing, Paris, France.

McKinley, James C., Jr. 2011. Beyoncé Accused of Plagiarism Over Video. *New York Times*, 10 October. http://artsbeat.blogs.nytimes.com/2011/10/10/beyonce-accused-of-plagiarism-over-video/?_r=0.

Pearson, Roberta, and Máire Messenger Davies. 2014. *Star Trek and American Television*. Berkeley: University of California Press.

Rainer, Yvonne. 2009. *Trio A*: Genealogy, Documentation, Notation. *Dance Research Journal* 41 (2): 12–18.

Ritter, Madeline, and Rupert Vogel. 2012. *The Value of Dance: Notes on Copyright*. Trans. C. Langer. In *Zeitschrift der Deutschen Vereinigung für gewerblichen Rechtsschutz und Urheberrecht*, 14 December. https://tanzfonds.de/en/magazin/the-value-of-dance-notes-on-copyright/.

Seibert, Brian. 2015. From a Fount of Grief, Endless Innovation. *New York Times*, 23 January. http://www.nytimes.com/2015/01/25/arts/dance/martha-graham-dance-tackles-new-versions-of-lamentation.html.

Sutton, Benjamin. 2015. When Arty Music Videos Rip Off Artists. *Hyperallergic*, 19 February. http://hyperallergic.com/184095/when-arty-music-videos-rip-off-artists/.

The Balanchine Foundation. 2002. The George Balanchine Trust. Accessed 24 February 2015. http://balanchine.org/balanchine/02/gbftrust.html.

Taylor, Diana. 2003. *The Archive and the Repertoire: Performing Cultural Memory in the Americas*. Durham: Duke University Press.

Vincs, K., J. McCormick, R. Vincs, D. Skovli, S. Taylor, K. Wallace, B. Lin, and P. Divers. 2014. *The Crack Up* (Live Performance). Melbourne, VIC.

What Is the Streisand Effect? *The Economist*, 15 April. Accessed 10 December 2015. http://www.economist.com/blogs/economist-explains/2013/04/economist-explains-what-streisand-effect.

CHAPTER 16

Preservation and Paradox: Choreographic Authorship in the Digital Sphere

Hetty Blades

16.1 Introduction

In dance, questions of authorship and ownership are closely related to issues of documentation, preservation and heritage. The much-cited ephemerality of performance (Phelan 1993; Siegel 1972, 1) and absence of universal notation system means that, as with other forms of performance based culture, documentation is important for allowing access for future generations and generating a tangible heritage. Choreographers often develop idiosyncratic and novel ways of preserving and inscribing their work (Cvejić in De Keersmaeker and Cvejić 2012; Van Imschoot 2012). Chosen modes of documentation and transmission often become part of a choreographer's artistic identity and demonstrate, to a certain extent, the way that they view their role as an author, and their relationship to their work. Choreographers restrict the transmission and re-staging of their work to varying degrees, with some exercising strict control and others allowing their work to circulate freely. Equally, some choreographers choose to publically articulate the intended meaning, stimuli and processes of their work, whilst others remain quiet. The range of approaches reveals something of the complexities of

H. Blades (✉)
Centre for Dance Research, Coventry University, Coventry, UK

© The Author(s) 2018   301
S. Whatley et al. (eds.), *Digital Echoes*,
https://doi.org/10.1007/978-3-319-73817-8_16

preserving dance. The form not only escapes universal inscription, but also has few standardized practices governing its production, documentation and circulation. In particular contemporary dance practitioners are frequently motivated by a desire for originality, resulting in a field rich with variety, not only in terms of choreographic style, but also in strategies for documentation, preservation and transmission.

The development of the internet and widespread access to recording technology has contributed significantly to the range of approaches used by choreographers to share and document their work. Furthermore, the circulation and apparent stabilization of dance through digital technologies requires choreographers to (re)think their relationship to their own work, foregrounding questions such as: What does it take to adequately transmit, re-perform and preserve my work? And, how will it be remembered? In response to these questions, the first part of this chapter discusses contemporary dance authorship and outlines how the relatively recent passing of some major figures in the development of Western contemporary dance has ignited questions concerning choreographic authorship and cultural heritage. As dance scholar Sally Gardner points out, '[w]ith the demise since the start of the twenty-first century of several seminal choreographers, it is timely to pursue the issues and questions of the modern dance legacy' (2014, 230). In response to this situation, I discuss how the work of Merce Cunningham (1919–2009) and Pina Bausch (1940–2009) is being preserved and 'protected' through online mechanisms. The second part of the chapter considers the ways in which such issues are being handled by living artists, focusing on how Flemish choreographer Anne Teresa De Keersmaeker negotiates her relationship to her own work. I examine De Keersmaeker's authorial positioning during the 'referencing' of her choreography by pop star Beyoncé Knowles and the subsequent development of the online project *Re:Rosas! The fABULEUS Rosas Remix Project* (*Re:Rosas!*). Both of these examples involve De Keermaeker's seminal work *Rosas danst Rosas*, which premiered in 1983 and is widely known via a film version of the work by Thierry De Mey from 1997. Furthermore, both cases highlight the role of the internet, demonstrating how the online circulation of dance pose important questions about what it might mean to preserve, author and own a work of dance art.

16.2   Choreographic Authorship and Ownership

The role of the choreographer is littered with complexities. Dance and law scholars Charlotte Waelde, Sarah Whatley and Mathilde Pavis (2014) describe the collaborative nature of the process of dance-making in which the dancers instantiate the ideas of the choreographer, but where ownership shifts as the dancers imprint their interpretation and individual artistry on the work, and shifts again as the work is performed in a public shared environment before an audience. (2014, 7)

As articulated here, dance making involves dancers, each of whom bring their own unique body and movement style, not to mention creative ideas. This means that other than choreographers making solos on themselves, choreography is essentially a collaborative act. However, despite its collaborative nature, contemporary dance convention tends to isolate a single person as the 'author' of a work or set of practices. Furthermore, as dance theorist Laurence Louppe points out, even in collectives such as Grand Union, who later became known as Judson Dance Theater,[1] decisions often come down to an individual choice (2010, 179). Dance theorist Anthea Kraut further suggests that some contemporary and postmodern choreographers used strategies such as improvisation, chance procedure, a method whereby the elements of the choreography are determined by chance, rather than by the choreographer; and pedestrianism, or 'everyday' movement, 'to distance themselves from the modernist emphasis on authorial invention', but that nevertheless these artists continue to be recognized as the author of their works (2016, 266). Graham McFee (2011) makes a similar claim, although articulated slightly differently. He suggests that it is incorrect to refer to dancers as 'artists', not because they do not have artistic skills, but because we tend to distinguish between the dancers and the choreographer when attributing value, responsibility and ownership.

So, the author-concept appears to be strong in dance, indeed Louppe goes as far as to suggest that authorial signature is fundamental the concept of a dance 'work' (2010, 179–80). Difficulties in conceptualizing a dance work with no author are perhaps due to the way that works are made and transmitted on and with the body. Whilst scores are frequently used to document and instigate movement, they do not usually hold the same work-determining weight as musical scores and texts of plays. They also vary greatly in terms of how strictly they constrain the work. Some scores might aim to document every single detail, but more often than not, they are used as a form of stimuli. This means that the (re) formation of the 'work' requires more than the activation of a score, it depends upon a choreographer, or proxy (such as a rehearsal director, or re-stager), making choreographic decisions to fill in the gaps in memory and/or documentation. Furthermore, dance works tend to be relatively fluid entities. Whilst some follow a 'closed' work model where each instance of the work aims toward an ideal 'original' form, many are much more 'open' (Rubidge 2000). As the work is embodied by different dancers there will inevitably be deviations to the movement vocabulary and style. Changes might be made to the work to reflect evolving cultural contexts, requiring choreographic decision-making. For a work to evolve and undergo revisions at the direction of the choreographer is relatively common.[2]

The close relationship between a choreographer and their work means that some interesting problems arise when they die, leaving behind a corpus of work residing in the bodies and memories of dancers, and through idiosyncratic documentation. The question of what happens to a contemporary choreographer's work, and who might be qualified to oversee restagings has also been around for some time.[3] Referring to a well-known dance pioneer, Gardner points out that, '[t]his has been a question, confronted in different ways, since the death of Isadora Duncan in 1927' (2014, 231). However, the past two decades have proved a particularly interesting time in dance history, due to the deaths of key figureheads, including Martha Graham (1894–1991) as well as Cunningham and Bausch. Such artists were instrumental in the development of Western contemporary dance, which was established in both the USA and mainland Europe in the first half of the twentieth century (Jowitt 2011). Each of these choreographers were considered avant-garde and set out to challenge existing conventions (Copeland 2004; Franko 1995; Servos 1981). Although different in style, American choreographers Graham and Cunningham both challenged the traditions of classical ballet. This first wave of contemporary choreography is often referred to as 'modern' dance, and was challenged in the 1960s and 1970s by the 'postmodern' choreographers of Judson Dance Theatre. Bausch was based in Germany and her style has slightly different roots, but equally questioned that which came before. She is widely credited with developing 'tanztheater' (dance theatre), drawing on theatrical narratives, characters and costuming alongside movement.[4]

Following in the tradition of their early modern dance predecessors, such as Doris Humphrey and Jose Limon, these three artists clearly demonstrate the common singularity of dance authorship suggested by Louppe and McFee. Graham, Cunningham and Bausch are all well known; their choreographic styles are closely related to their artistic identities and easily identifiable. In the case of Graham and Cunningham their styles evolved into codified techniques, widely taught in European and American training institutions. Although not entirely straightforward, movement idioms can be codified thorough a process of naming and standardizing specific sets of movements. This allows for certain features of an artist's choreographic practice to outlive them through the body-to-body transmission that occurs between teachers and their students. However, there is something intuitively more complex about a choreographer's relationship to their own work(s). This is perhaps due to the fluid nature of dance. The author of a book or painting formulates a single, relatively stable entity, which can be bought, sold, touched and physically located within the world, even if, as is the case with novels, this physical form has many different formats. Choreographers, on the other hand, author more fluid entities.[5]

Perhaps as a result of this fluidity, as hinted at by Kraut (quoted above), choreographic authorship seems to be considered somehow different to authorship in other areas. For example, Gardner writes:

> Inherent to issues of modern dance memory, in particular, is that individual authorship, and the location of authorial value or of a work's identity in or as the bodily 'flesh' of works or idioms, has not been widely acknowledged or accepted. Despite the early twentieth-century emergence and subsequent ongoing creative production of modern dance as an individualized rather than social dance, the idea of a dance artist in the modernist sense (as the inventor of a body) is not widely recognized. (Gardner 2014, 230)

This position seems in some ways paradoxical to the previous suggestion that singular authorial signatures are common in dance practice. It seems that whilst the author-concept is strong in in terms of how we attribute ownership, the bodily, unfixed nature of dance means that the recognition of a choreographer's corpus is more complex. Louppe traces the root of the issue, suggesting that, 'the act of choreography, considered as a simple spectacle, has inherited a traditional foundation' (2010, 235), and that the temporality of dance in performance has prevented the choreographic work from becoming recognized as a 'fully fledged artistic act' (2010, 235). So, whilst we attribute individual authorship to choreographic works, the nature of dance means that choreographers are not recognized in the same way as the creators of more stable works of art.

The fluidity of dance works means that their circulation is almost impossible to entirely constrain. For example, once a dancer has learned the steps, structure or concept of a dance it exists in their body. They can go on to perform, remake and teach this work. Furthermore, choreography can be copied from performances, videos and scores. This situation means that each choreographer must decide how best to constrain their works, which changes can be made, and who is allowed to perform it. During a choreographer's working life these can be decided on a case-by-case basis. For example, Cunningham, Bausch and Graham each had their own companies, which performed works made only by themselves. A number of these works remained in the repertoire for many years, meaning that they were performed by multiple different casts. Bausch's work *Cafe Muller* for instance, premiered in 1978 and was performed until 2013. However, the place of the work within the repertoire was not consistent; it was performed every year between 1980 and 1988 and then not at all between 1988 and 1992 (Tanztheater Wuppertal Pina Bausch n.d.). Each restaging would have inevitably involved some minor or major alterations and revisions, which could be decided by Bausch. But what happens when the head of the company is no longer there? Can the company never perform another new work? Does it mean that the works within the repertory cannot be revised? Furthermore, who is responsible for making such decisions?

16.3   Legacies

Dance scholar Carrie Noland discusses how the Cunningham Dance Foundation started establishing a 'Legacy Plan' a couple of years before the choreographer's death (2013, 85). The way that the plan was put into place before Cunningham's death is important; for example arts writer Lizzie Feidelson points out that the plan had Cunningham's 'blessing' (2013). The strategy for preserving Cunningham's legacy involves, 'a set of initiatives intended to preserve while making available to other companies over fifty years of choreographic production as well as a unique method of training dancers' (Noland 2013, 85). The foundation, under the direction of Trevor Carlson, felt that the company should not continue without Cunningham. Therefore, upon his death it was decided that it would cease to exist on 1 January 2012. The Legacy Plan included a two-year Legacy Tour, which involved eighteen works and toured to fifty cities around the world (Noland 2013, 85). It also involved the development of Cunningham's 'Dance Capsules', a form of online archive.

The capsules document eighty-six of Cunningham's works. They are arranged in reverse chronological order on the homepage. Selecting a capsule leads the user onto a new page, which includes metadata concerning the credits for the choreography, music, décor, costumes, lighting and the date and venue of the first performance. The Cunningham Company archivist David Vaughan provides a brief synopsis for each work. In the right-hand corner of the screen are scrolling images of the work in performance. Below is a catalogue of 'assets' divided into 'public' and 'private'. Full access must be obtained via written request to the foundation, whereas limited sources are openly available. Public assets include detailed production credits, such as the original cast lists and information about the running time, music and so forth. Sometimes excerpts of the music are also available, as is footage from Cunningham's film series, *Mondays with Merce*. The private assets include extensive choreographic notes (fifty-five in the case of Cunningham's 1983 work *Roaratorio* for example), alongside video clips, reviews, production notes and so forth.

The distinction between the public and private assets can be understood as distinguishing between those assets (public) that merely provide enough information to reference the work, and catch a glimpse of its aesthetic, and private assets which might enable a staging of the work. The capsules have clearly been developed to allow for Cunningham's works to be re-instantiated. Feidelson suggests that the eighty-six works were selected depending on whether there was enough material about to allow for it to be re-performed (2013), yet these re-stagings are tightly controlled by the Cunningham Trust.

Noland points to the paradoxical relationship between preservation and the ideal of the avant-garde. She writes that,

> The notion of 'legacy' presupposes the perseverance of an essential core, and preserving this core requires technologies of storage, reproduction, and transmission as well as institutional support. The impulse to preserve, however, comes into conflict with the structure and ideology of the avant-garde itself, which demands the rejection of the recent in favor of the new, a fundamentally self-sacrificial and open attitude toward the future as a blank unknown. (Noland 2013, 86)

Such paradoxes are at the heart of dance preservation. The 'essential core' seem particularly relevant in relation to Cunningham's 'dance capsules', which are described as containing 'complete documentation of a

Cunningham work' (Merce Cunningham Trust n.d.). The notion of completeness suggests that even though moments of performance cannot be exactly replicated, the work has a set of essential properties, which can be fully captured. The implication is that the transmission of these properties will allow for the work to be 'authentically' re-enacted. The strategy of the Merce Cunningham Trust to gather the relevant information to enable the works to live on, yet to keep this information gated, generates another paradox whereby the circulation of the work is both enabled and restricted.

A similar claim for completeness is found in the description of the Pina Bausch archive, which claims to include, 'Pina Basuch's complete artistic legacy' (Pina Bausch Foundation n.d.). At the time of writing the archive is still under construction and exists only as an outline on the website of the Pina Bausch Foundation, however the strategy and framework for the development of the archive is interesting. The collection appears extensive; materials will be organized into eighteen categories, such as; 'Moving Image/Audio-Visual Material', 'Workbooks', 'Props', 'Costumes' and so forth. The introductory text explains, 'After her death, her son Salomon established the charitable Pina Bausch Foundation on August 3rd, 2009 in which he has placed her entire artistic legacy in accordance with her wishes' (Pina Bausch Foundation 2009). Reprised here are the notions of completeness or entirety, and the foregrounding of Bausch's role in the decisions made about the continuation of her work.

Unlike the Cunningham Company, Bausch's company Tanztheater Wuppertal remains active. The company continue to perform Bausch's works, and in 2015 for the first time the company commissioned three new works by Tim Etchells, François Chaignaud and Cecilia Bengolea, and Theo Clinkard (Anderson 2015). However, despite opening up the repertoire, the preservation strategies are repeatedly framed in relation to Bausch; indeed the archive project is titled, 'An Invitation from Pina' (Pina Bausch Foundation n.d.). It is logical and respectful to emphasize the wishes of the choreographer and also perhaps has underlying political implications. Recalling the suggestions quoted above it can be argued that foregrounding the choreographer is a way to combat or overcome the lack of acknowledgment for authorial value that Gardner (2014, 230) and Louppe (2010, 235) suggest is inherent to dance.

The questions about legacy raised by the deaths of Cunningham and Bausch can be seen as having a direct impact on living choreographers, who have also turned their attention to questions of how best to document, transmit and protect their work. 'Postmodern' artists such as Yvonne

Rainer and Trisha Brown, recently took steps to ensure that their work continues in accordance with their wishes.[6] Gardner discusses Yvonne Rainer's approach, suggesting, 'Rainer is still active as a choreographer but she is also self-consciously aware of her own mortality, and of what that mortality might mean for her body of work' (2014, 230). Gardner draws comparisons between Graham and Rainer. She suggests that, 'Graham was known as having an uncompromising approach to authorship or her works and was notorious for seeking to govern the broader lives and thoughts of her dancers' (2014, 233). On the other hand, Rainer's approach was initially more open. For example, her seminal work *Trio A* was choreographed in 1966, during Rainer's time as a member of Judson Dance Theatre. Judson's postmodern framework often focused on pedestrian movement, performed by people without dance training. Gardner suggests that Rainer was initially happy for *Trio A* to be handed over to others, in the 'democratic spirit of the times' (2014, 233). However, she goes on to say that Rainer's 2009 essay, '*Trio A*: Geneology, Documentation, Notation', demonstrates a shift in thinking, suggesting that the essay shows that Rainer has become 'obsessive' and more like Graham in her control of the work, 'after realizing how far the transmission of her dance could take her work away from its intended values' (2014, 233). Rainer's response to this realization was to qualify a number of dancers as 'custodians' of the work, who are trusted by Rainer to handle its transmission by overseeing re-stagings. This situation further highlights the complex set of paradoxes at the heart of dance preservation and transmission. At its very core *Trio A* was democratic in spirit and a challenge to hierarchical structures, yet in its careful preservation is has become an entity, trusted only in the hands of experts.

Importantly, Rainer's strategy preserves the centrality of body-to-body transmission. Handing over the custody of the work to a small number of dancers means that the circulation of *Trio A* can only be 'legitimately' learned directly from these authorized 'transmitters'.[7] The method of handing works down from dancer to dancer is common in dance practice. Whilst some companies use codified notational systems to inscribe works, this practice is relatively rare, conventionally, dance works are circulated through dancers and choreographers teaching movement material to new dancers. The widespread use of video recording has shifted this practice somewhat, as companies now often rely upon a combination of living memory and recorded representation to restage works. By removing the possibility for dancers to 'authentically' stage *Trio A* via the notated score, or a video recording, Rainer is re-establishing the central role of body-to-body transmission, and consciously limiting the potential for the work to circulate.

Rainer's approach is interesting partly because this moment in the history of contemporary dance, in which key figures are negotiating questions of legacy, coincides with the expansion of the internet, a tool which many choreographers are utilizing in order to negotiate the slippery terrain of preservation and heritage. The potentials of the internet for dissemination have ushered in multiple new ways to share and preserve work. Yet these potentials also pose a unique set of problematics.

16.4   DE KEERSMAEKER'S ONLINE OFFERING

In 2011 Anne Teresa De Keersmaeker was at the centre of a plagiarism row with pop star Beyoncé Knowles, whose video for the song *Countdown* (2011) features movements that are strikingly similar to sections of De Keersmaeker's works *Rosas danst Rosas* (1987) and *Achterland* (1990). De Keersmaeker claimed that Knowles had plagiarized her work, and threatened legal action (Yeoh 2013). However, Adria Petty, the co-director of the music video strongly denied this claim, explaining how she showed Knowles multiple videos as inspiration (McKinley 2011). Indeed the *Countdown* video is made up almost entirely of 'references' to other cultural icons and dance routines, Knowles is quoted as claiming, 'I was also paying tribute to the film, "Funny Face" with the legendary Audrey Hepburn' and 'My biggest inspirations were the '60s, the '70s, Brigitte Bardot, Andy Warhol, Twiggy and Diana Ross' (in McKinley 2011).

This is not the first of Knowles's videos to use existing choreography. For example, the movement in the video for *Single Ladies (Put a Ring On It)* (2008), derives directly from Bob Fosse's *Mexican Breakfast* (1969). Cultural theorist Philippa Thomas points out that this caused outcry amongst the public when the similarities were revealed, despite the fact that the use of Fosse's work was publically acknowledged by Knowles (2014, 293). It seems that the practice of borrowing, referencing and reusing is common in music video production, and that slightly different rules seem to apply to those governing more traditional artistic practices. Music videos are developed to illustrate or support a song, rather than being an individual work in their own right. Whilst they often contain choreography, the choreographer is rarely considered the author of the video, which is usually referred to as belonging to the singer or group whose song it illustrates. Furthermore, as a form that was invented for mass circulation, music videos have always engaged in a process of transmission, re-embodiment and re-enactment.[8]

Whilst those viewers familiar with the references used might see the *Countdown* video as an intertextual pastiche, unfamiliar viewers will perhaps assume that the choreography, styling and so on is original to Knowles and Petty, raising complex issues around ownership, copyright and dance (see Kraut 2016; Waelde et al. 2014; Yeoh 2013). However, leaving these questions aside for the time being, I want to highlight the central role of the internet in this scenario. *Rosas danst Rosas* was originally made as a stage work. It is a dance for four women; De Keersmaeker danced in the original version, alongside Adriana Borriello, Michèle Anne De Mey and Fumiyo Ikeda, who are credited as co-creators (Rosas n.d.) It was De Keersmaeker's third work and the first one for her company Rosas, which went on to become hugely successful. In 1997 De Mey and De Keersmaeker developed a film version of the work, which is set in an empty architectural school (Rosas n.d.). Multiple sections of this film exist on YouTube, thus allowing viewers around the world access to the work, in a way that was unimaginable at the time of its conception. It seems safe to assume that it was this film that Petty showed to Knowles, indeed the scenes in the *Countdown* video take place within a similar setting.

De Keersmaeker's response to the challenges of the internet, foregrounded by the *Countdown* case, was particularly interesting. In 2013 she and Rosas teamed up with *f*ABULEUS, a Belgian arts production organization to develop *Re:Rosas!* This is a website featuring specially recorded films in which De Keersmaeker and Samantha van Wissen, who features in the film version of the work, lead viewers through a simplified version of the 'chair section' or 'second movement' of *Rosas danst Rosas* (Re:Rosas 2013), one of the sections that appears in the *Countdown* video. In stark contrast to De Keersmaeker's response to Knowles, this site encourages viewers to develop their own versions of the work. These can then be submitted to the site, which houses a large collection of the videos. The project was originally created to coincide with the thirtieth anniversary of the work in 2013. It was intended to be a temporary project in order to collect videos for an exhibition in the Kaaitheater in Brussels (Artslant n.d.). Two hundred and fifty films were gathered for the event (Impulsetanz n.d.), and the huge response to the project meant that they chose to keep the site active. At the time of writing there are 372 videos on the site and they continue to be added.

The homepage articulates the premise of the site, telling users, 'it's your turn. Dance your own *Rosas danst Rosas*, make a video film of it and post it on this site' (Re:Rosas 2013). Below are four YouTube videos, titled, 'Welcome', 'Movements', 'Structure' and 'Choreography'. In the first video De Keersmaeker speaks to the camera to introduce the work and explain the instructions to users. The 'Movements' video entails van Wissen teaching the five phrases that make up this section of the work, labelled A, B, C, D and E. Each movement is articulated in detail. The camera work contributes to the level of detail; close-ups are used to demonstrate the position of the hands, van Wissen's focus and so on. The 'Structure' video demonstrates how the five phrases are organized in the work. De Keersmaeker joins van Wissen to show how the dancers interact with one another. Lastly, in the 'Choreography' video van Wissen is accompanied by three more female dancers, who enact the entire section, whilst text, inscribed over the top of the video demonstrates how the components come together to form the choreography. On another page the background and structure of the work is briefly articulated, illustrated by photographs, diagrams and three films. In the first film, De Keermsaeker outlines the original, more complex structure of the section using a chalkboard to help her communicate the arrangements. Below this film is an interview with De Keersmaeker and a clip of this section of the work in performance.

This project functions as a form of choreographic score by breaking down the movement and structure. The choreographic elements are extracted from other performative components, such as costume and staging. The original music is also provided. The introductory text reads:

> Anne Teresa De Keersmaeker and dancer Samantha van Wissen will teach you the moves, step by step, from the second part of the performance. After that it becomes your dance: *you dance Rosas*. In a different setting, with a huge number of dancers … any way you like! (Re:Rosas n.d.)

This proposition, combined with the nature of the information given, means that the framework, although implicit, is quite clear: the movement, music and structure are set, suggesting that these are the 'essential core' (Noland 2013, 86) of the work, but that creativity is invited in relation to context, cast and other components, such as the camerawork, costumes and so forth. Picking up on the site's subtitle, Claire Frisbie, marketing manager at Brooklyn Academy of Music, suggests that the project is, '[m]odeled after the practice of so many musicians who upload parts of their songs to the internet for DJs to remix' (2013). However, users are not entirely let loose; there are some features of the work that must be maintained.

Another important difference to musical remixing is that unlike DJs, who can use direct recordings, anyone wishing to remix the work must first activate the movement through their own bodies, opening the work up to vastly varied corporealities. Whilst the practice of learning choreography from video is commonplace, this inevitably leads to questions about the importance of bodily transmission, who has the authority to 'transmit' such knowledge (Gardner 2014) and whether recorded version of the work is 'authentic'. The practice of learning dance routines from music videos, on the other hand seems not to face such questions, perhaps because of the way that they are developed to circulate via digital media, and exist wholly in digital form thus avoiding the apparent dichotomy between 'live' and recorded performance that exists for dance and other performing arts that have a tradition of being instantiated on stage.[9] For example, the wide circulation of the *Single Ladies* (2008) video is discussed by Thomas (2014), who explains how the choreography was reperfomed in multiple social contexts. This was encouraged by Knowles's record label, Columbia Records, who held a competition in 2009, in which members of the public competed for a cash prize by submitting their own versions of the dance routine from the video (Thomas 2014, 295). The rules very clearly stipulated that entries must copy the choreography exactly (Thomas 2014, 295). Although there is no prize on offer in the *Re:Rosas!* project, other than the posting of each participant's video on the site, the project clearly echoes the call of Columbia Records. The transmission of contemporary dance works online mean that they enter into a new form of circulation, and differences in genre or style between music videos and contemporary dance works do not mean that they will be treated differently by viewers.

De Keersmaeker's invitation seems to recognize this transition. *Rosas danst Rosas* is explicitly relocated into a space of fragmentation and reconfiguration. However, this is not necessarily a radical act on behalf of De Keersmaeker, rather it can be understood as an acknowledgement of the new space in which dance works find themselves. As dance scholar Harmony Bench suggests:

> social media enable the emergence of new social dance practices defined not by music genres or by movement vocabularies, but by modes of composition and circulation within social media environments. (Bench 2010, 184)

This is an important articulation in relation to *Rosas danst Rosas,* because as the case with Knowles demonstrates, distinctions between conventional 'high' art such as theatre dance and popular culture forms are reconfigured in the neutralizing sphere of the virtual.

Bench focuses on the way in which online choreographies are inherently social, articulating the concept of 'social dance-media', suggesting that some online choreographic works utilize the participatory nature of the internet in order to 'reconfigure dance as a site of social exchange and engagement by providing the vehicles for sharing and circulating dance' (2010, 184). She draws a clear distinction between these choreographies and those developed for the stage, suggesting '[a]s a hybrid form, social dance-media differentiates itself from stage-based choreography by insisting upon public engagement and participation' (2010, 184). However *Re:Rosa!* muddles this distinction by re-situating the stage work *Rosas danst Rosas* as a work of social dance-media. This is not the case for any stage work that is documented online; in social dance-media the choreographic component must reflect social media strategies, insomuch as the choreographer must integrate users as collaborators, rather than merely commentators (Bench 2010, 185). This framework is very evident in *Re:Rosas!* which depends essentially upon interaction from participants.

Whilst *Re:Rosas!* is not the first online project to engage the public in choreographic activity, it does have some unique features due to De Keersmaeker's positioning. Bench articulates three forms on online choreography; 'crowdsource', 'flash' and 'viral' (2010, 184). Of these, 'crowdsourcing' seems to be the concept that most closely relates to the site. Although including the public, or non-professional dancers in performance work is not a new phenomenon, Bench suggests that crowdsourcing choreography offers something different insomuch as it is a 'process of harnessing the knowledge and creative input of a widespread population rather than an expert few' (Bench 2010, 187). She suggests that whilst performers who are in work for the stage or screen operate under the direction of a choreographer, crowdsourcing has a more democratic process. *Re:Rosas!* can be understood as reliant on crowdsourcing, as it depends on participation from public groups. Yet, Bench's articulation that crowdsourcing decentralizes power is problematized by De Keersmaeker's strong authorial stance. In some ways the participants are entirely free from De Keersmaeker's command once they have learned the steps, and in this sense the project can very much be read as a process of harnessing knowledge and creative input. Yet, the participants are working under direction from De Keersmaker and van Wissen. The very precise choreography is articulated in detail. De Keersmaeker and van Wissen are very clearly 'experts', meaning that a hierarchical structure is maintained.

Yeoh suggests that, 'choreographers are more concerned with the proper re-presentation of their works rather than its economic exploitation' (2013, 99). But how can 'proper re-presentation' be maintained when works are circulated and re-embodied around the world? De Keersmaeker's project offers an innovative way to preserve the work. Rather than gating the choreography, and protecting its essential core, De Keersmaeker fragments the work, and scatters its pieces into the virtual sphere, allowing the choreography to be replanted in numerous bodies. Yet, perhaps paradoxically, the project allows her to articulate the movement in accordance with her wishes. Although this site offers a form of score, the articulation of movements is not removed from the subjectivity of the body. Users learn to mimic van Wissen's corporeality rather than an 'objectified' or removed rendering through notation or inscription. De Keersmaeker's release of the work can be understood not as a form of surrender, but a way to exercise control. Furthermore, the interactive nature and usability also allows the work to circulate, reaching new audiences and perhaps eclipsing its status as 'the work Beyoncé stole'.

Re:Rosas! stands in contrast to the more conventional archival approaches by the Merce Cunningham Trust and Pina Bausch Foundation. Firstly, the work is not 'complete'; it is only a small section that is released for 'remixing'. Although mentioned briefly, the site does not feature much contextual, choreographic and production detail. The multiple categories present on the Bausch archive, and extensive metadata in Cunningham's Dance Capsules are not needed, as the aim of this site is not intended to allow for an exact reconstruction, but instead to invoke further choreographic acts, which stand in relation to De Keersmaeker's. Thomas suggests that the internet facilitates partial knowledge of 'texts', such as music videos, and that, 'this partiality is what allows discourses of "authenticity" back into a space of fracturing and mutability' (2014, 290). The complexities of the notion of authenticity in dance are highlighted here, as the work is not reproduced in accordance with its original form, yet each new version is authentically a version of the work. But why is it that these instances have a different relationship to the work than Knowles's version? I suggest this is due to De Keersmaeker's authorization. Her invitation to 'remix' the work allows for it to be authentic without being complete. De Keersmaeker's invitation gives these versions a different weight to non-authorized enactments of the choreography. The closer an instance of the work is to the choreographer, the more likely we are to consider it authentic. The way that the authorial invitation legitimizes the remakes intuitively seems to provide them with a unique ontology and relationship to *Rosas danst Rosas*, thus demonstrating the centrality of the choreographer in contemporary dance practice.

16.5   Conclusion

Re:Rosas! demonstrates features of De Keersmaeker's authorial positioning. She encourages creative re-working, liberating the work from its original context and structure, yet somewhat paradoxically, this centralizes her role in the work. It allows her to articulate a correct version of the work in great detail, limiting the potential for mis-renditions.[10] Rather than resisting the circulation and use of the choreography in the populist sphere of the internet, De Keersmaeker places the work within the online culture of transmission and re-embodiment. The project both preserves and transfigures *Rosas danst Rosas*. This approach offers a novel approach to the cultural heritage of dance. Instead of following a conventional archival approach which aims to exhaust the features of the work, documenting it in its entirety, *Rosas danst Rosas* is documented and constrained, yet simultaneously released from its original form. Its heritage is formed through fragments and remnants of the work, preserved in the bodies of the site's participants.

In various ways, each of the cases discussed in this chapter demonstrate a drive to position the choreographer at the centre of their work. This can be understood as response to the situation described by Gardner (2014, 230) and Louppe (2010, 235), who suggest that choreographic corpuses are under-recognized, due largely to the temporality of performance and the ontological fluidity of dance. Fixing features of dance works through archiving and the authorization of experts, allows for the choreographer to maintain some control over the persistence and re-performance of their work. Furthermore, the use of technology enables preservation and transmission to be approached in an ever-increasing variety of ways. It is clear that choreographers think about their relationship to their work in different ways, meaning that as the drive to preserve continues, so too does the inherent idiosyncrasy of dance documentation. Furthermore, technological strategies for the preservation of performance based cultural heritage reveal the paradoxical nature of dance preservation; the desire to enable the work to live on is coupled with restrictions, and the open transmission of choreography is simultaneously an act of constraint.

Notes

1. Judson Dance Theatre were a group of dance artists working in New York in the 1960s and 1970s who were instrumental in the development of Western contemporary dance, including artists such as Yvonne Rainer, Steve Paxton, Deborah Hay and Lucinda Childs, amongst many more.
2. Sarah Whatley (2005) discusses this process in the work of UK choreographer Siobhan Davies.
3. For example, Helen Thomas (1995) discusses the restaging of early modern dance pioneer Doris Humphrey's work.
4. See Climenhaga (ed.) (2012) for an extensive overview of the development of tanztheater.
5. See McFee (1992, 2011) and Pakes (2013), amongst others, for considerations of dance ontology.
6. In 2013 it was announced that Brown was to retire and that her company would commence a three-year tour, as well as establishing archival practices (Trisha Brown Company n.d.). Brown sadly died in March 2017.
7. The idea of a dance 'transmitter' is explored in depth by Gardner (2014).
8. Bench (2014) discusses this phenomenon in relation to Michal Jackson's *Thriller* (1983).
9. The notion of 'liveness' has been considered by Auslander (1999), Pavis (1992), Phelan (1993) and Varney and Fensham (2000), amongst others.
10. It is important to mention that between 2012 and 2015 De Keersmaeker collaborated with performance theorist Bojana Cvejić to publish three detailed 'scores', each of which document a total of seven works in great detail (2012a, 2012b, 2012c).

References

Anderson, Zoe. 2015. Tanztheater Wuppertal Commissions. Accessed 29 October 2015. http://www.dancing-times.co.uk/dance-today-news/item/1813.

Artslant. n.d. Open Call for Re:Rosas! Accessed 20 April 2016. http://www.artslant.com/la/articles/show/35542.

Auslander, Philip. 1999. *Liveness: Performance in a Mediatized Culture*. London: Routledge.

Bench, Harmony. 2010. Screendance 2.0: Social Dance-Media. *Participations* 7 (2): 183–214.

———. 2014. Monstrous Belonging: Performing "Thriller" After 9/11. In *The Oxford Handbook of Dance and the Popular Screen*, ed. Melissa Blanco Borelli, 393–411. New York: Oxford University Press.

Climenhaga, Royd. 2012. *The Pina Bausch Sourcebook: The Making of Tanztheater*. Abingdon, Routledge.

Copeland, Roger. 2004. *Merce Cunningham: The Modernizing of Modern Dance.* New York and London: Routledge.

De Keersmaeker, Ann Teresa, and Bojana Cvejić. 2012a. *A Choreographer's Score: Fase, Rosas danst Rosas, Elena's Aria, Bartok.* Metacarfonds: Brussels.

———. 2012b. *A Choreographer's Score: En Atendant and Cesena.* Metacarfonds: Brussels.

———. 2012c. *A Choreographer's Score: Drumming and Rain.* Metacarfonds: Brussels.

De Mey, Thierry. 1997. *Rosas danst Rosas* [film]. Produced by Avila & Sophimages.

Feidelson, Lizzie. 2013. The Merce Cunningham Archive: The Dancer or the Dance? *N+1 Magazine,* 16. Accessed 29 October 2015. https://nplusonemag.com/issue-16/essays/the-merce-cunningham-archives/.

Franko, Mark. 1995. *Dancing Modernism/Performing Politics.* Bloomington and Indianapolis: Indiana University Press.

Frisbie, Claire. 2013. The Internet *Danst Rosas*: Anne Teresa De Keersmaeker for the YouTube Generation. *BAM Blog,* 16 October. Accessed 29 October 2015. http://bam150years.blogspot.co.uk/2013/10/the-internet-danst-rosas-anne-teresa-de.html.

Gardner, Sally. 2014. What Is a Transmitter? *Choreographic Practices* 5 (2): 229–240.

Impulsetanz. n.d. Dance Your Own 'Rosas danst Rosas'. Accessed 29 October 2015. https://www.impulstanz.com/en/news/aid1643/.

Jowitt, Deborah. 2011. Introduction. In *Fifty Contemporary Choreographers,* ed. Martha Bremser and Lorna Sanders, 1–18. Abingdon: Taylor & Francis.

Kraut, Anthea. 2016. *Choreographing Copyright: Race, Gender and Intellectual Property Rights in American Modern Dance.* New York, NY: Oxford University Press.

Louppe, Laurence. 2010. *The Poetics of Contemporary Dance.* Trans. S. Gardner. Southwold: Dance Books.

McFee, Graham. 1992. *Understanding Dance.* London: Routledge.

———. 2011. *The Philosophical Aesthetics of Dance: Identity, Performance and Understanding.* Southwold: Dance Books.

McKinley, James C., Jr. 2011. Beyoncé Accused of Plagiarism Over Video. *New York Times,* 10 October. Accessed 29 October 2015. http://artsbeat.blogs.nytimes.com/2011/10/10/beyonce-accused-of-plagiarism-over-video/.

Merce Cunningham Trust. n.d. Merce Cunningham Dance Capsules. Accessed 29 October 2015. http://dancecapsules.mercecunningham.org/?8080ed.

Noland, Carrie. 2013. Inheriting the Avant-Garde: Merce Cunningham, Marcel Duchamp, and the "Legacy Plan". *Dance Research Journal* 45 (2): 85–121.

Pakes, Anna. 2013. The Plausibility of a Platonist Ontology of Dance. In *Thinking Through Dance: The Philosophy of Dance Performance and Practices,* ed. Jenny Bunker, Anna Pakes, and Bonnie Rowell, 84–101. Southwold: Dance Books.

Pavis, Patrice. 1992. *Theatre at the Crossroads of Culture*. London: Routledge.

Phelan, Peggy. 1993. *Unmarked: The Politics of Performance*. London and New York: Routledge.

Pina Bausch Foundation. n.d. Archive. Accessed 29 October 2015. http://www.pinabausch.org/en/archive.

Rosas. n.d. Rosas. Accessed 29 October 2015. http://www.rosas.be/en/rosas.

Rosas and fABULEUS. 2013. Re:Rosas: The fABULEOUS Rosas Remix Project. Accessed 29 October 2015. http://www.rosasdanstrosas.be/en/.

Rubidge, Sarah. 2000. Identity and the Open Work. In *Preservation Politics*, ed. Stephanie Jordan, 205–215. London: Dance Books.

Servos, Norbert. 1981. The Emancipation of Dance: Pina Bausch and the Wuppertal Dance Theatre. *Modern Drama* 23 (4): 435–447.

Siegel, Marcia. 1972. *At the Vanishing Point*. New York: Saturday Review Press.

Tanztheater Wuppertal. n.d. Company. Accessed 10 February 2018. http://www.pina-bausch.de/en/.

Thomas, Helen. 1995. *Dance, Modernity and Culture*. London: Routledge.

Thomas, Philippa. 2014. Single Ladies, Plural: Racism, Scandal and "Authenticity" Within the Multiplication and Circulation of Online Dance Discourses. In *The Oxford Handbook of Dance and the Popular Screen*, ed. Melissa Blanco Borelli, 289–303. Oxford: Oxford University Press.

Trisha Brown Company. n.d. Company: About. Accessed 29 October 2015. http://www.trishabrowncompany.org/?section=6.

Van Imschoot, Myriam. 2012. Rests in Pieces: On Scores, Notation and the Trace in Dance. Accessed 29 October 2015. http://www.make-up-productions.net/media/materials/RestsInPieces_Myriam%20VanImschoot.pdf.

Varney, Denise, and Rachel Fensham. 2000. More-and-less-than: Liveness, Video Recording, and the Future of Performance. *New Theatre Quarterly* 16 (1): 88–96.

Waelde, Charlotte, Sarah Whatley, and Mathilde Pavis. 2014. Let's Dance! But Who Owns It? Accessed 26 April 2016. https://ore.exeter.ac.uk/repository/handle/10871/16903.

Whatley, Sarah. 2005. Dance Identity, Authenticity and Issues of Interpretation with Specific Reference to the Choreography of Siobhan Davies. *Dance Research* 23: 87–105.

Yeoh, Francis. 2013. The Copyright Implications of Beyoncé's Choreographic 'Borrowings'. *Choreographic Practices* 4 (1): 95–117.

CHAPTER 17

Dance and Law: From Indifference to Rapport

Charlotte Waelde

17.1 Current Policy and Legal Framework: From Indifference

In 2015, DanceUK, the "National Voice for Dance" in the UK estimated that the dance economy employed circa 30,000 people; that there were around 200 dance companies in the UK; and pointed out that dance plays a central or supporting role in many other art forms, such as music and theatre.[1] UK National statistics estimated that there were 3414 employed dancers and choreographers as of early 2014.[2] So while dance may be a comparatively small sector of the creative industries economy, which, in early 2015, was estimated to be worth £76.9 billion per year,[3] it is nonetheless a very important part.

The dance community has followed a very different path compared to other parts of the creative industries such as the music industry, a sector that has been strongly commercial. In 2015, UK Music estimated that the music industry made a £3.5 billion contribution to the UK economy made up of: £1.6 bn from musicians, composers and songwriters; £634 m from recorded music; £662 m from live music; £402 m

C. Waelde (✉)
Centre for Dance Research, Coventry University, Coventry, UK

© The Author(s) 2018
S. Whatley et al. (eds.), *Digital Echoes*,
https://doi.org/10.1007/978-3-319-73817-8_17

321

from music publishing; £151 m from music representatives; £80 m from music producers, recording studios; £1.4 bn the value of exports.[4] The music industry, by contrast to the dance community, is made up of tiers of individuals and organizations with interests in the creation, development and exploitation of music. These include the artists themselves— singers, songwriters, musicians— those involved in one way or another in the exploitation of the music-record companies, managers, promoters publishers, distributors, broadcasters among others, along with a host of collecting societies such as PRS for music[5] and MCPS[6] which represent the interests of different parties involved in the business. By comparison the dance community has much less presence. DanceUK is an important umbrella organization calling itself the "national voice for dance",[7] the National Dance Network is "a meeting point of organisations whose primary role is the development of dance in the context of presenting, programming and commissioning",[8] and dancers would be eligible to be members of Equity, but there is very little other support and no industry bodies established to exploit dance.

There will be a myriad of reasons for this, not least of which is suggested in the terminology used: the music *industry*, and the dance *community*. Having worked with dancers and choreographers over the past seven years or so, the community feel is obvious. Yes, there are highly ambitious dance companies, dancers and choreographers, but generally the community is close, supportive and without exception devoted to the art-form. What is important, particularly to those who work alone or in small groups, is the process of creation of the dance and all that brings with it.[9] Another key reason for the difference lies in the ephemerality of dance. Many dancers and choreographers are of the view that the dance is fixed or "set" in the "memories and bodies of the dancers" where the bodies are considered material objects.[10] Any form of record would be an anathema: the dance is meant only to be ephemeral—to exist at the time of performance and fixation would ossify the work.[11] Such an approach means that a dance can draw an audience at the moment of performance— but not beyond: a business model would thus depend on live performance. This is in stark contrast to the music industry where performance of music is also ephemeral, but the capture of the music, and exploitation of recorded music, has for many years provided the largest part of the income stream for the industry.[12]

However, deep cuts, past and future, in public funding for the arts must necessarily lead to changes. In 2010–11 public grant in aid funding to the

Arts Council stood at £450 million.[13] In 2011–12 it was reduced by 14 per cent to £388 million; in 2012–13 by 7.5 per cent to £359 million; in 2013–14 by 3 per cent to £348 million and in 2014–15 to £343 million.[14] The strong direction given by the Arts Council[15] is to ensure that "The Arts are resilient and innovative."[16] A way to achieve that is through "strengthening business models in the arts, helping arts organisations to diversify their income streams including private giving".[17] Participants are strongly urged to diversify their strategies in a number of ways including in their approach to creativity, to their workforce and in responding to audiences and markets. Dance is no exception to these ambitions. In two reports in 2009 and 2010 the dance sector in the UK was mapped and a number of proposals made about the relationship between this sector and the Arts Council.[18] In the 2010 report in a series of interviews with dancers it was noted that the dance community could take better advantage of commercial opportunities that arose which could in turn be based at least in part on more coordination and knowledge sharing.[19] Specifically on the dance pages of the Arts Council site it is stated that the organization will:

> support[ing] the development of entrepreneurial skills to ensure that companies, artists and producers have a deeper sense of their markets and how to position themselves.[20]

The law that supports the ways in which the music industry is organized commercially is the law of copyright. Can that same law be used to develop a business model for dance?

17.1.1   What Is the Law of Copyright?

The law of copyright was first put on statutory footing in the UK in 1709 in the Statue of Anne.[21] The impetus for this Act came from the development of the printing press: suddenly it was possible to publish books and for these to be put into circulation. But it became difficult for either the author, or the publisher, to exert any form of control over circulation of copies. The Act therefore granted the author the sole right and liberty of printing books—a right that could be assigned to the publisher— for a period of fourteen years from first publication.[22] If the author was alive at the end of that period it was renewed for another fourteen years. From then on copyright was considered to be a creature of statute, the parameters of which are set by the legislature. Over the ensuing years the law was extended in response to new developments and technologies including art and drama, sound recordings, films, photographs, and the term of protection was extended (in Europe) for authorial works to seventy years after the death of the author. Although copyright is territorial, which means that the law extends to the territory in which it is enacted,[23] agreement to be found in a series of international conventions[24] and agreements[25] to which the majority of countries in the world have signed up, means that copyright is recognized and can be enforced in many territories around the world.

Because books, music, software, dance and other works are both non-excludable and non-rivalrous, meaning that individuals cannot be effectively excluded from use, and that the use by one individual does not reduce availability to others, so a mechanism is needed to enable the owner to exert control over the works. And this is what copyright does: it gives to the owner of the copyright in the work a number of exclusive rights to control copying, issuing copies to the public, renting or lending the work, performing showing or playing the work in public, communicating the work to the public and adapting the work.[26] As the owner has these exclusive rights, so she can licence or assign them to others who can, in turn, exercise them with the consent of the owner.

The law of copyright does not however give complete monopoly power over the work. The rights of the owner are limited in a number of ways through a series of limitations and exceptions that are built into the law mainly for public policy reasons. These rights are said to balance the interests of the user of with those of the owner of the copyright and generally allow the user to use parts of a work protected by copyright without payment or permission. In the UK they include fair dealing for the purposes of non-commercial research and private study; criticism, review, quotation and news reporting; caricature, parody or pastiche.[27] There are also a number of measures in the UK legislation that allow works to be used for those with disabilities,[28] for the purposes of education,[29] by libraries and archives[30] and for the purposes of public administration.[31] Each of these limitations is bounded by stringent criteria set out in the Act that need to be followed if copyright is not to be infringed. In addition it should be remembered that copyright protects the expression of ideas, but not ideas themselves. This can be a challenging distinction to grasp in some cases as the boundary between ideas and expression is opaque in law, but it is another example of where the law balances those who have interests in the copyright framework.

In thinking about copyright it is also important to remember that, in the UK, the author is the first owner of copyright unless she is an employee and acting in the course of her employment. If this is the case, then the employer will be the first owner.[32] In the UK the owner is free to licence or assign her copyright to a third party. This often happens in the music business, where the musician, singer and song-writer will assign copyright to a record company. All of the copyright ownership is then consolidated in the hands of one entity. But the author does retain moral rights in the work (where applicable). The main moral rights in the UK are the right to be identified as the author of the work,[33] and the right to object to derogatory treatment of a work.[34] These rights last for as long as copyright subsists in the work.[35] As with the exceptions and limitations to the copyright monopoly, these moral rights are limited in a number of different ways, but their existence means that interests in a work protected by copyright can be split as between the owner and the author. From this discussion it can be seen that the law of copyright seeks to balance three interests: those of the author, the copyright owner and the public interest.

While the copyright legislation is relevant for dance, historically dance has been almost entirely absent from our copyright discourse particularly in the UK. One is hard pushed to find case law on copyright and dance. What there has been has included questions of ownership of copyright by a choreographer under the 1911 Copyright Act[36]; questions of infringement of the copyright in an Oscar Wilde story when adapted in the form of a ballet[37]; and a finding that a dramatic work must be capable of being performed to be protected by copyright.[38] Neither has there been much focus on dance in our law literature, although there was some excitement recently over a dance performed by Beyoncé that seemed to draw heavily on earlier work by the choreographer de Keersmaeker.[39] Other jurisdictions have paid more attention to this art form and the place of copyright in its exploitation. In the US for instance dance was put on the legal map as a result of a court case concerning the ownership of dances by the choreographer, Martha Graham.[40] This spawned much literature and seemed to result in a greater appreciation of copyright in dance, at least in the US.

The dance community has seemed hesitant about asserting rights. That is not because those involved in the dance community do not know about copyright but, as noted above, it seems rarely to be of concern for their artistic endeavour. What is rather more important, particularly to those who work alone or in small groups, is the process of creation of the dance and all that brings with it.[41]

17.2   Dance and Copyright: To Rapport

But now there is increasing reason why the two, dance and copyright, should move closer.

When thinking about copyright in a dance, there are three preliminary steps that need to be undertaken: the work needs to be identified; legal originality needs to be assessed; the work needs to be fixed. The first important step is to identify the work of dance. Under the Copyright Designs and Patents Act 1988 (CDPA), the current copyright legislation in the UK, a work has to fall into a particular category in order to be protected by copyright: for our purposes, a dance must fall into the category of dramatic work.[42] Legal guidance on what qualifies as a dramatic work is sparse. It seems that a dramatic work can't be purely static and should have movement, story or action[43] and should be capable of being performed[44] but, in law, we know little beyond that.

The second important step is to assess who makes the right sort of legal authorial contribution to that work to be considered by the law to be the (or an) author of the work. To identify who the author is, it is necessary to consider who has exerted the right sort of originality in the work of dance. In terms of the level of originality required for copyright to subsist, this has historically been very low in the UK, requiring only "skill, labour and effort" and that a work should not be copied.[45] This, in turn, has meant that few works have been denied protection. It is important to identify who has made the right sort of original contribution to the work because the person(s) who contributes the right sort of originality is regarded as the author of the work. There seems a clear assumption in the dance community that the choreographer is the author of the dance and the owner of the copyright in it.[46] But subjective assumptions of authorship, and what the law says, are often two different things. The one British case to have considered the question, *Massine v de Basil*[47] noted above, was decided under the 1911 Copyright Act which included a reference to "choreographic work" as did the 1956 Copyright Act. The CDPA however says nothing about choreography or choreographic work but does provide that author of a dramatic work is the person who creates that work.[48] That would require an analysis of who has expended the right sort of skill, labour and effort into what the law recognizes as the work. Difficult questions however lie at the interface between the authorial input necessary to be considered an author for the purposes of copyright, and the input that instead interprets a work and is thus in the nature of performance. How much of the dance should be considered personal to the dancer as opposed to fixed on the body by the choreographer is the key question. The more that the creation of the dance is an iterative, collaborative process, the more such input is likely to be recognized by the law as being of the right sort of originality to be considered authorial whoever has made that input—whether dancer and/or the choreographer. And when assessing who has made the right sort of authorial input, it is important to remember, as noted above, that ideas are not protected by copyright, but only the expression of the ideas. But there is a fine and difficult line in law in deciding, for dance, where the line between idea and expression as between the dancer and choreographer lies in the process of creating the dance.

The third step is to consider the requirement of recording of the work. Although there is no requirement for recording of a work for copyright to subsist in the international framework,[49] the law in the UK does require that the work be fixed[50]: copyright only arises at this point. What form fixation takes is left open and needs only to be "in writing or otherwise".[51] Traditionally fixation has been thought of as being in writing, reflecting the historical text-based roots of copyright law. For dance, one of the notation systems such as Laban or Benesh would qualify, both of which have relatively modern origins, having been invented in the mid twentieth century. More modern examples of dance fixation include film and video, computer animation, motion capture and holography.[52]

But this raises challenges in law for dance: the paradox is that fixation is the key to copyright protection for works of dance, but at the same time presents a high hurdle. To gain the protection of copyright what has to be captured is *a* version of the work, whatever the participants and the community might think about the ephermerality of the work and its ossification, or however challenging notation systems might be for a true representation of a dance. If there is no fixation, there is no copyright.

17.2.1   Changing Laws

The legal question of what is a work of dance—or a dramatic work—is currently complicated by the development of jurisprudence from the Court of Justice (CoJ) around both the categorization of works, and in relation to the level of originality needed for the subsistence of copyright. The CoJ case law seems to challenge the criteria of both *work* and *originality* in a way that appears to conflate the two.[53] The CoJ has stressed that the European scheme of protection for copyright protects works where the subject matter is original in the sense of being the author's intellectual creation.[54] What the work is called, in other words for our purposes whether it is a work of dance being a subset of the category of dramatic works, is irrelevant, although it seems that a work would need to fall under the International Berne Convention categories of a literary or artistic work.[55] The standard of originality for all types of work is the same: it is one of intellectual creation.[56] To reach this level the author should express her creative ability in an original manner by making free and creative choices,[57] and stamp her "personal touch" on the work.[58] Where choices are dictated by technical considerations, rules or constraints which leave no room for creative freedom, then these criteria are not met.[59]

With the new case law from the CoJ mentioned above, it seems that the concept of "work" as we have understood it in the law of copyright may no longer be relevant. If so, then this may leave space for hitherto unprotected elements, or combinations of elements, to be considered as suitable for protection by copyright. There could however be challenges for some dances in relation to the "dictated by technical considerations" proviso. Some works that have historically been protected may no longer receive copyright status because they are limited by their technical function. An example from music is the skill, labour and effort exerted in updating musical scores to recreate the music of a baroque composer: the input may be considered to be dictated by technical requirements and therefore may not capable of protection by copyright.[60] By analogy, would the recreation of an historic dance to conform to an original production now earn its own copyright protection?—arguably not if its re-creation was dictated by the technical requirements of the original choreographer.

17.3   Summary

Much of the discussion above has been relevant to modern and contemporary dance. On this, the law is clear: the dance is protected by copyright once it is recorded in one form or another. Although there is no legal definition of dance, from a legal perspective there would be few dance routines that would fall outwith protection. This is because, despite what the dance community might think, artistic quality is not a criterion of protection. If it is a dance, then it will be protected. A traditional dance, such as a waltz or a tango that is recorded on a film, will be protected only in relation to the particular rendition of the dance. In other words, the owner of the copyright in the film could prevent third parties copying the film without permission, but other dancers—whether amateur or professional—could not be prevented from dancing a waltz, or dancing a tango. These are dances that have been in existence for very many years and as such deemed to be in the public domain and thus free for all to reproduce.

More challenging, from a legal perspective, is to determine who is the author of the dance. Where the dance is "laid on the body of the dancer" by the choreographer, leaving little room for the dancer to stamp her own intellectual individuality on the work, then the author in law is likely to be the choreographer. By contrast, where the choreographer leaves room for the dancer to express her own individuality, then the law is likely to regard either the choreographer and dancer as joint authors of the copyright in the dance, or the dancer as the author of the copyright in the dance, with the choreographer as the person who has given instructions or ideas but whose input may not be of the right kind for her to be considered an author in law. This is an outcome which is likely to be at variance with what might be thought to be the position by those who work in the dance community.

17.4   DANCE AND DIGITIZATION

The variety and ubiquity of digital technologies now means that the ways in which a dance might be made accessible to audiences is limited only by the imagination. As more and more opportunities open up, so new business models will emerge that could be embraced by the dance community as they respond to the edict "commercialize to survive". And it will be the law of copyright that forms the bedrock of those models; the ways in which income might be generated is limited only by our imagination. Social media in particular offer many diverse ways in which exploitation can occur. No longer are we tied to, say, royalty streams from licensing recorded forms of the dance. Consider for instance the YouTube clip of the opening ceremony of the Paralympics.[61] Imagine that each time the clip is viewed, advertisements appear; each time that advertisements appear, the advertisers make a payment to YouTube; each time a payment is made this is shared between "owners".[62] Why should David Toole, who features in the clip, as an owner of the copyright in his dance, not be entitled to a share of that income? His argument would be so much more powerful from the perspective of an owner of the copyright in the dance as he would be on equal terms with equally as powerful and entitled copyright owners in the many other layers of copyright that make up the spectacle. So this may not be a form of exploitation that is currently much used, but it is potentially a lucrative one.

Other challenges will arise. Characterized by convergence, hybridity and the blurring of disciplinary boundaries, digital dance projects frequently involve a range of creatives who may make claims on the works, including programmers, designers, coders, engineers and new media artists. Choreographers may employ digital tools to create choreographic objects that reveal much about their own making process. While identifying authorship within these new digital creativities might be challenging, it is what is required of the law: and the law will step in and ascribe authorship in accordance with its terms—terms that may not accord with assumptions within the dance community or what it might be felt is equitable in the circumstances of each project given the many layers of creative input. As we move forwards into these challenging times, it would well befit the dance community proactively to address these issues to ensure that they do not become hurdles in the future.

17.5   DANCE AND OUR INTANGIBLE CULTURAL HERITAGE

A final point arises in relation to dance and our cultural heritage. As has been noted by others, there is a dearth of representations of dance in our memory institutions. But thinking about representations of dance in our cultural heritage is changing. One of the challenges of the past has been around the ephemeral nature of the art form along with the enduring view in the community that the dance should not be captured and ossified, as discussed above. It is also likely part of a wider phenomenon in UK heritage circles in which intangible cultural heritage has not been considered a part of our cultural heritage on its own terms. Where it is present it has tended to be as an adjunct to tangible objects.[63] That however is now shifting, most particularly with the development of the international legal framework particularly in the form of the UNESCO Convention for the Safeguarding of the Intangible Cultural Heritage 2003. This Convention places obligations on States that sign up to it to safeguard intangible cultural heritage. While the UK is not currently a signatory, as thinking around the importance of intangible cultural heritage develops (and possibly political pressure—163 states are party to the Convention as of October 2015) it may well decide to sign up.

This thinking has started in the dance community. In her blog post of 21 May 2015 for the *Guardian*, "Stepping out of the past: modern dance's heritage debate", Judith Mackrell[64] reported on discussions at a panel convened by Rambert to explore issues around if and how contemporary dance should become a part of our cultural heritage. Some choreographers and dancers remain adamantly opposed to the capture and preservation of dance: dance is "of the present moment"; its "slippery" nature resists commodification; and a slavish approach to reproducing the past could lead to a sacrifice of effectiveness of the work and of its integrity—all arguments that have been noted above. For some the mere mention of the word "heritage" conjured up images of "crumbling castles". For others, safeguarding our dance heritage was as important as safeguarding classics from music, art and literature, although it is recognized that there are significant practical and theoretical challenges.

What makes it possible for dance to become part of our cultural heritage is its capture in some fixed form. And, as has been discussed above, as soon as it is captured in some fixed form, then questions over copyright arise.

17.6   Conclusion

We are at an important moment in time when thinking about the relationship between dance and copyright. Our age of austerity means that efforts need to be made to find creative ways in which new revenue streams can be found to support dance. Often these may depend on fixing the dance in some way. As soon as the dance is fixed, questions over copyright come to the fore. These new exploitation models are likely to depend on copyright which in turn will determine the legal author and owner of the work, and thus the person able to control the dance. If those legally entitled to the copyright in the work are not the ones best placed to exploit it, then the participants can enter into contracts to determine who should own the rights. Careful analysis will need to be made of the rights flowing from increasingly convoluted digital dance projects—but nothing is insurmountable so long as it is factored into thinking at the start of a project. Experience from other sectors—such as the music industry—tells us that where ownership is not clear from the start, the majority of problems arise down the line where money starts to be made from the musical work. Because the law is likely to determine authorship and ownership in a way that differs from industry assumptions, and because revenue follows ownership of copyright, so those who the law does not consider owners are not entitled to share in revenues. That is when the musicians, singers and song-writers resort to the courts.[65] Had ownership of copyright been agreed at the outset, then litigation would have been unnecessary.

These questions will become increasingly pressing in the dance community as digital technologies are more and more integrated into the artform and more and more creatives are involved in projects. But a significant advantage, in addition to the possibility of finding new revenue streams, is that dance, in captured form, will be able to find its rightful place within our intangible cultural heritage.

NOTES

1. Dance UK Dance facts, accessed 19 October 2015, http://www.danceuk.org/resources/dance-facts/.
2. Creative Industries Economic Estimates, January 2014, accessed 19 October 2015, https://www.gov.uk/government/uploads/system/uploads/attachment_data/file/271008/Creative_Industries_Economic_Estimates_-_January_2014.pdf.
3. "Creative industries now worth £8.8 million an hour to the UK economy", accessed 19 October 2015, https://www.gov.uk/government/news/creative-industries-now-worth-88-million-an-hour-to-uk-economy.
4. "True Value of the Music Industry to the UK Economy Revealed", accessed 19 October 2015, http://www.ukmusic.org/news/true-value-of-music-industry-to-uk-economy-revealed. This is a music industry report. It was well received by Government departments including the Intellectual Property Office.
5. PRS for Music, accessed 19 October 2015, https://www.prsformusic.com/Pages/default.aspx.
6. PRS for Music Royalties, accessed 19 October 2015, http://www.prsformusic.com/creators/memberresources/mcpsroyalties/pages/mcps.aspx.
7. Dance UK, accessed 19 October 2015, http://www.danceuk.org.
8. National Dance Network, accessed 19 October 2015, www.nationaldance.co.uk.
9. Charlotte Waelde and Phillip Schlesinger, "Music and Dance: Beyond Copyright Text?" (2011) 8: 3 *SCRIPTed* 257, accessed 19 October 2015, http://script-ed.org/?p=83.
10. Martha Traylor, "Choreography, Pantomime and the Copyright Revision Act of 1976," *New England Law Review* 16: 227 (1981): 237.
11. See for instance Paul Théberge, "Technology Creative Practice and Copyright," in *Music and Copyright*, ed. Simon Frith and Lee Marshall (Edinburgh: Edinburgh University Press, 2004, 2nd ed.), 139, 140.

12. This changed in the wake of digitization and the challenges with dissemination of works on the Internet. More emphasis was replaced on live music. See David Byrne, "The Internet will suck all the creative content out of the world," 11 October 2013, *Guardian*, accessed 19 October 2015, http://www.theguardian.com/music/2013/oct/11/david-byrne-internet-content-world.

13. "Supporting vibrant and sustainable arts and culture", accessed 19 October 2015, https://www.gov.uk/government/publications/2010-to-2015-government-policy-arts-and-culture/2010-to-2015-government-policy-arts-and-culture.

14. This is not the only source of funding for the Arts Council. The national lottery gives significant amount of money via the Arts Council to support the arts. Total funding including lottery funding in 2010–11 was £601 million. In 2014–15 it was expected to be £605 million.

15. The Arts Council Plan 2011–15, accessed 19 October 2015, can be found at http://www.artscouncil.org.uk/media/uploads/pdf/Arts_Council_Plan_2011-15.pdf. The plan implements the Council's strategic vision 2011–21 "Achieving Great Art for Everyone", accessed 19 October 2015, available at http://www.artscouncil.org.uk/media/uploads/achieving_great_art_for_everyone.pdf: accessed 19 October 2015.

16. Arts Council Plan p. 7.

17. Ibid.

18. "Dance Mapping," 30 September 2009 and "Joining up the dots: Dance agencies: thoughts on future direction," 26 May 2010, accessed 19 October 2015. Both available from: http://www.artscouncil.org.uk/what-we-do/supporting-artforms/dance/.

19. "Joining up the dots", accessed 19 October 2015, p. 26.

20. http://www.artscouncil.org.uk/what-we-do/supporting-artforms/dance/.

21. The Statute of Anne, accessed 19 October 2015, http://archive.org/stream/thestatuteofanne33333gut/33333.txt.

22. Ibid., p. 6.

23. The UK law, the Copyright Designs and Patents Act 1988 (CDPA) as amended extends to England, Wales, Scotland and Northern Ireland—see though s 304.

24. E.g. Berne Convention for the Protection of Literary and Artistic Works 1886.

25. Agreement on Trade Related Aspects of Intellectual Property Rights 1994.

26. CDPA ss 16–21. For secondary infringement see ss 22–6.

27. CDPA ss 29, 30, 30A.

28. CDPA ss 31A–31F.

29. CDPA ss 32–36A.

30. CDPA ss 37–40A.
31. CDPA ss 40B–44A.
32. CDPA ss 9–11.
33. CDPA s77.
34. CDPA s 80.
35. CDPA s 86.
36. *Massine v. de Basil* [1936–45] MacG CC 223.
37. *Holland v. Vivian Van Damn Productions Ltd.* [1936–45] MacG. Cop. Cas. 69 (Ch. D.).
38. *Norowzian v. Arks Limited*, [2000] F.S.R. 363 (C.A.). Tom Rivers, "Norowzian Revisited" [2000] *E.I.P.R.* 389. Richard Arnold, "Joy: A Reply" [2001] *I.P.Q.* 10.
39. "Split screen: Beyonce 'Countdown' vs Anne Teresa De Keersmarker", accessed 19 October 2015, http://www.youtube.com/watch?v=PDT0m514TMw. Francis Yeoh, "The Copyright Implications of Beyoncé's 'Borrowings,'" *Choreographic Practices* 2013, 4 (1): 95–117; Luke Jennings "Beyoncé v De Keersmaeker: can you copyright a dance move?" *Guardian*, 11 October 2011, accessed 19 October 2015, http://www.theguardian.com/stage/theatreblog/2011/oct/11/beyonce-de-keersmaeker-dance-move. The story continues with developments that are highly relevant for this discussion: Judith Mackrell "Beyoncé, de Keersmaeker—and a dance reinvented by everyone", 9 October 2013, *Guardian*, accessed 19 October 2015, http://www.theguardian.com/stage/2013/oct/09/beyonce-de-keersmaeker-technology-dance.
40. *Martha Graham School and Dance Foundation Inc. v Martha Graham Center of Contemporary Dance, Inc.*, 43 Fed. Appx. 408 (2nd Cir. 2002); *Martha Graham School and Dance Foundation Inc. v Martha Graham Center of Contemporary Dance, Inc.*, 374 F.Supp.2d 355, 363 (S.D.N.Y. 2005); *Martha Graham School and Dance Foundation Inc. v Martha Graham Center of Contemporary Dance, Inc.*, 466 F.3d 97 (2006); Anne Braveman, "Duet of Discord: Martha Graham and her Non-Profit Ballet over Work for Hire", *Loyola of Los Angeles Entertainment Law Review*, 2005, 25: 471; Sharon Connelly, "Authorship, Ownership and Control: Balancing the Economic and Artistic Issues Raised by the Martha Graham Copyright Case", *Fordham Intellectual Property, Media & Entertainment Law Journal*, 2006, XV: 837.
41. Waelde and Schlesinger, "Music and Dance: Beyond Copyright Text?".
42. CDPA s 3(1).
43. *Creation Records v News Group* [1997] EMLR 444.
44. *Norowzian v. Arks Limited* [2000] F.S.R. 363 (C.A.).
45. *University of London Press v University Tutorial Press* [1916] 2 Ch. 601.

46. Waelde and Schlesinger, "Music and Dance: Beyond Copyright Text?";
Agnes De Mille, *And Promenade Home* (Boston, Toronto: Little, Brown
and Company, 1956), at 256. "[T]he choreographer is glued immobile as
a fly in a web and must watch his own pupils and assistants, suborned to
steal his ideas and livelihood. Several dancers made paying careers out of
doing just this"; Graham McFee, *The Philosophical Aesthetics of Dance:
Identity, Performance and Understanding* (Alton: Dance Books 2011).
47. [1936–45] MacG CC 223.
48. CDPA s 9(1).
49. Berne Convention Article 2.2 leaves fixation to members of the Union.
50. This is so the extent of the monopoly claimed may be known to others.
Tate v Fulbrook 1908 1 KB 821 at 832.
51. CDPA s 3(2).
52. Each of which may have separate protection in their own right.
53. Mireille van Eechoud, "Along the Road to Uniformity: Diverse Readings
of the Court of Justice Judgments on Copyright Work", 3(1) (2012)
J.I.P.I.T.E.C. para 60; Christian Handig, "The 'Sweat of the Brow' is Not
Enough!—More Than a Blueprint of the European Copyright Term
'Work'," [2013] *E.I.P.R.* 1; Andreas Rahmatian, "Originality in UK
Copyright Law: The Old 'Skill and Labour' Doctrine Under Pressure"
[2013] *I.I.C.* 3; Eleonora Rosati, "Towards an EU-Wide Copyright?
(Judicial) Pride and (Legislative) Prejudice" [2013] *I.P.Q.* 46; Justine Pila,
"An Intentional View of the Copyright Work" (2008) *Modern Law Review*
71; Christian Handig, "*Infopaq International A/S v Danske Dagblades
Forening* (C-5/08): is the Term 'Work' in the CDPA 1988 In Line With
The European Directives?" (2010) *E.I.P.R.* 32(2), 53.
54. Case C-5/08 *Infopaq International A/S v Danske Dagblades Forening*
(Infopaq) paras 33 38. See also Case C-393/09 *Bezpečnostní softwarová
asociace* para 45 What is not protected is expression which is limited by its
technical function. Case C-406/10 *SAS Institute Inc. v World Programming
Ltd* paras 38–40. Case C-145/10, *Painer v Standard VerlagsGmbH et a*l.
In the UK see *SAS Institute Inc.v World Programming Ltd* [2013] EWHC
69 (Ch.) para 27.
55. Case C-5/08 *Infopaq International A/S v Danske Dagblades Forening*,
Case C-393/09 *Bezpečnostní softwarová asociace* paragraph 45; Joined
Cases C-403/08 and C-429/08 *Football Association Premier League and
Others*; Eleonora Rosati, "Originality in a Work, or a Work of Originality:
The Effects of the Infopaq Decision", *E.I.P.R.* 2011, 33(12), 746. Estelle
Derclaye, "Wonderful or Worrisome? The Impact of the ECJ Ruling in
Infopaq on UK Copyright Law" (2010) E.I.P.R. 32(5), 248.
56. See the references in Note 55.

57. *Infopaq*, para 45; *Bezpečnostní softwarová asociace*, para 50; *Painer*, para 89, *Football Dataco* para 38.

58. *Painer*, para 92; *Football Dataco* para 38.

59. *Bezpečnostní softwarová asociace*, paras 48 and 49, *Football Association Premier League and Others*, para 98; *Football Dataco* para 39. See also the articles at Note 55.

60. *Sawkins v Hyperion Records Ltd*, [2005] EWCA 565.

61. "Birdy—Birdy Gerhl (Anthony and The Johnsons Cover) accessed 19 October 2015, http://www.youtube.com/watch?v=vhZVKYV8kGw.

62. This is what happens with many YouTube videos.

63. Laurajane Smith and Emma Waterton, "'The Envy of the World' Intangible Heritage in England", in *Intangible Heritage,* ed. Laurajane Smith and Natsuko Akagawa (Abingdon: Routledge, 2009), 289–91. The authors quote an extract from an interview with a representative from English heritage as follows: INTERVIEWEE: The UK has not said that it will ratify [the 2003 Convention] and I think it will be quite a long time before it does. INTERVIEWER: What are the reasons for that? INTERVIEWEE: It is just difficult to see how you could apply a convention of that sort in the UK context…it is not relevant…it just does not fit with the UK approach… I think it would be very difficult to bring in a convention that says we are actually going to list this sort of stuff and protect it. What are the obvious examples you come up with? Morris Dancing? As intangible heritage and so on? The UK has no intangible heritage. (Interview 1, English Heritage, 4 July 2005) at 297.

64. Judith Mackrell, "Stepping Out of The Past: Modern Dance's Heritage Debate", *Guardian*, 21 May 2015, accessed 19 October 2015, http://www.theguardian.com/stage/dance-blog/2015/may/21/modern-dance-the-heritage-debate-rambert-ben-duke-farooq-chaudhry.

65. *Sawkins v Hyperion Records Ltd* [2005] EWCA 565; *Brown v Mcasso Music* [2005] FSR 40; *Coffey v Warner/Chappell Music Ltd* [2005] EWHC 449; *Fisher v Brooker* [2006] EWHC 3239; *Fisher v Brooker* [2008] EWCA Civ 287; *Fisher v Brooker* [2009] UKHL 41; Luke T. McDonagh "Rearranging the roles of the performer and the composer in the music industry: the potential significance of Fisher v Brooker", *I.P.Q.* 2012, 64; Dominic Free, "Beckingham v. Hodgens: The Session Musician's Claim to Music Copyright", 96 *Ent. L R*, 2002, 1(3), 93–8; Richard Arnold "Reflections on 'The Triumph of Music'; Copyrights and Performers Rights in Music" [2010] *I.P.Q.* 153.

Index[1]

[1]Note: Page numbers followed by 'n' refer to notes.

Printed by Printforce, the Netherlands